Statehood, Territory, and International Spaces

Queen Mary Studies in International Law

Edited by

Malgosia Fitzmaurice

VOLUME 53

The titles published in this series are listed at *brill.com/qmil*

Statehood, Territory, and International Spaces

By

Giovanni Distefano

BRILL | NIJHOFF

LEIDEN | BOSTON

Originally published in French as *Droit international des espaces. Morceaux choisis*, deuxième edition, Editions Pedone, Paris, 2022.

Library of Congress Cataloging-in-Publication Data

Names: Distefano, Giovanni, author.
Title: Statehood, territory, and international space / by Giovanni Distefano.
Description: Leiden ; Boston : Brill, 2025. | Series: Queen Mary studies in international law, 1877-4822 ; volume 53 | Includes bibliographical references and index. | Summary: "Statehood, territory and international spaces are at the heart of a specific branch of international law: the international law of territory. International territorial disputes and their settlement are examined from the standpoint of legal titles: acquisition and loss of territorial sovereignty, use of force (annexation, conquest), the right of peoples to self-determination (and secession), ius cogens norms etc"– Provided by publisher.
Identifiers: LCCN 2024033741 (print) | LCCN 2024033742 (ebook) | ISBN 9789004708587 (hardback) | ISBN 9789004708594 (ebook)
Subjects: LCSH: Jurisdiction, Territorial. | Self-determination, National. | Sovereignty. | Secession. | Jus cogens (International law) | Territory, National.
Classification: LCC KZ3675 .D53 2024 (print) | LCC KZ3675 (ebook) | DDC 341.4/2–dc23/eng/20240724
LC record available at https://lccn.loc.gov/2024033741
LC ebook record available at https://lccn.loc.gov/2024033742

Typeface for the Latin, Greek, and Cyrillic scripts: "Brill". See and download: brill.com/brill-typeface.

ISSN 1877-4822
ISBN 978-90-04-70858-7 (hardback)
ISBN 978-90-04-70859-4 (e-book)
DOI 10.1163/9789004708594

Contents

Abbreviations

AFDI	Annuaire français de droit international
AILC	American International Law Cases (ed. by Francis Deák: First series (1783–1979); Bernard Reams: Second Series (1979–1989)), Dobbs Ferry, NY: 1982 and 1992, Oceana
ARSIWA	ILC Text of Articles on the International Responsibility of States for Internationally Wrongful Acts (2001)
Bruns	Fontes Iuris Gentium, Repertory of the Diplomatic Correspondence of European States (1856–1878), Berlin, 1837
CCI	Italian Civil Code
CIL	Customary International Law
CJEU	Court of Justice of the European Union
CTS	*Consolidated Treaty Series 1648–1919* (by Clive Parry, Oxford, 1969)
Digest of International Law	Digest of International Law, (ed. by Marjorie Whiteman), Washington D.C., 1963
Distefano, Gaggioli, Hêche, 2016	*Convention de Vienne de 1978. Commentaire article par article et études thématiques*, ed. by G. Distefano, G. Gaggioli, A. Hêche, Bruylant, Brussels, 2016
ECtHR	European Court of Human Rights
EEZ	Exclusive Economic Zone
FCC	French Civil Code
GE 1949	1949 (Four) Geneva Conventions
Hackworth	Digest of International Law, (ed. by Green H. Hackworth), Washington, 1940–1944
I.C.J.	International Court of Justice
ICC	International Criminal Court Statute
ICC	Rome Statute establishing the International Criminal Court
ICJ Statute	Statute of the International Court of Justice
IHL	International Humanitarian Law
ILM	International Legal Materials
ILR	International Law Reports
LNTS	League of Nations Treaty Series
LoN	League of Nations
MFA	Minister for Foreign Affairs
Moore	A Digest of International Law as Embodied in Diplomatic Discussions, Treaties and other International Awards, the Decisions of Municipal Courts and the Writing of Jurists (ed. by Bassett Moore), Washington D.C., 1906

NRG	Nouveau recueil général de traités, conventions et autres transactions remarquables : servant à la connaissance des relations étrangères des puissances et états dans leurs rapports mutuels (ed. by Georg Friedrich von Martens and al.), Göttingen : 1843-, Dieterich.
Official Journal	League of Nations Official Journal
P.C.I.J.	Permanent Court of International Justice
P/I 1977	First Protocol (1977) to the four Geneva Conventions (1949)
P/II 1977	Second Protocol (1977) to the four Geneva Conventions (1949)
Pasicrisie	Pasicrisie internationale: Histoire documentaire des arbitrages internationaux (ed. by Henri La Fontaine), Bern, Stämpfli and Cie, 1902
PCA	Permanent Court of Arbitration
PIL	Public International Law
PMC	Permanent Mandates Commission (of the League of Nations)
Prassi italiana	Prassi italiana di diritto internazionale, Prima serie (1861 1887), Seconda serie (1888–1918), Terza serie (1919–1925), NewYork:1970, 1980, 1995, Oceana
PYIL	Polish Yearbook of International Law
RBDI	Revue belge de droit international
RCADI	Collected Courses of The Hague Academy of International Law
RDILC	Revue de droit international et de legislation comparée Recueil des arbitrages internationaux (ed. by Albert Geouffre Lapradelle; Nicolas Politis), Paris, Pedone, 1905
RGDIP	Revue générale de droit international public
Rivista	Rivista di diritto internazionale
SCC	Swiss Civil Code
SCOTT	*Cases on International Law Principally Selected from Decisions of English and American Courts* (ed. by James Brown Scott), St. Paul, West Publishing Company, 1922
UN	United Nations
UNC	United Nations Charter
UNCLOS	United Nations Convention on the Law of the Sea (1982)
UNGA	United Nations General Assembly
UNSC	United Nations Security Council
UNTS	United Nations Treaties Series
UNTS	United Nations Treaty Series
VCLT 1969	Vienna Convention on the Law of Treaties (1969)
VCSS 1978	Vienna Convention on Succession of State in Respect of Treaties (1978)
YILC	Yearbook of the International Law Commission

Table of Cases

Arbitral Awards

Permanent Court of International Justice (P.C.I.J.)

International Court of Justice (I.C.J.)

European Court of Human Rights

International Criminal Jurisdictions

Court of Justice of the European Union

Municipal Law Cases

Introduction

The title of this course, somewhat syncretic, even kaleidoscopic, may seem abusive, even presumptuous, but I was looking for a sufficiently neutral and broad designation in which I could have embedded all the themes that have fascinated me for more than two decades. The subject of this course can be summed up in the following triad: State, (land) territory and public international law. This title thus encompasses disparate domains that share a common denominator, i.e., space conceived, as Jean Combacau and Serge Sur remind us,[1] as both a space and a thing.[2]

But can "international law of territory" be considered a branch of public international law? It is certainly not a legal order in its own right,[3] because it is not distinguished from the international legal order,[4] as a sub-system, by the presence of institutions that are specific to it. But it is certainly a branch of public international law, or rather, it is one of the branches that traditionally contribute to the training of the generalist in public international law, in the same way as the internist in medicine. Not only because of its importance in the doctrine, but also because the "PIL generalist" resort to use his knowledge and forge his own analytical toolbox.

The title of this book, pivoting on a triad, reflects the numerous shortcuts which have been dictated by the brevity of the oral course, eventually mirroring the varying degree of depth of the different themes that will be dealt with.

Given these specificities,[5] I have opted for a bird's eye view, trying to cover as many phenomena as possible, in short, a panorama that might appear sometimes superficial or even banal. However, by painting this picture, I hope to draw the reader's attention to one or other of the themes discussed and why not arouse passions in this field.

---

1 Jean Combacau, Serge Sur, *Droit international public*, 1st edn, Paris, 1993, 396.

2 See *infra* Part 1. Chapter 1. Section A.

3 On the difference between "branch" and "legal order" in international law, see Giorgio Balladore-Pallieri, "Le droit interne des organisations internationales", *RCADI*, vol. 127 (1969-II), 1–36.

4 See Santi Romano, *The Legal Order* (Transl. from Italian, 1917), London / New York, Routledge, 2018, paras. 33–34, at 66–69.

5 As far as possible, I have tried in this writing not to betray the approach as well as the "oral" origin of the course given in Paris for the IHEI in March 2016.

 | DOI:10.1163/9789004708594_002

The term "spaces" (in English one could say "spatial law", or even "international law of spaces"[6] not to be confused with "space law")[7] ought to be preferred to the more restrictive term "territories"; in fact, the latter generally only designates spaces – land and sea – where a State, or even a group of States or an international organisation, exercises sovereignty or sovereign rights (for example: land territory, internal waters, the territorial sea, *etc.*), whereas in other spaces, where no State enjoys sovereignty – territorial, in fact – one speaks of "zones" (EEZ) or "areas" (the "Area" or "Seabed").[8] In the same vein, and following an ancient doctrinal tradition inspired by Roman law (*res habilis* and ownership), the term "territory" would include only those spaces susceptible to state appropriation by a State. However, for the sake of brevity and simplicity we will use the expression "international law of territory"[9] in this book, bearing in mind its limitations, hence comprising all other "spaces" over which no State sovereignty is wielded.

In this perspective, spaces could be subdivided according to their status in terms of state appropriation: (a) *res nullius*, i.e. not subject to the territorial sovereignty of a state and therefore susceptible to appropriation; (b) *res domini*, i.e. subject to the territorial sovereignty of a state or group of states; (c) *res omnium*, i.e. spaces that are not susceptible to state appropriation, therefore *extra commercium*, and over which, therefore, only the personal dimension of state sovereignty can be exercised (e.g. the High Seas); d) *res communes*,[10] subject to the sovereignty of all States or of a group of States (as in the case of the "condominium"); e) *common heritage of humanity*, i.e. spaces that belong not only to humanity as a whole but must be exploited solely for its well-being (the Moon, celestial objects and cosmic space as well as Antarctica and the Area), in short the *res publica*.

The structure of this course is articulated in three parts, like a piano sonata; these three parts correspond to what one could call respectively: physiology, pathology and therapy in the apprehension of space by PIL. In the first part

---

6 This is also the title of a symposium held in May 2016 at the Graduate Institute (Geneva) in honor of Professor Lucius Caflisch.

7 This would be the "Law of Outer Space".

8 ICJ, Military and Paramilitary Activities in and Against Nicaragua (Nicaragua v. United States of America), Merits, Judgment, *I.C.J. Reports 1986*, para. 212, at 111.

9 The so-called "law of territory", see: Marcelo Kohen, Mamadou Hébié, 'Territorial Disputes', in *The Cambridge Companion to the International Court of Justice*, ed. by C Espòsito and K Parlett, CUP, Cambridge, 2023, 332. We considered it appropriate to add the adjective "international".

10 With regard to *res communes* et al., see: JA Pastor Ridruejo "Le droit international à la veille du 21ème siècle: normes, faits et valeurs", 274 *RCADI* (1988), 257 – 265.

we will look at the usual techniques of creation, extinction and modification of territorial titles. This part is nowadays mainly useful for the settlement of classical territorial disputes; it includes the essential tools of the internationalist – counsel or judge – called to solve a territorial dispute.

In contrast, in the second and third parts we will try to examine space as an object of dispute (territorial polemology) and as a means of dispute resolution (territorial irenicism) respectively. These two parts roughly reflect Wolfgang Friedmann's bipartition between the *right of coexistence* and *the right of cooperation*.[11] Space is no longer a source of disputes but becomes a means of resolving them: from an object of conflicts of interest *to an* object where the notion of "community of interest", first identified by the PCIJ in the *Oder Commission* case (in 1929), takes shape.[12] Space, and we are not just talking about rivers, lakes, outer space, the "Area", *etc.* – which will not be studied in this volume – thus becomes a means by which cooperation between States is achieved in order to attain common goals such as international peace and security.[13] As a slogan, one could speak in the third part of the course of fragmented sovereignty, whereas the second part of the course witnesses the triumph of omnipotent sovereignty.

In other words, and more concretely, the internationalist is hardly helpless in the face of the needs of international politics and the technical expectations of diplomacy; there is enough inventiveness[14] in public international law to find the appropriate legal solution (or regime) to resolve, defuse or prevent sovereignty conflicts in the broadest sense. This approach, which underlies the 'right of cooperation' in territorial matters, is the subject of the third and final part, territorial irenicism.

In this respect, we could speak of the 'desacralization' of territory, but we prefer, with less emphasis and more correctly, to use the term 'deterritorialization' of spaces, i.e., the subtraction of these spaces from the exclusive exercise of the sovereignty of a State. In this respect, from the end of the 19th century onwards, we have seen the emergence of legal regimes that gradually transcended *exclusiveness* as a distinctive element of sovereignty, as Huber put it

11 Wolfgang Friedmann, *The Changing Structure of International Law*, New York, 1964.

12 See *infra* Part 3. Chapter 8. Section C.

13 These are the goals that are foremost in Article 1er of the UN Charter.

14 As a historical apostil, it is worth noting that the Eastern Question, especially after the break-up of four empires in the wake of the First World War, provided the jurists of European chancelleries with material that could sharpen their skills in concocting original solutions designed to defuse or even prevent bloody territorial conflicts. See *Commentary on the Covenant of the League of Nations* (ed. R Kolb), Brussels, 2015.

so well in the de Palmas case. In this regard, we could randomly mention: the collective protectorate (on the mandate of the European Concert, as was the case for the island of Crete), the neutralisation of certain Ionian islands initially under British protectorate, later transferred to Greece; the League of Nations (hereafter: LoN) Mandates, the international cities and territories of Danzig, Tangier and the Memel territory, with all their differences; or, most eloquently, the direct international administration by the LoN of the Saar territory and the Leticia region. After the Second World War, we find these same legal concepts: from (admittedly aborted) international cities such as Trieste and Jerusalem, to the trust administration of the United Nations, via direct international administration under Chapter VII of the UNC.[15] Therefore, the representation of space as a focal point for the covetousness of states and for conflicts between them is reductive and even misleading. It illustrates only one part of this course, the polemological dimension[16] of international law of territory, i.e. the "territorial obsession" decried, and relativized, by Georges Scelle,[17] which is embodied in the "right of coexistence" according to W. Friedmann's binary typology.[18] This visceral attachment to territory, as an expanse for exercising sovereignty in its almost ancestral and animal dimension[19] has been heretofore, it is a truism, the major cause of all the conflicts known to humanity.[20]

15 A small footnote: despite a certain (pugnacious) vulgate, the LoN's experience in this area has not been as disastrous as it is sometimes portrayed.

16 "This place is mine; 'I am of this place', says the albatross, the patas monkey, the green sunfish, the Spaniard, the great horned owl, the wolf, the Venetian, the prairie dog, the three spined stickleback, the Scotsman, the skua, the man from La Crosse, Wisconsin, the Alsatian, the little-ringed plover, the Argentine, the lungfish, the lion, the Chinook salmon, the Persian", Robert Ardrey, *The Territorial Imperative*, 1966, 274.

17 Georges Scelle, "Obsession du territoire. Essai d'étude réaliste de droit international", in *Symbolæ J.H.W. Verzijl*, Leiden, 1958, 347–361.

18 W Friedmann, "General course in public international law", 127 *RCADI* (1969-II), 80.

19 See the magnificent study by Ardrey (286): 'And finally we must know that the territorial imperative – just one, it is true, of the evolutionary forces playing upon our lives – is the biological law on which we have founded our edifices of human morality [...] Whether morality without territory is possible in man must remain as our final, unanswerable question.

20 Fortunately, there are still conflicts today which, while unresolved, are picturesque. One need only think of the territorial dispute between Denmark and Canada over a 1.2 km islet (called "Hans") on which there is a periodic ceremony (on both sides, at obviously different times) of "taking down" the flag of the neighbor opposite and replacing the bottle of schnapps with whisky, and "vice-versa" (*La Presse*, Canada, November 11, 2015), hence the "Whisky War" attributed to this conflict. This curious dispute was finally settled on 14 June 2022 by the sharing of the buried islet by a treaty concluded in Ottawa. Or, perhaps more revealing of the passions – both good and bad – that the earth's crust arouses, the Norwegian government's 2016 gift to Finland of the top of the highest mountain (named

It is necessary to recall, if need be, the conflict in Ukraine triggered on 24 February 2022 by the aggression of the Russian Federation, which is still raging today, and which will inevitably disrupt and poison international relations for decades to come. Therefore, states must do everything possible, hence territorial irenicism, to "heal the scars of history"[21] which are the inter-state borders[22] of which, on the other hand, international law gives an aseptic definition:

> The general theory that a boundary represents the line of separation between areas of State sovereignty, not only on the earth's surface but also in the subsoil and in the superjacent column of air.[23]

A final word of caution; the reader will notice that some examples or historical/concrete situations can be seen through different prisms at the same time. For example: the issue of the "Turkish Republic of Northern Cyprus" will be examined both from the perspective of the puppet state, the non -collective recognition, the legal title/use of force, and even the right to self-determination of peoples; the question of Kosovo will be examined from the angle of indirect international administration, secession, remedial secession, direct international administration; the status of Palestine will be dealt with from the perspective of the right to self-determination of peoples, non- collective recognition, use of force / legal title; the status of Somaliland can be examined from

---

"Halti"), most of which lies in the territory of the latter. This border adjustment would have been a "gift" to celebrate the 100th anniversary of Finland's declaration of independence from the Russian Empire. The proponents of such an anniversary gift, however, seem to be sticking to their guns (*The Independent*, 16 October 2016).

21 Denis De Rougemont, "Aspects culturels de la coopération dans les régions frontalières, texte présenté lors de la Première confrontation européennes des régions frontalières, 29 juin-1er juillet 1972", in Institut universitaire d'études européennes (ed.), *L'Europe des Régions III*, Geneva, 1972, 71.

22 It should be remembered that the etymology of the word 'frontier' (from the Latin *frons, frontis*), in Latin languages, refers to the military front line, opposing two opposing arms: '*to make frontier*, means to put oneself in battle to fight, to defend oneself', *Littré* (https://www.littre.org/definition/frontière). In ancient Greece: "What is a space between two armies, marked – in a totally voluntary way – by a boundary marker? A space-time of equilibrium in the middle of a war, an intermediate space around which time has come to a standstill. A pause to be prolonged, a place that no one must invade, because any combat would lead to victory, and thus to the control of the terrain by the army of the victors", Norbert Loraux, *La tragédie d'Athènes. La politique entre l'ombre et l'utopie*, Paris, 2005, 156–157 [our translation].

23 ICJ, Frontier Dispute (Benin/Niger), Judgment of 12 July 2005: *ICJ Reports* 2005, para. 124, at 142.

the angle of secession as well as *de facto* state. We could multiply the examples, but we risk being particularly tedious. This multi-layer approach tells us that, despite our initial hesitations about the appropriateness of the title of this course, the links between the different themes seem to be strong enough to ensure the conceptual coherence of the subject, summarized by the label 'international law of territory'.

Introductory Note to This Edition

This volume is derived from the second edition of a book written in French and published by Pédone in November 2022 ("Le droit international des espaces: morceaux choisis"). The underlying approach has remained the same as we wished to maintain the spirit that originally animated it, i.e., that of a course taught – as visiting professor at IHEI (Paris) in March 2016 – to a group of passionate students.

Prolegomena: State, Sovereignty and Spaces

In view of the aims of this volume, it will by no means be a question of investigating in depth these three flagship concepts of public international law; much more modestly and usefully, we shall confine ourselves to sketching out instrumental definitions of these three *dramatis personae* of this book. The international order, as any other legal order, is composed by a plurality of subjects. The latter may be roughly divided in territorial and non-territorial entities. Among the territorial ones the State stands out, as the primary and original subject of the contemporary international order. The consubstantiality between international law and State is so obvious that it has often been questioned in doctrine which of the two was the first to appear from a chronological point of view.

According to a traditional division of time, with the Peace of Westphalia in 1648 there was the definite completion of a process that had begun four centuries before, to say the least. In other words, the State, as territorial entity, emerges as a defined and primary subject of the contemporary international order. This horizontal character of the new international order presupposes the centrality of the territory and the effective deployment of sovereign powers over it.

A State: the Monad of Contemporary Public International Law

Starting with the state, it must be said at the outset that, as we shall see below, international law, except for certain special cases,[1] most of the time bows to its actual existence. Nevertheless, it provides us with the criteria for verifying its existence as the primary subject of the modern international order. In search of these criteria, we should refer to Article 1 of the Convention on the Rights and Duties of States signed in Montevideo on 26 December 1933:

> The state as a person of international law should possess the following qualifications: a) a permanent population; b) a defined territory; c) government; and d) capacity to enter into relations with the other states.[2]

1 See *infra* Part 2.

2 Although it is an international treaty with a regional focus, it stands as the only treaty-law attempt to define a State to date.

 | DOI:10.1163/9789004708594_003

Three elements, therefore, enveloped by a fourth, decisive one, sovereignty, which is succinctly expressed by the capacity to enter into international legal relations with other states and other subjects of the international order, i.e. *treaty-making power*. The latter implies two other equally important capacities, namely the capacity to participate in the general mechanisms of international responsibility as well as that of diplomatic representation (active and passive).[3] The combination of these three capacities in a political organisation of a human grouping with a territorial base allows us to speak of a state in the sense of international law. The litmus test of the existence of a state is therefore sovereignty, the second character of these prolegomena and a truly chameleonic concept, malleable and ductile in the light of circumstances. According to the inescapable dictum of arbitrator Max Huber in the Island of Palmas case:

> Sovereignty, in the relations between States signifies independence. Independence, in regard to a portion of the globe is the right to exercise therein, to the exclusion of any other State, the functions of a State.[4]

In a language close to formal logic and in a rigorous conceptual sequence, Max Huber identifies sovereignty with independence and equates it with two qualities: the *fullness* and exclusiveness of the exercise of state functions over a part of the land territory. A land space that is characterised by these two attributes is therefore State territory within the meaning of PIL. Going further up the equation, we find independence, which means both the direct submission of the state to international law (i.e. *immediacy*) and its *equality* vis-à-vis other states. The former is thus the vertical limit of sovereignty, embodied in Article 2 § 7 UNC, while the latter expresses its horizontal limit, sanctified by Article 2 § 1 of the UNC.

The two pillars of the contemporary international legal order are the principle of sovereignty and the principle of territoriality. Both are derived from the horizontal structure of the international system, which has started to come into being during the Twelfth Century.[5] The dominant paradigm of sovereignty

3 Giovanni Distefano, *Fundamentals of Public International Law. A Sketch of the International Legal Order*, Leiden, 2019, 60–68.

4 Island of Palmas Case (Netherlands/USA), Award of 4 April 1928, 2 *RIAA*, 83. That sovereignty is constrained by international law and is not antinomic to it is revealed by the following passage in this award: "Territorial sovereignty ... has a corollary duty: the obligation to protect within the territory the right of other States, in particular their right to integrity and inviolability in peace and in war, together with the rights each State may claim for its nationals in foreign territory", *ibid.*, 839.

5 Distefano (2019), 74–89.

absorbs the latter to the concept of independence. The principle of territoriality presupposes and implies a subjective right on the State, that is to say the *ius excludendi alios*.[6] Therefore, territorial sovereignty is conceived as a State's right to obtain that other States (as well as other subjects of PIL) abstain themselves from carrying out the functions related to State sovereignty on foreign territory. This subjective right of exclusiveness is opposable *erga omnes* and its essential requirement is based on the effectiveness of the sovereignty that a State exercises in its own territory and within its boundaries.

If it is true that "territory"[7] is a sub-species of the more general concept of "space", characterised, as we have seen, by the radiance of the (territorial) sovereignty of one (or even several) State(s), it is necessary to define the latter. Now, space 'can be apprehended in two ways, as an expanse and as a thing, and lends itself respectively to two kinds of powers, personal and real. It is from this fundamental distinction that we must start in order to identify the two kinds between which space is divided'.[8]

This definition of space, which we adopt here, has the great merit, in addition to its conceptual precision, of explaining a very wide range of territorial situations and regimes that will be examined later in this volume.[9] On the one hand, as a space, it makes it possible to apprehend the international dimension of sovereignty, since it sees it as one of its dimensions, the spatial one, alongside the personal one.[10] On the other hand, it takes into account the real law aspects of sovereignty, insofar as the latter is a right necessarily *erga omnes*, i.e., a right over a thing opposable to any other subject of the international legal order.[11] In other words, and from this perspective, territorial sovereignty

---

6 *Supra* note 4.

7 It is not insignificant to note that, contrary to the accepted vulgate, the term 'territory' might not derive from 'land' (*terra*), but from the verb '*terrere*', i.e., to exercise terror (M de Vaan, *Etymological Dictionary of Latin and the other Italic Languages*, Leiden, 2008, 616). Consequently, 'territorium' would indicate the space where the state exercises its monopoly of legal violence or, if one prefers, its sovereignty. In the same sense, the *Oxford English Dictionary* would retain the aception deriving from 'terrere' (to frighten): a neighbouring register, according to Isidore of Seville, the territory (*territorium*) was thus called almost to say *tauritorium*, i.e. the spaces trampled and crushed by the plough and the oxen: 'the ancients, in fact, demarcated the territories and possessions by tracing a furrow' (*Etymologiae* (624–636), Book XIV, V, 22).

8 Combacau, Sur, 396 [our translation].

9 See *infra* Part 3.

10 "Sovereignty encompasses both elements of personal allegiance and territoriality", ICJ, Sovereignty over Pedra Branca/Pulau Batu Puteh, Middle Rocks and South Ledge (Malaysia/Singapore), judgment of 23 May 2008: *ICJ Reports* 2008, § 79, at 40.

11 "By real rights we mean here, as in civil law, rights that are enforceable against any other person, as opposed to merely conventional rights, which exist only with respect to the

is an objective legal situation which, if it is in conformity with the law, is opposable *ipso jure* to any other subject of international law.

B Territory

The territorialization of international system eventually consecrated– in the wake of an historical process unfolding since the Twelfth Century – by the 1648 Munster and Osnabruck Treaties respectively, represents undoubtedly the lasting legacy of the Peace of Westphalia. It suffices to think to Art. 2 (1) of UN Charter which spells out the 'sovereign equality' of Member States, as the fundamental principle on which the UN has been built upon. Therefore, one can argue that the international order is heretofore essentially a territorial order.[12] The great number of territorial disputes (territorial and maritime), as well as the fact that they represent a significant part of international adjudication, confirms the existence of a true 'territorial obsession'.[13]

i *The Different Components and the Characteristics of State Territory*

Traditionally, State territory is composed ('*ab inferos et usque ad sidera*') by land territory (mainland) and its subsoil, internal waters and their soil and subsoil, and by the suprajacent column of air (airspace). These spaces constitute the State territory strictly speaking.[14] It needs to be distinguished by other spaces on and within which riparian States exercise rights and competences which, although flowing from State sovereignty, must not be confused with the latter: Continental shelf and the EEZ. As far as the main features of the territory are concerned, it is generally recognized by the doctrine and consolidated practice that the territory must be (a) stable, (b) delimitated and (c) continuous. The first characteristic refers to the permanence of the residing population,

other parties to the agreement. Property, easements, mortgages, in civil law, are real rights. In international law ... territorial sovereignty, in any case, also has this character", ICJ, Free Zones Case, 1929, Pleading of Mr Logoz (Switzerland), C 17-I (I), 949. As will be seen below, the acquisition of title to territorial sovereignty by legal fact bears a striking resemblance to the customary process (see *infra* Part 1. Chapter 3. Section D). In the Sovereignty over Pedra Branca/Pulau Batu Puteh, Middle Rocks and South Ledge (Malaysia/Singapore) case, paras. 137 (at 56), 139 (at 57), 222–223 (at 80), the Court nevertheless hastens to distinguish sovereignty from (state) ownership in international law.

12 On the territorial character of the international legal order, see the classical considerations of Raymond Aron, *Guerre et paix entre les Nations*, Paris, Calmann-Lévy, 1984, 187.

13 Scelle (1958), 137–361.

14 See Article 3 of the UNGA Resolution 3314 (XXIX) "Definition of Aggression".

thus excluding the phenomenon of nomadism. With regard to the second one, it has not to be interpreted in a restrictive manner when it is affirmed that the state's territory has to be clearly delimited. Indeed, there exist quite a few States whose borders are not clearly limited in their entirety and nevertheless their existence is not put into question.[15] Finally, the third one refers to the continuity of State's territory. However, State territory may be composed by many islands (Japan), by two territorial spaces separated by the sea (Malaysia), as well as by the territory of another State but still having access to High Seas (e.g. Oman and the peninsula of Musandam; Russia and Kaliningrad).

The aforementioned territorial situations must be though distinguished from enclaves, that is State territories which are completely surrounded by another State or States territory (for instance, the Italian enclave of Campionc in Swiss territory or Madha, the enclave of Oman in United Arab Emirates,[16] or subsets of former enclaves between Bangladesh and India).[17] These situations, although rare, does not bring prejudice to the quality of State territory of these "spaces". In the same vein, one should remind that nowadays there are only two truly enclaved States, *i.e.,* Lesotho, which is entirely surrounded by the territory of one single State, namely the Republic of South Africa, and the San Marino, completely encircled by Italy.

ii *The Legal Relationship between State and Territory: a Sampling of Theories on Territorial Sovereignty*

When scholars speak about the legal relationship between State and territory, they refer to the legal nature of the state's territory in international law. Leaving aside the problem, although valid, of the legal nature of territory in municipal order, there are mainly four theories – developed by international jurisprudence – which try to tackle this question.

Territorial sovereignty is the link between the State and its own territory, and this is precisely due to the horizontal structure of the modern international legal order. However, sometimes these normative categories collide with territorial situations which go beyond the cultural context where they have been elaborated, that is Europe.

---

15 PCIJ, Advisory Opinion, 4 September 1924, in *Reports of P.C.I.J.*, Series B 9, at 10.

16 Zoran Nikolic, *The Atlas of Unusual Borders* (Collins 2019), 138–139.

17 These very peculiar territorial situations – consisting in some cases of third-degree enclaves – came to an end in 2015 by virtue of the 2015 "Land Boundary Agreement" (August 1), through the formal exchanges of no less than 162 enclaves (https://mea.gov.in/Uploads/PublicationDocs/24529_LBA_ MEA_Booklet_final. pdf).

In 1975, the International Court of Justice, following General Assembly request, rendered an advisory opinion on the legal situation in the Western Sahara (formerly a Spanish colony). In that occasion, the Court could not resort to the same legal construction adopted in the Island of Palmas arbitration case in order to fully understand the situation at hand. This was because the situation concerned a case where the territory was not only undefined, but it varied according to the wander of nomad population residing thereon. The the existence of these nomad tribes prevented a legal crystallization of the territory and therefore the establishment of territorial sovereignty.

The link between sovereign and territory – meaning the territorial sovereignty – was displaced in that case by the personal relationship (*'lien juridique d'allégeance personnel'*) between the sovereign and the abovementioned populations. Consequently, the sovereign exercised only one of the two competences composing the notion of sovereignty, namely the *ratione personae* one, whereas the territorial competence was absent precisely because of lack of a territory.[18] From the foregoing, it stems that the concept of territorial sovereignty adequately refers only to a legal order rooted on its territorial character, as it is the case of the international legal system.

1 The Theory of the Territory-Object (*Eigentumstheorie*)

For the sake of birthright one ought to commence with this theory which, more than the other ones, betrays an evident Roman law legacy, which can be resumed as follows: *'Quidquid est in territorio, est etiam de territorio'*.[19] Traces of this theory can be found, with all the due terminological and conceptual precautions, in the less recent international jurisprudence and doctrine.[20]

According to this theory, the relationship between a State and its territory is precisely the same as the one between the individual and a subject of the national legal system. To put it differently, the territorial sovereignty of the State is a kind of property of international law, that is, an exclusive power of disposing of a territory as is the power to dispose of goods within the municipal legal

---

18 I.C.J, Advisory Opinion, October 1975, in *I.C.J. Reports* 1975, 12 ff.

19 'Whatever is in the territory is indeed of the territory', Aaron X Fellmeth, Maurice Horowitz, *Guide to Latin in International Law*, 2nd edn, 2021, Oxford, 252.

20 On the legal character of the territory in international law, see Louis Delbez,' Le concept d'internationalisation', in *RGDIP* 1967, 5–62, 10.

order. Therefore, there is no difference between the two legal relationships, nor there is a difference in international law between *dominium* and *imperium*.[21]

The right of a State over a territory – implying the power to dispose of it – is an absolute right since it is opposable *erga omnes* and it is also concrete (real), for it refers to goods or things. Real rights, belonging to the family of absolute rights, confer to their holders sometimes full real rights (ownership), some other times limited real rights (over a thing belonging, in terms of ownership, to another subject, *infra* Part 3. Chapter 8. Section D). Hence, the State is the holder of the *ius excludendi alios*, *i.e* the *imperium strictu senso*, and of the *ius abutendi atque fruendi* (*i.e* right to dispose of and exploit a thing, in other words the *dominium*). Grotius[22] had already pointed out the coincidence between *imperium* and *dominium*, and subsequent jurisprudence tended to support this authoritative view.

This conceptualization certainly enjoys the merit of having convincingly apprehended the legal nature of certain activities exercised by a State over a territory (for example, the cession, the sale, the lease, other forms of concession, etc.). The abovementioned situations, therefore, are examples of all those situations that can be included in the normative category of real rights that in national law are drawn near the right to property. However, this theory reveals the traditional legal construction according to which the State right of sovereignty was interlaced with the (absolute) sovereign (monarch), who exercised a real right of disposal and enjoyment – close to ownership – over the territory.

Critics to this reasoning are twofold. First, it is not adequate in dealing with the phenomenon of multiple ownerships on the same territory, that is to say State's and individuals' (or legal corporations'). The supporters of the theory, though, tried to answer that even if the two ownerships stem from the same title, they refer to different levels: the level of national law – private law ownership – for individual's ownership, and that of international law for the State's ownership. However, it is the second criticism that proves to be fatal to this theory, because the relationship between the state and its territory is not reduced to a simple property relationship. It goes far beyond that, and territorial sovereignty turns out to be a composite concept which, despite some affinities with the notion of property in domestic law, cannot be fully assimilated to it. This

---

21 Giuseppe Sperduti, 'Sovranità territoriale, atti di giurisprudenza ed effettività in diritto internazionale', *Riv. Dir. Intern.* 1959, 491–425 at 401, 417. With regard to the derived concepts of "condominium" and "coimperium", see *infra* Part 3. Chapter 8. Section D.

22 Hugo Grotius, *De iure belli ac pacis, Libri tres*, Amsterdam, Vol. I, Ch. III, para. VIII (transl. from Latin: *The Rights of War and Peace*, Book I, 260–267, Indianapolis, 2005).

theory represents then another attempt to embed a political phenomenon in patrimonialist and private-law schemes that end up debasing it.

2 The Theory of the Territory-Subject (*Eigenschaftstheorie*)

According to this conceptualization, State territory is considered by PIL as one its constitutive elements, together with the population and the government.[23] Unlike the previous theory, this one stresses the perspective of the 'essence' (or existence) rather than that of 'possession'. This theory, though particularly popular in Germany,[24] faced some difficulties to influence publicist doctrines of other European countries. While the theory of the territory-object betrays an evident private law analogy, the theory of the territory-subject stems from public law.

The main problem with this approach is represented by its inability to explain the immanence of the State notwithstanding the changes of its territorial basis. In other words, if one of its constitutive element changes, State's personality should change accordingly, hence having an impact on the existence of the State. Moreover, it does neither explain some events of the international life of a State which imply a divorce between sovereignty on the one hand and its exercise on the other, or between sovereignty of a State and ownership by another (*infra* Part 3. Chapter 8. Section A). In addition, the theory under scrutiny considers only the territorial dimension of State sovereignty, leaving aside the personal dimension, that is, governmental authority that a State may exercise on its nationals abroad. On the other hand, the colonial territories were excluded from this legal construction since they were not fully considered as state's own territory, neither under international law nor under national law.

The supporters of this theory were therefore compelled to construct unpersuasive logical fictions in order to grasp these phenomena.

3 The *Kompetenztheorie*

The 'Vienna School of Legal Thought' endeavored to improve the theory of territory-subject and to 'purify' the legal concept of territory, hence contributing to the "demystification" [25] of the State.

23 In Re Duchy of Sealand, Judgment of Administrative Tribunal of Cologne (RFG), 3 May 1978, in 80 *ILR*, 685 (relevant fragment).

24 Karl Friker, *Vom Staatsgebiet*, Tübingen, Verlag der H Laupp'schen Buchhandlung 1857, *passim*.

25 Eric Suy, 'Réflexions, sur la distinction entre la souveraineté et la compétence territoriale', in *Internationale Festschrift für Alfred Verdross*, München-Salzburg, W Fink, 1971, 495.

According to this way of thinking, the territory is nothing more than one of the two jurisdictions (or competences) encompassed by State sovereignty, namely the territorial jurisdiction (*ratione loci*) and the personal one (*ratione personae*).[26] This idea of State's territorial sovereignty prefers the term 'jurisdiction', adopted in other international instruments of normative character, especially in the Twenty-First Century, for example the Covenant of the League of Nations (Art. 15 (9)) and the UN Charter (Art. 2(7)).

4 A Syncretic Theory

Each of the abovementioned theories hold some truth to the extent that each of them points out some specific aspects of the legal relationship existing between State and territory. According to the prevailing legal theory, the territorial state can be conceived as space and thing at the same time: 'In international law, the sovereignty expresses itself both as the exercise of the real right over the territory and as the manifestation of the exclusive power of government on the territorial community'.[27] From the abovementioned it follows that the territory is the object of two different types of powers: personal and real at the same time.[28] As a land, the territory is the place 'where the *imperium* is exercised'; whereas, as a good, it can be subject to appropriation and to the exercise of *dominium*.[29]

In a nutshell, the State holds a real right, which is akin to the right to ownership under municipal law. Consequently, it (the right) may become State's possession according to the different ways provided for by international law (*infra*, Part 1. Chapter 1–3), in the same manner as an individual becomes the owner of a good under national law. This is the first pillar of the theory, which allows to grasp those specific territorial situations (reminiscent of private law) concerning the separation between sovereignty and its exercise as well as between sovereignty and property. These territorial situations are instead considered as aberrations by the *Kompetenztheorie*, which is thus unable to apprehend them correctly.

---

26 Hans Kelsen, *Pure Theory of Law* (Transl. from German, 2nd revised and enlarged ed. (1960), Berkeley, 1967), 10–15, 286–291.

27 Court of Appeal of Rome, 23 (25) June 1965, in P Picone, B Conforti, *La giurisprudenza italiana di diritto internazionale pubblico. Repertorio 1960–1987*, Naples, Jovene, 1988, 110 [our translation].

28 Jean Combacau, Serge Sur, *Droit international public*, 5th edn, Paris, Montchrestien, 2001, 398–400.

29 Pasquale Paone, *Contributo allo studio della tutela giuridica internazionale dell'attività statale*, Milan, Giuffré, 1961, 160–165, 172–174.

On the other hand, the second basis of the theory under exam refers to the territory as a space. To put it differently, it considers it as a dimension where the State exercises its sovereignty, that is, its territorial jurisdiction. Indeed, the State exercises its powers not *on* the territory itself (*dominium*) but rather *within* the space subject to its sovereignty (*i.e., imperium*) and regarding individuals and legal corporations therein. This space would constitute the sphere of territorial validity of State's jurisdiction, that is to say, its territorial jurisdiction.[30]

Therefore, the two aspects of territorial sovereignty (*imperium* and *dominium*) are indissolubly united in the light of this theory: international legal order recognizes the State to hold the right to exercise governmental authority in a specific area. This is to say that all the other subjects of international law other than the State itself are excluded. This conceptualization, whose intrinsic consistency can be hardly challenged, takes knowledge of the historical evolution of the international legal order and the idea of State, since early Middle Ages in Europe.

iii *State Succession and Territorial Changes*

This section deals with the different types of territorial changes that can be observed in international relations. The question of the validity of these changes of sovereignty, to which Article 6 VCSS 1978[31] refers will be examined later in the light of the overarching principles of the international legal system (*infra* Part 1. Chapters 1–3 and Part 2. Chapters 5–6).

In accordance with Art. 2 (1) (d) of the VCSS 1978, "succession of States" means the replacement of one State by another in the responsibility for the international relations of territory', which would translate in view of Montevideo's formula that there has been a succession of sovereignty over the territory concerned. As the ICJ did not fail to make clear:

> A State succession is one of the ways in which territorial sovereignty passes from one State to another.[32]

For the purposes of the present study, State successions can be distinguished according to a criterion which is, at least in theory, quite simple: the survival – or

30 Rolando Quadri, 'Le navi private nel diritto internazionale' (1939), in *Scritti Giuridici*, Vol. 1, Milan, Giuffré, 1988, 72; Combacau, Sur, 396.

31 For a commentary, see: G Gaggioli, 'Article 6', in Distefano, Gaggioli, Hêche, 2016, Vol. 1, 181–225.

32 Land, Island and Maritime Frontier Dispute (El Salvador/Honduras: Nicaragua intervening), Judgement of 11 September 1992, *I.C.J. Reports 1992*, para. 399 (at 598).

not – of the State affected by the territorial changes. In other words, that the latter *continues* to exist, notwithstanding territorial changes, so that its legal personality as a State is *identical* to that before State succession. Based on this criterion, six scenarios can be identified.

1 Secession

Whereas, as we will see below, there is no right to secession in international law,[33] this term of art refers to the 'separation of any part of the territory of a State [while] the predecessor State continues to exist' (Art. 35 VCSS 1978).[34]

In other words, the State affected by the separation is *identical* in its legal personality notwithstanding its territorial area has diminished. Conversely, this kind of State succession has given birth to a new State (or new States). This case must be very carefully distinguished from that, sometimes abusively and erroneously assimilated to that of a 'newly independent Stat' within the framework of the right of peoples to self-determination. The cases of Pakistan/Bangladesh, USSR (after 1991), Ethiopia/Eritrea, Sudan/South Sudan, illustrate, for instance, this kind of State succession.[35]

This scenario, regulated by article 16 VCSS 1978 with regard to succession to treaties,[36] is characterized by the existence of a people living on a 'non-self-governing territory' entitled by PIL to determine its fate on the international legal scene. Unlike the case of secession where there is *one and only* territory, here we are faced with a (dominant) territory illegally occupying another territory (the non-self-governing territory). Hence, in this scenario, governed by the right of peoples to self-determination, there is no *separation* of a part of the territory of a State, but the emancipation of a *distinct* territory, under illegal occupation by the former.[37]

2 Extinction of States through Dissolution (or Dismemberment)

This situation is similar to the previous to the extent that one or more States separate from an existing one. However, unlike it, in this case 'part or parts of the territory of a State separate to form one or more States' (Art. 34 (1) VCSS 1978), but the *predecessor State* ceases to exist. Hence, new States replace the

33 *Infra* Part 2. Chapter 6. Section B.

34 For a commentary, see: Victor Mikulka, 'Article 35', in Distefano, Gaggioli, Hêche, 2016, vol. 2, 1209–1228.

35 See *infra* Part 2. Chapter 6. Section B.i.

36 For a commentary, see: E Henry, 'Article 16', in Distefano, Gaggioli, Hêche, 2016, vol. 1, 561–612.

37 See *infra* Part 2. Chapter 6. Section A.

latter by succeeding to its sovereignty.[38] We may speak of voluntary dissolution, such as the dismemberment of Czechoslovakia (31 December 1992), or involuntary dissolution, such as the Socialist Federal Republic of Yugoslavia (successively after 1992) or Austria-Hungary (at the latest after the Armistice of Villa Giusti on November 3rd, 1918). Hence, contrariwise to the case of secession, there is no continuity (no continuator State), but the new States are successors of the defunct State.

3 Extinction of States through Merger (Unification)

This situation contemplates the merger of two or more existing States giving birth to a new State possessing a new international legal personality. The State thus emerging is the successor of the defunct States which disappear: 'two or more States unite and so form one successor State' (Article 31 (1) VCSS 1978). The unification normally presupposes a voluntary character, as the legal avenue leading to it is generally an international treaty; if the latter has been concluded under the threat or use of force, is then invalid by virtue of article 52 VCLT 1969.[39] The case of North and South Yemen merging into a unified State illustrate this situation:

> On the 26th of May 1990 [...] there shall be established between the State of the Yemen Arab Republic and the State of the People's Democratic Republic of Yemen (both parts of the Yemeni Homeland) a full and complete union, based on a merger, in which the international personality of each of them shall be integrated in a single international person called "the Republic of Yemen".[40]

Another example, though transient, may be cited, that of the United Arab Republic (UAR), formed by the merger of Syria and Egypt in 1958.[41] This

38 For a commentary, see: Veronika Bilkova, 'La succession aux traités internationaux suite à la dissolution des fédérations ex-socialistes après 1990', in Distefano, Gaggioli, Hêche, 2016, vol. 2, 1805–1852.

39 With regard to the threat or use of force and the creation of territorial titles or titles of sovereignty, see *infra* Part 2. Chapter 5.

40 'Agreement on the Establishment of the Republic of Yemen', 30 *ILM* (March 1991), 822. The "new" Yemen did not have to apply for membership at the UN, but it was considered by its Secretariat: note of August 7, 1990 (ST/CS/SER.A/31).

41 A joint communiqué was signed by the two heads of State on February 1, 1958, 'wherein was set forth a "Proclamation of the United Arab Republic"' (*Digest of International Law*, Vol. 2, 230–231), which thus became the founding act of this – loose and ephemeral– Union of States.

unification lasted, though, only three years as in 1961, Syria withdrew from the UAR, Egypt retaining the latter denomination.

4 Extinction of States through Total Annexation (or Absorption)

This situation refers to the extinction of a State by way of its absorption into another State. Previously better known as total annexation, this case implies the disappearance of a State and the enlargement of the absorbing State the international legal personality of which remains unaffected, hence identical to that before the absorption. In other words, this State extends its sovereignty to the entirety of the annexed State. This form of State succession highlights, perhaps in a more vivid way, the issue of legality[42] for it presupposes that the absorbed State *voluntarily* relinquishes its statehood and hence its international legal personality. Such a consent is normally enshrined in a treaty which rather ironically represents the swansong of its international legal existence. The "re-unification" of Germany and the parallel extinction of the German Democratic Republic in 1990 clearly illustrates this form of State succession.

5 (Partial) Annexation

Unlike the previous situation, we here faced to what was generally termed, especially before 1945 – and the UNC – "partial annexation", that is to say the extension of State sovereignty on part of the territory of another State that continued to exist, although diminished in its spatial ambit (Art. 15 VCSS 1978).[43] Akin to the situation previously examined, here too the issue of the legality of this form of State succession is particularly compelling. In effect, alongside the prohibition of the threat or use of force, another peremptory norm of international law must be complied with for the extension of sovereignty to be considered as valid: the right of peoples to self-determination (infra Chapter 2. Section E). In other words, the obligation on the ceding State to consult at the very least the population living on the territory affected by the cession. Furthermore, in the light of these two norms of *ius cogens* (of more later, *infra* Chapter 2), the cession can only occur through explicit or implicit relinquishment by the ceding State of its sovereignty over the concerned area. This *abandonment* usually takes place through a so-called territorial treaty of cession or sale. Especially in the past, this means of transferring territories between States, either after a war or in time of peace ranked amongst the most frequent: USA, for instance, conspicuously enlarged its territory during the

---

42 See *infra* Part 2. Chapter 5.

43 For a commentary, see: Attila Tanzi, Lucrezia Iapichino, 'Article 15', in Distefano, Gaggioli, Hêche, 2016, vol. 1, 543–555.

XIX century through the acquisition of Alaska (from Russia), Louisiana (from France), Florida (from Spain), or after a war (Philippines from Spain).

6 Newly Independent States

By this term of art, contemporary international law refers to a 'successor State the territory of which immediately before the date of the succession of States was a dependent territory for the international relations of which the predecessor State was responsible' (Article 2 (1) (f) VCSS 1978).[44] In other words, and by taking into account the State practice, this typology of States, which is characterized by a special regime within VCSS 1978,[45] comprises not only States that emerged from the decolonization process but also those States that were previously under the LoN Mandate (*infra* Part 3. Chapter 9. Section A) régime and UN Trusteeships regime (*infra* Part 3. Chapter 9. Section B). All of these situations fall generally within the compass of the right of peoples to self-determination, which will be investigated, in relation to territorial sovereignty and territorial disputes later in this volume (*infra* Part 2. Chapter 6. Section A).

---

44 For a commentary, see: Lorenzo Gradoni, 'Article 2', in Distefano, Gaggioli, Hêche, 2016, vol. 1, 112–120.

45 See: Etienne Henry, 'Article 16', *ibid.*, 561–612.

PART 1

The Technique: Creation, Extinction and Modification of Title of Territorial Sovereignty

CHAPTER 1

The Concept of Legal Title

> How can a state acquire or lose its title to territorial sovereignty? From a methodological point of view, the approach adopted will be eminently jurisprudential not only in order to paint a vivid picture of the applicable law, but also because this branch of international law of territory has been profoundly shaped by international tribunals so that in some respects the applicable body of rules is ultimately a scholarly distillation of PIL throughout the decades.

The centrality of this polysemous and protean concept is obvious.[1] There is no question here of dwelling on the etymology, however fascinating, of the term and concept of title in legal science.[2] Instead, we will focus on the characteristics of this specific kind of legal title, namely territorial title. In order to do this, it is useful to distinguish two definitional pairs of territorial title, articulated in a cascade. Firstly, the dichotomy between title/right and title/entitlement. The second element of this concept refers to title as the root of the subjective right insofar as it focuses on the conditions ("entitlement") that must be met by a legal subject in order to become the holder of a subjective right. Despite its sometimes-inaccurate usage, it is this meaning of title that should be the focus of our attention here and on which the second dichotomy is grafted, namely that between title/source and title/evidence. The former refers to "any fact, act or situation that is the cause and basis of a right"[3] while the latter refers to any "[d]ocument invoked to establish the existence of a right or a quality".[4]

1 As Judge Georges Abi-Saab observed in his Separate Opinion attached to the ICJ Chamber judgment in the Frontier Dispute (Burkina Faso/Mali) case, "[t]his frantic quest for a 'written legal title', at the cost of going to any length", Judgment of 23 December 1986, *ICJ Reports* 1986, § 13, 111.

2 See in this regard our considerations in: *L'ordre international entre légalité et effectivité*, Paris, 2002, 58–91.

3 *Dictionnaire de la terminologie du droit international*, ed. by Jules Basdevant, Paris, 1960, 604.

4 *Ibid.*, 605.

 | DOI:10.1163/9789004708594_004

These two meanings of the concept of title acquire their full meaning at the moment of their ascertainment by the judge,[5] i.e., at the phenomenological stage, whereas the first dichotomy – title/source and title/right – is situated at the level of the construction of legal title, i.e., at the ontological stage. Leaving aside the phenomenological aspect,[6] it is appropriate to dwell on this last dichotomy, and more precisely on the notion of title/source, which is the only one that needs to be addressed here. This is 'the source or ground of possession',[7] or, in other words, '*titulus est iusta causa possidendi quod nostrum est; or, it is the means whereby the owner of lands hath the just of his property*'.[8] The emphasis is on both the way the owner has taken possession of the thing in question and the lawfulness of that possession, with *just* here clearly referring to *iusta causa*, i.e., in conformity with the law (*ius-tus*). Moreover, *just title* in Anglo-Saxon law designates, in the wake of Roman law, the title by virtue of which one acquires a thing by prescription (the *usucapio* of Roman law).[9] The only true legal title would therefore be the one that unites in the same legal subject both the right to possess a certain thing and its actual possession.[10] We have therefore established that legal title is the *justification* (in the etymological sense), the *causa*, the fact, the presupposition of the legal acquisition by a legal person of the right of ownership.

A quick look at the normative texts that make up the *Corpus iuris civilis reveals* that any transfer of ownership that requires the actual taking of possession of the thing or land is subject to the distinction between *titulus adquirendi* and *modus adquirendi*. The 'fact' which gives rise to the personal obligation is worded: *iustus titulus, iusta causa, iustum initium*. This is precisely the function of the 'titulus', to be the 'iusta causa' that would legally justify the creation or extinction of the subjective right. *Iusta*, therefore, in the sense that Roman civil law attributed to this term,[11] i.e. 'in accordance with the

5 "The notion of title may also and more generally refer to any means of proof capable of establishing the existence of a right as well as to the very source of that right", ICJ, Frontier Dispute Case, 1986, § 18, at 564.

6 See: Distefano, 2002, 393–434.

7 *Black's Law Dictionary*, 6th edn, St. Paul, 1990, 1487.

8 William Blackstone, *Commentaries on the Laws of England*, Vol. 1, London, 1765–1769, 195 [emphasis added].

9 *Black's Law Dictionary*, 866.

10 See the Fama Case (High Court of Admiralty, 1804), in *Scott*, 183: "[T]o complete the right of property, the right to the thing, and the possession of the thing itself, should be united … that there should be both the jus in rem, and the jus in re".

11 In the strict sense, the adjective *iustus* designated a thing that was legitimate (*Lexicon Totius Latinitatis*, Vol. II, 972): "Iustus est legitimus"; but also, and this meaning proves to be very interesting, it can qualify, in the strict sense, a thing that is (or is done) according

law'.[12] On the other hand, '*modus*' is used to indicate the manner in which the transfer of ownership takes place, i.e. the actual taking of possession. Both elements are thus required for this kind of transfer of sovereignty to take place validly and to produce legal effects *erga omnes*, specific to territorial rights.[13] This distinction between the two conditions or elements is crucial for a satisfactory conceptualisation of territorial title. Austin expresses well both the unfortunate confusion between the concepts, but also the need for terminological precision:

> I shall use indifferently, 'mode of acquisition, title, cause, investitive event,' etc. : unless I attach specially a more special meaning ... By Roman Lawyers, and in the language of the derivative systems, titulus never means a title in the sense of mode of acquisition ... In the sense in which the term 'Titulus' is used by the Roman Lawyers, it denotes, not a mode of acquisition, but a condition necessary to the efficacy of a mode of acquisition.[14]

In the light of the aforesaid, we can conclude that the term 'titulus', from which the present forms in the Indo-European languages derive, had a very restricted meaning in Roman law. It constituted one of the two conditions required to bring about the transfer of ownership in a strictly legal manner. Consequently,

---

to law: *secunda certa iura*; *Thesaurus Linguae Latinae*, 1970, Vol. VII, 2, fasc. The expression *iustus titulus* would seem to be, according to some (e.g.: Joseph-Louis-Elézéar Ortolan, *Explication historique des Instituts de Justinien*, 4th édn, Tome 1er, Paris, 1850, 459 and note 4), less recent than that of *iusta causa*. Nevertheless, there is some doubt in this respect, and a careful analysis of the texts does not dispel it. On the Greek archetype of the prelegal notion of "causa", see "aition" and "fault" in Anaximander. Anaximander's Cosmic Justice reminds us that the Greek concept of 'cause' is originally the same as that of 'fault' [Hermann Diels, *Die Fragmente der Vorsokratiker*, Berlin, 1903, 12 B1], thus shifting the perspective from legal imputation to physical causation.

12 Moreover, the 18th century philosopher and jurist Giovanbattista Vico, under the heading "Formae, modi, caussae. Cur 'Caussae' dictae?" (*Universi iuris uno principio et fine uno* (1720), caput CXVII, in *Opere giuridiche. Il diritto universale*, Florence, 1974, 137), based on the etymology of 'causa', derived from 'cavere', concludes that laws and jurists are often referred to as 'cavere', since they protect subjective rights ... in accordance with the objective law in force, hence the term 'modi, caussae, cavissae'.

13 See: Giuseppe Carnazza Amari, *Elementi di diritto internazionale*, Vol. 2, Milan, 1874, 186–187.

14 John Austin, *Lectures on Jurisprudence, or the Philosophy of Positive Law* (1863), Lect. LV, London, 1885, 885, 886: "Certain classes of titles, or of modes of acquisition, have concise names: as, for example, 'occupancy', 'alienation', 'praescription' and so on", 896: the coincidence between 'titles' and 'modes of acquisition' could not be more obvious.

it is important to distinguish as clearly as possible between the possession of the thing (or *adprehensio physica*) and the title *to* it (*titulus adquisitionis*), with regard to changes of ownership. This need to combine the right to possess a thing (or occupy land) *with* the possession (or *occupatio*) itself (or the physical acts that make it possible) is the very foundation of any legal order.[15] However, some authors[16] are still struggling in these mists and fail to detect this fundamental requirement of the legal order: conceptual myopia is thus perpetuated.

It is from these terms that we will build our concept of legal title. The first represents the legality of the territorial transfer while the second refers to the requirement of the effectiveness of the territorial transfer. There will be legal title when its two constituent conditions (or components) are found to be united in the same State. In this concept of legal title, legality and effectiveness merge.

A The So-Called "Modes of Acquisition" of Title to Territory

From the outset, the reader should be aware that the expression 'modus adquirendi' is hardly of Romanist origin but was developed by modern civil jurists. Roman jurisconsults preferred not to build a unified system, but spoke in each case, and depending on the circumstances, of *solutio, redemptio, adquisitio* of rights or obligations. Modern civil law is familiar with this same crucial differentiation and builds on it the edifice of private law as regards the transfer of property. Indeed, the acquisition is called 'à titre originaire'[17] when the subjective right (property) arises as a new right in the holder. The salient feature of this type of acquisition is that it is *independent of the acquirer's* will to acquire; the latter's volition can possibly only be taken into account if he intends to renounce the acquisition. Examples of this "mode of acquisition" include occupation, accession, usucapio, "possession by a third party in good faith",

15 Pasquale Fiore, *Nouveau droit international public suivant les besoins de la civilisation moderne*, Paris (translated from Italian by Paul Pradier-Rodière), 1868, 378–379.

16 See, among other authors: Thomas J Lawrence, *The Principles of International Law*, 5th edn, Oxford, 1920, 169, according to which there are as many titles as there are modes of acquisition and sources of title; Arrigo Cavaglieri, "Règles générales du droit de la paix", 26 *RCADI* 1929-I, 413, which supports the conceptual and functional identity between legal title and mode of acquisition of territory; Pasquale Fiore, *Il diritto internazionale codificato e la sua sanzione giuridica*, 5th edn, Turin, 1915, 444–459.

17 See: ICJ, Maritime Delimitation and Territorial Questions between Qatar and Bahrain (Qatar v. Bahrain), Judgment of 16 March 2001, *ICJ Reports* 2001, paras. 99 et seq.

in relation to movable property.[18] On the other hand, derivative acquisition is said to occur when the following two conditions are met: a) the existence of a *relationship*[19] between the acquirer (the holder *in fieri*) and another subject (the previous holder); b) the ownership (by the transferor) of the right to the thing or, at most, the power of disposal. If one of the two elements is missing, the acquisition in favour of the acquirer will not take place. Typical cases of derivative acquisition are the contract of transfer of ownership and the succession *mortis causa*. Finally, subjective rights can be created by *law*.[20] Therefore, to say that subjective rights are created *ope legis*, means that the title (legal causa) of the transfer of rights lies elsewhere than in the will of a subject to transfer a right and the reciprocal will of another subject to acquire it.

Internationalist doctrine trickles down and changes direction, but it ends up in the wake of the legacy of Roman law, especially since one of the 'founding fathers' of the discipline, Grotius,[21] maintains this distinction, and Pufendorf follows suit.[22] Subsequent doctrinal literature is limited to receiving this legacy and from then on, this systematisation constitutes an obligatory passage in any textbook or work on the subject: this tradition (in the Latin sense of the word) is perpetuated as a sign of reverence[23] and is only very rarely broken. This is

18 It should also be noted that acquisition by original title bears some relation to, but does not coincide with, *non domino* acquisition, where the transferor is not endowed with the power of disposition over the right in question. The reference here is to usucapio, the acquisition of movable possession by a third party in good faith. See further note 41.

19 'A Thing becomes ours from a derivative Acquisition, either by the Deed of another, or by Vertue of some Law' (Grotius, 1625, Book II, Ch. VI, § 1.1, 566).

20 Examples are: legal usufruct (active) servitudes, mortgage, *ex lege* obligation claim rights (e.g. right to maintenance), *etc*.

21 Grotius, Book II, Ch. III, VI–VII. According to Carl Schmitt, *Le Nomos de la terre dans le droit des gens du* jus publicum europaeum (trans. from German, 1950), Paris, 2001, Ch. II.3, 137–138, this distinction of private law is not old. The said author would have it go back to the above-mentioned chapter of Grotius' work.

22 Samuel Pufendorf, *De iure naturae et gentium libri octo*, 1672 [reprinted in *Classics of International Law*, No. 17, Washington, 1934], Book IV, Ch. IV, § 1.

23 In particular: Sir Hersch Lauterpacht, *Private Law Sources and Analogies of International Law*, London, 1927, § 104 (in full consistency with the spirit of the work, as this author does not deviate in any way from the analogy with Roman private law); Carlo Giuseppe Raggi, "Diritti reali (diritto internazionale pubblico)", in *Novissimo Digesto Italiano*, Vol. 5 (Appendix), 757–758; Guido Fusinato, *Le mutazioni territoriali, il loro fondamento giuridico e le loro conseguenze*, Parte Prima, Lanciano, 1885, 26–42 (original modes), 43–48 (derivative modes); Balladore Pallieri (1962), 450; Ernst Nys, "L'acquisition du territoire et le droit international", 36 *RDILC* 1904, 365–406; Mark Frank Lindley, *The Acquisition and Government of Backward Territory in International Law*, London, 1926, 1–3 (a paradigm of this tradition; exhaustive list); James L Brierly, *The Law of Nations*, 6th ed. (by Humphrey Waldock), Oxford, 1963, 163–173; Fiore (1916), Book III, Title III; Franz von Liszt, *Le droit*

so even though neither State practice nor international and domestic jurisprudence corroborates this distinction.

Like a snowball, the a-critical repetition of this classification becomes apodictic and no longer controversial. However, even among some of the authors who defend it, doubt creeps in. Many questions remain regarding the plausibility and consistency of this classification.[24] In this respect, this classification does not shed any light, it even contributes to thickening the mists hence leading the doctrine to observe, without preconceptions, that:

> the traditional modes of acquiring State territory – discovery, occupation, prescription, accretion, cession, and subjugation (or conquest) – together with their corresponding modes of losing State territory are insufficient to do more than provide theoretical explanations of the holding of unchallenged territory has been demonstrated frequently.[25]

It is therefore for reasons that have to do with the specific characteristics of international society that international law departs[26] from the precepts of Roman law. It is quite logical that this should be the case, since it was in a legal

---

international. Exposé systématique (trans. from the German, after the 9th ed.), Paris, 1928, § 10, at 99–100; Kent McNeil, *Common Law Aboriginal Title*, Oxford, 1989, 10–11; Sir Robert Jennings, *The Acquisition of Territory in International Law*, Manchester, 1963, 3, 7; Giuseppe Barile, *I diritti assoluti nell'ordinamento internazionale*, Milan, 1951, 197; Giulio Diena, *Diritto internazionale pubblico*, Parte prima (Diritto internazionale pubblico), 3rd edn, Naples, 1930, 255; Lawrence, § 74, at 140–150; Gabriel Audinet, "Annexion, cession et démembrement de territoires", in *Répertoire de droit international*, Paris, 1929–1931, Vol. 1, § 3–7 (modes originaires); § 8–15 (modes dérivés); Austin, 899–905; Giulio De Dominicis, *Gli acquisti originarî e derivativi di territorio*, Milano, 1914; Stefan Verosta, "Gebietshoheit und Gebietserwerb in Völkerrecht", ÖJZ 1954, 241–280; Georges Abi-Saab, "La pérennité des frontières en droit international", 64 *Relations internationales*, 1990, 343; Prospero Fedozzi, *Introduzione al diritto internazionale e Parte generale*, in *Trattato di diritto internazionale*, Vol. 1, Padova, 1938, 413–422; Cavaglieri (1929), 402; Santiago Torres Bernardez, "Territory, Acquisition", in *Encyclopedia of Public International Law*, Vol. 10, Amsterdam, 1987, 496 ff; Georges Abi-Saab, "Cours général de droit international public", 207 RCADI, 1987-VII, 70.

24 "In any case the dual classification *oversimplifies* the situation, and the modes described as 'derivative' are so in rather different ways", Ian Brownlie, *Principles of Public International Law*, 4th edn, Oxford, 1990, 132 [emphasis added].

25 A Munkman, "Adjudication and Adjustement -International Judicial Decision and the Settlement of Territorial and Boundary Disputes", 46 BYIL 1972–1973, 93–94.

26 As one eminent jurist wisely observed: "The law of international dominion -or perhaps it would be better to say international 'seisin'-is not the law of anyone civilized country or a *quintessence* of the land laws of all civilized countries", Sir John Fischer Williams, "Sovereignty, Seisin, and the League", BYIL, Vol. 17 (1926), 32 [emphasis added].

system that referred to ownership and not to sovereignty that these "modes" were developed and drawn upon. However, the analogy between these two normative concepts is not and should not be perfect. For the legal relationship between the state and its territory is not entirely comparable to (and cannot be reduced to) that between the *res* and the individual. The latter could exist without the former, whereas the state cannot *exist* without territory (at least in the medium or long term).[27]

Not only does this classification not stand up to the criticism mentioned earlier, but it is also not supported by State practice, international jurisprudence and the most qualified doctrine (Article 38 (1) (d) ICJ Statute). Let us begin with the arguments put forward by the latter.

According to some authorities, this classification would represent one of the remnants of the patrimonialist theory of territorial sovereignty.[28] In fact, the reality of the acquisition (or loss) of title to territorial sovereignty is too complex and multifaceted to be frozen[29] in patrimonial schemes that are drawn, by analogy, from private law, and that were conceived and responded to very different requirements. In fact, other elements contribute to the dynamics of the creation and extinction of titles, namely the behaviour of third States, of States directly concerned by the territorial change, the analysis of the legal fact, the effectiveness, *etc.*

It is precisely on these aspects that the jurist must focus his attention, as this classification is only a subterfuge that leads to investigative laxity and speculative fearfulness.[30] Hence the important role played by the study of state practice[31] and the history of international legal relations. It is therefore important

27 The question of "drowning states" remains hitherto unresolved and partially unexplored. See *infra* Part 2. Chapter 7. Section D.

28 Santi Romano, "Clipperton" (1930), in *Frammenti di un dizionario giuridico*, Milan, 1983, 37 (although in a more nuanced way). See also Distefano (2002), 33–37.

29 See Charles De Visscher, "Observations sur l'effectivité en droit international public", 62 *RGDIP* 1958, 604.

30 "Many of the standard textbooks, and particularly those in English, classify the modes of acquisition in a *stereotyped way* which reflects the preoccupation of writers in the period before the First World War. According to this analysis (if the term is deserved) there are five modes of acquisition ... *Labels are never a substitute for analysis* ... A tribunal will concern itself with proof of the exercise of sovereignty at the critical date or dates, and in doing so will not apply the *orthodox analysis to describe its process of decision* ... The orthodox analysis does not prepare the student for the interaction of principles of acquiescence and recognition with the other rules ...", Brownlie (1990), 131–132 [emphasis added]. It should be noted that 'orthodox analysis' has and still has followers [see supra note 23].

31 Moreover, this classification is corroborated by the examination of State practice: 'The assumptions underlying this distinction appear, however, to be completely unrelated to

to give more weight to the specific characteristics of each territorial change by trying to extrapolate general rules only with great caution:

> The analysis of the problem in historical perspective puts the emphasis on consolidation of title as a process. Moreover, it underlines the two typical characteristics of titles to territory. It brings out their initial relativity and the growing multiplicity of their constituent elements in their movement towards absolute operation. Such an historical analysis also explains the unsatisfactory character of any attempt to put the operative rules into the strait jacket of private law analogies.[32]

This passage illustrates above all the *credo of* the doctrine which sees in the creation of legal title that specific phenomenon which is the 'complex juridical fact'.[33] This 'individualisation' of cases does not mean the surrender of theory and conceptualisation. On the contrary, it is a matter of using the appropriate tools.

International and domestic jurisprudence[34] support this conclusion, with the latter preferring to base their *ratio decidendi* on other elements (briefly

---

the elements that can be drawn from an unprejudiced analysis of international practice', Mario Giuliano, "I diritti e gli obblighi degli Stati", in *Trattato di diritto internazionale*, Vol. III, Book 1, section 1, Padua, 1956, 96 [our translation].

32 G Schwarzenberger, G. "Title to territory: response to a challenge", in *International Law in the Twentieth Century*, New York, 1969, 290. In the same sense: DHN. Johnson, "Consolidation as a root of title in international law", *Cambridge Law Journal*, Vol. 13 (1955), 217.

33 "International jurisprudential practice sets great store by the the conduct of States. A State's silence, its consent, its acquiescence, any waiver of its rights, any protest, any effect of estoppel upon its actions, all represent important elements in the creation or extinction of a title over a territory", ICJ, Delimitation and Territorial Questions, 2001, § 69, at 168 (joint dissenting opinion of Judges Bedjaoui, Ranjeva and Koroma) See *infra* Part 1. Chapter 3. Section D.

34 See Case Concerning the Frontier between British Guiana and Brazil (Brazil v. United Kingdom), Award of 6 June 1904 by His Majesty King Victor Emmanuel III of Italy, *RIAA*, Vol. XI, 68; Island of Palmas Case, 829; Case Concerning the Frontier between Galicia and Hungary near Lake 'Meerauge' (Austria v. Hungary), Award of 13 September 1902 by Judge Winkler (President), *RIAA*, Vol. 829; Case concerning the Frontier between Galicia and Hungary near the so-called 'Meerauge' Lake (Austria v. Hungary), Award of 13 September 1902 by Judges Winkler (President), de Mniszek-Tschoznicki, Lehoczcki, in Baron Descamps and C Renault, *Recueil international des traités du XXème siècle,* Paris, 1902, 730–752; ICJ, Legal Status of Eastern Greenland (Norway v. Denmark), judgment of 5 April 1933, *ICJ Reports* A/B 53, 45–47; ICJ, Minquiers et Ecrehos (France/United Kingdom), Judgment of 17 November 1953, *I.C.J. Reports* 1953, 47; The Indo-Pakistan Western Boundary (Rann of Kutch) (India/Pakistan), Award of 19 February 1968, *RIAA*, vol. XVII, 528, 563.

outlined above) rather than on 'models' or 'modes' whose theoretical weakness has already been highlighted.[35] We are also pleased to note that in the latest edition of Oppenheim there is a significant, albeit muted, reversal of the value and scope of these 'modes of acquisition':

> When Grotius laid the foundations of modern international law, state territory was still, as in the Middle Ages, more or less identified with the private property of the monarch of the State. Grotius and his followers applied, therefore, the rules of Roman law concerning the acquisition of private property to the acquisition of territory by states.[36] Nowadays, however, the acquisition of territory by a state normally means the acquisition of sovereignty over such territory. In these circumstances the Roman law scheme of 'modes' concerning the acquisition of private property are no longer wholly appropriate. It is still necessary, however to expound these 'modes' of acquisition because they are still relevant to explain titles that go back in history, as so many titles to territory do; and because the new law has developed out of the old, so that the old is necessary to an understanding of the new law.[37]

This "overturning" is revealing and of interest to us in many respects. It is argued that the "modes" of acquisition, although now obsolete and replaced by the new body of rules on the subject, must be used in accordance with the principle of intertemporal law.[38] This principle implies that, in order to assess the legal situation, it is necessary to use the rules that were applicable at the time the facts occurred and not those that would be in force at the time the dispute arises or is settled. The two principles of intertemporal law were delineated by Max Huber in the famous case of the Island of Palmas:

35 "[T]he importation of the *niceties* from the law of property into the field of international law confuses rather than aids in resolving the instant problem", United States v. Ushi Shiroma, 85 [emphasis added]. Similarly: Case of the Canton of Valais v. Canton of Ticino (Switzerland, Federal Supreme Court, Public Law Chamber), judgment of 2 July 1980, *Revue Suisse de droit international et européen*, Vol. 37 (1981), 231.

36 See *supra* notes 21 and 22.

37 *Oppenheim's International Law*, 9th ed (by Sir Robert Jennings and Arthur Watts), Vol. 1, Oxford, § 242, 679 [emphasis added]. For a better appreciation of doctrinal change: Sir Robert Jennings (1963); in the same sense, namely 'modes of acquisition' as material rules, and hence their historical evolution and application to past territorial changes: Combacau, Sur, 408.

38 See Giovanni Distefano, "Time Factor and Territorial Disputes", in *Research Handbook on Territorial Disputes*, ed. by Marcelo Kohen and Mamadou Hebié, Elgar, 2017, 394–416.

> The same principle which subjects the act creative of a right to the law in force at the time the right arises [1st principle], demands that the existence of the right, in other words its continued manifestation, shall follow the conditions required by the evolution of law.[39]

While the application of the principle of intertemporal law in international law is not problematic, the same is not necessarily true for its application to so-called territorial 'modes'. This is because the application of this principle is based on an erroneous conception of the normative nature and scope of these "modes". In fact, the latter are only cognitive categories and do not constitute rules of international law and as such cannot benefit from the intertemporal law principle. They represent only logico-historical categories to which the jurist was accustomed to have recourse according to the Romanist teaching he had received, with the aim of explaining territorial changes. As we have seen, these 'modes of acquisition' are constantly rejected by international courts, and always have been. They have only been referred to in a preliminary manner and international courts have not built their *ratio decidendi* on them. We have already seen how they have been "parachuted" into the doctrine of international law, but they have not enjoyed the same success in international fora and in state practice. These "modes" are therefore not normative categories, but at best they allow the international judge to "apprehend" and legally "construct" the "facts" that are consequently amalgamated by the legal title.

The lawyer uses these 'modes' as 'Kantian spectacles';[40] they are therefore descriptive categories derived by analogy from private law, whereas in domestic law they represent normative categories because they are enshrined in statute and not only in doctrine, as is the case in international law. The civil codes list the 'modes' by which subjects of law acquire ownership of things.[41] However, there is nothing of the sort in international law, whether treaty or customary. And case law practice shows this absence. These modes are, therefore, descriptive categories in the international order, while they are prescriptive categories in domestic orders.[42] Other elements, which we will see below,

---

39 Island of Palmas case, 845. Similarly: ICJ, Land and Maritime Boundary between Cameroon and Nigeria (Cameroon v. Nigeria; Equatorial Guinea intervening), judgment of 10 October 2002, *ICJ Reports* 2002, para. 205, at 405.

40 To borrow the telling image shaped by Bertrand Russell, *History of Western Philosophy*, 2nd edn, London, 1961, 680.

41 See e.g., Arts. 711–717 FCC; Arts. 655 ff SCC; Art. 922 CCI.

42 We can therefore say about the 'modes' of acquisition what has been said about the distinction between legal norms and legal propositions by Kelsen (1967), 71. The authorship of the distinction between prescriptive and descriptive categories seems to lie with John

and which can be included under the heading of "perfection of title", are and remain fundamental for the purposes of the normative understanding of territorial phenomena.

Instead of resorting to 'modes' of acquisition (of territory, of territorial sovereignty, *etc.*) we prefer to speak of certain legal facts [*lato sensu*][43] whose evaluation, assessment, which can only be legal, is to be sought in the legal order where these facts are deemed to produce predetermined legal effects. Thus, many considerations come to mind concerning the acquisition of title *to the extension*[44] of territorial sovereignty, considerations that it would be pointless to try to fit at all costs into rigid private law schemes. For this would deprive them of their flexibility with regard to specific situations that present themselves to the jurist and the judge in international law. These facts, which we will investigate later in this study, constitute the factual description of the material process recognised by international law as capable of creating (and extinguishing) a legal title.

We have therefore thought it appropriate to replace the "modes" of acquisition by legal concepts which are already well established in international law and which we will use to explain territorial changes.

The so-called 'cession' mode is reduced to the legal concept of the (territorial) treaty, which will be examined below [Part 1. Chapter 2]; the so-called 'acquisitive prescription' mode can be explained with the help of certain concepts such as acquiescence, estoppel, renunciation or absence of protest, the peaceful nature of the 'material fact' of occupation, *etc.* [Part 1. Chapter 4. Section B.iii]; the so-called mode of occupation is identified through the notion of the effectiveness of the material fact generated jointly with the *animus occupandi* and the *nullius* character of the territory [Part 1. Chapter 4. Section A];

Stuart Mill, "Essays on Nature", in *Three Essays on Religion*, New York, 1874, 11–15: "Those who say that we ought to act according to Nature do not mean the mere identical proposition that we ought to do what we ought to do" (12).

43 See *infra* Part 1. Chapter 3.

44 This is an expression that we favour and that will be frequently used from now on, as it highlights the *irradiation of* territorial sovereignty beyond the original spatial sphere. We will see later that it is not territorial sovereignty that is transferred from one state to another in relation to a territorial base, but rather the withdrawal of one and the *immediate* extension of the other. This felicitous formulation is also found in state practice, as can be seen from the diplomatic note sent on 19 August 1887 by M Barros Gomes, Portuguese Minister for Foreign Affairs, to M Maurice de Bunsen, French Plenipotentiary in Lisbon, on the subject of the Zambezi River Basin Controversy, in Herbert Arthur Smith, *Great Britain and the Law of Nations*, London, 1935, 10: 'such a country has acquired or legalized its titles *to extend its sovereignty* and civilizing influence throughout the immensely vast regions of Africa, to the benefits of all nations in general' [emphasis added].

the so-called mode of accession is apprehended through the concept of the transfer of title *ope naturae*;[45] the so-called modes of forcible annexation and conquest can alternatively be apprehended in law through the concepts of nullity and, exceptionally, of consent and recognition [Part 2. Chapter 5]; the so-called mode of jurisdictional attribution (i.e. adjudication)[46] is replaced by the simple analysis of the value and effects of the jurisdictional decision. All other phenomena of transfer of territorial sovereignty that are either discarded or included in the "modes" find their explanation through the analysis of the conducts of States and the construction of a "complex juridical fact" [Part 1. Chapter 3. Section D].

Traditional 'modes' of acquisition are therefore theoretical redundancies, superfluous and harmful in the process. They are at most icons, verbal expressions, and even representations of the mind. Moreover, they do not describe certain phenomena that remain unexplained: the birth of new states, States' conducts as a source of legal title, annexation and conquest,[47] *etc.* In this respect, their normative scope is therefore extremely limited. However, these 'modes' are convenient shortcuts to *describe* certain cases of territorial changes: images to express certain territorial phenomena intellectually. We cannot deny that, viewed from this perspective, they can be of some use. However, we must admit that their normative scope always ends up overlapping, thus sliding from the descriptive to the prescriptive level. This drift, whether voluntary or involuntary, misleads the reader who approaches the theme of territorial changes.

B Towards a New Articulation of the Concept of Title to Territorial Sovereignty

We have already had the opportunity to investigate the different meanings of the term 'title'. In this chapter, it is appropriate to go further in order to really construct the concept of legal title with the help of certain theoretical and jurisprudential contributions. Common Law, imbued with the proverbial pragmatism, has delved into this direction and some very interesting discoveries have been made. According to Austin, the concept of title, *stricto sensu*, refers

45 The cases that fall into this category will not be discussed in this investigation because of their marginal usefulness for our purpose.

46 The presence of the latter, as an autonomous "mode" (in its own right) within the traditional classification, is far from being unanimously accepted by the doctrine.

47 Norman Davies, *Vanished Kingdoms*, London, 2011, 729–739.

only to subjective rights that are created through a fact and not directly by law, *i.e. ipso iure*:[48]

> I apply the term *title* to every fact whatever, *through* which the law confers or extinguishes a right, or imposes and exonerates from a duty;[49]
>
> [T]he right arises of necessity through a *title*: through a fact distinguishable from the law conferring the right, and to which the law annexes the right as a consequence or effect.[50]

The concept of title must be used because few subjective rights are created directly by the mere effect of the law, or the rule of law, i.e., *ipso iure*. It follows that the concept of title has a crucial function because it makes it possible to discern, in a given situation, which of the facts (or events)[51] is capable, in accordance with the law, of creating a subjective right in favour of a legal subject. The title thus makes it possible to select certain facts, to the detriment of others, with a view to creating (or extinguishing) a right (or an obligation). It is the prism *through* which the bundle of rights and obligations emanating from the law (in this case, public international law) reaches the various addressees, creating rights and obligations for them, who thus become holders of these rights.

It can be inferred that any subjective right,[52] any obligation must always have a *title*, or legal basis, on which it depends and to which it is attached. The title is therefore the *justification of* the subjective right or obligation. The belonging, the imputation, of the subjective right to the subject of law is commonly called entitlement. This close correlation between fact(s), title and the right that arises from it is elegantly highlighted by Salmond: "every right involves a title or a source from which it is derived. The title is the *de facto* antecedent, of which the right is the *de iure* consequent".[53] The (objective) law

48 For example, the sovereign rights that the coastal State enjoys over 'its' continental shelf exist *ope legis*, i.e., by the mere existence of an international legal rule providing for them (Article 76 UNCLOS). No other fact is required by law for these subjective rights to be conferred.

49 Austin, 880.

50 *Ibid.*, 879.

51 Jeremy Bentham, *Traités de législation civile et pénale*, Vol. 1, Ch. XV, Paris-Geneva, 1802, 281.

52 In our case, the expression "right of territorial sovereignty" refers to a bundle of competences, rights, faculties, powers and obligations that are usually subsumed under this term.

53 Sir John Salmond, *Jurisprudence*, 9edn (ed. by JL Parker), London, 1937, § 120, at 473.

attributes to certain facts, through the prism of title, certain legal effects which may be either (subjective) rights[54] or obligations.[55] Conversely, such rights or obligations may be extinguished or modified by this same means:[56] we will then speak, depending on the case, of the right of territorial sovereignty or of certain minor territorial rights[*infra* Part 3. Chapter 8. Sections A–C]. It is therefore important to distinguish the title from the subjective right on which it is based, otherwise the cause and effect may be confused.[57] This cannot be repeated often enough, given that the doctrine[58] and the language of the case law are not very attentive in this respect. Consequently, in territorial disputes, the title (by its presence, absence and 'weight') acquires a fundamental importance. The validity of a claim of a territorial right obviously depends on the quality of the title:[59] to present a title in support of one's claims, thence the formula: fact > title > claim.

54 "A title: that is to say, certain facts or events by reason of which the right has become vested on its owner", Salmond, § 73, at 293.

55 See: George Whitecross Paton, *A Textbook of Jurisprudence*, Oxford, 1946, § 60, at 231.

56 This is precisely the 'gradation' of legal title [see *infra* Part 1. Chapter 1. Section C].

57 "Though employed in various ways, it [the title] is generally used to describe the manner in which a right of real property is acquired, or the real right itself. In the first sense, it refers to the conditions necessary to acquire a valid claim to land; in the second it refers to the legal consequences of such conditions. *These two senses are not only interrelated but inseparable: given the requisite conditions, the legal consequences or rights follow as of course; given the rights, conditions necessary for the creation of those rights must have been satisfied. Thus, when the word 'title' is used in one sense, the other sense is necessarily implied ... When necessary to distinguish between these two aspects of title, the former will be referred to as 'entitling conditions' and the latter simply as 'rights'*", McNeil, 10 [emphasis added]; Austin, 977; Brownlie, 123.

58 See Andrea Gioia, *Titoli storici e linee di base del mare territoriale*, Padua, 1990, 19, 95, 147.

59 "The claimant ... tries to prove that a right of possession is and has been with him. He uses the rule of international law, together with a factual evidence, in support of his case", Norman Hill, *Claims to Territory in International Law and Relations*, London, 1945, 26; Emer de Vattel, *The Law of Nations or Principles of Natural Law* (1758; translated from French), Book I, Ch. XXIII (Liberty Fund: 2008), Indianapolis, § 283, 245; Sir Humphrey Waldock's Third Report on the Law of Treaties, *YILC*, Vol. Gowlland-Debbas, "Collective Responses to the Unilateral Declarations of Independence of Southern Rhodesia and Palestine: An Application of the Legitimizing Function of the United Nations", *BYIL*, Vol. 67 (1990), 152; Antony M Honoré, "Ownership", in *Oxford Essays in Jurisprudence* (ed. by AG Guest), Oxford, 1961, 134, "a title to a thing is a claim [*stricto sensu*]"; Balladore-Pallieri, 455; JHW, Verzijl, *International Law in Historical Perspective*, Vol. III, Leiden, 1970, 297.

C Strength or Relative Weight of Territorial Title: the 'Gradations' of Legal Title

Since title to territorial sovereignty constitutes the basis of an *erga omnes* right, the States concerned contribute, by the most varied means (*acta* or *facta concluenti*), to the perfection of the title,[60] thereby extending its opposability.[61] From this perspective, we speak of absolute title and relative title:[62] this "gradation"[63] is a function of the (active and/or passive) contribution of States to the creation (or extinction) of territorial title.

In the gradation of legal title, reference is made here to the "formal criterion" as opposed to the "substantive criterion", which we will discuss below.[64] In fact, we are no longer looking at the content of the subjective right of which the legal title is the foundation, but at the legal title itself, whose degree of perfection we are measuring. We are therefore looking at the degree of capacity

60 "I]mperfect title is made *absolute*", Ward v. Broadwell (1854), in *AILC* (1783–1968), Vol. 4, 30 [emphasis added]; "[the title invoked]has been perfected into a complete title", United States v. Arredondo, Supreme Court of the United States, AILC (1783–1968), Vol. 3, 195.

61 'The archetype of this principle can be found in the Roman law rule on possession: Nemo sibi ipse causam possessionis mutare potest' (Paulus, L.3 § 19, de acq. vel am. poss. 41). See in the same vein: Arbitration between Germany and the United Kingdom relating to Lamu Island, award of Baron Lambermont, decision of 17 August 1889, *RIAA*, vol. XXVIII, 244. As it has been rightly noted: "the fact that an interested State puts forward a certain *legal* interpretation or *qualification* entails its *acceptance of* the *legal consequences* of that interpretation, including those to its detriment. Moreover, today'*s self-interpretation mortgages tomorrow's*", Georges Abi-Saab, "'Interprétation' et 'Auto-Interprétation': Quelques réflexions sur leur rôle dans la formation et la résolution du différend international", In *Recht zwischen Umbruch und Bewahrung. Festschrift für Rudolf Bernhardt*, Berlin, 1995, 19 [emphasis added; our transation]. One of these legal consequences is precisely the opposability of the situation of which the State that has given the qualification. Therefore, the latter will no longer be able to go back on its validity (enforceability against it), thereby contributing to the perfection of this situation because it extends its enforceability against it. Validity, based on the quantity and quality of the cooperation of the various States, is thus supported.

62 "T]he more absolute a title becomes, the more it rests on multiple foundations", George Schwarzenberger, "Titles to Territory: response to a challenge", in *International Law in the Twentieth Century*, New York, 1969, 90. Similarly: Vincenzo Bellini, "Il principio generale dell'effettività nell'ordinamento internazionale", 27 *Annuario di diritto comparato e di studi legislativi*, 1957, 225–369.

63 In Common Law, for example, a clear distinction is made between the various *gradations of* legal title: "There are several stages or degrees required to form a complete title to lands and tenements", Blackstone, Book II, Ch.13, 195. See also: AD Hargreaves ("Terminology and Title in Ejectment", *Law Quarterly Review*, 1940, 392) who speaks of "perfect title".

64 See *infra* Part 3. Chapter 8.

of the title (formal criterion) to generate a subjective right, regardless of the content of the latter (substantive criterion). For example, a concession treaty in administration (minor territorial right, from the standpoint of the substantive criterion) only constitutes a complete legal title (formal criterion) when the administering State actually exercises the rights and powers vested in it by the agreement and in accordance with it.

From the point of view of the "formal criterion", we therefore speak of absolute title,[65] relative title[66] and *inchoate title*. The former refers to a quasi-unassailable title that gives rise to a subjective right and the latter to a title whose degree of perfection must be measured against another competing title for the same subjective right. Finally, the term incomplete or deficient title refers to a legal title that lacks one or more elements to finally give rise to a subjective right.[67]

A title which, by its very nature, is incomplete and needs to be perfected, is the "*inchoate title*"[68] (from the Latin "*inchoare*": to begin, to start), i.e., a title incipient, in the making. In the Island of Palmas case, the Sole Arbitrator Max Huber referred to it in the following terms: "an 'inchoate title', an *ius ad rem*, to be completed eventually by an actual and durable taking of possession within a reasonable time".[69] It is therefore a title inchoate which international

---

65 Lindley, 27. Or 'perfect title': Jones v. United States (1890), in *AILC* (1783–1968), Vol. 3, 259; or 'full title', Protocol of the Mixed Commission (Germany and Great Britain) established on 15 July 1886, in *Pasicrisie*, 280.

66 "[R]elative or lesser title", McNeil, 13.

67 "The term 'incomplete title' has been used interchangeably with 'imperfect title', 'equitable title' and 'inchoate title'", Chichimacha Tribe of Louisiana v. Harry L. Laws Co (1982), in *AILC* (1979–1986), Vol. 2 (Second Series), 17.

68 Under the entry 'inchoate' *Black's Law Dictionary* (761) gives the following meanings: "Imperfect; partial; unfinished; *begun but not completed*". The character of incompleteness is thus particularly evident.

69 Island of Palmas case, 845. However, the expression *ius ad rem* used by the Swiss jurist is not very happy. For the notion of "inchoate title" refers to a right which the holder enjoys in a *nullius* territory. Consequently, we are not faced with a State demanding that another State cede a parcel of its territory, but with the obligation incumbent on the other States to respect the right that the State has to take possession, within a reasonable time, of this territory *sans maître*. Therefore, to the protection of the right to proceed with the effective taking of possession and to complete it. This is precisely the precision (not only terminological) provided by Barile (1951, 227, note 217). On the other hand, it would be a question, strictly speaking, of deficient, incomplete *ius in re*. In the past, Barbeyrac referred to the "facts (investitures)" which could generate, for the benefit of the State in question, an embryonic, imperfect title. This is the case, he wrote, when the said State manifests, by conclusive acts, its intention to extend its public power over territories sans maître, in short, when it displays, by concrete measures, its *animus occupandi* [see *infra* Part 1. Chapter 4. Section A]: "Another thing that should be noted is that the effect that we

law requires to be completed within a reasonable time by the actual taking of possession of the territory.[70] And since an *inchoate title* is not sufficient in itself to give rise to a subjective right, it follows quite naturally that the legal title that will eventually be completed will be composed only in part by the *inchoate title*. Other 'investitive' facts must be added to it, thus giving rise to a 'complex' fact capable of achieving the desired result. The *inchoate title* is therefore a perfect illustration of the notion of perfecting legal title, and hence its 'composite' structure. As we have just seen, a 'proto-title' (*inchoate title*) is not 'as good' as an absolute title, or even a relative title, provided that the latter is characterised by a minimum of effectiveness.[71] But what are the legal facts that international law recognises as capable of creating an *inchoate title*? What are the legal effects produced by the birth of such a title? How does this imperfect title materialise? What rights does the State holding *inchoate title* enjoy by virtue of such title? The doctrine is unanimous as to the facts that can generate an *inchoate title*: discovery,[72] symbolic and/or formal taking of

---

attribute here to a simple declaration of will is reduced to preventing those who could not have the same intention. But it has never been claimed that this is sufficient to acquire a full right of ownership that henceforth excludes all claims of others. If, being within reach of taking physical possession of the thing of which one has shown a desire to take possession, one did not do so, one would give the impression that one did not care and that one had changed one's mind. The desire to appropriate, and the signs one gives of this to exclude competitors, tend by themselves to the enjoyment of the right, which one cannot have without possession. Thus, as soon as one neglects to procure this enjoyment, one renounces the right one has just acquired; and the others, who let themselves be warned, recover theirs", Charles Barbeyrac, *Notes à la traduction de oeuvre de Pufendorf: Le droit de la nature et des gens ou système général des Principes les plus importants de la morale, de la jurisprudence et de la politique*, Vol. 1,er, Ch. IV, § 2, Basel, 1771, 580 (note 2; our translation).

70 Vattel had already mentioned this type of title: "When therefore a nation finds a country uninhabited and without an owner, it may lawfully take possession of it: and after it has sufficiently made known its will in this respect, it cannot be deprived of it by another nation. Thus navigators going on voyages of discovery, furnished with a commission from their sovereign, and meeting with islands or other lands in a desert state, have taken possession of them in the name of their nation: and this title has been usually respected, *provided it was soon followed by a real possession*", Emer de Vattel, Book 1, Ch. XVIII, § 20, at 214 [emphasis added]. The doctrine in its wake hardly hesitated to adopt such an embryonic concept of title; in particular: Mark F Lindley, *The Acquisition and Government of Backward Territory in International Law*, London, 1926, 9–16; Jürg Fisch, *Die europäische Expansion und das Völkerrecht*, Stuttgart, 1984, 444, 447–490 (who speaks of 'Titel *a priori* und *a posteriori*'); Fusinato, 37; Jan De Louter, *Le droit international public positif*, vol. 1, Oxford, 1920, 348; Brierly (1963), 165–166.

71 "An inchoate title however cannot prevail over a definitive title founded on continuous and peaceful display of sovereignty", Island of Palmas case, 869.

72 "Title by settlement, like title by discovery, is of itself an *imperfect title*, and its *validity will be conditional* upon the territory being vacant at the time of the settlement, either as

possession,[73] blessing of the premises, hoisting of the flag, agreements on "spheres of influence".[74] In other words, what is lacking is actual occupation; *inchoate title* refers to a beginning of possession[75] which is in the process of being finalised: a still fluctuating legal situation (*schwebende Rechtslage*).[76] However, international law protects certain rights of the titular state; in particular, the titular state enjoys a kind of right of pre-emption[77] over the territory in question.[78] This is precisely to enable the state to complete its title,

never having been occupied, or has having been abandoned by the previous occupant", Sir Travers Twiss, *The Law of Nations Considered as Independent Political Communities: on the Rights and Duties of Nations in Time of Peace*, Oxford,1884, 123 [emphasis added].

73 "[T]he mere fact of seeing a land, without any act, even symbolic", Island of Palmas case, 843; 'In effect, when navigators have met with desert countries in which those of other nations had, in their transient visits, erected some monument to shew their having taken possession of them, they have paid as little regard to that empty ceremony, as to the regulation of the popes, who divided a great part of the world between the crowns of Castille and Portugal', Emer de Vattel, Book 1, Ch. XVIII, § 208, 215.

74 See also *infra* Part 3. Chapter 8. Section E.

75 "[O]f the territories over which states only claimed inchoate title resulting from discovery and formal possession", Roberto Ago, *Il requisito dell'effettività dell'occupazione nel diritto internazionale*, Rome, 1934, 116 [our translation]. State practice seems to confirm this view. In this regard, it is useful to reproduce here the reply of Mr. Gallatin, Plenipotentiary of the United States of America, to his English counterpart, Mr. Addington, at the time of the territorial dispute between the two States concerning the validity of the title of sovereignty in the Oregon region: "Prior discovery gave a right to occupy, provided that occupancy took place within a reasonable time and was ultimately followed by permanent settlement, and by the cultivation of the soil", Sir Travers Twiss, 168.

76 See Romano, "Clipperton" (1930), 38: "[U]no stato di pendenza e di aspettativa"; Mario Giuliano, "I diritti e gli obblighi degli Stati", in *Trattato di diritto internazionale*, Vol. III, Padua, 1956, 209.

77 This right of pre-emption is guaranteed by international law to the State holder of the inchoate title, and other states must refrain, always for a reasonable period of time, from undertaking acts of possession or occupation of the territory in question, which could impede the taking of possession of the territory by the state holding the right.

78 State practice is full of such examples, especially during the height of the colonisation of distant lands (e.g., the *Scramble for Africa*). Rules were needed in order to delimit as clearly as possible the land *sans maître*, even before an actual occupation could be established. The Berlin Conference of 1885 responded precisely to this need by establishing a conventional system of creating 'inchoate title' through 'notification' and other 'pre-emption' procedures. It should be noted, however, that long before this date, states, through the so-called spheres of influence agreements and agreements with native chiefs, had been able to avoid conflicts arising from the application of the fundamental rule in such cases that is *prius in tempore potior in iure* (Codex 54 *De Regulis Iuris* in 6 to 5, 12). A discovery or the beginning of an occupation could therefore not be tainted by successive similar acts. This is what the Minister of Foreign Affairs and illustrious Italian jurist, Mr. Mancini, had to say in a dispatch addressed to the Italian plenipotentiary in Berlin for

which can only be done through an effective taking of possession.[79] Thus, the state is obliged to establish itself and manifest a state presence[80] within a reasonable time:

> [W]*hatever rights Spain may have had to the sovereignty of Sulu and its dependencies, those rights must be considered as having lapsed owing to the complete failure of Spain to attain a de facto control over the territory* claimed.[81]

In this case, Spain, through certain protectorate agreements[82] (with the Sultan of Sulu) and spheres of influence[83] (with the other European Powers with special interests in the region) had managed to create an *inchoate title* for itself with regard to this archipelago. However, it could not or did not complete it, due to the lack of *animo imperii* occupation, and therefore, the other Powers (notably England) considered themselves released from the obligation to refrain from carrying out, in their turn, acts of occupation.

In the Bulama Island case, the sole arbitrator was confronted with a very particular situation, which in two respects, in particular, serves as an introduction to two aspects relating to legal title that we shall study below: a) the relative weight of each title put forward by the Parties and b) the 'multititular' character of the international legal order with regard to the creation and extinction of legal titles. According to the Tribunal's findings:

the above-mentioned Conference, Mr. De Launay, quoted in *Prassi italiana*, Prima serie (1861–1887), Vol. II, para. 841.

79 See e.g., the Clipperton Island case (France v. Mexico), award of 28 January 1931 by King Victor Emmanuel III of Italy, *RIAA*, Vol. II, 1109.

80 A Verdross, B Simma, *Universelles Völkerrecht. Theorie und Praxis*, 3rd edn, Berlin, 1984, 672. 'Prominent British writers on international law agree that an inchoate title cannot for an indefinite time constitute a bar to the occupation by another State', Geoffrey Marston, "Abandonment of Territorial Claims: the Cases of Bouvet and Spratly Islands", 57 *BYIL* 1986, 342. As an example for the determination of this "reasonable period", the eminent Italian jurist Fiore ((1916), 444–459) proposed a period of 25 years. This period of time betrays the influence of the civil law codifications of Western countries on the length of time necessary to recover the acquisition of property by way of usucapio [see *infra* Part 1. Chapter 4. Section B.iii].

81 Dispatch from Earl of Derby to the English Ambassador in Berlin, Lord Odo Russell, 17 January 1876, in *Bruns*, B.1.2 (1871–1878), § 602.

82 Treaty of 1836. It should also be noted in the process that the Sultan of Sulu will successively conclude a similar agreement with England, causing numerous problems as to the scope of these acts and its credibility as a Contracting Party. On the notion of international protectorate, see *infra* Part 3. Chapter 8. Section G.i.

83 Protocol of 1885.

> the said Island of Bulama and the said mainland opposite thereto were discovered by a Portuguese navigator in 1446; that long before the year 1792[84] a Portuguese settlement was made at Bissao on the river Jeba, which said settlement has ever since been maintained under Portuguese sovereignty ; ... that the Island of Bulama is adjacent to the mainland and so near to it that animals cross at low water;[85] *in 1752 formal claim was made by Portugal to the Island of Bulama, which claim has ever since been asserted*; ... hat the British title is derived from an alleged cession by native chiefs in 1792, at which time the sovereignty of Portugal had been established over the mainland and over the Island of Bulama; that the Portuguese Government has not *relinquished* its claim, and now occupies the Island with a Portuguese settlement of about seven hundred persons ; ... and that none of the acts done in support of the British title have been *acquiesced* in by Portugal.[86]

Portuguese sovereignty was finally recognised by the Tribunal, which based its *ratio decidendi* on the following facts: (a) Portuguese *inchoate title* derived from discovery; (b) Portuguese *inchoate title* derived from contiguity; (c) maintenance of the claim and actual occupation at the time of the arbitral settlement; (d) these facts corroborate the absence of acquiescence on the part of Portugal. Great Britain could only claim inchoate title based on an agreement with the native chieftains.[87] However, this title was not enforceable against Portugal because it was granted at a time when the Portuguese title had already been completed or, at the very least, was being perfected. Consequently, and if one follows Max Huber,[88] British *inchoate title* (if it had existed) could hardly prevail over the, very relative, Portuguese title. It therefore follows that the judge called upon to settle the dispute is necessarily led to determine the weight of the titles in dispute. That is to say, their *respective* capacities to generate the subjective right for which they are competing.

The perfection of legal title in the case of territorial transfers that take place without a treaty act, or in any case when the latter is not the only juridical

84 Date of the first English claim.

85 An additional grounds – based on contiguity – which could give rise to *another* inchoate title, independent of the one resulting from the discovery, for the benefit of Portugal.

86 Arbitral award between Portugal and the United Kingdom, regarding the dispute about the sovereignty over the Island of Bulama, and over a part of the mainland opposite to it, Decision of 21 April 1870, *RIAA*, vol. XXVIII, 138–139 [emphasis added].

87 See *supra* note 72.

88 See *supra* note 71.

cause of the territorial transfer, takes the form of a complex juridical fact. For example, in the case of the discovery of an island *sans maître*, the State is in possession of an *inchoate title*, i.e. an *ius in re* deficiency.[89] If the State persists in its claim to the island and thus continues the effective occupation, the incomplete title that is the *inchoate title* will be incorporated, as a constituent element, into the complete title that arises precisely from the actual occupation. The different elements that make up the legal title contribute, each for its part and according to its "weight", to making it more *effective*, or even to making the territorial situation supported by the title in question more *effective*.

We still have to face a corollary problem to that of absolute/relative title, namely that of the relative weight of legal titles. This notion, so essential in this field of public international law, is the logical consequence of the "multititular" character of this legal system in relation to the establishment of territorial titles. It would indeed not be intelligible in a "unititular" system.

By "multititular", *common* law jurisprudence means a plurality of 'sources' of title to ownership (and thus of claims based on them), sources of title that are different and independent of each other. It is thus envisaged that several *'roots of title'* develop in a distinct and competing manner, giving rise to claims that are equally legitimate, at least initially. In a process comparable to parthenogenesis, legal title can give rise to other legal titles that grow out of this common 'trunk'. As a result, several competing 'roots of title' can spring from the same common trunk. In this system, 'absolute titles' or 'better titles' can only emerge (or be generated) as a result of the confrontation between competing titles and the *catharsis* of the jurisdictional settlement of disputes. Honoré thus described the functioning of a 'multititular' system in relation to the creation (and extinction) of subjective rights:

> [T]hat several persons may have titles to the same thing; thus a new possessor has, under some systems of law, *a better right to possess than any later possessor of the thing not deriving the title from an earlier possessor … Hence there may be problems of priority of title.*[90]

89 See *supra* note 69.

90 Honoré, 135 [emphasis added]. Herbert W Ballantine, "Title by Adverse Possession", *Harvard Law Review*, Vol. 32 (1918), 135–152.

It follows that the possibility of acquiring a title without the consent, express or implicit, of the previous holder may lead to the situation where titles continue to exist independently while strengthening or weakening over time.[91]

The 'disadvantages' linked to the dia-chronic character of 'multititular' systems naturally lead to the problem of the 'critical date',[92] whose role is particularly important in this case. This dynamic inherent in the conflict of legal titles and their respective maintenance and extinction was clearly described in the Minquiers et Ecrehos case by Judge Levi Carneiro in his separate opinion attached to the judgment:

> In my opinion, while the French original title – consisting at most in the mere institution of an unproven and doubtful suzerainty, … the English original title – deriving from the probably unconditional Norman conquest – was strengthened, consolidated, legitimised, in the course of successive treaties and the almost uninterrupted occupation of the whole of the Channel Islands and, finally, by the assertion of national sovereignty when political feudalism disappeared.[93]

91 "[T]he later acquisition may have the effect either of divesting the earlier or of creating a second, *concurrent title*; in the latter event, the two titles may continue indefinitely to run concurrently, or the *earlier* may lapse or become unenforceable after a period of time", Honoré, 136 [emphasis added].

92 On this key concept of the jurisdictional settlement of territorial disputes, see Distefano (2018), 397–416.

93 ICJ, Minquiers and Ecrehos, 96–97. "The events after 1925 or 1937, as the case may be, are thus essentially intended to show that, *in the face of Argentine claims* [to certain Antarctic areas], the United Kingdom did not abandon but actively *maintained its title to* the territories in question", Antarctic Cases (United Kingdom v. Argentina; United Kingdom v. Chile): *I.C.J. Pleadings* 1956, § 35 (Application against the Argentine Republic; emphasis added); "The Court notes that, in respect of a situation which could only be *strengthened* with the passage of time, the United Kingdom Government refrained from formulating reservations", Fisheries case (United Kingdom v. Norway), Judgment of 18 December 1951: *I.C.J. Reports* 1951, 139 [emphasis added]. "In Qatar, therefore, the authority of the Al-Thani gradually spread, while that of the Al-Khalifa progressively shrank", Joint Dissenting Opinion of Judges Bedjaoui, Korova and Ranjeva attached to the Judgment of the International Court of Justice in the Case concerning Maritime Delimitation and Territorial Questions between Qatar and Bahrain, 2001, § 104. Similarly: ICJ, Sovereignty over Pedra Branca/Pulau Batu Puteh, Middle Rocks and South Ledge (Malaysia/Singapore), 2008, § 290.

We thus observe that not only is international law a "multititular" system,[94] but that legal title is not something immutable, fixed forever. Instead, territorial title evolves, changes, interacts with new facts and competing titles.[95] Moreover, it is like a sponge, because new facts or legal acts become embedded in it, grafted onto it with the aim of weakening or strengthening it, always in relation to other rival titles; hence the adjective 'relative'. The legal title is thus composed of several elements held together by the fact that they all tend towards the achievement of a certain goal. It is an aggregate of conclusive acts and facts, an efficient cause in the Aristotelian sense, whose raison d'être is precisely the achievement of a result, of a legal situation, namely the creation or extinction of a subjective territorial right. The Minquiers and Ecrehos case illustrates these characteristics in many respects and was undoubtedly settled using the concept of 'best title' and the German concept of the 'relative force' of title.[96]

On the contrary, in *unititular* systems, one can only conceive of one common source with regard to the legality of possession (and the claim to title). The conflict between titles is here only dia-chronically conceivable, i.e., the most recent title in dispute can only prevail by erasing the title from which it originates. The antecedent title is thus replaced by its substitute, which is the fruit, if we may use this expression, of its womb. In this system the title thus immediately becomes 'absolute' or the 'best title' following the erasure of the previous title. Thus, unlike the *multititular* system, absolute titles can be created whose *erga omnes* opposability and validity are immediately and

94 "[I]nvoking prescription would therefore involve adopting a totally different basis for determining the boundary", Kasikili Island / Sedudu (Botswana / Namibia) Case, Judgment of 13 December 1999, *ICJ Reports* 1999, § 91, at 1101.

95 It should be stressed in this respect that the relationship between 'time' and territorial title is at least fourfold: a) evolution of the rules governing the acquisition and loss of territorial sovereignty; b) creation and maintenance of territorial titles over time; c) conflicts between territorial titled over time in a 'multititular' system; d) critical date. The first two dimensions can be subsumed under the single heading of "intertemporal law" and only the third will be more specifically tackled in this book, while b) and d) have been the subject of another study (*supra* note 92).

96 See in this sense: Sir Gerald Fitzmaurice, "The Law and Procedure of the International Court of Justice. Points of Substantive Law. Part II", 32 *BYIL* 1955–1956, 64–65; The Indo-Pakistan Western Boundary (Rann of Kutch) between India and Pakistan, 528–569. See the diplomatic correspondence between Brazil and Britain on the issue of Trinidad Island from 20–22 July 1895, in *NRG*, 2nd series, Vol. 21, 637, where the intertwining of these two concepts can be observed.

automatically established.[97] Quite obviously, the so-called "unititular" systems refer to a primitive conception of the legal order and, in particular, of the mechanisms of creation and extinction of subjective rights. This is why both domestic and international legal orders are "multititular" systems.

These considerations are essential for understanding the notions of "*better title*" and "*relative strength/weight*": concepts that international tribunals resort to when adjudicating territorial disputes, which are ultimately conflicts between titles.[98] In fact, the international order, impregnated with flexibility[99] in its functioning, can only be a "*multititular*" legal system. The conceptual link between the "multititular" of international law[100] and the concept of the "best title" is revealed as follows:

> [T]he concept of title employed to solve disputes approximates to the notion of the better right to possess familiar in common law. The operation of the doctrines of prescription, acquiescence, and recognition makes this type of approach inevitable, but in any case tribunals will surely favour an approach which reckons with the limitations inherent in a procedure dominated by the presentation of evidence by two claimants, the result of which is not automatically opposable to third states.[101]

Territorial disputes arise, in general, as soon as two or more titles compete for the same territorial base, a territorial (or delimitation) dispute being nothing more than a conflict between legal titles in relation to their respective weights, in the first place, and their respective spatial extents, secondly.[102]

---

97 "[I]f the title to a thing is in A, no title to it can be acquired (independently) by B, except by a process which divests A. There is only one 'root of title' for each thing … and the present title can ultimately be traced back to that root", Honoré, 137.

98 ICJ, Kasikili Island / Sedudu Case (Botswana / Namibia), § 91 (at 1101).

99 "[I]t emerges that multititular systems are more flexible than unititular systems", Honoré, 141.

100 The legal concept of 'disputed possession' so typical of international (and common law) law finds its foundation and plausibility in the 'multititular' character of the international legal order [see *infra* Part 1. Chapter 4. Section B.ii].

101 Brownlie, 124. The problem of the relative effect of res judicata will not be studied here. It suffices to point out that this relativity is further highlighted by the relativity inherent in the character of the titles involved [G Distefano (2002), 435–451].

102 "If the *relative strength* of these different claims may be *tested* by the result of that remarkable contest, that of continuity westward must be pronounced to be *the stronger of two*", diplomatic dispatch from US Secretary of State N Calhoun, sent on 3 September 1844 to the British Ambassador in Washington, M Pakenham, regarding the Oregon Territory dispute, quoted in *Moore*, Vol. 1, 264–265 [emphasis added]; the oral argument of Mr Volterra

If the settlement of the territorial dispute is entrusted to a jurisdictional body, the latter will assess the *weight* and *strength* of one title in relation to the other.[103] In this respect, it is worth recounting a passage from that sacred book in the matter, the award in the Island of Palmas case:

> If a dispute arises as to the sovereignty over a portion of territory, it is customary to examine which of the States claiming sovereignty possesses a title – concession, conquest, occupation, etc. – *superior to that which the other State might possibly bring forward against it*.[104]

It must be said from the outset that the "weight" of each title is measured only in relation to that of the competing title, hence the adjective "relative".[105] Again, the reality with which an international court is confronted and on which it is called upon to rule is often complex, and here more than in domestic

---

(Bahrain) in the Maritime Delimitation and Territorial Questions case, 2001, CR 2000/13 (meeting of 13 June 2000), § 144.

103 "[S]overeignty should be accorded to that Party which has demonstrated in its own conduct the *greater degree* of continuous effective control, jurisdiction or possession", The Dubai-Sharjah Border Arbitration (PCA), Award of 19 October 1981, *ILR* Vol. 91, § 9 [emphasis added]. In the same sense: Temple of Preah Vihear (Cambodia v. Thailand), Judgment of 15 June 1962 (Merits), Pleadings, Documents, Correspondence, 1962, Vol. II, 525.

104 Island of Palmas case, 838–839 [emphasis added]. The practice of international tribunals provides us with a rich harvest of precedents: Boundary Delimitation case (United States of America v. United Kingdom), award rendered on 10 January 1831 by King William 1st, *RIAA*, vol. XXVIII, 42; The Indo-Pakistan Western Boundary (Rann of Kutch) between India and Pakistan, 528: "a judgement has to be rendered on the relative strength of the cases made out by two parties"; ICJ, Temple of Preah Vihear, 30; Arrangement for the Settlement of Differences between the Sultan of Muscat and the Sultan of Zanzibar, and the Independence of their respective States, Decision of 2 April 1861, *RIAA*, vol. XXVIII, 109–113; Territorial Sovereignty and Scope of the Dispute (Eritrea and Yemen), Award of 9 October 1998, *RIAA*, vol. XXII, paras. 455, 496, 509; ICJ, Maritime Delimitation and Territorial Questions between Qatar and Bahrain, 2001, § 203 [although the Court declined to apply it *in specie*].

105 "It is often not so much a question of establishing the absolute merits of one of the contentions involved – each of which frequently has its strengths and weaknesses – as of assessing the relative value of the claims in the search for the 'better title'", De Visscher (1958), 604 [our translation]. In the case of the Legal Status of Eastern Greenland, 46, PCJ expressed itself in the following eloquent terms: "In most of the cases involving claims to territorial sovereignty which have come before an international tribunal, there have been two competing claims to sovereignty, and the Tribunal has had to decide which of the two is the stronger ....[the] superior claim"; see also: Arbitral Tribunal for Dispute over Inter-Entity Boundary in Brcko Area (Sprska Republic v. Federation of Bosnia and Herzegovina), award delivered the 14 February 1997, 36 *ILM*, 1997, § 75 (at 421).

legal systems, it is hardly possible to establish a rigid casuistry of precedents, because of the unique character of each case (*"einzigartig und einmalig"*).[106] All the more so as one cannot resort to the privatist and patrimonialist classification of the modes of acquisition of territory.[107] In the light of this aspect of legal title, we are in a position to formulate a critique of the rigid doctrinal orthodoxy in the classification of the modes of acquisition of title to territorial sovereignty, whose relevance for the purposes of *the ratio decidendi* is derisory.

The key principle behind the concept of the "relative force" of title derives from the horizontal and "anarchic" structure of the International Community, where, in the absence of a superior ("absolute") entity, territorial disputes are generally settled on a relative basis strictly circumscribed by the disputing Parties.[108] It can be argued that this is often due to the content of the arbitration agreement through which the Parties submit their dispute; indeed, it is the arbitration agreement itself (which establishes and delimits the competence and powers of the body) that specifies that the disputed territory can only belong to one or the other of the Parties before the judicial body.[109] It is therefore not surprising that the international tribunal, bound only by the legal titles involved, is obliged to settle the dispute on a relative basis. It is bound by the compromise from which it draws its powers and from which it cannot deviate. Moreover, if he is, as some authors claim,[110] a mere organ of the Parties, he

106 "[E]ach territorial problem has its own specific characteristics", The Dubai-Sharjah Border Arbitration, § 190. This is even more evident in maritime delimitation controversies. See to this effect the statements of the Arbitral Tribunal in the delimitation of the maritime boundary between Guinea and Guinea-Bissau, award rendered on 14 February 1985, *RGDIP*, Vol. 89 (1985), 521.

107 "[T]he importance of showing a better right to possess in contentious cases, i.e. of relative title, is *obscured* if too much credit is given to the five 'models'", Brownlie, 132 [emphasis added]. The position taken by the eminent English jurist (which we fully share) is all the more significant in that it remains an isolated voice within the Anglo-Saxon doctrine that gives disproportionate importance to these "models". However, we are pleased to point out that the latest (9nd) edition of Oppenheim's influential textbook (1992) marks a shift, albeit a muted and extremely cautious one, but which is certainly significant (§ 242, 679, see *supra* note 37 the relevant passage quoted at 86). See also: Munkman, 37.

108 See e.g., the arbitration agreement of 1st March 1895 by which Guatemala and Honduras referred their territorial dispute to an arbitral tribunal. There is a clear reference to the concept of relative strength of the titles invoked and their respective values: "las lineas demarcadas en documentos públicos no contradictos par otros de *igual clase* y de *mayor fuerza*, dando a cada uno el *valor* que le corresponda según su antigüedad y *eficacia júridica*" (Art.VI), in *Pasicrisie*, 506. In the same vein: ICJ, Temple of Preah Vihear, Pleadings, Documents, Correspondence, 1962, Vol. II, 525.

109 See the separate opinion of Judge Koojimans in the case of Maritime Delimitation and Territorial Questions between Qatar and Bahrain, 2001, § 77 (at 170).

110 M Miele, *L'aggiudicazione di territori nel diritto internazionale*, Milan, 1940 (and *passim*).

must faithfully perform the obligations to which he is subject by virtue of the agreement. This is another reason why territorial disputes are adjudicated on a relative basis. This aspect was clearly pointed out by Huber in the ubiquitous Island of Palmas case:

> The possibility for the Arbitrator to found his decision on the relative strength of the titles invoked on either side must have been envisaged by the Parties to the Special Agreement, because it was foreseen that the evidence produced as regards sovereignty over a territory in the circumstances of the island in dispute might prove not to be sufficient to lead to a clear conclusion as to the existence of sovereignty.[111]

The principle of the relativity of the *res iudicata* (sanctified moreover by Article 59 of the Statute of the International Court of Justice) is inextricably linked to that of the 'relative force' of the legal title.[112]

Owing to the particular construction of the International Community, the participation of its members (States directly concerned as well as, where

111 Island of Palmas case, 869. The Guiana Boundary Case (Brazil, Great Britain), Award of 6 June 1904 (*RIAA*, vol. XI, 22), the Arbitrator was confronted, in various sectors of the boundary, with the very relative weakness of the titles involved, or even their virtual non-existence, and was therefore unable to establish which of the two was the 'better title': "That it does not appear from the documents produced to Us, which have been weighed and duly considered, that there are historical and legal claims on which to found thoroughly determined and well-defined rights of sovereignty in favour of either of the contending Powers over the whole territory in dispute, but only over certain portions of the same; That not even the limit of the zone of territory over which the right of sovereignty of one or of the other of the two Parties may be held to be established can be fixed with precision; *That it cannot either be decided with certainty whether the right of Brazil or of Great Britain is the stronger*" [emphasis added]. Hence, it turns out that the minimum threshold of 'best title', even moderated by the 'relative' character, is not always met.

112 See Continental Shelf case (Libya v. Malta), judgment of 3 June 1985: *I.C.J. Reports* 1985, § 21. In the case of land-based territorial disputes, the principle has long been established: see, e.g., The Guiana Boundary Case (1904), *supra* note 111. Finally, it is worth recalling that until the decision of 13 September 1990, neither the ICJ nor its predecessor had granted a request for intervention under Article 62 of the Statute. In the above-mentioned judgment, Nicaragua had been allowed to intervene in the proceedings. However, even in this case the principle of the relativity of res judicata is still valid, as the Chamber had to affirm in the Land, Island and Maritime Frontier Dispute (El Salvador/Honduras), Application to Intervene, Judgment, 13 September 1990, *ICJ Reports* 1990, para. 102 (at 135–136): '[T]he intervening State does not become party to the proceedings, and does not acquire the rights, or become subject to the obligations, which attach to the status of a party, under the Statute and Rules of Court, or the general principles of procedural law'.

appropriate, third States)[113] in relation to territorial changes is essential for their validity in law and the only bulwark against the principle of naked and raw effectiveness.

We shall examine, in turn, the meaning of the relative title/absolute title dichotomy on the one hand in situations featuring a legal relationship (*legal act*) between two States (treaty of cession or sale) and, on the other hand, in situations where the *causa* of the change of territorial sovereignty resides in a *legal fact* (transfer of territory in the absence of a treaty).[114] For any territorial change subsequent to the establishment of the public power on the so-called original territory must be based on a legal title which may vary from case to case.

---

113 "[A]lthough it[recognition by third States] cannot be considered as valid recognition of Colombia's sovereignty over …, it tends to *support* Colombia's argument", Territorial and Maritime Dispute (Nicaragua v. Colombia), Judgment of 19 November 2012: *I.C.J. Reports* 2012, § 95 (at 660). Similarly: Territorial and Maritime Dispute between Nicaragua and Honduras in the Caribbean Sea (Nicaragua v. Honduras), Judgment of 8 October 2007, *I.C.J. Reports* 2007, paras. 220–226 (at 724–727).

114 The constituent elements of the situation to which we are referring here may be (and often are) legal acts which on their own would not be considered capable of creating (or extinguishing) a territorial title, but which, taken as a whole, constitute the "legal fact" on which the title is based. Consequently, it is very often a "complex" juridical fact (the "efficient cause") which draws its effectiveness from the existence and synergy of its various components.

CHAPTER 2

Acquisition and Loss of Title of Territorial Sovereignty by Conventional Juridical Act: the Territorial Treaty and Its Specificities

In a nutshell, territorial changes can take place by the following means: a) by unilateral legal act (occupation of *terra nullius*, renunciation, *etc.*); b) by conventional legal act (treaty of cession or sale); c) by legal fact; d) or by the simple operation of the rule of law (*ipso iure*) in conjunction with natural events (*ope naturae*).[1]

The general theory of law has long been aware of the distinction between legal acts and legal facts. The former is a manifestation of will emanating from one or more subjects of a given legal order (hence the sub-distinction between unilateral and conventional acts) aimed at producing the legal effects intended by the authors.

The legal fact is, instead, any event – not a fact of Nature – to which a norm *attributes* a legal effect. By exclusion, the legal fact would therefore be everything that is not a legal act. It refers to all those phenomena that are not voluntary activities of man: "I call *legal facts* those events by virtue of which legal relationships begin or end".[2]

However, for some, including the distinguished Italian jurist Bobbio,[3] this second meaning would be a simple specification of the first. That is to say: within the legal fact in the broad sense – that is to say, as a cause of legal

1 See *supra* note 45.

2 Friedrich Karl von Savigny, *Traité de droit romain* (trans. from German), 2nd edn, vol. III, Paris, 1856, § 104, at 3 [italics in text].

3 See in particular: Norberto Bobbio, "Fatto normativo" [Normative fact], in *Enciclopedia del diritto*, Vol. XVI, Milan, 1967, 988–995. 'The term legal fact is a name of a kind and also a name of a species, i.e. it encompasses both the general category of non-voluntary facts and voluntary facts, *as well as the species of non-voluntary facts as distinguished from acts*. From the distinction between facts and normative acts derives a definition of source of law that is more articulated than the one already given: sources of law are those facts or acts to which the legal system attributes the suitability or *capacity* (*where 'suitability' refers to 'facts' and 'capacity' to acts*) to produce valid norms of the system' (991; emphasis added; our translation). The same authority is still right when he states elsewhere that even this distinction between act and fact does not allow us to resolve the major question of the naturalness or spirituality of law (*La consuetudine come fatto normativo*, Padua, 1942, 23).

 DOI:10.1163/9789004708594_005

effects – a distinction would be made between the legal act and the legal fact (in the strict sense), that is to say, the legal fact which is not a legal act.

In this section, we will study the territorial treaty as an example of a conventional legal act conveying territorial titles. The disposition of territorial titles by means of conventional legal acts does not, in fact, pose insurmountable problems from the theoretical point of view.[4] However, this particular kind of treaties has some peculiarities that deserve to be examined more closely.

A The Principle of Stability and Permanence of Borders

In this respect, the International Court of Justice was confronted a few decades ago with a quite interesting problem. The question was whether the treaty and the boundary it established shared the same existence and suffered the same vicissitudes. In other words, the question was whether the treaty having been terminated, the boundary established thereby would also follow the same fate. The principal judicial organ of the United Nations had to express itself in these eloquent terms:

> A boundary established by treaty thus acquires a permanence which the treaty itself does not necessarily possess. A treaty may cease to be in force without the permanence of the boundary being affected ... where a boundary has been agreed, its persistence does not depend on the survival of the treaty by which the boundary was agreed.[5]

In this respect, the International Court of Justice used the principle of the stability and permanence of borders as a *deus ex machina*, which is certainly one of the most powerful principles of judicial policy. It should nevertheless be noted here that this principle, *ratio legis* of the international legal order

4 But this doctrinal opinion cannot be shared: "Titles based upon cession are usually so clear that legal disputes regarding them *are not frequent*. There have been controversies over the extent of the ceded area", N Hill, *Claims to Territory in International Law*, London, 159. For, as we shall see at once, many controversies have arisen and continue to arise concerning the application of a treaty conveying territorial title, even if only by its mere interpretation. See Distefano (2002), 419–434.

5 Case concerning the Territorial Dispute (Libyan Arab Jamahiriya/Chad), judgment of 4 February 1994: *ICJ Reports* 1994, § 73. Moreover, it should be recalled that the termination of the treaty has no retroactive effects, thus not "affecting any right, obligation or legal situation of the parties created by the execution of the treaty before it was terminated" (Article 70 § 1 (b) VCLT 1969).

in matters of territorial situations, is certainly at the origin of certain specific characteristics of the territorial treaty. For example, in the VCLT 1969 – and the general international law on the subject which it surely codifies in this regard[6] – a fundamental change of circumstances as a ground for terminating a treaty (Art. 62) cannot be invoked "if the treaty establishes a boundary" (para. 2 (a)).[7] Therefore, the famous "clausula rebus sic stantibus"[8] does not apply in the case of boundary treaties or boundaries[9]otherwise established.[10] VCSS 1978 goes even further as it extends the application of the principle of stability and permanence of frontiers to all treaties establishing territorial regimes (Art. 12 "Other territorial regimes").[11] State practice and international tribunals[12] are in line to corroborate the strength of this rule, which is so essential in treaty relations between States: in the interests of the security of international relations, of course. As for the nature of this rule, which some claim to be of customary origin, let us confine ourselves to assuming that it is a logico-historical principle inherent in the very construction of the international legal order. A general principle of international law which "pervades" certain rules of this legal order, among which is precisely that of the fundamental change of circumstances and modifies its operative field as well as the modalities of application.

---

6 See, e.g. Fisheries Jurisdiction Case (United Kingdom v. Iceland), Judgment of 2 February 1973 (Jurisdiction): *I.C.J. Reports* 1973, § 36–43; Case concerning the Gabčíkovo-Nagymaros Project (Hungary/Slovakia), Judgment of 25 September 1997: *I.C.J. Reports* 1997, § 95 (at 104).

7 For the scope (extension) of the term "frontier", see *YILC*, 1982, Vol. II, Part II, 62, § 5: 'The term 'frontier' usually refers to the limit of a State's land territory, but it is conceivable that it may be taken in a broader sense to refer to various lines which fix the spatial limits of the exercise of various jurisdictions. In this regard, one need only think of spatial legal regimes such as the territorial sea, the contiguous zone, the continental shelf, the Exclusive Economic Zone, *etc.*'.

8 See Aymeric Hêche, "Les conditions d'application de la *clausula rebus sic stantibus*", *RBDI*, 2014/1, 322–354; Distefano (2019), 538–542.

9 See, inter alia, Tadeusz Jasudowicz, "The Prohibition to Apply the *rebus sic stantibus* Norm with Respect to Treaties Establishing National Frontiers", 8 *Polish Yearbook of International Law* 1976, 155–181; Ludwig Gelberg, "The Warsaw Treaty of 1970 and the Western Boundary of Poland", 76 *AJIL*, 1982, 128.

10 See *infra* Part 1. Chapter 3.

11 See also *infra* Part 3. Chapter 8. Sections B–C.

12 "Whether it is a land boundary or a continental shelf boundary, the operation is essentially the same: it has the same inherent element of stability and permanence and is subject to the rule that a boundary treaty is not affected by a fundamental change of circumstances", Aegean Sea Continental Shelf case (Greece v. Turkey), Judgment of 19 December 1978 (Jurisdiction): *ICJ Reports* 1978, § 85 (at 36).

B *Nemo plus iuris ad alium transferre quam ipse haberet*

This formula from Roman private law,[13] which has also been known in other slightly different formulations as a result of successive codifications, places an inescapable limit on the scope of effectiveness of the territorial treaty: a state may only cede (to another state) what it possesses as a sovereign. This rule, which is obviously found in modern civil law, is uncontroversial. It is rather its application in detail, i.e., the exact determination of what a State possesses, that is controversial but not the principle itself. As was stated in peremptory terms: "It is evident that Spain could not transfer more rights than she herself possessed".[14] Better still, a state cedes its titulus with all its riches and weaknesses (causes of invalidity, its territorial extension and ambiguities) as well as all the claims it could make in this respect; the acquiring state therefore entirely succeeds to it.

Indeed, it is strongly suggested that any transfer made by someone who is not the owner of the thing (*a non domino*) is void. This rule can be seen from the perspective of *titulus adquirendi* and *modus adquirendi*. The transfer of territory to another State, when the legal title (*titulus adquisitionis*) is sorely lacking, does not constitute a breach of the form of transfer (modus *adquirendi*). The absence of legal title, which is supposed to be conveyed by the treaty, however, renders the alleged territorial transfer ineffective and unenforceable in law. For the sake of consistency with the other sections of this book, we cannot avoid pointing out that State practice,[15] international[16]and municipal[17] jurisprudence as well as doctrine[18] corroborate, if need be, what can be termed a truism.

13 'No one can transfer more rights (to another) than he himself have', Fellmeth, Horwitz, 204.

14 Island of Palmas case, 857.

15 See Earl of Malmesbury's dispatch to Baron Brunnow, dated 29 October 1858, regarding the territorial rights ceded by the Sublime Porte to Russia by the Treaties of Carlowitz (1699) and Passarowitz (1718), quoted in *Bruns*, FB11 § 984.

16 Arrangement for the Settlement of Differences between the Sultan of Muscat and the Sultan of Zanzibar, 109–113; Award between the United States and the United Kingdom relating to the rights of jurisdiction of United States in the Bering's sea and the preservation of fur seals, Decision of 15 August 1893, *RIAA*, vol. XXVIII, 268–269; Libyan American Oil Co (LIAMCO) v. Government of the Libyan Arab Republic, Award of 13 April 1977, 62 *ILR*, 200; Island of Palmas Case, 842.

17 Chichimacha Tribe of Louisiana, 18; American Insurance Co. and al. V Canter (US Supreme Court, 1828), in *Scott*, 189.

18 See, among other authors: Abi-Saab (1990), 347; Honoré (1961), 118.

C The Principle of the Relative Effect of Treaties

We are concerned here with an issue that is very closely related to the previous one. The principle of the relative effect of treaties, which is referred to in the adage "Pacta tertiis nec nocent nec prosunt", may be based on the principle of the independence and equality of States: one of the founding principles of the current edifice of the international legal order. Whether one considers the normative force of the agreement from the subjective angle ("the will as a source of rights and obligations") or from the objective angle ("the expectations created among the circle of addressees of the rules contained in the treaty"), the answer is the same: a treaty creates neither rights nor obligations vis-à-vis third parties. This principle is part of the common heritage of jurisprudence and positive law, so that it can be found in all legal systems.[19] International law is no exception, and the PCIJ reiterated this principle in the following terms: "A treaty creates rights only between the States which are Parties to it; in case of doubt, rights do not arise from it in favour of other States".[20]

The basis (the *ratio iuris*) of this principle can be found not only in the principle of the equality and independence of States but also in a customary rule or, by analogy, in the general principles of law "recognised by civilised nations" [within the meaning of Article 38 (1) (c) ICJ Statute]. As the question of its nature is far beyond the scope of our investigation, it suffices to say that this principle, which is unsurprisingly codified in Art. 34 VCLT 1969,[21] is not open to dispute. It is more interesting, however, to see how this principle affects territorial transfers and the creation of legal titles.

In this respect, as we said earlier, there is an evident affinity between the previous question and the present one. Indeed, if it is true that by means of an agreement a State can only transfer what it legally possesses, it is no less true that in case it disposes of something of which it does not enjoy ownership, the rights of third parties would not be affected. In the Island of Palmas case, sole arbitrator Max Huber rather easily rejected the American argument that since the island of Palmas was mentioned in the Peace Treaty (by which the

---

19 "Agreements have effect only between the contracting parties; they do not harm third parties, and they benefit them only in the case provided for by Art. 1121", Art. 1165 FCC; see also Art. 1372 CCI.

20 Case concerning Certain German Interests in Polish Upper Silesia (German v. Poland), judgment of 25 May 1926: *PCIJ Reports* A 7, 29. In this sense, and *expressis verbis*: Gulf of Fonseca Case (Costa-Rica v. Nicaragua), Central American Court of Justice, award delivered the 30 September 1916, 11 *AJIL* 1917, 199.

21 See: Distefano (2019), 452–461.

United States of America succeeded to all Spanish titles to the said island), the Netherlands should have protested if they felt that the island belonged to them or that their interests were prejudiced. The arbitrator links the two principles when he states that:

> [T]he cessionary Power never envisaged that the cession, in spite of the sweeping terms of Article III, should comprise territories on which Spain had not a valid title, though falling within the limits traced by the Treaty. It is evident that whatever may be the right construction of a treaty, it cannot be interpreted as disposing of the rights of independent third Powers.[22]

Indeed, the provisions of this treaty could not 'convey' any title, since while the form of the transfer valid, the very substance of the territorial right was missing. Spain could not cede a *titulus adquisitionis* to the United States of America since it did not have any in the territory concerned. In the light of the concept of legal title, it can be said that while the form of the transfer (i.e., the treaty in this case) is valid in law, the *titulus adquirendi*, the cause of the *negotium* is lacking as it relates to non-existent (sovereign) rights of the transferor.[23]

This is what is meant by the formula *res inter alios acta*, which therefore does not call for a reaction from all those who could enjoy (and do enjoy) absolute rights over the thing, the object of the transfer.[24] Consequently, one can imagine the two principles that we have just briefly reviewed (the relative

22 Island of Palmas case, 857 [emphasis added]. Similarly: Sovereignty over Pedra Branca/Pulau Batu Puteh, Middle Rocks and South Ledge (Malaysia/Singapore), § 64; ICJ, Territorial and Maritime Dispute (Nicaragua v Colombia), 2012, § 162 (at 685).

23 The treaty is therefore 'absolutely null and void' in the sense attributed to it by modern civil law (FCC 1111; CCI 1418). In the Delagoa Bay case, the arbitrators concluded in this sense since the treaties that England intended to invoke "involved the transfer of another's property; the territories in question had belonged to Portugal for three centuries" (161).

24 This is the meaning that Max Huber rightly attributed to the silence of the Netherlands following the conclusion of the Madrid Peace Treaty, which the United States of America tried in vain to pass off as an 'acquiescence' to Spanish and American claims. However, it was a *res inter alios acta* and, as a result, nothing could be disposed of about the possible rights or claims of third states without their consent or approval in some form. In other words, if the island belonged to the Netherlands, the treaty could not take it away from them; if, on the contrary, it did not belong to them, nothing could transfer it to them: 'Id quod nostrum esse sine facto nostro ad alium transferri non potest' (D.50, 17, 11 Pomponius V ad Sabinum). Bluntschli, on the other hand, makes the condition of the invalidity of the treaty dependent on the protest of 'the state whose prior rights are threatened' (97).

effect of treaties and the impossibility of transferring a territorial right without legally holding it) as two aspects of the same question. Both principles constitute impassable limits to the effectiveness of the treaty for the purposes of territorial transfer, which the practice of international and domestic courts has well underlined, as is apparent from this case before a Dutch court:

> The Münich Pact of September 29, 1938, between Germany, Italy, Great Britain and France, which provided for the transfer by Czechoslovakia of part of her territory to Germany, was void under international law, *since the four Powers purported to dispose of territory and subjects of a State which was not a party to that agreement.*[25]

The territorial titles of third States may also be affected if, by a treaty, State A cedes territories to State B in respect of which another State C had, under a previous treaty, a right of pre-emption: a kind of *inchoate title*.[26] However, this embryonic title of *ius ad rem* (for it is still a personal right and not yet an absolute right) may be violated by the subsequent conclusion of a treaty ceding the territory in question. This would result in a violation of the first treaty by the ceding State, whereas if the occupation by State B were to be effective, it would be no less valid, i.e., enforceable *erga omnes*. Since State B would have both the *titulus adquisitionis* (i.e., the cession treaty with State A) and the *modus adquirendi* (i.e., the actual occupation); it would thus enjoy full and perfect legal title.

D Agreements with 'Native Rulers'

The question we are now going to address can be summarised in the following terms: what is the legal value of a treaty concluded between a colonial power and the local potentate for the purpose of establishing territorial titles

25 Nederlands Beheers-Instituut v. Nimwegen and Männer, District Court of Arnhem, award delivered the 17 January 1952 (Court of Appeal, 18 November 1952), 18 *ILR*, 250 [emphasis added]. The same observations apply to the Molotov-Ribbentrop Pact of 23 August 1939: AP Gureckas, "Lithuania's Boundaries and Territorial Claims between Lithuania and Neighbouring States", 12 *New York Law School of International and Comparative Law Journal* 1991, 123–124. On this treaty, from the standpoint of non-recognition, see *infra* Part 2. Chapter 5. Section B.i.

26 *Oppenheim's International Law*, 1992, § 247; Lindley, 168–169.

for the benefit of the former?[27] What was its legal value at the time of conclusion and, subsequently, in an inter-temporal law perspective – especially following the emergence of certain principles such as the right of peoples to self-determination?

It is important from the outset to set out a few milestones in order to delimit the field of investigation, but above all to indicate the extremes between which the various doctrinal and jurisprudential positions oscillate. As is often the case, the most radical positions are found in the literature, while the case law generally prefers to stick to more nuanced statements. A clearly Euro-centric view is displayed by Liszt:

> Nomadic Negro [sic!] tribes do not constitute States, in the sense of international law, even when they are under the hereditary rule of their chiefs; consequently treaties with them cannot form the basis of derivative acquisitions of territory, but may be used exclusively as testimony or as an indication that one State has established itself earlier than another in the territory mentioned in such treaties, and that, consequently, it has acquired for itself that territory by way of occupation.[28]

This view still seems to reflect the *opinio iuris communis* at the beginning of the last century if one is to believe Max Huber who, in the Island of Palmas case, attributes the same meaning to the 'contracts' concluded between the East India Company and the local chiefs. These 'contracts' only had evidential value for the purpose of establishing effectiveness; they were solely instrumental to prove the effectiveness of the Dutch presence in this territory: *prius in tempore potior in iure*.[29]

In the light of the construction of the concept of legal title, it can be maintained that, according to Max Huber, these agreements lacked the *titulus adquisitionis*. Instead, they were considered as evidence of *modus*, i.e., of the effectiveness of the occupation, because in the eyes of the International Community of the past, these peoples were hardly considered as independent

27 The more specific question that is part of the present theme, namely that of the colonial protectorate, will be studied later in this volume: Part 3. Chapter 8. Section G.

28 Liszt, 106 [our translation]. Some would consider these compacts as nothing more than mere morality: Lawrence, 162.

29 "The fact that these contracts were renewed from time to time and appear to indicate an extension of the influence of the suzerain, seems to show that the regime of suzerainty has been effective", Island of Palmas case, 856.

states.[30] That is to say, they were legal subjects who could enjoy the title to territorial sovereignty and could therefore establish treaty-making power with European states.[31] Similarly, in the Legal Status of Eastern Greenland case, the PCIJ implicitly denied international legal personality to native peoples when it stated:

> Conquest only operates as a cause of loss of sovereignty when there is war between two States and by reason of the defeat of one of them sovereignty over territory passes from the loser to the victorious State. *The principle does not apply in a case where a settlement has been established in a distant country and its inhabitants are massacred by the aboriginal population.*[32]

According to some authors, State practice has been reluctant to recognise these "agreements" as anything other than proof of the effectiveness of the State's presence (or of some authority).[33]

However, even during the 19th century, there were authorities that went beyond these arguments. Some authors classify agreements with native chieftains as legal facts that can give rise to an *inchoate title*. But it is mainly in relative terms that the value of such an agreement must be weighed against other 'facts or acts' that may constitute presuppositions for the establishment of territorial title. An arbitral body is thus called upon to weigh the relative value of such agreements against other competing state actions. For example,

---

30 In relation to the dispute between the United States of America and Great Britain concerning the latter's title and territorial claims to the coastline inhabited by the "Mosquito Indians", the diplomatic note from Mr. Marcy of the United States Department of State to the Representative of the United States of America in London, Mr. Dallas (dated 24 May 1856) is eloquent: 'It cannot be alleged by her [London] *that those Indians constitute, or are competent to constitute, an independent State, admissible as such into the family of Sovereign Powers*', quoted in *Bruns*, FB11 § 979 [emphasis added]. The British had in fact entered into a protectorate agreement with the country's native chiefs; this was met with a reaction from the United States of America, which considered it contrary to previous stipulations with Britain.

31 The 'capacity to conclude treaties' (Art. 6 VCLT 1969) is precisely one of the three legal capacities whose possession qualifies an entity as a subject of international law (Distefano (2019), 60–68).

32 PCIJ, Legal Status of Eastern Greenland, 46–47 [emphasis added].

33 In the dispute over territorial rights to the island of Santo Domingo, see the diplomatic note of José Fabio Melgar, Spanish Minister of Foreign Affairs, sent on 24 August 1861 to all the Latin American republics: 'The Cabinet of Madrid has accepted the proposals made to it by General Santa-Ana, and basing itself on *an alleged contract which lacks the value of an international pact*', quoted in *Bruns*, FB11 § 1049 [emphasis added].

a claim based on such an agreement was frequently found to be in conflict with a competing claim based on the so-called *hinterland* (or "spheres of influence") theory:

> [M]ost of the treaties concluded with barbarian sovereignties are of very poor value as conventions of the law of nations [... however they give] a priority of occupation over territories to which a hinterland settlement between two powers cannot remove the *res nullius* character in relation to a third occupant.[34]

Therefore, according to this view, these agreements are still only means of proof of effectiveness; in short, from the "formal" point of view they are not comparable to treaties between States. What changes, however, is the (quantitative) "weight", in terms of effectiveness, attributed to these agreements, while not qualifying them as conventions between independent States. Diplomatic practice and that of international tribunals[35] do not dissent from this doctrinal trend, since there are many examples of these agreements being assimilated to discovery or even symbolic occupation,[36] for the purpose of creating an embryonic, imperfect title.[37]

---

34 Frantz Despagnet, *Cours de droit international public*, 3rd edn, Paris, 1905, 117, 123 [our translation]. On the nature and legal effects of agreements establishing spheres of influence, see *infra* Part 3. Chapter 8. Section E.

35 For example, in the Bulama Island case (139), England had claimed among its 'titles' that based on the 'alleged cession by native chiefs in 1792'. The value of the *inchoate title was* in no way contested, but this embryonic title had to fade in the face of Portugal's earlier effectiveness on the island. The arbitral tribunal in the Eritrea-Yemen case considered the 'various local agreements Italy made with local rulers' as evidence of title (1998, § 468).

36 See *infra* Part 1. Chapter 4. Section A.

37 See e.g., the "diplomatic instructions" given on 21 November 1884 by the Italian Minister of Foreign Affairs – and eminent jurist – M Mancini, to the Italian Plenipotentiary at the Berlin Conference of 1885, M de Launay, concerning Italian interests and claims in the Bay of Assab: "The Italian Government has not yet taken any steps to resolve the problem of the Bay of Assab. de Launay, concerning Italian interests and claims in the Bay of Assab: ... *secondly, at the discovery or first occupation, the title of the compact stipulated with the native chiefs having, without opposition, the full sovereign right over the territory in question, can be considered equivalent*; thirdly, it is necessary that within a certain period of time the title of the actual performance of agricultural work, or of a civil industry be added', quoted in *Prassi italiana*, Prima serie, Vol. II, § 840 [emphasis added; our translation]. See also the diplomatic note from the Italian Foreign Minister, M Blanc, to the British Ambassador in Rome, Mr Clare Ford, sent on 19 October 1894, concerning the French proposal to the Negus Menelik to neutralise Ethiopia and place it under protectorate. The Minister speaks in this regard of "diplomatic title" and "paper title", quoted in *Prassi italiana*, Seconda serie (1887–1918), Vol. II, § 2328. The concept of "paper title" was

However, from an intertemporal perspective of law, it can be argued that these agreements, as long as they fulfil the same requirements imposed on treaties between States,[38] are considered by the most qualified publicists as true conventions between independent States creating rights and obligations. It is true that the most enlightened doctrine is constantly flowing and changing its slope, but this tendency began in the literature towards the end of the 19th century, at the very moment when the Berlin Congress of 1878 began, which consecrated the *Scramble for Africa*:

> Moreover, even savage populations, *although rudimentarily structured*, always and regularly possess *a certain organisation*, by virtue of which they enjoy the right to be considered, *at least in this respect, as independent political associations*.[39]

This view is largely supported by the Diamond Deposits case, in which the Umpire had no difficulty in considering certain tribes in southern Africa as organised groupings with an awareness of the concept of sovereignty. This implied both a regime of order, maintained by means of organised force and justice, and the *ius disponendi*, the right, derived from territorial sovereignty, to dispose of territory, one of the attributes of international legal personality.[40] Consequently, the international case law[41] and State practice[42] reflect

---

also referred to in Maritime Delimitation and Territorial Questions (Qatar v. Bahrain), ICJ, 2001, CR 2000/22 (meeting of 28 June 2000), § 10 (oral argument by Mr Volterra (Bahrain)).

38 This was held by the Arbitral Tribunal in the Lamu Island case (243).

39 Fusinato, 31 [emphasis added; our translation]. Also: Combacau, Sur, 409; A Truyol y Serra (*Histoire du droit international public*, Paris, 1995, 110), who argues that these treaties also included a recognition of the international legal personality of native peoples. 'From all this the conclusion follows that the barbarians in question can not be barred from being true owners, alike in public [i.e., imperium] and in private [i.e., dominium] law', Francisco de Vitória, *De Indiis* (1532), Part I, § 328 (ed. by Ernest Nys, New York, 1964, Oceana Publications, 125).

40 West Griqualand Diamond Fields Case (Republic of South Africa v. Griqua and Betchuana Tribes), Award of 17 October 1871, in *Recueil des Arbitrages internationaux*, vol. II, 692.

41 E.g., in the Delagoa Bay case (161), where the conventions stipulated between England and certain kingdoms ("regule") of the coast were placed on the same level as treaties between States, the Arbitral Tribunal applied the same rules of general international law relating to the law of treaties.

42 See e.g., the Portuguese diplomatic note on the territorial rights that Portugal intended to claim as a result of, among other 'causes', the conclusion of treaties with the local chiefs of the populations that inhabited the coasts of the Bay of Lourenço Marques (Delagoa Bay): '3° In the conventions and acts of recognition successively reiterated, since centuries, *by the chiefs of the villages that inhabited that coast, and that had always recognised*

this theoretical, cultural and civilisational shift. Thus, from the perspective of the construction of the concept of legal title, it can be maintained that native populations did have *titulus adquisitionis*, which could be regularly transferred through agreements with the Western Powers. As the International Court of Justice had no difficulty in declaring:

> On the contrary, such agreements with local rulers, whether or not considered as an actual "cession" of the territory, were regarded as derivative roots of title, and not as original titles obtained through by occupation of *terrae nullius*.[43]

From the perspective of intertemporal law, it can be argued that while the question of the legal value of such agreements for the purposes of establishing legal title may still be open to discussion, the question of the legal value of such agreements is not,

> The principle of intertemporal law requires that the legal consequences of the treaties concluded at that time in the Niger Delta [at the end of the 19th century] be given effect today, in the present dispute.[44]

These treaty commitments are now considered, by some authorities,[45] to be on a par with conventions between European states, thus creating rights and

---

the sovereignty of the Crown of Portugal', quoted in *Bruns*, FB12 § 594 [emphasis added; our translation]. In the interminable dispute between Spain and the other European powers (especially England), there were several treaties concluded by the latter, at different times, with the Sultan of Sulu (the supreme authority of the political entity known as the Sulu Archipelago). These agreements, sometimes of protectorate, sometimes of pure and simple submission to the foreign power, were obviously in contradiction with each other. These parallel commitments, and their effective scope, were at the centre of diplomatic correspondence for at least thirty years, during which time Spain sought, in vain, to consolidate its effective presence on the islands. However, what interests us is that the legal value of the agreements in question was never the subject of controversy, and their validity in international law was never contested. See in this regard: *Bruns*, FB12 § 602–607; Smith, § 4 (35–45), *supra* note 82.

43 ICJ, Western Sahara Case, 1975, § 80 (at 39). Similarly: ICJ, Land and Maritime Boundary (Cameroon v. Nigeria; Equatorial Guinea intervening), 2002, § 201 (at 402).

44 ICJ, Land and Maritime Boundary (Cameroon v. Nigeria; Equatorial Guinea intervening), 2002, § 205 (at 405).

45 An extremely brilliant thesis has been devoted to this question, which is highly recommended reading for all readers wishing to delve deeper into the subject: Mamadou Hébié, *Souveraineté territoriale par traité. Une étude des accords entre puissances coloniales et entités politiques locales*, Paris, 2015.

obligations. It has even been argued from some quarters that they are null and void on the basis of the unequal character of the Contracting Parties: in short, they are, it is argued, 'treaties of leonine character'.[46] In any case, the treaties of cession, submission or vassalage with the European Powers were considered in all respects valid by the courts of these States;[47] all the more so as these conventions appeared in the collections of international treaties of these Great Powers.[48] It can therefore be concluded that in no case did these treaties constitute a mere subterfuge to obviate a lack (or insufficiency) of effectiveness in the occupation of the territories.[49] These agreements were therefore considered, at least by the chancelleries of the European states, to be genuine treaties capable of conveying territorial titles on the international plane.[50] It is certain, however, that the European powers, faced with a well-established authority over the territories they intended to conquer, employed "softer" means to achieve their objective. Indeed, it was not uncommon to find that these treaties, often drafted in the language of the Great Power alone, concealed under obscure terminology (sometimes impenetrable and often poorly translated) real annexations under the guise of agreements of international representation or even friendship.[51]

46 Morse Bradford, Hamid Kazi, "American Annexation of Hawaii: an Example of the Unequal Treaty Doctrine", 5 *Connecticut Journal of International Law*, 1990, 407–456; Alessandro Pulvirenti, "The overthrow of the Hawaiian Kingdom: Did international law permit the threat of the use of force? 26 *Revue Suisse de droit international et européen* 2016, 581–604.

47 See also, for the colonial protectorate, *infra* Part 3. Chapter 8. Section G.

48 'In the last century and even earlier, European powers and the United States concluded hundreds of treaties with native peoples. They were considered to be rights-producing (especially if they dealt with rights to the benefit of the European side of civilisation) and were included in the official collections of treaties concluded by the states in question', Tullio Scovazzi, "*Kawanatanga* e *Rangatiratanga*: a proposito del trattato di Waitangi", 77 *Rivista* 1994, 732. Also: Evangelos Raftopoulos, *The Inadequacy of the Contractual Analogy*, Athens, 1990, 136. *Contra*: RR Robbins, "The Legal Status of Aden Colony and the Aden Protectorate", 33 AJIL 1939, 705.

49 "In none of these cases does the status of the territory even appear to have been questioned on the ground that the ruler lacked international personality and therefore did not have the capacity to make a cession", McNeil, 119.

50 [S]uch rulers [of Africa] were accepted as being capable in international law not only of holding title to territory, but of transferring it to other Parties', Malcolm Shaw, *Title to Territory in Africa*, Oxford, 1986, 45.

51 See, e.g., the Treaty of Uccialli of 2 May 1889 between Ethiopia and Italy. See, e.g., the Treaty of Uccialli of 2 May 1889 between Ethiopia and Italy, which is still held up as an example of "fraud" as a cause of invalidity in treaty law. The question revolves around the exact translation of an Amharic term, whose semantic ambivalence created a hermeneutical

E The 'Plebiscite' as a Condition for the Validity of Territorial Change

Plebiscites are inspired by the principle of the right of peoples to self-determination, which is one of the purposes and principles set out in the second paragraph of Article 1 UNC.[52] However, it is important to stress that historically the plebiscite was certainly one of the first manifestations of this principle, and even its archetype, especially in the original version of the principle of nationalities.[53]

The practice of plebiscites dates back *roughly* to the French Revolution[54] although there are earlier examples. Indeed, the plebiscite argument made it possible to reconcile the doctrine of the *Constituante* (decree of 22 May 1790 by which France renounced to its territorial conquests) with the alleged will of the populations of the conquered territories. This argument was later abandoned by France, which preferred to replace it with the policy of "natural boundaries"[55] which better suited the new expansionist aims of the revolutionary government. This argument of diplomatic policy was taken up again in Italy during the *Risorgimento* in order to give a popular consecration to the annexations carried out by the Kingdom of Sardinia.[56] In fact, diplomats did not skimp on arguments and fine words in order to justify the *Realpolitik* of their States on this new principle; in short, they tried to integrate this principle, considered at the time to be very dangerous for the stability of the State regimes,[57] as a new

---

conflict between the two Contracting Parties: Tullio Scovazzi, "*Iccialacciual*: sulla divergenza fra i testi del Trattato di Uccialli", 76 *Rivista* 1993, 5–25.

52 On the question of the right to self-determination of peoples in international law of territory, see below: Part 2. Chapter 6.

53 *Della nazionalità come fondamento del diritto delle genti di Pasquale Stanislao Mancini* (edited by Erik Jayme), Turin, 1994.

54 Plebiscites of the County of Avignon (1791) as well as of Savoy, Mulhouse, Hainaut and the Rhineland (1792).

55 Merlin de Douai report of 30 September 1795 on the annexation of Belgium.

56 In this respect, a distinction can be made between the plebiscites held in Emilia, Tuscany (11–12 March 1860), Sicily (21 October 1860), the Marches and Umbria (1866) and finally Rome (1870), which were only internal legal acts (and therefore not of "international concern"), and the plebiscites in the provinces of Venice and Mantua, which were ceded to France and then returned to Italy "subject to the consent of the populations duly consulted". The latter plebiscites were in fact provided for in the 1866 Treaty of Prague (*NRG*, Vol. 18, 344).

57 It should not be forgotten that in the name of the principle of nationalities, a prodrome of the principle of the right of peoples to self-determination, the populations of Palermo, Naples, Madrid and Cadiz (1820) revolted against their oppressors: a prelude to the insurrections of 1848 which set the whole of Europe ablaze. In this respect, it is worth reproducing a passage from a diplomatic note from the Count of Rechberg (Vienna) to Prince de Metternich, the Austrian ambassador in Paris, concerning the Duchies of Schleswig

foreign policy instrument, with the aim of finally neutralising it. To this end, it is useful to reproduce the diplomatic dispatch sent by the French Minister of Foreign Affairs, M Drouyn de Lhuys, to the French ambassador in London, the Prince de La Tour d'Auvergne (6 April 1864), with regard to the question of the duchies of Schleswig and Holstein: "Whatever form it takes, *national assent is at the origin of all sovereignties*. It is their strength and stability".[58]

This was echoed in the diplomatic note from the French ambassador in Berlin to the aforementioned Minister of Foreign Affairs, which reported the words of the Prussian Chancellor Bismarck on this subject:

> [A]ny solution to the Duchy affair had to be considered from several points of view: the rights of the disputing Princely Houses, European political expediency, and *last but not least,* the wishes of the inhabitants.[59]

The principle of nationalities in the form of a plebiscite was first applied in Greece (1st January 1822) and Belgium (25 August 1830).[60] Again, the cession of Nice and Savoy by the Kingdom of Sardinia to France was sanctioned by a plebiscite (15–22 April 1860) in accordance with Article 1 of the Treaty of Turin of 24 March 1860, according to which the High Parties had stipulated that the cession was to be carried out "without any constraint of the will of the populations".[61]

After WWI it is worth recalling the plebiscites prescribed by the Treaty of Versailles of 28 June 1919: in Schleswig (1920), Upper Silesia (1921) and the

---

and Holstein, in which absolutely *legitimate* fears are expressed concerning the application of the principle of nationalities: "It is superfluous, I think, to develop for you the reasons that make us fear any new application of the principle that the popular will must constitute the basis of the public law of Europe. You know all the dangers to which Austria would be exposed if it were admitted as a rule that States must be formed or broken up according to the doctrine of nationalities and the judgments of universal suffrage. We have always avoided considering the Danish-German dispute as a quarrel of nationalities. It is a question of international law which we believe must be resolved by seeking to reconcile diverse rights and conflicting interests", quoted in *Bruns*, FB11 § 1061.

58 Quoted in *Bruns*, FB11 § 1062 [emphasis added; our translation].

59 Quoted in *Bruns*, FB11 § 1063 [our translation; italics in the text]. See also § 1003.

60 "What, indeed, is the rule of conduct which has been followed by the Powers in the affairs of Greece and Belgium? How have the Cabinets proceeded in the Moldo-Valacan Principalities, and even recently in the question of the Ionian Islands? Did they not agree to question the national wish, and did they not agree to consecrate it?", diplomatic dispatch from M Drouyn de Lhuys to the French ambassador in Vienna, the Duke of Gramont, sent on 8 April 1864 (still concerning the Duchies of Schleswig and Holstein), *Bruns*, FB11, § 1003 [our translation].

61 See in this regard *Bruns*, FB11 § 1042.

Saarland (1935). As a result of the referendum results, parts of Schleswig and Upper Silesia were allocated to Denmark and Poland respectively, while the Saarland, administered by the League of Nations, was returned to Germany.[62]

In contrast, WWII peace treaties provided for only one plebiscite: that relating to the Italian territories of Tende and La Brigue (Art.2 of the Peace Treaty of 10 February 1947 with Italy). These territories, following the referendum of 12 October 1947, passed to France. The agreement of 12 December 1953 between Great Britain and Egypt provided for a plebiscite in the Sudan[63] to determine the fate of the territory, which was jointly administered[64] by these two states – in reality by the former – on the basis of a treaty of 1899: its attachment to Egypt or the constitution of an independent state. Finally, although the plebiscite was not held, Sudan became eventually an independent state (1st January 1956).

The attachment of Tende and La Brigue to France allows us to emphasise that the latter was obliged to organise this plebiscite not only from the point of view of international law, but also by the French Constitution of 27 October 1946, which, in its article 27 § 2, stipulated that 'no cession, no exchange, no addition of territory is valid without the consent of the populations concerned'.[65] Again, in accordance with this provision, the cession of the French Establishments of Chandernagor (Chandannagar), perfected by the treaty of 2 February 1951, was preceded by a plebiscite held on 19 June 1949, the result of which was favourable to the attachment to India.[66]

In this case, if the obligation to hold a plebiscite is enshrined in the constitution of one of the Parties affected by the territorial transfer, failure to do so may have two major legal effects. On the one hand, under domestic law this would constitute an unlawful act, on the other hand, under international law – and in particular the law of treaties – it could represent a ground for "relative" invalidity of the cession treaty within the meaning of Article 46 of the Vienna Convention on the Law of Treaties. From the point of view of the concept of

---

62 On the Saarland during the direct international administration, see *infra* Part 3. Chapter 10. Section A.i.

63 *UNTS*, Vol. 161, 157.

64 On the Anglo-Egyptian *condominium* in Sudan, see *infra* Part 3. Chapter 8. Section D.

65 See: Suzanne Bastid, "*Le rattachement de Tende et de la Brigue*", 53 *RGDIP* 1949, 321–340.

66 The cession to India of the other French establishments was, however, carried out without a plebiscite. See on this subject: Alain Coret, "La cession de l'Inde française", *Revue juridique et politique de l'Union française*, 1955, 577–590, 697–712. See also: Re Georger and Teivassigamany (France, Council of State), decision of 27 June 1958, 26 *ILR*, 114–115.

legal title it can be argued that in this case the *titulus adquisitionis* of the treaty will not be perfected until the plebiscite has taken place.[67]

The doctrine has long debated whether, in the absence of an internal norm or a treaty commitment, there was a rule of general international law requiring states to hold a plebiscite before effecting territorial transfers by means of treaty legal acts. Grotius had to argue that, following a war:

> But that the entire Sovereignty may be firmly alienated, the Consent of the Whole Body of the People is required; which may be done by their Representatives, whom they call Orders or States. And that any Part of the Kingdom may be firmly alienated a twofold Consent is required, both of the Whole Body, and especially of that Part which it was united against its Will.[68]

However, according to some authors, state practice could not support the strength of such a norm in general international law,[69] while another minority view, following the Delft jurist's lead, argues that denying the population a say in its fate is tantamount to violating the principle of the right of peoples to self-determination.[70]

67 See in this regard: Kazi Mukhlesm Rahman v. Bangladesh and Another (Bangladesh Supreme Court, Appellate Division), decision of 3 September 1974, 70 *ILR*, 48.

68 Book III, Ch. XX, § V.2, 1554.

69 Malcolm Shaw, "Territory in International Law", 13 *Netherlands Yearbook of International Law* 1982, 87–88; De Louter, 329: "if, by international treaty, these States have lawfully disposed of their territory, the subjects can neither individually nor collectively revolt against this fact"; Liszt, 103: "The validity of an acquisition of territory is not subject to the assent of the inhabitants of that territory (plebiscite)" [our translation]; "The principle that the wishes of a population are to be consulted when the territory which they inhabit is ceded has not been adopted into international law, and can no longer be adopted into it *until title by conquest has disappeared*", William Edward Hall, *A Treatise on International Law*, 8th edn, Oxford, 1924, 49 [emphasis added].

70 See (*ante litteram*): Fusinato, 47–48: according to whom the requirement of a plebiscite, both among the citizens affected by the "territorial change" and among former citizens, was required by international law; Zinedine Meriboute, "L'annexion en droit international contemporain", *Revue de droit international et sciences diplomatiques et politiques*, Vol. 64 (1986), 38: "legal transfers of territories, which would presuppose that there is an agreement on the transfer between the States concerned and, *above all*, the exercise of the right to self-determination of the populations of the territory changing sovereignty" [our translation].

Without elaborating further on this, and in the silence of the international and domestic courts,[71] one can only follow the opinion of two distinguished jurists when they state:

> [I]t cannot be said that international law makes it [viz. Le plebiscite] a condition of every cession that it should be ratified by a plebiscite. In the modern law, however, the plebiscite has to be seen rather as a device for securing compliance with the principle of self-determination enshrined in the Charter of the United Nations.[72]

In the light of the right of peoples to self-determination,[73] it seems to me that it is inconceivable today, and therefore invalid under international law, that a state should be able to cede a (inhabited) part of its territory without consulting the population concerned (by the transfer), or even its entire population.

71 See: The Berubari Union and Exchange of Enclaves (Supreme Court, India), award delivered the 14 March 1960, 53 *ILR*, 201–203.

72 *Oppenheim's International Law* (1992), § 248.

73 See *infra* Part 2. Chapter 6. Section A.

CHAPTER 3

Acquisition and Loss of the Title of Territorial Sovereignty by Juridical Fact

The absorption of the fact into the legal title ('fact-in-law')[1] is carried out precisely by means of those legal rules that provide for the creation (extinction or modification) of territorial titles.[2] However, the jurist (in particular the judge) is not a stranger to this phase of law creation. He contributes to it and even plays a decisive role, due to the very nature of the 'legal fact'.[3] Seen from this angle, it is not possible to ignore the extreme affinity that this problematic reveals with the phenomenon of customary law. What, if we want to quote a famous quotation, was described in these terms, imbued with a very English pragmatism: "One precedent creates another. They soon accumulate and constitute law. What yesterday was fact, today is doctrine".[4]

Indeed, the points of contact between the creation (or extinction, or modification) of a territorial title by legal fact and the phenomenon of the emergence of a customary rule are numerous. The 'mystery' of their creation, or their refractory nature to any systematisation, are the common denominator of 'customary rules' and 'legal facts'. The 'difficulty' consists precisely in finding a 'place' for them[5] and an explanation that satisfies the mind. These two

1 '[T]he vast tides cast by the social milieu against the law', Jean Touscoz, *Le principe d'effectivité dans l'ordre international*, Paris, 1964, v [our translation]. See also, in addition to this chapter, *infra* Part 1. Chapter 4.

2 See: ICJ, Sovereignty over Pedra Branca/Pulau Batu Puteh, Middle Rocks and South Ledge (Malaysia/Singapore), 2008, paras. 120–122 (at 50–51).

3 "The fact is less an *observation* than a *construction* of the mind. Strictly speaking, facts do not exist ready-made in nature like clothes in a tailor's shop, and the role of the scholar is not to call them up one by one according to the needs of his discipline, but rather to *create* them in some way by isolating them abstractly from the complex whole of which they are a part", André Lalande, *Vocabulaire technique et critique de la philosophie*, 13rd edn, Paris, 1980, 339. Similarly: Patrick Nerhot, "Le fait du droit", 31 *Archives de philosophie du droit* 1986, 272; Nicola Abbagnano, *Dizionario di filosofia*, Turin, 1971, 380.

4 Junius, 'Dedication to the English Nation', in *The Letters of Junius*, 1769–1771 (quoted in *Bartlett's Familiar Quotations*, 14th edn, 1968, 1091a).

5 "His approach in no way replicates that of the actors *who supposedly generated* the rule. Their actions were in pursuit of concrete ends, but they had *no intention of promoting norms and principles*. It is the interpreter, after the fact, who draws out this unsuspected component of the actors; and he does so in the light of a present problem which, like an unexpected light, gives *the scattered facts of the past a new meaning*", Peter Haggenmacher, "The Doctrine of

 | DOI:10.1163/9789004708594_006

phenomena remain for the most part hidden from theoretical investigation, and the jurist can merely note their vigour.[6] That is to say, the actual existence of the rule or territorial title, following the occurrence of certain "qualifying facts", chosen and ordered by the "observer".[7]

This introduction served the purpose of providing the conceptual framework within which the following reflections will be developed: the elements (or "facts") that will be studied hereafter are the elements that, in turn and each time in different ways and degrees, taken alone or together, compose the *investitive legal fact* of the *titulus*. The latter will thus be a *complex juridical fact* through which the creation, extinction and modification of territorial titles take place.[8] These "legal facts" will be studied under the magnifying glass of the various concepts that legal science has developed for the purpose of apprehending the phenomena of creation of law other than those induced by the will [see *supra* Part 1. Chapter 2]; that is to say, States' conducts which cannot be subsumed under the category of conventional legal acts.[9]

It is not, therefore, a question of studying the facts or categories of facts that are likely to create a legal title, but of studying the different ways in which certain 'legal facts' of States are *dressed up* by the science of law. Therefore, for

---

the Two Elements of Customary Law in the Practice of the International Court", *RGDIP*, Vol. 90 (1986), 114 [emphasis added]. For this to make sense, the so-called two-element theory of custom must be overcome or at least set aside. This is what is proposed by the proponents of the "spontaneous law" theory, according to whom, "[Custom] is truly a process of *spontaneous* and to some extent *mysterious production* of law", Giuseppe Sperduti, *La fonte suprema dell'ordinamento internazionale*, Milan, 1946, 201. See also: Distefano (2019), 306–318.

6 Roberto Ago, *Scienza giuridica e diritto internazionale*, Milan 1950, 81 [as well as: "Science juridique et droit international", 90 *RCADI* 1956-II, 851–958].

7 See the brilliant studies by Giuseppe Barile: "La rilevazione e l'integrazione del diritto internazionale non scritto e la libertà di apprezzamento del giudice", *Comunicazioni e studi*, Vol. 5 (1953), 141–229; "Interpretazione del giudice e interpretazione di parte del diritto internazionale non scritto", in *Scritti in onore di Tommaso Perassi*, Vol. 1, Milan, 1947, 137–172.

8 "A title may consist of a fact which is deemed *one and invisible*, and is said to be simple. Or a title may consist of a fact which is *not* deemed one and invisible, but is esteemed a number of single and invisible facts compacted *into a collective whole, and may then be called complex*", Austin, 886 [emphasis added].

9 That the "attitudes" of States, as distinct from "volitional acts", may be sources of rights and obligations for States is a principle that does not suffer from any discussion, as we shall try to explain below. Consequently, one cannot agree with the *obiter dictum of* the Federal Supreme Court of Switzerland in the Canton of Valais case (*Revue Suisse de droit international et européen*, Vol. 37 (1981), 234), when it states that: 'There is no general principle of public international law or Swiss domestic law according to which a subject of law would be bound by its own actions. This shows that there is no hesitation in undermining the objective character of any legal order in which legitimate expectations are protected' [our translation]. See in this respect the pertinent observations of Abi-Saab (1995), 19.

example, acquiescence and estoppel are not legal facts, but 'narrative models', i.e. 'normative categories' used to give meaning and significance to certain States' conducts.[10]

In the field that concerns us here, these different normative categories and institutions that we will study below (A-D) are for the jurist (especially the judge) so many utensils, different clothes that allow him to apprehend certain behaviours and attitudes of the States in order to derive legal effects from them for the purposes of creating or extinguishing a *titulus adquisitionis*.[11] The *modus adquisitionis*, on the other hand, is always the same, namely the actual occupation of the territory concerned.

A Acquiescence

Under this heading we will study acquiescence as a 'narrative model', i.e., as a 'normative category' used to bestow meaning and significance to certain state attitudes. This concept is often confused with other institutions or legal concepts in such a way that it is difficult to delineate its precise contours.[12] Before doing so, we believe it appropriate to reproduce two passages from the case law of the International Court of Justice, as they are often cited for this purpose and, moreover, highlight this similarity of legal concepts raised by the absence of protest or, again, "circumstantial silence":

> [I]t is clear that the circumstances were such as called for some reaction, within a *reasonable period of time,* on the part of the Siamese authorities, if they wished to disagree with the map or had any serious question to raise in regard to it. They did not do so, either then or for many years, and

10 See Distefano (2019), 598–620.

11 It is therefore not inaccurate to say that international law of territory is a formidable test bed for any internationalist who nourishes the desire to be a generalist in this multifaceted province of jurisprudence.

12 Equally undeniable is the fact that the concept of acquiescence represents the inspirational model for all those other normative categories with which it is often confused; hence we begin this section with it. A monumental thesis has recently been brilliantly defended by Dr. Aymeric Hêche (*Acquiescement. Etude de droit international public*, Ph.D. Thesis presented and defended at the Faculty of Law of the University of Neuchâtel, June 2022, Brussels, 2023). It undoubtedly makes a valuable contribution to the study of this protean notion of public international law, which is as widely used by States as it is deserted by the doctrine. This study thus fills a deplorable gap in the investigation of this polyphonic notion, despite its muteness, of public international law.

> thereby must be held to have *acquiesced. Qui tacet consentire videtur si loqui debuisset ac potuisset.*[13]
>
> The conduct of Honduras vis-à-vis earlier *effectivités* reveals an admission, recognition, acquiescence, or other form of tacit consent to the situation[14]

This last fragment is very revealing because it alone highlights all the other institutions to which the concept of acquiescence has been linked. Doctrine is often divided on the question of whether the concept of acquiescence has an autonomous legal force or whether, on the other hand, it requires the assistance of other elements or concepts in order to produce certain legal effects. These, in our case, would consist in the creation, extinction or even modification of territorial titles. Consequently, it is necessary first of all to clear the ground by comparing it precisely to these other concepts in order to reach a definition by exclusion of this "polyphonic" notion.[15]

Some have equated acquiescence with tacit agreement, and this is surely the oldest of the doctrinal currents that attempt to enshrine any creation of law in the concept of consent (whether express or tacit).[16] Now, if it is true that consent and acquiescence are two distinct 'phenomena',[17] it is no less true, as Sperduti rightly maintains, that they are equivalent in the legal effects they generate.[18] Another current, denying the concept of acquiescence its own

---

13 ICJ, Temple of Preah Vihear, 23 [emphasis added].

14 ICJ, Land, Insular Boundary Dispute, 1992, para. 364 (at 577) [emphasis added].

15 Hêche, para. 841.

16 See in particular: Vattel, Ch. XXII § 286; Giuseppe Sperduti, "Sovranità territoriale, atti di disposizione di territoriale ed effettività nel diritto internazionale", 42 Rivista 1959, 419 (more nuanced and oscillating between tacit pact and acquisitive prescription); *Black's Law* Dictionary, 25; Sir Gerald Fitzmaurice, "The Law and Procedure of the International Court of Justice, 1951–4: Points of Substantive Law. Part II", 32 *BYIL* 1955–1956, 27–30; Schwarzenberger, 300; Giuseppe Biscottini, *Le manifestazioni unilaterali di volontà nell'ordinamento internazionale*, Rome, 1943, 113–115; Arrigo Cavaglieri, "Il decorso del tempo e i suoi effetti sui rapporti giuridici internazionali", 5 *Rivista* 1926, 187 (the author introduces for this purpose the concept of "*bonus vir*" for the purpose of determining silence as a tacit manifestation of will); Ian C McGibbon, "The Scope of Acquiescence in International Law", 31 *BYIL* 1954, 145. *Contra*: Maurice Bourquin, "Les baies historiques", in *Mélanges Georges Sauser-Hall*, Neuchâtel-Paris, 1952, 37–51. With regard to tacit agreement, see *infra* Part 1. Chapter 3. Section C.

17 Moreover, to reduce acquiescence to a juridical act (thus an act of will) would have meant the negation of any dogmatic autonomy of the former: a superfluous duplication.

18 Giuseppe Sperduti, 'Prescrizione, consuetudine e acquiescenza in diritto internazionale', 44 *Rivista* 1961, 8. The ICJ sometimes seems to waver between the two concepts: "[T]he Court considers that the *conduct of Somalia* [...] in relation to its maritime boundary with Kenya [...] in particular its alleged absence to protest against Kenya's claim [based on

normative autonomy, makes it one of the elements required by the institution of usucapio, which, of course, it accepts as a right of citizenship in the international order.[19] This doctrinal position is further corroborated by a certain jurisprudential practice.[20] Some people would still lump it together with customary law.[21] However, there is certainly some truth in this, as even passive attitudes can be taken into account in the 'establishment' of a customary rule. However, this would confuse the result with the means of proof that is acquiescence.[22] On the other hand, there is no doubt that acquiescence,[23] in the international order, is originally a "general principle of law" within the meaning of Article 38 § 1 c) of the Statute of the International Court of Justice, even if it has since been enshrined in customary international law.

But what about the concept of acquiescence and its capacity to create, erase or modify territorial titles? Answering this question would inevitably lead to raise questions about its alleged normative autonomy. Acquiescence occurs only when a subject is "silent" when it should be reacting, provided that the "fact" in question possesses a certain notoriety,[24] to activities of public power conducted by another state.[25] This is referred to as "circumstantial silence". The

---

acquiescence – tacit agreement], does not establish Somalia's clear and consistent *acceptance* of a maritime boundary at the parallel of latitude", Maritime Delimitation in the Indian Ocean (Somalia v. Kenya), Judgment of 12 October 2021: *ICJ Reports* 2021, § 80 (at 236) [emphasis added].

19 See among others: Sperduti (1959), 419; Percy E Cobbett, *Law and Society in the Relation of States*, London, 1951, 108: "[acquiescence is] really the foundation of the modern law of prescription". *Contra* PK Menon, "International Boundaries. A Case Study of the Guyana-Surinam Boundary", 27 *ICLQ* 1978, 767 (who, while admitting acquisitive prescription in international law, is careful to distinguish it from acquiescence).

20 Arkansas v. Tennessee (U.S. Supreme Court), decision of 3 June 1940, *ILR*, Vol. 9, 113: "the area in question should now be deemed to be within the boundaries of Tennessee *by virtue of prescription and the acquiescence* on the part of Arkansas in the exercise of dominion and jurisdiction over that area ... since Tennessee had continuously performed various acts of public authority" [emphasis added]; Indiana v. Kentucky (U.S. Supreme Court), AILC (1783–1968, Deak), Vol. 3, 239: "acquiescence [in the exercise of dominion and jurisdiction]" [emphasis added]; Indiana v. Kentucky (U.S. Supreme Court), *AILC* (1783–1968, Deak), Vol. 3, 239: "acquiescence [100 years] can only be regarded as a recognition of the right of Kentucky too plain to be overcome.

21 Sir Gerald Fitzmaurice, "The General Principles of International Law Considered from the Standpoint of the Rule of Law", 92 *RCADI* 1957-II, 122.

22 See: Yehuda Blum, *Historic Titles in International Law*, The Hague, 1965, 60 [*passim*].

23 Hêche, paras. 995–1001, 319.

24 According to a medieval brocade: "vigilantibus non dormientibus iura subveniunt", that is to say: 'The law supports the waking, not the sleeping', Fellmeth, Horwitz, 306.

25 Such as "collection of taxes", ICJ, Land and Maritime Boundary (Cameroon v. Nigeria; Equatorial Guinea intervening), 2002, paras. 223–224.

Roman law maxim cleverly cited by the International Court of Justice in the Temple case[26] codifies an ancient axiom.[27] But it is precisely on the aspect of "circumstantial silence" that we should focus our attention. Moreover, this condition is expressed by the last part of the maxim that is sometimes neglected, namely: *si loqui debuisset ac potuisset*. That is, if the subject had to do it (because his title was in danger) and if he could do it (the requirement of the notoriety of the 'fact'). Acquiescence necessarily presupposes knowledge of the fact in relation to which the subject does not react,[28] as further evidenced by Article 45 VCLT 1969 which envisages the loss of a State's right to invoke a cause of nullity, extinction or suspension 'by reason of its conduct' and 'after having become aware of the facts'.[29]

It is therefore not 'silence' as such, but silence *characterised* by a well-defined factual and normative context:[30] this is a demonstration that most

---

26 ICJ, Temple of Preah Vihear, 23. Similarly: Maritime Delimitation in the Indian Ocean (Somalia v. Kenya), paras. 36–89.

27 Codex 43 (De Regulis Iuris in 6to), 5, 12. See in this regard the admirable and penetrating reflections of Guido Donatuti, "Il silenzio come manifestazione di volontà", in *Studi in onore di Pietro Bonfante*, Vol. 4, Milano, 1930, 461–484 [according to the analysis of this eminent Romanist, and following a thorough Benedictine work on the sources of Roman law, silence is only valid as *"patientia", and* not as a manifestation of will; § 4]. Indeed, the emphasis is on the circumstances surrounding the 'silence' of the entitled party (the holder), as we learn elsewhere in the Digest (50, 17, 142) from a fragment of the jurist Paulus: *Qui tacet, non utique fatetur: sed tamen verum est eum non negare*. This formula was moreover 'canonised' by the decretal of Boniface VIII (lib. V, tit.12, reg.43), to which we can oppose another formula, also taken from a sacred text, which is the following: 'Apples of gold in a silver case, a word spoken at the right time' (Bible, Book of Proverbs, Ch. XXV, v. 11).

28 ICJ, Sovereignty over Pedra Branca/Pulau Batu Puteh, Middle Rocks and South Ledge (Malaysia/Singapore), 2008, § 243; ICJ, Maritime Delimitation in the Indian Ocean (Somalia v Kenya), § 84.

29 Article 45 ARSIWA has been drafted almost verbatim with the only – important – difference that it elegantly eludes the question of the passage of time, whereas Article 45 VCLT 1969 mentions "reasonable time". In this respect, we cannot help but notice that the VCLT 1969, which specifies – as is appropriate for a codification convention – in a careful manner, time limits, mechanisms and procedures, opens up an abyss in the spirit of finesse in this provision, by the adjective "reasonable".

30 This condition was noted by Prince Gortchakov in his Memorandum of 27 October 1856 concerning Russian territorial rights in the Black Sea: 'Now, in matters of law, if it is a question of transferring any territory from one possessor to another, it is necessary that the Treaty of Peace [in this case, the Treaty of Paris of 1856] authorise this change by a clearly expressed stipulation. *Silence does not legitimise either abandonment on the one hand or acquisition on the other*', quoted in *Bruns*, FB11 § 1130 [emphasis added]. In Roman law, silence could be expressed in the following attitudes: *'non contradicere'*, *'non repugnare'*, *'non dissentire'* to a proposal of another; or to be *'praesens et non contradicere'*, *'praesens et*

legal facts are 'complex facts'. This characteristic of 'circumstantial silence' was highlighted by a decision of the Federal Supreme Court of Switzerland:

> Based on a traditional Anglo-Saxon concept, the law of nations uses the term "acquiescence" to refer to the principle that passive acceptance of a situation can give rise to a legal relationship; this term corresponds roughly to the notion of "qualifiziertes Stillschweigen."[31]

This sentence is really important because it lists the conditions required by international law to be able to speak of "acquiescence" in a specific situation. According to the judges of the Federal Supreme Court of Switzerland, the *ratio iuris* of this concept must be sought in the principle of *good faith*:

> "Acquiescence" means the silence that has been observed with regard to a legal claim made by another subject of law and which has the effect that, according to *the principle of good faith*, this passive attitude can only be interpreted as constituting a tacit recognition. *It is thus the interpretation and legal qualification of a passive attitude based on the principle of good faith.*[32]

As for the passage of time, this is a necessity inspired by the requirement of security of legal relations; it is therefore a requirement of proof of circumstantial silence'. It must be observed and recorded by the judge for a fairly long period of time:

> The time factor plays an important role, since it is this factor which, as a general rule, gives the absence of an objection to the claim made by another subject of law the character of a tacit acceptance.[33]

non recusare', '*praesens et non dissentire*', '*praesens et non exsequi*', or only '*praesens*', '*sciens et non contradicere*' to an opposing act. See Donatuti, 461 [*passim*].

31 Case of Canton of Valais v. Canton of Ticino, 233 [our translation; the Federal Supreme Court of Switzerland quotes Karl Strupp, Hans-Jürgen Schlochauer, *Wörterbuch des Völkerrechts*, 2nd edn, Berlin, 1960–1962, Vol. III, 391].

32 Case of Canton of Valais v. Canton of Ticino, 233 [our translation].

33 *Loc. cit.* This passage echoes the Roman law maxim: "*Longo silentio res gabetur pro derelicto*", Gotofr.L.15 § 21 (*de damno infecto*).

However, it must be repeated that Time does not extinguishes, creates or modifies territorial title, but it is the conducts of the States concerned *over time* that give birth to territorial titles:

> The Court considers that although Nicaragua's conduct falls short of recognition of Colombia's sovereignty …, it nevertheless affords some support to Colombia's claim.[34]

The passage of time has also been referred to as a 'condition of acquiescence',[35] but it is primarily a means of evidence:[36]

> [*T*]*ime favours* those who have acted, creating a situation that is advantageous to them or doing what is necessary to destroy a threat directed against them. On the other hand, it *does a disservice to* those who have remained *inactive*, confining themselves to making more or less futile claims or protests or falling asleep in a *deceptive security*.[37]

From this point of view, it is clear that the function of "acquiescence" can be "constitutive", i.e., it transforms into a situation of law a situation of fact that is contrary *per se to* the law (in force); in other words, acquiescence can undoubtedly modify a "conventional [pre-existing] title".[38] It should nevertheless be pointed out, if need be, that States may by treaty "sterilise" the effects of acquiescence by setting it aside (derogating) in their *inter se* relations. By way of example, we may mention Article IV § 2 of the Antarctic Treaty (1 December 1959):

34 ICJ, Territorial and Maritime Dispute (Nicaragua v. Colombia), 2012, § 90, at 659.

35 Jean Barale, "L'acquiescement dans la jurisprudence internationale", 22 *AFDI* 1965, 405.

36 'The passage of time does not in itself contain any legal element, it cannot in itself be productive either of the emergence or extinction of legal claims', Cavaglieri (1926), 169 [our translation]; ICJ, Military and Paramilitary Activities in and against Nicaragua, 1984, paras. 43–51.

37 Emile Giraud, "Le droit international public et la politique", 110 *RCADI* 1963-I, 476 [emphasis added ; our translation]; in the same vein: Marie-Claude La Rose, "Le litige canado-américain au sujet de l'île de Machias Seal", 2 *Revue Québécoise de droit international* 1985, 316. 'The idea that the passage of time *alone* would constitute law has, in our view, no place in international law", Maritime Delimitation and Territorial Questions case, Argument by Mr Salmon (Qatar), CR 2000/5 (meeting of 29 May 2000), § 3.

38 Land and Maritime Boundary (Cameroon v. Nigeria, intervening Equatorial Guinea), 2002, § 68; ICJ, Land, Island and Maritime Frontier Dispute, 1992, § 80.

> No acts or activities taking place while the present Treaty is in force shall constitute a basis for asserting, supporting or denying a claim to territorial sovereignty in Antarctica or create any rights of sovereignty in Antarctica. No new claim, or enlargement of an existing claim to territorial sovereignty in Antarctica shall be asserted while the present Treaty is in force.[39]

It is now appropriate to say a few words about the context in which this phenomenon known as 'acquiescence' takes place and about the characteristics it must have in order for the 'legal fact' it captures to produce legal effects. For it is indeed the context, from an "objectivist" perspective that we are focusing on here, that qualifies acquiescence as producing legal consequences.[40] However, it should also be remembered that States rarely display an attitude free of contradiction in territorial matters; in short, they very rarely speak with one voice.[41]

State practice, international tribunals and the literature provide information on the – mostly passive[42] – attitudes that can be taken into account for the purpose of "establishing" acquiescence as a "legal fact". Diplomatic protest,[43]

---

39 *UNTS*, Vol. 402, No. 5778, 75.

40 *"Georgia further asserts that the State asserting the claim must make a showing of acquiescence by the neighbouring State. Inaction, in and of itself, is of no great importance; what it is legally significant is silence in the face of circumstances that warrant a response"*, Georgia v. South Carolina (U.S. Supreme Court), judgment of 25 June 1990, 91 *ILR*, 449 [emphasis added].

41 Munkman, 77–78.

42 Barale, 403; "[E]ven negative conduct ... is in my opinion, quite sufficient for this purpose, *if the facts are clear*", Individual op. cit. of Judge Sir Gerald Fitzmaurice in the Temple of Preah Vihear case, 1962, 55 [emphasis added]; "The Court further notes that these Honduran activities, which may be regarded as effective and may be presumed to have been known to Nicaragua, were not known to Nicaragua. 55 [emphasis added]; 'The Court further notes that these Honduran activities, which may be regarded as effective and which may be presumed to have been known to Nicaragua, had not given rise to any protest on the part of Nicaragua', ICJ, Territorial and Maritime Dispute between Nicaragua and Honduras in the Caribbean Sea (Nicaragua v. Honduras), 2007, § 208. It is worth recalling that the judge must scrutinise such conduct.

43 See the joint separate opinion of Judges Basdevant and Levi-Carneiro in the Minquiers et Ecrehos case (71); Lamu Island case, 244; Ch. De Visscher (1960), 254; cf. the Memorandum of the Portuguese Government reiterating Portuguese titles to a portion of the West African coast (cited in *Bruns*, FB11 § 595): 'The scope of the declaration is clear: Portugal did not want the non-occupation of the disputed territories to be interpreted as *a tacit waiver of its rights*. We shall see how *twenty-nine years* later the British government interpreted the declaration referred to' [our translation; emphasis added]. Regarding the dispute over certain Alaskan territories, which saw Russia and Great Britain clash, see the 'confidential memorandum' addressed on 23 November 1822 by Count Lieven to the Duke

the absence of a challenge (protest)[44] or of an "appropriate reaction",[45] or "belated",[46]also in relation to "internal acts" of the other States concerned.[47] But the protest[48] must go far beyond the paper

of Wellington, reporting on the attitude shown by England: 'England has *not protested* against this provision either. She has not even *protested* against the new settlements which the Russo-American Company has been able to form south of the 55th degree, in virtue of this privilege [emphasis added], quoted in: Smith, 5 (see also 66). See also the dispatch of the Italian Minister of Foreign Affairs, the Marquis of San Giuliano, sent on 12 July 1912 to the Italian Minister of War, M Spingardi, on the subject of British acquiescence in Italian claims to the North African territories bordering Egypt: '*acquiescence* which, as far as England is concerned, acquires all the more value, since it had *amicably complained against our primitive declaration*', quoted in *Prassi italiana,* Seconda serie (1887–1918), Vol. II, § 2220 [our translation; emphasis added]; cf. the diplomatic dispatch from the Italian Foreign Minister, M Tittoni, sent on 30 October 1906 to the Italian Ambassador in London, the Marquis of San Giuliano, reaffirming the need for the Italian Government to protest about certain English actions in the Upper Juba Territories: 'so as to prevent the British from seriously damaging our interests in that region through our acquiescence', quoted in *Prassi italiana,* Seconda serie (1887–1918), Vol. II, § 2329 [our translation]. It is interesting to note in this regard that the Italian territorial rights to which the Minister was referring were minor territorial rights, namely rights arising from the so-called spheres of influence agreements. This passage also supports the view that the rules governing the life of titles are the same whether they are "minor" territorial rights or territorial sovereignty.

44 "Nicaragua never protested against Colombia's exercise of sovereignty over the islands throughout a period of more than 150 years", ICJ, Territorial and Maritime Dispute (Nicaragua v Colombia), 2012, § 75 (at 654).

45 See the joint separate opinion of Judges Basdevant and Levi-Carneiro in the Minquiers and Ecrehos case (81); California v. Nevada (1980), *AILC* (1979–1986, Reams), Vol. 2 (Second Series),3–7; ICJ, Land, Island and Maritime Frontier Dispute, 1992, paras. 67, 284; The Indo-Pakistan Western Boundary (Rann of Kutch) between India and Pakistan, 531; Island of Palmas, 869; Island of Bulama, 138–139; Judge Armand-Ugon's dissenting opinion in the Sovereignty over Certain Frontier Land, 1959, 44; Judge Luchaire's Separate Opinion in the Frontier Dispute case, 1986, 654; Antarctica (United Kingdom v. Argentina), Order of 16 March 1956): *ICJ Reports* 1956, § 24; The Dubai-Sharjah Border Arbitration, paras. 206, 211; Brownlie, 160–161; Sir Robert Jennings (1963), 36; De Visscher (1967), 109; Jean-Pierre Ferrier, "Le conflit des îles Paracels et le problème de la souveraineté sur les îles non habitées", 21 *AFDI* 1975, 193, 194; Cavaglieri (1926), 203.

46 See: ICJ, Island of Timor Case (Netherlands v. Portugal), Award of the PCA of 25 June 1914, *RIAA*, Vol. 11, 504; United States v. Louisiana and Others (U.S. Supreme Court), Judgment of 26 February 1985, *ICLA* (1979–1986, Reams). Vol. 2 (Second Series), 423; Arbitral Award Made by the King of Spain on 23 December 1906 (Honduras v. Nicaragua), Judgment of 18 November 1960: *I.C.J. Reports* 1960, 213; T Kotani, "A Theoretical Approach to the problem of the Kurile Islands", 24 *Japanese Annual of International Law* 1981, 10–11.

47 ICJ, Maritime Delimitation in the Indian Ocean (Somalia v. Kenya), paras. 77–80.

48 "The most common means in international law of safeguarding one's rights is protest: it is very often encountered in practice", Paul Verykios, *La prescription en droit international public,* Paris, 1934, 99 [our translation]. But if the protest is not followed by punctual and repeated acts of contestation and attempts at settlement, it loses force and dies out. The

protest,[49] and it must exhaust all avenues for the peaceful settlement of international disputes[50] set out in a non-exhaustive manner in Article 33 of the UNC.[51] And if necessary, if the situation in dispute threatens peace and security, the Parties may "bring the territorial dispute to the attention of the Security Council or the General Assembly" (UNC 35).[52] Moreover, the State may bring an application before the International Court of Justice even in the absence of a title of jurisdiction, the hypothesis of *forum prorogatum not being* excluded *a priori*.[53] These are "facts" of state which can hardly be interpreted as an acquiescence of the state to the claims of the other state or to a certain territorial situation.

---

length of time during which the protest must expand and become qualitatively stronger is subject to assessment on a case-by-case basis. The commencement of direct negotiations or talks between the parties to the conflict must be interpreted as an acknowledgement by the state in control of the territory that a dispute does exist and that therefore its territorial title could not be formed in accordance with international law. In short, that it has not been able to join to its *modus adquisitionis* the *titulus adquisitionis* (which always remains with the dispossessed state). See in this regard: Thomas R Mattair, *The Three Occupied UAE Islands. The Tunbs and Abu Musa*, Abu Dhabi, 2005.

49 Paul Heilborn, *Das System des Völkerrechts entwickelt aus den Völkerrechtlichen Begriffen*, Berlin, 1896, 376, who speaks of "papieren Protest", in counterpoint to "paper title". For structural reasons, paper protests can hardly affect the validity of the title in formation. McGibbon (I.C. "Some observations on the part of protest in International Law", 30 *BYIL* 1953, 294–299) provides us with an overview of the conditions under which a protest can actually be effective. The formula "paper claims" has also been used, with the same meaning, in oral pleading by Mr Paulsson (Bahrain) in the Maritime Delimitation and Territorial Questions case, CR 2000/11 (meeting of 8 June 2000), § 107.

50 However, the Court wishes to obserbe that "it is unreasonable and unrealistic to expect a State that was ravaged by civil war and had no functioning government to have lodged formal diplomatic protests against purported claim to a boundary line" (ICJ, Maritime Delimitation in the Indian Ocean (Somalia v. Kenya), § 46). This alleviation of the requirement of a prompt, constant and firm protest in the case of "failed States" (infra Part 2. Chapter 7. Section C) is noteworthy.

51 The obligation to negotiate therefore underpins the effectiveness of the concept of protest. See in this sense: M Khadduri, 'Iraq's Claim to the sovereignty of Kuwait', 23 *New York University Journal of International Law and Politics* 1990, 4.

52 See in this sense PK Menon, "Title to Territory: Traditional Modes of Acquisition by States", 72 *Revue de droit international et des sciences diplomatiques et politiques* 1994, 30–32. For, 'not even protest, however clear and prompt it may be, is always effective and sufficient in itself for the lasting safeguarding of rights disregarded by the deed of others', Cavaglieri (1926), 202.

53 In accordance with Article 38 § 5 of the ICJ Rules.

B Estoppel

In the limited space available to analyse this legal concept, it is important to highlight its distinctive features, particularly in comparison with the other 'narrative models' discussed in this chapter. The legal notion of *Estoppel* finds its conceptual origin in Anglo-American law;[54] according to *Black's Law Dictionary*:

> "Estoppel" means that a party is *prevented* by his own acts from claiming a right to *detriment* of other party who was entitled to *rely* on such conduct and has acted *accordingly*.[55]

Three cumulative conditions emerge from this definition: a) it is impossible to change one's representation (or to go back on one's previous position); b) if the Party(ies) concerned have relied on it; c) and if this change causes prejudice to the Party(ies).[56] The distinctive feature of this kind of *estoppel* is indeed the knowingly fraudulent conduct of one of the Parties which acts with the intention of entrapping the other.[57] Thus, *estoppel by representation* was delineated by the Federal Supreme Court of Switzerland:

> An estoppel is created when one party, *relying on the assurances or conclusive acts* of another, has been *induced* to perform acts which have legal effect and which would be *prejudicial to* him if that other party were subsequently permitted to disclaim them. The characteristic effect of estoppel is that, when the above conditions are met, *the subsequent attitude of the other party cannot be taken into account*, irrespective of whether that attitude is in itself well-founded or not.[58]

---

54 Francesco Francioni, "La consuetudine locale nel diritto internazionale", 54 *Rivista* 1971, 411.

55 *Black's Law Dictionary*, 551 [emphasis added]. It appears that the etymology of this word goes back to Old French, as the *Oxford English Dictionary* attests ('app. ad. OF. estoupail, estouppail bung or cork, f. estouper').

56 The element of prejudice – suffered by the change of attitude – is central to the legal concept of *estoppel* and makes it possible to differentiate the latter from acquiescence: ICJ, North Sea Continental Shelf, 1969, 26; ICJ, Case concerning the Delimitation of the Maritime Boundary in the Gulf of Maine Region (Canada v. United States), Judgment of 12 October 1984: *ICJ Reports* 1984, § 145, at 309.

57 See in this sense Derek W Bowett, "Estoppel before International Tribunals and its Relation to Acquiescence", 33 *BYIL* 1957, 186.

58 Case of the Canton of Valais v. Canton of Ticino, 234 [our translation; emphasis added].

A State is thus "stopped"[59] from invoking a right (which it has failed to assert), on a judgment (in other words, the principle of *res iudicata*, also known as *estoppel by record*, or *collateral estoppel*[60]), on a representation of facts (on which the other Party has relied). The *ratio iuris* of estoppel is undoubtedly the principle of good faith which permeates it and without which it would hardly be conceivable. We are indeed in the field of the "objectivity" of the law, of the *legitimate* expectations that it must protect and that arise for certain subjects of law following certain attitudes of other subjects of law. This is the place where the will has less hold, where the "volitional phenomenon" is difficult to detect. Hence the impossibility of establishing this concept in a consensual (even tacit) scheme, unlike the concept of acquiescence where attempts have been made, albeit erroneously,[61] to do so.

In the same vein, *estoppel* should be distinguished from other normative categories to which it has been linked. First of all, from acquiescence:[62] a State that acquiesces is, because of *estoppel*, prevented from reversing its position. In this scheme, acquiescence is upstream while *estoppel* is downstream, shielding the legal situation, otherwise the other party would be harmed.

59 "Great Britain is stopped by the fact that it did not recognize the Tinoco government during its incumbency", Aguilar-Amory and Royal Bank of Canada Claims (Tinoco case), Great Britain v. Costa Rica, award delivered on January 12, 1922, *RIAA*, Vol. 1, 377.

60 "*Collateral estoppel forecloses* relitigation of all issues litigated in a prior proceeding", Occidental of Umm Al Qaywayn Inc. v. Cities Service Oil Co. et al (U.S. District Court), judgment of 18 July 1975, 66 *ILR*, 179 [emphasis added].

61 See especially Antoine Martin, *L'estoppel en droit international public*, Paris, 1979, 306: 'It can therefore be said at most that the principle of good faith is *mediately at the* basis of the institution of *estoppel*, in the sense that it constitutes the basis of the implicit agreement whose binding nature a court will sanction, if need be, through the procedural means of *estoppel*' [our translation]. What are then the reasons for resorting to the notion of the agreement, albeit by interposing good faith, as long as estoppel only comes into play in the configuration of *foreclosure*, i.e. as *allegans contraria non est audiendus*? (*infra* note 66).

62 "[I]n most cases the State which purports to acquire the right is losing nothing: on the contrary the detriment is all on the other side, so that *the doctrine of estoppel cannot operate to protect the State which has been placed in an improved position as a result of the silence or inaction of another*", Bowett (1957), 201 [our emphasis]. See also: Delimitation of the Maritime Boundary in the Gulf of Maine Area (United States of America v. Canada), Judgment of 12 October 1984: *I.C.J. Reports* 1984, paras. 128–131 (at 304–305); Francisco Villagran Kramer, "Actos convencionales y no convencionales – ratificación, aquiescencia y estoppel", in *El derecho internacional en un mundo en transformacion*, Vol. II, Montevideo, 1994, 982. *Contra* Barale, 424; IC McGibbon, "The Scope of Acquiescence in International Law", 31 *BYIL* 1954, 147.

Again, the concept of *estoppel must be* distinguished from usucapio, provided that the latter is accepted as a legal right in the international order.[63] To this end, it should be recalled that *estoppel* is always the consequence of a legal fact that has come into being as a result of conclusive attitudes of the Parties (whether this is called "acquisitive prescription" or not). From this point of view, it cannot be equated with usucapio; rather, *estoppel* would represent its procedural counterpart, i.e., *foreclosure*, to which we shall come back later.[64]

Once these distinctions have been made, it is necessary to determine the status of *estoppel* in international law. At the outset, one might be tempted to say that since the concept of "estoppel" is known by this designation only in the legal orders of the *Common Law* countries, it would be difficult at first sight to classify it among the "general principles of law" within the meaning of Article 38 § 1 lit. c of the Statute of the International Court of Justice.[65] The prodromes of its jurisprudential emergence in this branch of international law must be sought in a few cases that should be mentioned here.

In the Temple of Preah Vihear case, although the Court did not name it expressly, it appears repeatedly both in the Parties' Memorials and, successively, in the individual opinions of certain judges. In the latter respect, it is the separate opinion of Vice-President Alfaro, which will have a decisive impact on subsequent international jurisprudence:

> Whatever term or terms be employed to designate the principle such as it has been applied in the international sphere, its substance is always

63 In this sense: Schwarzenberger, 301: "Acquisition of title in this manner may be called title by way of acquisitive prescription. It shares with extinctive prescription the legal effect of creating an *estoppel against third states whose claims have become stale.* [emphasis added]; Menon (1978), 768; Jacques Bentz, "Silence as a manifestation of will", 67 *RGDIP* 1963, 89; Henry W Ballantine, "Title by Adverse Possession", 32 *Harvard Law Review* 1918, 136. According to Bowett (1957), 201, who would admit the concept of acquisitive prescription in international law, it would differ from the concept of estoppel in that it does not require (subjective) good faith, whereas the latter would be required. We shall return later to usucapio and its status in the international legal order (see *below* Part 1. Chapter 4. Section B.iii.).

64 "It] is contended that the Republic of Mexico is *estopped* from asserting the national title over the territory known as 'El Chamizal' by reason of the undisturbed d, uninterrupted, and unchallenged possession of said territory by the USA ... since the Treaty of Guadalupe Vidalgo", El Chamizal Case (United States of America v. Republic of Mexico), Award rendered on 15 June 1911 by the Mixed Arbitral Commission, *RIAA*, Vol. 11, 328 [emphasis added].

65 *Contra*: Menon (1994), 33 (but this is more a *petitio principii* than an argument). On estoppel being a 'general principle of law' within the meaning of Art. 38 (1) c) ICJ Statute, see: G Distefano (2019), 559–579.

> the same: inconsistency between claims or allegations put forward by a State, and its previous conduct in connection therewith, is not admissible (*allegans contraria non audiendus est*). Its purpose is always the same: a State must not be permitted to benefit by its own incosistency to the prejudice of another State (*nemo potest mutare consilium suum in alterius injuriam*).[66]

In the light of the above, two functions of the principle of *estoppel* in international law of territory can be identified. The first is as a *cause of title*, or legal cover for the "facts" of states, creating, extinguishing or modifying territorial titles. The doctrine is divided in this respect.[67] However, in addition to a few honourable mentions in landmark cases brought before the World Court,[68] it is not daring to detect a recent trend in its jurisprudence that would tend to admit it in international law of territory. However, the credit for establishing *estoppel as a* principle of substantive law undoubtedly goes to the arbitral tribunal in the *La Palena* case between Argentina and Chile:

> there is in international law a principle, which is moreover a principle of substantive law and not just a technical rule of evidence, according to which 'a State party to an international litigation is bound by its previous acts or attitude when they are in contradiction with its claims in the litigation'.[69]

---

66 ICJ, Temple of Preah Vihear, 1962, 40. In this sense: Christian Dominicé, "A propos du principe de l'estoppel en droit des gens", in *Recueil de droit international en hommage à Paul Guggenheim*, Geneva, 1968, 327–365.

67 Among the deniers: G Goldstein, "Canadian Perspectives on Public and Private International Law Relating to Territorial Control", 28 *Canadian Yearbook of International Law* 1990, 40; Sir Robert Jennings (1963), 42: "It is doubtful whether *estoppel or preclusion* can ever be itself a root of title to sovereignty. It may assist in the determination of a title on some other ground but *there probably is no such thing as a title by estoppel*" [emphasis added]. *Contra* Cobbett, 108; Schwarzenberger, 297; Separate opinion of Judge Sir Gerald Fitzmaurice, Temple of Preah Vihear Case, 62–63.

68 See e.g., North Sea Continental Shelf case, 1969, § 30; Elettronica Sicula (ELSI) case between the United States of America and Italy, judgment of 20 July 1989: *I.C.J. Reports* 1989, § 54–55.

69 The Palena case (Argentina/Chile), arbitral award of 9 December 1966, *RIAA*, vol. XVI, 164 (the quotation is taken from the separate opinion of Vice-President Alfaro in the Temple of Preah Vihear case, see *supra* note 66).

The International Court of Justice has since overcome the hesitations displayed in the Temple of Preah Vihear case and seems to have accepted, in the wake of *La Palena* case, this substantive construction of the estoppel principle.[70]

The second signification, namely the procedural aspect of this rule, embodies the legal impossibility for the state that has adopted a certain attitude to change it subsequently. Jurisprudence also knows a notion that explains this eminently procedural phenomenon: *foreclosure*. The State is then foreclosed "to blow hot and cold"[71] during a jurisdictional procedure.[72] In its procedural configuration, the *estoppel-foreclosure* rule finds its *ratio iuris* in the maxim *allegans contraria non audiendus est*,[73] whereby a Party is foreclosed from benefiting from its inconsistency to the detriment of the other Party who relied on the latter's conduct or representations.[74] This rule represents a "preliminary"

70 ICJ, Sovereignty over Pulau Ligitan and Pulau Sipadan (Indonesia / Malaysia), judgment of 17 December 2002: *I.C.J. Reports* 2002, paras. 226–228; ICJ, Maritime Delimitation in the Black Sea (Romania v. Ukraine), judgment of 3 February 2009: *ICJ Reports* 2009, § 72, at 88.

71 *"Ex eodem ore calidum et frigidum efflare"*. This sentence is taken from a fable by Aesop (Hausrath, 35), in which the satyr befriends a man whom he later distrusts when he realises that the man is using his breath both to warm his hands and to cool the broth. There is no shortage of parallels in European languages in this respect. In addition to the above-mentioned English expression, there are: "souffler le chaud et le froid", "Kalt und Warm aus einem Munde blasen", "soffiare caldo e freddo".

72 The question remains whether outside the jurisdictional phase, e.g., during negotiations, states can change their position or whether they are bound by their own previous actions. In one case, an arbitral tribunal had to express itself in the following terms: 'Granted that a party cannot be held to attitudes taken up in the course of negotiations -involving, as is often the case, concessions and renunciations offered for the sake of reaching an agreement- the same is not true of an initial position taken up at the outset of the negotiations, for this reflects, at least *grosso modo*, the way in which that party assesses its rights and obligations on the juridical plane', American Independent Oil Co, decision of 24 March 1982, 66 *ILR*, 575.

73 This principle is a general principle of law within the meaning of Article 38 § 1 (c) of the Statute of the International Court of Justice and would have its counterpart in Muslim law (see separate opinion of Judge Ammoun in the North Sea Continental Shelf cases, 1969, § 22).

74 "Whatever term or terms be employed to designate this principle such as it has been applied in the international sphere, its substance is always the same: inconsistency between claims or allegations put forward by a State, and its previous conduct in connection therewith, is inadmissible [... Finally, the legal effect of the principle is always the same: the party which by its recognition, its representation, its declaration, its conduct or its silence has maintained an *attitude manifestly contrary to the right is claiming before an international tribunal is precluded from claiming that right* (*venire contra factum proprium non valet*). "ICJ, Temple of Preah Vihear, 40 (individual op. of Judge Alfaro; emphasis added); ICJ, Territorial Dispute (Libyan Arab Jamahiriya/Chad), 1994, 96–100 (individual op. of Judge Ajibola); ICJ, Norwegian Fisheries, 1951, 172 (dissenting opinion

exception, a legal barrier to the creation and exercise of procedural rights and obligations, within the actions/exceptions dynamic.[75] International and domestic jurisprudence[76] as well as the doctrine[77] converge in this sense. Finally, it should be noted that these two meanings of the principle of estoppel are hardly irreconcilable; on the contrary, they are two different expressions of the same principle.

C Tacit Agreement

From the very outset, a distinction must be made in this section between: (i) a tacit agreement proven by the subsequent practice of the States parties to a territorial treaty and leading to the modification or even to the extinction of the latter and (ii) a tacit agreement, unrelated to a pre-existing formal treaty instrument, but instead conveying autonomously territorial titles.[78]

Even unwritten treaties, such as tacit agreements, are supposed to create rights and obligations against the subjects of international law,[79] because, notwithstanding the 'evidentiary value [of the written form]',[80] "no law prescribes a

of Judge Sir Arnold McNair); ICJ, Military and Paramilitary Activities in and against Nicaragua (Nicaragua v. United States), Judgment of 26 November 1984 (jurisdiction of the Court and admissibility of the application): *ICJ Reports* 1984, § 44–51; ICJ, Frontier Dispute (Burkina Faso/Mali), 1986, 654 (separate opinion of Judge Luchaire).

75 See Jurisdiction of the Courts of Danzig, Advisory Opinion of 3 March 1928: *P.C.I.J. Recueil* B 15, 26.

76 See e.g. Arbitration between Great Britain and Portugal as regards questions relative to the delimitation of their spheres of influence in East Africa (Manica Plateau)(Portugal v. United Kingdom), Award of 30 January 1897, *RIAA*, vol. XXVIII, 318; Beagle Channel Arbitration Case (Argentina v. Chile), Award of 18 February 1977, 52 *ILR*, § 171 ("preclude or foreclose"); Advisory Opinion concerning the Delimitation of the Polish-Czechoslovak Boundary (Jaworzina case), 6 December 1923: *ICJ Reports,* B 8, 39 (a form of "auto-estoppel", i.e. self-interpretation).

77 See, among other authors, Villagran Kramer, 976, 978.

78 See in general, on this notion in international law of territory: Giovanni Distefano, "L'accord tacite ou l'univers parallèle du droit des traités", 18 *QIL. Questions of International Law* 2015, 17–37. This section thus draws heavily on that article.

79 'An agreement between states, in the broad sense, can be constituted with legally binding effect whatever the manner of manifestation of their will', Anzilotti (1964), 311. Likewise: Matteo Decleva, *Gli accordi taciti internazionali*, Padua, 1957, 5–21.

80 Philippe Gautier, "Article 2 – 1969 Convention" in O Corten and P Klein (eds), *The Vienna Conventions on the Law of Treaties*, vol. I, Oxford, 2011, 38. Also: Samuel B Crandall, *Treaties. Their Making and Enforcement*, Washington, 1916, § 6 (at 5); *Hall's International Law*, ed. P Higgins, Oxford, 1924, § 109 (at 383).

special form for agreements between independent States".[81] Indeed, what matters, beyond[82] (and despite) the forms in which the will of States is expressed, is that States wanted to commit themselves in (international) law by creating rights and obligations. The basis for the binding nature of tacit agreements lies, like any other commitment, whatever its form,[83] in *bona fides*[84] in international relations between states.

i *Tacit Agreement Modifying or Terminating Territorial Treaties*

In this case, conclusive States' conducts, relating to a previous conventional legal act to create, modify and extinguish rights and obligations in accordance with (written) treaty law. In other words, tacit consent – although "not in written form"[85] – does not create rights and obligations in perfect isolation, but rather it is grafted onto a written treaty and in dialogue with it. The legal effects of tacit agreement are therefore considered and governed by the law of treaties.

While it is undisputed[86] that the subsequent practice of States parties to a treaty is a powerful element of the general rule of treaty interpretation codified in Article 31 § 3 (b)) VCLT 1969,[87] the question of whether such practice can lead to the modification or even termination of the treaty,[88] is still a matter of some debate in the literature, despite the fact that the case law is relatively

81 Lamu Island, 243 [our translation]; ICJ, Nuclear Tests (Australia v. France), judgment of 20 December 1974, *I.C.J. Reports 1974*, § 45 (at 267–268). Almost *verbatim*: ICJ, Temple of Preah Vihear (Cambodia v. Thailand), Judgment of 26 May 1961 (Preliminary Objections), *ICJ Reports* 1961, 31.

82 *Hall's International Law*, § 109 (at 383).

83 ICJ, Nuclear Tests, § 46 (at 268).

84 Danish reply in the case of the Legal Status of Eastern Greenland, C 63, 856.

85 ICJ, Maritime Delimitation in the Indian Ocean (Somalia v. Kenya), 2021, § 51.

86 Conclusion 7 of the Text of the "Draft Conclusions on subsequent agreements and subsequent practice in relation to the interpretation of treaties", provisionally adopted by the ILC (2014), UN Doc. A/69/10, 179–192.

87 International jurisprudence in international law of territory has not skimped in this respect and very often relies on this powerful method of treaty interpretation: ICJ, Pulau Ligitan / Pulau Sipadan, 2002, paras. 37–38, 59–61. See also: Giovanni Distefano, "L'interprétation évolutive de la norme internationale", 115 *Revue générale de droit international public* 2011, 373–396.

88 PA Sereni, *Diritto internazionale*, vol. I, Milan, 1966, 123 (which correctly distinguishes this phenomenon from "desuetude"). The tacit abrogation of a treaty by subsequent practice must also be distinguished from the tacit (or implicit, or even implied) abrogation resulting from the conclusion by States of a *later* treaty incompatible with an *earlier* one (Art. 59 VCLT 1969).

constant and uniform.[89] It is not our intention here to delve into the debates surrounding this question, and even less to delve into what we have called the *Via Dolorosa* of article 38 of the ILC's Draft articles which served as the basis for the VCLT 1969[90] and which envisaged precisely this scenario. Instead, we will limit ourselves to indicating some conceptual elements of this mode of modification[91] of international treaties in the light of international case law. The afore-mentioned (now defunct) provision ("Modification of treaties by subsequent practice") was formulated in the following terms: "A treaty may be modified by the subsequent practice of the parties in the application of the treaty when such practice establishes their agreement to modify the provisions of the treaty".[92] This draft article, which was eventually discarded by the Diplomatic Conference in Vienna, envisaged,[93] as the preparatory work within the ILC clearly shows, subsequent practice as "evidence" of a tacit agreement aiming to modify a written treaty. In other words, the behaviour of states *in the application of the treaty* has the effect of proving their 'mutual dissent' (*mutuus dissensus*), i.e., the opposite of the 'mutual consent' at the origin of the treaty. The legal plausibility of the existence of such a treaty modification procedure would be explained by the concern to adapt, through a very flexible process, the normative reality to changes in the factual environment. In order to avoid the premature obsolescence of international agreements, legal logic would recognise the normative value of subsequent state practice insofar as it gives rise to a tacit agreement to modify a written treaty. Mutual dissent is unearthed by the interpreter (e.g., the judge) from the analysis of subsequent practice, with certain *facta* or *acta concludenti* enabling him to establish whether the treaty has indeed been modified. From the standpoint of international jurisprudence, the case concerning the interpretation of the Air Services Agreement is the landmark case. The Arbitral Tribunal, chaired by Roberto Ago, argued that subsequent practice – carried out in this case by state organs that were not vested with *treaty-making power* – is 'a possible source of a subsequent modification,

89 *Oppenheim's International Law*, 1992, § 624 (at1254), according to which both oral and tacit agreements may modify written treaties.

90 Giovanni Distefano, "La pratique subséquente des Etats parties à un traité", 40 *AFDI* 1994, 41–71.

91 Extinction would also seem possible: Distefano (1994), 67–70.

92 *YILC*, vol. II (1966), 257.

93 However, as the preamble (last paragraph) of the 1969 VCLT states: "the rules of customary international law will continue to govern questions not regulated by the provisions of the present Convention"; therefore, it is not at all impossible to consider tacit agreement – arising from the practice of applying a treaty – as a modality for the modification (and termination) of written treaties.

arising out of certain actions or certain attitudes, having a bearing on the juridical situation of the Parties and on the rights that each of them could properly claim'[94] and reached the conclusion that the relevant conduct of states facts proved an "informal agreement".[95]

Case law and state practice provide us with a rich harvest of precedents. We need only mention a few of them here, starting with the most significant examples, not only because they relate to the UN Charter, but also because in all these cases the treaty in question does indeed provide for a formal procedure for its amendment (Arts. 108–109 UNC). Firstly, Article 12 of the UNC, a central provision in the arrangement of the respective competences of the Security Council and the General Assembly in the maintenance of international peace and security. General Assembly resolution 377 (V), "Uniting for Peace", and the subsequent practice of the bodies concerned, and the Member States have tacitly modified the articulation of competences between the General Assembly and the Security Council. The International Court of Justice noted this in the Wall in Palestine case.[96] Secondly, it is well known that the text of Article 27 § 3 of the Charter, relating to the voting procedure within the Security Council, no longer corresponds to the real norm, since the abstention of a permanent member during the adoption of a resolution is *in fact* equated to a positive vote ("concurring vote") and this against any possible hermeneutic acrobatics of this provision allowing to reconcile the letter of the article ("affirmative vote") with its real content. Fortunately, in this case too, the International Court of Justice, by ascertaining the tacit modification,[97] has helped to dispel any doubts. Thirdly, the same applies to Article 42 of the Charter, which provides that the Security Council, in the exercise of its primary responsibility for the maintenance of international peace and security, "may *take such action by air, sea, or land forces as may be necessary*" [emphasis added]. However, in order to better adhere to the new normative reality of this provision, the italicissed part of the sentence should be replaced by the following fragment: "authorise any Member State to use all necessary means". This new practice of the Security Council, which has met with no resistance

94 Case concerning the Interpretation of the Air Transport Services Agreements between the United States of America and France (France/United States), Award of 22 December 1963, *RIAA*, Vol. XVI, 63.

95 *Ibid.*, 69. See also, in the past, and in the same vein: Serbian/Brazilian Loans (France/Yugoslavia; Brazil/Yugoslavia), judgments of 12 July 1929, *P.C.I.J. Reports* A 20/21, 38.

96 ICJ, Legal Consequences of the Construction of a Wall in the Occupied Palestinian Territory, advisory opinion of 9 July 2004: *I.C.J. Reports 2004*, paras. 24–32.

97 ICJ, Namibia 1971, § 22.

either from Member States or from other UN bodies, was put in place as early as 1990 by Resolution 678 (29 November 1990). It is henceforth undisputed that the delegation by the Security Council of the forcible implementation of its resolutions on the maintenance of international peace and security is consistent with the Charter. Is this to be understood as anything other than tacit agreement revealed by subsequent amending state practice – constituted both by the action of the Council's member states and the approval (in whatever form) by other UN member states? The doctrine, for its part, does not seem to be unaffected by the charms of '*tacit mutual consent*' amending a treaty and arising from its implementation practice.[98]

More specifically in international law of territory, international jurisprudence has not hesitated to refer to the subsequent practice leading to the modification of a territorial treaty. Starting with the "locus classicus" of the Temple of Preah Vihear case, where the ICJ considered Thailand's acquiescence-silence with regard to a geographical map annexed to the delimitation treaty it had just ratified with France (Cambodia's protecting power), as acceptance of its modification. Indeed, the Court declared that the:

> Thailand's subsequent conduct confirms and bears out her original acceptance [...] *Both Parties, by their conduct, recognized the line and thereby in effect agreed to regard it as being the frontier line.*[99]

Subsequent jurisprudence has easily followed the lead of the International Court of Justice. Suffice it to mention here the Eritrea-Ethiopia delimitation case:

> The conduct of one party must be measured against that of the other. Eventually, but not necessarily so, the legal result [consisting in a tacit agreement] may be to vary a boundary established by a treaty.[100]

98 Oppenheim, § 537 (at 571); Riccardo Monaco, Carlo Curti Gialdino, *Diritto internazionale pubblico*, 3rd edn, Turin, 2009, § 9.4 (at 177). See in general note 99 (page 63) of our article quoted above (note 90) as well as the dissenting opinion of Judge Ajibola attached to the ICJ judgment in the case between Cameroon and Nigeria (2002), 556–561.

99 ICJ, Temple of Preah Vihear, 1962, 33 [emphasis added].

100 Eritrea-Ethiopia Boundary Delimitation Decision, Decision of 13 April 2002, *RIAA*, Vol. 25, § 3.29 (at 117).

ii *Tacit Agreement as an Autonomous Source of Territorial Titles*

A set of conducts and attitudes consisting of tacit waivers, actions and reactions, claims and silences that *do not relate to a pre-existing written treaty* can just as easily give rise to a tacit agreement[101] carrying territorial rights or titles.[102] In this case, therefore, an implied agreement may 'arise from the conduct of the Parties'[103] and form the basis of territorial title.[104]

The stringent test[105] for establishing such an implied agreement has been stated by the Court as follows: 'Evidence of a tacit legal agreement must be compelling.[106] The establishment of a permanent maritime boundary is a matter of grave importance and agreement is not easily to be presumed'.[107] The Court in this case (between Nicaragua and Honduras) refuted the existence of a maritime boundary established by tacit agreement.[108] However, in a more recent case between Peru and Chile, it declared that 'an agreed single maritime

---

101 "[a] The German Government had severed on 5 November 1918, diplomatic relations with Russia, thus interrupting the execution of the Brest-Litovsk Treaty. The Russian Government declared a few weeks later in a radio manifesto "to all" that it regarded that treaty as abrogated. [b] The German Government by refraining from protesting against this unilateral declaration and from insisting on its contractual rights, as well as by evacuating the Russian territory occupied by Germany in accordance with that treaty, tacitly accepted this declaration. [c] The common intention of the parties to abrogate the treaty subsequently found expression in the fact that it was not mentioned in the Treaty of Rapallo of 16 April, 1922", Russian-German Commercial Treaty Case (German Reichsgericht), award delivered the 23 May 1925, 3 *ILR* 1925–1926, 355.

102 "In international jurisprudential practice, the conduct of States is greatly taken into account. The silence of a State, its consent, acquiescence, renunciation, protest, the estoppel that may affect its acts, constitute important elements in the creation or extinction of a title to a territory", collective dissenting opinion of Judges Bedjaoui, Koroma and Ranjeva appended to the ICJ Judgment in the Case concerning Maritime Delimitation and Territorial Questions between Qatar and Bahrain, 2001, § 69 (at 168).

103 ICJ, Sovereignty over Pedra Branca/Pulau Batu Puteh, Middle Rocks and South Ledge (Malaysia/Singapore), 2008, § 120 (at 50). In the following paragraph, however, the Court immediately resorts to the notion of acquiescence. In 2009, the ICJ appears to equate tacit agreement with a *modus vivendi* (Black Sea Delimitation, 2009, § 197, at (125)).

104 ICJ, Gulf of Maine, paras. 144–154 (at 309–312).

105 Individual opinion of Judge Owada attached to the judgment of the Court in the Maritime Dispute, 2014, § 12.

106 In a recent case, the ICJ stated: "The Court has set at a high threshold for proof that a maritime boundary has been established by acquiescence or tacit agreement", ICJ, Maritime Delimitation in the Indian Ocean (Somalia v. Kenya), 2021, § 52 (at 228).

107 ICJ, Territorial and Maritime Dispute between Nicaragua and Honduras in the Caribbean Sea, 2007, § 253 (at 735). This allowed the ICJ to naturally exclude a "line with a specific, limited purpose" or "provisional", such as that resulting from a *modus vivendi*.

108 The same was true, more recently, in ICJ, Maritime Delimitation in the Indian Ocean (Somalia v. Kenya), 2021, paras. 36–71.

boundary exists between the Parties"based 'on a tacit agreement' between them.[109] The Court does not know "when or by what means this boundary was agreed", but it notes, on the one hand, that the tacit agreement coalesced (the verb "crystallized" being used by the Court rather to indicate the customary process)[110] between 1947 and 1954 and, on the other hand, that it derives from an aggregate of disparate treaty acts and legal facts (State conduct) which all converge towards its emergence.[111] Moreover, the Court's conclusion is supported by the legal logic according to which subsequent treaties between the parties could not have been concluded in the absence of this tacit agreement; they therefore necessarily presuppose it.[112] Should temporal indeterminacy then really disturb us? Is it not connatural to the concept of tacit agreement revealed by conclusive States' conduct? Moreover, was this same Court more precise – and could it be more precise – in the Temple of Preah Vihear case?[113]

As for the territorial extent (external limit) of this delimitation, some criticism has been levelled at the ICJ, but its reasoning is consistent with the very nature of the tacit agreement, which is based on actual States' conducts and not on any alleged conception that the Parties may have had of the maritime space regimes of the time. The external limit must therefore be defined in the light of the intentions and purposes pursued by the Parties throughout their various conducts.[114] Admittedly, the Court admits to some "uncertainties" regarding the 80 nautical mile limit finally decided upon, but it considers, and it is difficult to prove the contrary, that it is supported by "the evidence presented to it".[115] With regard to the evidence on which the Court relies, it should be noted that the Court in 2007 did not provide with any precise criteria, let alone a legal formula or algorithm that could establish the existence of a tacit agreement.[116] The Court's silence in this regard should not come as too much of a surprise, as the 'scientific' character of international law does not depend on recourse

---

109 ICJ, Maritime Dispute, 2014, paras. 177 (at 91).

110 ICJ, North Sea Continental Shelf, 1969, para. 61 (at 39).

111 ICJ, Maritime Dispute, 2014, paras. 69, 91 (at 31, 39–40).

112 ICJ, Maritime Dispute, 2014, para. 100 (at 41). Also: statement of Judge Guillaume, para. 8. *Contra*: separate opinion of Judge Owada (paras. 12–21), dissenting opinion of Judge Sebutinde (paras. 4–10).

113 ICJ, Temple of Preah Vihear, 1962, 33.

114 Chile's surveillance of the disputed maritime spaces (ICJ, Maritime Dispute, 2014, paras. 126–129), Peru's lack of "protest" (para. 147), the "Bakula Memorandum" (paras. 136–142).

115 *Ibid.*, para. 151 (at 58). *Contra:* Declaration of Judge Donoghue (110–111).

116 The dissenting and separate opinions attached to the 2007 (Territorial and Maritime Dispute between Nicaragua and Honduras in the Caribbean Sea) and 2014 (Maritime Dispute) judgments do not shed any further light.

to the quantitative methods of the exact sciences (*more geometrico*). Legal science, embodying instead Pascal's *esprit de finesse*[117]does not bother with such "trifles". On the other hand, the Court emphasises the need to prove convincingly that the States have expressed their will *to be bound by law* and that a meeting of their consents to that effect has coalesced. As already noted above, such conclusive conduct (since it concludes that an agreement has emerged) may be sought both in their internal and external spheres of activity and may assume any form and emanate from any State organ. These criteria, if they can be called such, therefore appear to be applicable in any field of international law and are hardly exclusive to international law of territory; they therefore belong to the toolbox of the generalist internationalist.[118]

International jurisprudence is not short on tacit agreements as an autonomous source of territorial title. An arbitral tribunal, called upon to settle a maritime boundary dispute, stated that:

> Senegal considers that the practice subsequent to the 1960 [Franco-Portuguese] Agreement on Maritime Delimitation and the acquiescence of each State to the legislation of the other ... would therefore have given rise to *a tacit agreement or bilateral custom.*[119]

Territorial boundary disputes are obviously not left out, as the Taba case shows, where the Arbitral Tribunal correctly noted a tacit agreement: 'The parties to

117 Pascal, *Thoughts* (1670), I-512: 'There are then two kinds of intellect: the one able to penetrate acutely and deeply into the conclusions of given premises, and this is the precise intellect; the other able to comprehend a great number of premises without confusing them, and this is the mathematical intellect. The one has force and exactness, the other comprehension. Now the one quality can exist without the other; the intellect can be strong and narrow, and can also be comprehensive and weak. [...] In the one the principles are palpable, but removed from ordinary use; so that for want of habit it is difficult to turn one's mind in that direction: but if one turns it thither ever so little, one sees the principles fully, and one must have a quite inaccurate mind who reasons wrongly from principles so plain that it is almost impossible they should escape notice' (Transl. from French, Dutton, New York, 1958, Section I.2 and 1 (at 3, 1)).

118 Distefano (2002), 184–192.

119 Maritime Boundary Determination Case (Guinea-Bissau/Senegal), Award of 31 July 1989, 20 *RIAA*, § 83 (at 151; our translation; emphasis added). This case could have been included, by virtue of its *ratio decidendi*, in the previous sub-section insofar as the conduct of the States was in relation to a delimitation treaty and could as such easily be configured as a subsequent practice modifying it.

the Agreement of 1906, had by their conduct, agreed to the boundary as it was demarcated by masonry pillars'.[120]

In a similar vein, it has been correctly asserted that a boundary established by the principle of *uti possidetis* can be modified by the "tacit consent"[121] of the parties concerned or that an "express or tacit agreement between the Parties", arising from oil concessions, can form the basis of an autonomous title.[122]

D Historical Consolidation of Territorial Titles or the "Complex Juridical Fact"

i *The Concept and Its Genesis*

At the end of this section, we can argue that territorial titles are ultimately created and extinguished by what can be called a 'complex fact',[123] which refers to a set of unique and indivisible facts gathered into an aggregate aimed at creating or extinguishing territorial sovereignty.[124] The effectiveness of this cluster of facts depends on the circumstances.[125] As maintained in one of the most authoritative textbooks on public international law – *Oppenheim's International Law* – last edited by the late Professor Robert Jennings, a "complex fact" can:

> include continued and effective occupation and administration, acquiescence and/or protest, the relative strength or weakness of any rival claim, the effects of the inter-temporal law, the principle of stability in territorial title and boundaries, regional principles such as *uti possidetis*,

120 Taba case (Egypt/Israel), Award of 29 September 1988, 27 *ILM* 1988, § 233 (at 1488; emphasis added). Also: Lamu Island, 244; but most importantly: Eritrea-Ethiopia Boundary Delimitation Decision, 2002, paras. 3.6–3.13 (110–112).

121 "If the *uti possidetis juris* can be qualified by adjudication and by treaty, the question then arises whether it can be qualified in other ways, for example, by acquiescence or recognition […] The conduct of Honduras vis-à-vis earlier *effectvités* reveals an admission, recognition, acquiescence *or other form of tacit consent to the situation*", Land, Island and Maritime Frontier Dispute, 1992, paras. 67, 364 (at 401,577) [emphasis added].

122 ICJ, Land and Maritime Boundary (Cameroon v. Nigeria, Equatorial Guinea intervening), 2002, § 304 (at 448).

123 On the notion of "complex wrongful act" in the theory of responsibility of States for internationally wrongful acts, see Giovanni Distefano, "Fait continu, fait compose et fait complexe dans le droit de la responsabilité", 52 *AFDI* 2006, 1–54.

124 See *above* I.1.

125 The Indo-Pakistan Western Boundary (Rann of Kutch) between India and Pakistan, 553 (Opinion of the Chairman).

> geographical and historical factors, the attitudes of the International Community, and the possible requirements of self-determination, and also indeed the possibly unlawful origin of the original taking of possession, and that subjugation is no longer per se a recognisable title. The weight to be given to these factors and considerations, in the assessment of the total result in terms of a consolidated title, will vary with particular cases.[126]

The creation and extinction of territorial titles through a "complex fact"[127] is akin to what the literature calls "historical consolidation of title". This term was coined in the wake of the Court's decision in the Norwegian Fisheries case, where it stated:

> Norway has been in a position to argue without any contradiction that neither the promulgation of her delimitation Decrees in 1869 and in 1889, nor their application, gave rise to any opposition on the part of foreign States. Since, moreover, these Decrees constitute, as has been shown above, the application of a well-defined and uniform system, it is indeed this system itself which would reap the benefit of general toleration, the basis of an historical consolidation which would make it enforceable against all States.[128]

This statement by the Court sounds like a distant echo of what Denmark had argued thirty years earlier in the East Greenland case, where Charles de Visscher was unsurprisingly among its legal advisors.[129] Indeed, as has been convincingly noted, Professor de Visscher's analysis 'is a penetrating and illuminating observation of the way Courts actually tackle questions of title to territorial sovereignty',[130] even if this concept has not been 'spelled out as a

126 *Oppenheim's International Law*, 1992, § 275, at 716.

127 ICJ, Sovereignty over Pedra Branca/Pulau Batu Puteh, Middle Rocks and South Ledge (Malaysia/Singapore), § 276 (at 96).

128 ICJ, Norwegian Fisheries, 1951, 138. It is generally admitted attributing the construction of this concept to the eminent Belgian jurist who actually sat on the ICJ's bench at the time of the dispute.

129 "It is both its immemorial possession and the general and continuous assent by States to the assertion and exercise of Danish sovereignty, an expression of a will which, strengthened by the action of time, has gradually consolidated possession into a legally valid situation *erga omnes*", Reply of the Government of Denmark, PCIJ, Vol. 63, at 721 (22 July 1932), Case concerning the Legal Status of Eastern Greenland [our translation].

130 Sir Robert Jennings (1963), 26.

doctrine by any court, and there may be some danger in allowing what is basically a simple, and indeed obvious, idea to develop into a somewhat doctrinaire principle'.[131]

This theory – which aims to explain how territorial titles can evolve over time in the light of state conduct – has been positively received by subsequent doctrine and jurisprudence (both international and national).[132] However, the fascination with this construction – in particular its versatility and flexibility – is the flip side of the coin for its critics. Indeed, even authors who do not refute its merits feel the need to point out its (minor) drawbacks. Sir Robert Jennings wrote: "Historical consolidation is also *a voracious concept*, and it should be kept within bounds",[133] while Brownlie argued:

> However, it is probably confusing to overemphasise, and to lump together, this penumbra of equities by discovering the concept of consolidation. Apart from the concept of consolidation, the rate of social, economic, and other 'non-legal' considerations in the application by tribunals of the more orthodox legal principles is not to be denied.[134]

Indeed, contrary to its 'historical' name, this theory 'is in some measure a misnomer' in that it tends to 'increase the significance of relatively recent possession'[135] at the expense of a distant legal past … and of historical titles! In fact, and rather paradoxically, the emphasis is more on the recent past, i.e. the period immediately preceding the critical date, than on the more distant past.[136] Moreover, as one opponent of this theory rightly points out, historical

---

131 *Ibid.*, 27–28.

132 See: i.a.: ICJ, Land, Island and Maritime Frontier Dispute, 1992, § 345 (at 565); Civil Aeronautics Board and al. v. Island Airlines Inc, District Court (Hawaii), Judgement of 8 October 1964, 35 *ILR*, 79; Re Ownership of the Bed of the Strait of Georgia and Related Areas, British Columbia Court of Appeal, Judgement of 25 June 1976, 73 *ILR*, 202; Raptis and Son v. State of South Australia (High Court), Judgement of 27 June 1977, 69 *ILR*, 66 [Stephen J, Judge].

133 Sir Robert Jennings (1963), 27 [emphasis added].

134 Brownlie, 124.

135 Sir Robert Jennings (1963), 27.

136 In general, it should be noted in relation to temporal duration that 'every material situation calls for its own solution, based on the balancing of competing claims and depending on the area', ICJ, Land and Maritime Boundary (Cameroon v. Nigeria, Equatorial Guinea intervening), 2002, § 28, at 485 (dissenting op. of Judge Koroma). This bears a striking resemblance to the process of customary rule formation as depicted by the ICJ in the North Sea Continental Shelf cases (1969, § 74, at 44).

consolidation refers more to a process (i.e., duration)[137] in time rather than to an (instantaneous) act at a specific point in time, hence its close relationship with the notion of a 'critical period'.[138]

ii *Its Tormented Jurisprudential Life*

The Court's most recent pronouncement in this regard appears prima facie indisputable. Indeed, it appeared to reject Nigeria's argument based on 'historical consolidation', arguing that it 'has never been used as a basis of title in other territorial disputes, whether in its own or in other case law'.[139] ICJ further stated, on a more general basis, that:

> nothing in the *Fisheries* Judgement suggests that the "historical consolidation" referred to, in connection with the external boundaries of the territorial sea, allows land occupation to prevail *over an established treaty title*. Moreover, the facts and circumstances put forward by Nigeria with respect to the Lake Chad villages concern a period of some 20 years, which is in any event far too short, even according to the theory relied on by it.[140]

What can we infer from this? Firstly (and most importantly), even the proponents of this theory recognise that it cannot prevail "over established conventional title", since the latter takes precedence over pure effectiveness. On the contrary, this 'theory' or 'doctrine' plays its full role in cases where a competing (formal) title has not been fully established or where it has been eroded or weakened due to the acquiescence or lack of timely reaction of the titular State, hence the correlative and opposite, much less famous, notion of "historical weakening of title."

We are therefore not inclined to consider that the Court has thus completely and definitively removed this theory from the international lawyer's toolbox of territorial disputes. Less radically, the Court has clarified the scope of application of this theory and its relationship to established legal titles. In doing so,

---

137 Marcelo Kohen, "L'influence du temps sur les règlements des conflits territoriaux", in: *Le droit international et le temps*, Paris, 2001, 144.

138 Distefano (2017), 406–407.

139 ICJ, Land and Maritime Boundary (Cameroon v. Nigeria, Equatorial Guinea intervening), 2002, § 65 (at 352; emphasis added).

140 *Loc.cit.* [emphasis added]. In fact, one of the Court's judges aptly stated that this "is not a mere theory, let alone an invention, on the part of Nigeria" (Ajibola J dissenting, para. 134, at 581).

it can be argued that the ICJ did not fundamentally depart from what it had stated in the 1951 *Fisheries* case.[141] On the contrary, the Court took this opportunity to elucidate its thought on one of the most intriguing and yet elaborate theories it has ever delved into.[142]

Indeed, it can be argued that this theory has not been favoured by some scholars because of its incorrect or abusive use, which has led to misunderstandings or even to the erroneous construction that a title can be established by the mere passage of time. Or, alternatively, that with the passage of time, a formal (i.e., conventional) title can be eroded and eventually extinguished due to adverse effectivities.

It must be borne in mind that formal title is only one of the recognised means by which a State may acquire sovereignty over a territory and, as such, it does not exhaust all other means and, above all, it does not coincide with title itself. In this respect and with a view to ascertaining title to sovereignty, international tribunals have often relied on the protean States' conducts – i.e., acquiescence, estoppel, subsequent practice in the application of a territorial treaty, (lack of) protest, tacit agreement, *modus vivendi*,[143] etc., which may well give rise to a legal title, even if it is not "formal" (i.e., based on or conveyed by a treaty).[144]

This is what Judge Koroma may have had in mind when he observed that such situations are made up of a:

> complex of interests and relations [to a territory] being continuous and extending over many years plus acquiescence. Historical consolidation also caters where there has been a clear loss or absence of title through abandonment or inactivity on the one side, and an effective exercise of jurisdiction and control, continuously maintained, on the other.[145]

---

141 See in this respect paragraph 220 (at 414) of the Court's judgment, in which it does not appear to categorically refute "historical consolidation".

142 In this respect, the Court's considerations in the Kasikili Island/Sedudu case (1999, paras. 47–80, at 1075–1096) appear less adamant than those in the Land and Maritime Boundary case (2002, paras. 71–81, at 355–358).

143 The "modus vivendi" may even be established as "best title" in the absence of any other fact or act that could give rise to territorial title: ICJ, Frontier Dispute (Benin/Niger), 2005, paras. 85–88 (at 129–130); 98–99 (at 132).

144 See G Distefano, "La sentence arbitrale du 9 octobre 1998 dans l'affaire du différend insulaire entre le Yémen et l'Érythrée", 103 *RGDIP* 1999, 863–883. See *supra* Part 1. Chapter 3. Sections A–C.

145 ICJ, Land and Maritime Boundary (Cameroon v. Nigeria; Equatorial Guinea intervening), 2002, § 26 (at 485) (dissenting opinion of Judge Koroma).

In short, if a formal (i.e., treaty) title has not been established,[146] this means that another (competing) title has arisen by historical consolidation, eroding and eventually extinguishing it. For this purpose, it is necessary to prove the "acquiescence" of the former holder with regard to the initial "contra legem acts" of the other State. On the contrary, if such abandonment (consent of the titular state to relinquish its title) cannot be proven during the critical period vis-à-vis the other state, then the latter's[147] *effectivités* remain *effectively contra legem* and must therefore bow to the established (treaty) title.

Therefore, the "historical consolidation" of territorial titles may well constitute:

> a valid basis for territorial title, that is to say that proven long use, coupled with a *complex of interests and relations* … can have the effect of attaching a territory to a given State. In my opinion, founded on the jurisprudence of the Court [relevant references follow], historical consolidation, if supported by the requisite evidence, can be a sound and valid means of establishing territorial title in international law.[148]

This "complex set" of States' conducts and attitudes – conveniently subsumed under the formula "historical consolidation of title" – may ultimately attest to States concerned respective consent to relinquish title and their intention to acquire it with regard to the disputed territory, so that the validity of the territorial transfer is juridically established. But this, and it must be repeated again and again, is on the condition that the evidential facts support the existence of such consent – in whatever form it is expressed – on the part of the State holding formal title. If this is, as it seems, the correct construction of the historical consolidation, then, regardless of its actual usefulness and its 'label',[149] it does not seem to contradict Heffter's famous and often quoted '*Hundert Jahre Unrecht ist noch kein Tag Recht*'.[150] Indeed, according to the famous German

---

146 ICJ, Land and Maritime Boundary (Cameroon v. Nigeria; Equatorial Guinea intervening), 2002, § 223 (at 415).

147 The 'principle[of historical consolidation] has evolved over the years, side by side with *effectivités*', ICJ, Land and Maritime Boundary (Cameroon v. Nigeria, Equatorial Guinea intervening), 2002, § 135, at 582 (dissenting opinion of Judge Ajibola).

148 ICJ, Land and Maritime Boundary (Cameroon v. Nigeria, intervening Equatorial Guinea), 2002, § 8 (at 476) (dissenting opinion of Judge Koroma; emphasis added).

149 *Loc.cit.* Former ICJ President Sir Robert Jennings had further observed that: "the idea of historical consolidation is something more than a terminological reform. It opens the door to a mode of acquiring title that is, or at least may become, subtly different from what is found in the old learning about occupation and prescription", 1963, 25.

150 AW Heffter, *Das Europäische Völkerrecht der Gegenwart*, 5th edn, Berlin, 1867, § 12 (at 30).

jurist, acquiescence – which can be assimilated to historical consolidation (and of which it is surely one of the constitutive elements) – is one of the valid 'modes' of acquiring the title of territorial sovereignty: it expresses the 'tacit renunciation' of the state to the territorial title in the face of the asserted claims and behaviours of another state.[151]

A final remark is in order: as shown in the previous pages, Time is one of the two (factual) dimensions, together with space,[152] within which state (and thus human) activity takes place. Consequently, time and space are not recognised by public international law as facts of acquisition or cession that can *per se* create, extinguish or modify territorial titles. In other words, the acts or deeds of certain states to this effect must be seen in the context of Time, since they are deemed by public international law to be suitable to produce such legal effects on the title of territorial sovereignty.[153] Grotius had already grasped the true function of time as one of the dimensions of human thought and activity:

> Time, as such, having no Power to produce any Thing, for nothing is done by Time, tho' every Thing be done in Time.[154]

151 According to Oppenheim (*International Law. A Treatise*, 2nd edn, Vol. 1, New York, 1912, § 243, at 311 note 1), the dictum of Heffter (*supra* note 150).

152 In the light of the aforesaid, it is not at all surprising that, by completely reversing the perspective (from object to subject), time and space are, according to KANT, the two lenses ("spectacles") through which reality is observed (*De mundi sensibilis atque intelligibilis forma et principiis*, paras. 14.3 and 15). Both are, according to the German philosopher, 'intuitions' or a priori categories of the mind (*The Critique of Pure Reason*, Second Part, paras. 4.2 and 4.7). See *supra* note 40.

153 Distefano (2002), 244–313; Marcelo Kohen, *Possession contestée et souveraineté territoriale*, Paris, 1997, 127–154.

154 Grotius (1648), Book II, Chapter 4.1, at 483. Galileo used to warn the observer about the determining and measuring role played by time: "Omnia metire quaecumque licet et immensa ad mensuram tempestive redige" ["Measure what is measurable and render measurable in time what as yet is not"].

CHAPTER 4

The (Presumptive) Dilemma between Formal Legal Title and Effectiveness

In this section, we will review some paradigmatic cases of divorce between *titulus* and *modus*. In other words, these cases are characterised by the fact that one state possesses the *titulus* while another happens to effectively occupy the territory in question. However, in all these situations, the effective occupation *contra titulum* has not been achieved through the use of force or in defiance of another peremptory rule of the international order, such as the right of peoples to self-determination. These cases will be analysed, however, in Part 2. Here we are dealing with situations where the occupation contrary to the *titulus* has been carried out peacefully or by means of armed force at a time when, however, such force was not prohibited by international law. One must therefore examine the role of *contra titulum* effectiveness, in the creation, modification and extinction of territorial titles.

The principle of effectiveness is usually described by a maxim of Roman law: "*Ex facto oritur ius*"[1] often in counterpoint with the other maxim: "*Ex iniuria ius non oritur*".[2] Now, in a truly Manichean vision of the relationships between Law and Fact(s), one could imagine that the whole juridical phenomenon oscillates between these two extremes, as if around the two poles of an ellipse. It is as if Law were sailing between Scylla and Charybdis, as if from the same 'mouth' (the 'fact') there were both the legal and the un-legal (*Recht* and *un-Recht*), the right and its violation. This reductive conception of Law is the corollary of theories that postulate, as a metaphysical axiom, the irreducible *opposition* between law and fact.

Effectiveness permeates every branch of public international law; for example, when determining the nationality link in the context of diplomatic protection in cases of dual (or multiple) nationality of an individual, international tribunals refer to the criterion of the *most effective* nationality, namely 'that which accorded with the facts, that based on stronger factual

1 L.52 ad leg. Aquilia.

2 The origin of this saying remains mysterious, in the darkness of history.

 | DOI:10.1163/9789004708594_007

ties between the person concerned and one of the States whose nationality is involved'.[3] Effectiveness also plays a decisive role in the field of international state responsibility and more specifically in the attribution to a state of the conduct of individuals who become its *de facto* organs;[4] or as a condition for the existence of a government;[5] or even in the criteria for the existence of non-state armed groups in the context of a non-international armed conflict.[6] The principle of effectiveness is thus the nexus between law and fact in the process of creating legal rules or legal situations that are enforceable within a given legal order.[7]

In this chapter we intend to highlight the manifestations of this principle (can it be considered as such?) in relation to the creation, modification and extinction of a territorial title. Being confronted, from the outset, with the arduous task of defining effectiveness, we must confess our perplexity. Of course, we can console ourselves if it is true that even the illustrious Belgian jurist Charles De Visscher expresses himself in this way in this respect: "It [effectiveness] evades any general definition. It suggests both the idea of a certain tension and that of an ultimate adequacy between fact and law".[8]

These two aspects, which the distinguished Belgian jurist considered to be contradictory or, at least, as if they represented two very different sides of the same thing, are in fact one and the same. Now, the effectiveness of a rule, a situation, *etc.*, would represent the proof, the legal indication that such a rule, such a situation, has finally emerged from this whirlpool of relations between law and fact. It is therefore only on a case-by-case basis, in the light of each specific situation or field, that a more refined notion of this principle can be

---

3 ICJ, Nottebohm (Liechtenstein v. Guatemala), Judgment of 6 April 1955 (second phase): *ICJ Reports* 1955, 22. The Court spoke in this regard of a "*social fact* of attachment" (23; emphasis added). Subsequent case law has more fairly restricted the application of this rule to cases of dual nationality (*Flegenheimer*, *RIAA*, Vol. XIV, 327) where the private individual also possesses the nationality of the respondent State (see Article 7 of the ILC Text of Articles on Diplomatic Protection, 2006).

4 See Articles 4 and 8 ARSIWA. See also: Giovanni Distefano, Aymeric Hêche, "L'organe *de facto* dans la responsabilité internationale: *Curia, quo vadis*?", 61 *AFDI* 2015, 3–33.

5 Aguilar-Amory and Royal Bank of Canada claims (Great-Britain v. Costa Rica) (Tinoco case), arbitral award of 18 October 1923, *RIAA*, Vol. I, 381.

6 See. Article 1 (1) P/II 1977 and Article 8 (2) (f) ICC.

7 E.g., "No state will be found willing to recognise a change which does not have the characteristics of effectiveness and stability", Scipione Gemma, "Les gouvernements de fait", 4 *RCADI* 1924-III, 337 [our translation].

8 De Visscher (1958), 601.

obtained. With regard to the international legal rule, it has been pertinently stated that: "The requirement of effectiveness, as a condition for the existence and validity of the international norm, can only lead to a permanent revision of this norm".[9]

It is this permanent contradiction, inherent to all legal orders, which qualifies the principle of effectiveness; it is as if there were an *asymptotic* rapprochement between law and fact and, in this, effectiveness would constitute the "guardian" or, better still, the test which would make it possible to ascertain whether each time, from this permanent contradiction, a norm or a legal situation has arisen, *etc.*

With regard to territorial titles in particular, their validity is the result of a process over time during which, thanks to their effectiveness, they are strengthened (or weakened, or even extinguished) in relation to other competing titles. It follows that any "territorial title, whatever *its origin*, is based on the actual exercise of state functions by the person claiming it"[10] (*modus*) in accordance with the relevant rules of public international law (*titulus*).

If all competing titles should be "effective", "the title with the highest degree of effectiveness wins, which is considered the best title".[11] This proves once again the plausibility of the adjective "relative" that is usually attached to both the title and the weight of each title and, consequently, to the effectiveness that characterises them. The relativity of the "weight" of each title measured in relation to the criterion of effectiveness is an inescapable consequence of the structure of the international legal order and of the *erga omnes* character of the territorial rights on which the titles are based. For, only the confrontation between legal titles and between their respective spatial extents,[12] in the light of their "relative degree of effectiveness", can allow the assessment of the weight of each of them. It would not make sense, nor would it always be possible, to weigh up a territorial title *in abstracto*.

9 Monique Chemillier-Gendreau, "A propos de l'effectivité en droit international", 11 *RBDI* 1975, 39.

10 Combacau, Sur, 409 [our translation; emphasis added]; Sereni (1966), Vol. 1, 99–100; Ortolan, 200.

11 Touscoz, 228–229. Likewise: De Visscher (1960), 404–405.

12 See Oppenheim's *Oppenheim's International Law* (1992), § 253.

State practice,[13] international[14] and domestic courts[15] and the doctrine[16] are in tune in corroborating the primary need for the criterion of effectiveness for the purposes of determining the "best title" (relative!). The effectiveness of possession "qualified" by the conclusive and convergent attitudes of the States, including above all the "specially affected" States,[17] is embodied in a "complex juridical fact" in which both *titulus* and *modus adquisitionis* are found. It follows that effectiveness, and the fact that this situation is well known to be rooted in factual reality and that it is "tolerated", "accepted", or even "not contested" by the "particularly interested" States, makes this situation valid, i.e., opposable *erga omnes*, by the very fact of the perfection of the legal title in which these States have participated.

It has been observed in this respect[18] that a legal order *is*, as a whole, legitimate when it is *effective*, i.e. when most of its rules are respected most of the time by most of its addressees. The principle of effectiveness is therefore the necessary condition for the legitimisation of the legal system.

---

13 See the diplomatic dispatch of 17 January 1876 from Lord Derby to Lord Russel (in Berlin) concerning the Anglo-Spanish controversy over the effectiveness of the Spanish occupation of the Sulu Archipelago, cited in Smith, 40–41; the diplomatic note of 27 November 1876 from the Earl of Derby to Mr. Layard (in Madrid), cited in Bruns, FBl2 § 605, concerning the same dispute; the British Reply (Sir Austen Chamberlain) of 18 February 1929 to the British Government, cited in Bruns, FBl2 § 605. Layard (in Madrid), quoted in *Bruns*, FBl2 § 605, on the same dispute; the British Reply (Sir Austen Chamberlain) of 18 February 1929 to the Persian Ambassador in London, on the Bahrain Islands controversy, quoted in Smith, 71. On this long controversy it is recommended to consult the comprehensive work of Fereydoun Adamiyat, *Bahrein Islands; A Legal and Diplomatic Study of the British-Iranian Controversy*, New York, 1955; Gholam R Tadjbakhche, *La question des îles Bahreïn*, Paris, 1960.

14 See Beagle Channel Arbitration, § 168; Boundary Delimitation case, 42; Clipperton Island case, 1110; ICJ, Sovereignty over Certain Frontier Land (Belgium v. Netherlands), Judgment of 20 June 1959 (Merits): *ICJ Reports* 1959, 227–228; Island of Aves Case (Netherlands v. Venezuela), Award of 30 June 1865, *RIAA*, Vol. XXVIII, 122-123; British Guiana-Brazil Frontier Case, 19.

15 See Civil Aeronautics, 79–80.

16 See Antarctic cases, § 37; Ludovico M Bentivoglio, *La "debellatio" nel diritto internazionale*, Pavia, 1948, 30; Schwarzenberger, 298; André Decencière-Ferrandière, "Essai historique et critique sur l'occupation comme mode d'acquérir les territoires en droit international", 18 *RDILC* 1937, 362–370.

17 ICJ, North Sea Continental Shelf cases, 1969, para. 73.

18 Ruggero Meneghelli, *Il problema dell'effettività nella teoria della validità giuridica*, Padova, 1964, 88 ff. In the same sense: Sperduti (1956), 748–752; Antonio Cassese, *International Law in a Divided World*, Oxford, 1986, § 10 (at 27): "Force is the principal source of legitimation in the International Community".

However, it is not a sufficient condition,[19] since, as a general rule, while it is true that a legal order that is not effective is not legal,[20] it is also true that not every effective order is necessarily legal.[21] This is where the – albeit partial – answer to the question of the validity of the legal system must be sought.[22]

A The Effective Occupation of *terra nullius*

This is one of the scenarios we earlier referred to and which we said allowed the notion of the principle of effectiveness to be better and more concretely delimited; it appears in this context as 'a data already 'constructed', more refined'.[23] However, this situation now appears to be a textbook hypothesis, since today there are no longer any territories 'sans maître' in the sense of 'susceptible to appropriation by a state':[24]

19 See *infra* Part 2.

20 The principle (or 'criterion') of effectiveness was given a crucial function even in the feudal legal order, which proves that it is inherent in the concept of legal order and cannot be ignored. Blackstone reminds us in this respect that the effectiveness of the possession and exercise of certain personal and territorial powers was required "in order that there might be a person always on the spot to perform the feudal duties and services", 197. See Loizidou v. Turkey (40/1993/435/514), ECtHR, Merits, Judgment of 18 December 1996, para. 49.

21 Contrary to Kelsen, according to whom the effectiveness of the situation is a sufficient condition *per se* for its validity (1967, 211–214). That the *imperium de facto* [thus characterised by effectiveness] is attributive, among other 'facts', of the title to territorial sovereignty over the original territory [in short of the emergence of the state], no one can doubt. However, the principle of effectiveness thus constructed does not constitute a sufficient title [for lack of *titulus adquisitionis*] for the purposes of legalising the translation of territorial sovereignty. In short, the validity of the juridical title, given its dyadic structure (*modus* and *titulus*) must be sought elsewhere, precisely in the second element.

22 In order to highlight the artificiality and the temporary and 'endogenous' character of the *opposition between* law and fact, we can say that a lawful territorial situation was certainly first and foremost an effective situation and that the subsequent and contrary effectiveness will come up against a situation that was also, at the outset, an (only?) effective situation. Validity is therefore, as we shall see later [Part 2. Chapter 5], a dynamic concept that crystallises through contradictory, successive and concomitant effective situations in time. Moreover, the concept of validity in international law has degrees (like the 'forms' of invalidity), which vary in space and time under the pressure of the (social) forces generated by the very existence of the (international) legal order.

23 De Visscher (1958), 603.

24 PCIJ, Legal status of Eastern Greenland, 74.

> The expression "terra nullius" was a legal term of art employed in connection with "occupation" as one of the accepted legal methods of acquiring sovereignty over territory. "Occupation" being legally an original means of peaceably acquiring sovereignty over territory otherwise than by cession or succession, it was a cardinal condition of a valid "occupation" that the territory should be *terra nullius* – a territory belonging to no-one – at the time of the act alleged to constitute the "occupation."[25]

Consequently, the main interest of this situation must be sought in an intertemporal law perspective, i.e., during the jurisdictional settlement of territorial conflicts whose titles in dispute are based on the occupation of territories originally *terra nullius*.

Following the model set out above, the *titulus adquisitionis* is in this case twofold, since it is formed both by the *nullius* character of the territory *and* by the *animus possidendi* of the occupying state, i.e., the "serious and reasonable will"[26] to exercise the prerogatives of public power as a sovereign. The *modus adquisitionis* is always the same, i.e., the *actual* occupation of the land territory concerned (the "adprehensio physica"). As the PCIJ made clear:

> it may be well to state that a claim to sovereignty based not upon some particular act or title such as a treaty of cession but merely upon continued display of authority, involves two elements each of which must be shown to exist: the intention and will to act as sovereign, and some actual exercise or display of such authority.[27]

While the character *nullius* of the earth land does not call for any particular comment,[28] the condition of *animus possidendi* means both *intellectus*

25 ICJ, Western Sahara, para. 79 (at 39). The synonym formula "territorium nullius" is also resorted to from time to time: "Consequently, there is ground to admit that, when … France proclaimed her sovereignty over Clipperton, that island in the legal situation of *territorium nullius*, and, therefore, susceptible of occupation", Sovereignty over Clipperton Island case, arbitral award 28 January 1933, in 26 *AJIL* 1932, 393.

26 Memorandum sent by M Mancini, MFA of Italy, to his Consul General in Egypt, De Martino, on 27 March 1882 in which the Italian title to the Bay of Assab was set out, cited in *Prassi italiana*, Vol. 1, series 2, § 838 (at 722).

27 ICJ, Case concerning the Legal Status of Eastern Greenland, 45–46. Also: Island of Palmas Case, 839; Island of Clipperton Case, 393.

28 It can be either an inhabited territory but without a political organisation in the sense that was intended at the time (see *supra* Part 1. Chapter 2. Section D) or an uninhabited territory.

possidendi, i.e., the awareness of the occupation, as well as the intention to "act as sovereign"[29] by performing acts "à titre de souverain".[30]

The *modus adquisitionis*, i.e. the occupation of the territory, has been the subject of continuous jurisprudential refinement, the most important steps of which are outlined below. The occupation, carried out by State organs,[31] must be: a) effective; b) uninterrupted (in time); and c) permanent (in the way it is deployed). International jurisprudence furnishes an illustrative collection of acts that may embody effective occupation:

> The Court recalls that acts and activities considered to be performed *à titre de souverain* are in particular, but not limited to, legislative acts or acts of administrative control, acts relating to the application and enforcement of criminal or civil law, acts regulating immigration, acts regulating fishing and other economic activities, naval patrols as well as search and rescue operations.[32]

As for effectiveness, this cannot be assessed *in abstracto*, but depends on two different sets of criteria,[33] namely the *intrinsic* and *extrinsic* value of the

---

29 ICJ, Territorial and Maritime Dispute (Nicaragua v. Colombia), 2012, § 75 (at 654).

30 ICJ, Maritime Delimitation and Territorial Questions between Qatar and Bahrain, 2001, § 197 (at 99–100); ICJ, Pulau Ligitan / Pulau Sipadan, 2002, § 147 (at 685); ICJ, Territorial and Maritime Dispute between Nicaragua and Honduras in the Caribbean Sea, 2007, paras. 176–208 (at 713–722); ICJ, Territorial and Maritime Dispute (Nicaragua v. Colombia), 2012, § 80 (at 655). See also: Distefano (2019), 660–664.

31 In this respect, it should be noted – as the abundant literature shows – that even private or "chartered" companies such as the East and West India Companies (British and Dutch, for example) were entrusted by the States of nationality to carry out the occupation. See in this sense: Island of Palmas case, 858; Article 5 ARSIWA. See also the fascinating book on this issue: William Dalrymple, *The Anarchy. The relentless rise of the East India Company*, Oxford, 2019.

32 Territorial and Maritime Dispute (Nicaragua v. Colombia), 2012, § 80 (at 655). The Court refers to its earlier judgment in the case of Territorial and Maritime Dispute between Nicaragua and Honduras in the Caribbean Sea (Nicaragua v. Honduras), 2007, paras. 176–208 (at 713–722). In general, and except in special circumstances related to the intrinsic characteristics of the disputed territory (*infra* note 35), the construction of ligthtowers, buoys and other navigational aids 'are not generally considered to be a manifestation of State authority', ICJ, Case concerning Minquiers and Ecrehos, 71.

33 Diplomatic practice attests to the existence of both sets of criteria: "The only possession required is such as is reasonable under all the circumstances – in view of the extent of territory claimed, its nature, and the uses to which is adapted and is put", Note from Mr Olney, Secretary of State (US) to Sir Julian Pauncefote, British Ambassador, 22 June 1896 (*Moore*, vol. 1, § 81 (at 269)).

territory. These criteria allow us to assess the level of effectiveness required in each case.[34] The first group refers to the specific characteristics of the disputed territory[35]i.e., does it have strategic, economic, political, ideological, *etc.* value?;[36] or is it far from other possessions of the same state or other states with rival sovereignty claims? The second group, reflecting the *multititular* nature of international law of terrritory, concerns the presence, and in the affirmative case the relative weight, of competing titles and claims. In other words, the required level of effectiveness must be measured, in each case, by taking into account the 'absence [alternatively the presence] of any claim to sovereignty by another Power'.[37]

The combined use of these two sets of criteria for assessing the required level of effectiveness thus allows international tribunals to resolve sovereignty disputes where the occupation a territory *sans maître* has been claimed by one or both parties:

> [I]n many cases the tribunal has been satisfied with very little in the way of the actual exercise of sovereign rights, provided that the other State could not make out a superior claim [extrinsic criterion]. This is particularly true in the case of claims to sovereignty over areas in thinly populated or unsettled countries [intrinsic criterion].[38]

---

34 'International law is satisfied with varying degrees in the display of State authority, depending on the specific circumstances of each case', ICJ, Sovereignty over Pedra Branca/Pulau Batu Puteh, Middle Rocks and South Ledge (Malaysia/Singapore), 2008, § 67 (at 36). The Court relied on her predecessor's considerations in the Case concerning the Legal Status of Eastern Greenland, 46 [*supra* note 105].

35 For example, "The construction of navigational aids ... can be legally relevant in the case of very small islands", Maritime Delimitation and Territorial Questions (Qatar v. Bahrain), Judgment of 16 March 2001 (Merits): *ICJ Reports* 2001, § 197 (at 100).

36 ICJ, Pulau Ligitan/Pulau Sipadan, 2002, § 134 (pat 682); ICJ, Territorial and Maritime Dispute between Nicaragua and Honduras in the Caribbean Sea (Nicaragua v. Honduras), paras. 173–174; ICJ, Sovereignty over Pedra Branca/Pulau Batu Puteh, Middle Rocks and South Ledge (Malaysia/Singapore), 2008, § 66 (at 36); Clipperton Island Case, 394; Palmas Island Case, 841.

37 ICJ, Case concerning the Legal Status of Eastern Greenland, 50. Similarly: ICJ, Sovereignty over Pedra Branca/Pulau Batu Puteh, Middle Rocks and South Ledge (Malaysia/Singapore), 2008, paras. 62–65 (at 35–36); ICJ, Territorial and Maritime Dispute (Nicaragua v. Colombia), 2012, § 80 (at 655).

38 ICJ, Case concerning the Legal Status of Eastern Greenland, 46.

B The Paradigms of the Antinomy between Legal Title (*titulus*) and Effectiveness (*modus*)

i *Immemorial Possession*

This situation, also known as *praescriptio longi(-ssimi) temporis*,[39] describes a territorial situation whose origin lies in a time so remote that it is possible to assert that no legal title ever existed. Alternatively, it could more correctly be said that proof of a *titulus* contrary to effectiveness cannot be produced,[40] in which case the presumption becomes irrebuttable.[41] This legal category is especially suited to explain the legal title (and its territorial extension) of a state to its original spatial base.[42]

It thus differs from effective occupation, previously discussed, where the (two-headed) *titulus* was based on both the *res nullius* character of the territory and the *animus occupandi* of the state controlling the territory. In the case of immemorial possession, it *is presumed* that the territory has not been subject to prior sovereignty, because of the impossibility of proving this:

> Possession from time immemorial is understood as the form of possession where *no evidence can be adduced that the situation was ever different* and no living person has ever heard of a different state of affairs.[43]

Immemorial possession also differs, dare I say for the opposite reason, from usucapio in that, in this situation, which we shall examine later, the occupation is necessarily *contra titulum*. The actual occupation of the territory therefore derogates from a *titulus* belonging to another State. In a way, immemorial possession is situated, from the point of view of *titulus*, between the occupation of *terra nullius* and usucapio, the cursor sliding respectively between the (total) absence and the proven presence of a contrary *titulus*.

---

39 "There is an International Prescription whether it be called Immemorial Possession or by any other name", Sir Robert Phillimore, *Commentaries upon International Law*, Vol. I, § 258 (at 303).

40 "Lapse of time, in the case equally of nations as of individuals, robs the parties of the means of proof …", Sir Travers Twiss, *The Oregon Question Examined, in respect to facts and the Law of Nations*, London, 1846, 125.

41 Lübeck v. Mecklenburg-Schwerin, Staatsgerichtshof, decision of 6/7 July 1928, 4 *ILR*, 115–116: '*This immemorial possession justifies the presumption of its legality* as well as the attribution to Lübeck of these rights for the future' [emphasis added].

42 Case of the Frontier between Galicia and Hungary near the so-called "Meerauge" lake (Austria/Hungary), arbitral award of 13 September 1902, *RIAA*, Vol. XXVIII, 391.

43 *Loc. cit.* [emphasis added].

ii *Disputed Possession*

The situation governed by this denomination highlights, unlike the one to be considered in the next subsection, an irreducible antinomy, reflecting an irreconcilability between *titulus* (the right to occupy a territory) and *modus* (actual occupation). There is thus a divorce between the two elements of (complete) legal title: one state possesses the *titulus* while another state effectively occupies the *disputed* territory, but this possession has never been peaceful since it has always been *disputed* by the first state. It should also be noted that this occupation was not achieved by the use of force or, alternatively, it was achieved by force at a time when force was not prohibited: this case will be studied later in the volume [*infra* Part 2. Chapter 5].

However, in the case under consideration here, this tension between *titulus* and *modus* must be examined in the light of the requirement of legality, i.e., the right *to* occupy a territory, since, as has been said, "possession cannot be said to derogate from the right".[44] Consequently, the reunion of the two elements of territorial title may take place either with the titular State, which presupposes the end of the effective occupation *contra titulum* of the other State, or with the occupying State, which requires that the titular State renounce to its *titulus*. This renunciation may be manifested in various ways, provided that it is real and not presumed: explicit acceptance, acknowledgement, acquiescence or abandonment (proven by its *animus derelinquendi*). This renunciation, coupled with the *animus occupandi* of the other State, thus constitutes the *titulus* of the new territorial situation. In the absence of such a renunciation, mere occupation, however effective, remains *contra titulum* and cannot *per se* give rise to a valid territorial title enforceable *erga omnes*. This resistance of *titulus* to *material occupation* is a constant in any legal order, and especially in the international order, because, as has been rightly pointed out:

> It is the ultimate measure of the *effectiveness* of a legal system and of its total hold on society (what the English call the *acid test*) *to know whether it will eventually give in to effectivities contrary to* its prescriptions, or whether it will contain them or find *antidotes for* them or at least impose limits on the play of effectiveness.[45]

In an international order where the function of sanctions or guarantee, in the broad sense,[46] is dispersed among its members and where the centralised

44 Boundary Delimitation Case, 39. Similarly: "a *de facto* possession in itself cannot confer the power of disposing of title", El Chamizal Case, 115.

45 Abi-Saab (1995), 19 [our translation].

46 Distefano (2019), 16–19.

reaction to international wrongdoing is devolved *mainly to* the United Nations Security Council, which makes its triggering dependent on a discretionary determination of one of the three situations contemplated by Article 39 UNC,[47] the bringing together of the two elements of the title with the State holding the *titulus* may sometimes prove problematic. Moreover, the banning of armed countermeasures, introduced by Article 2 § 4 UNC,[48] paradoxically harms that same State, as prophetically foreseen by Hans Kelsen.[49] At the same time, in a systemic perspective, "courts must now be precluded from requiring, as *additional measures of self-help*, that protests should now be supported by force or a show of force".[50] One of the longest-running – and still very much alive – territorial (and international) disputes is that between Argentina and the UK over sovereignty over the Falkland Islands (Malvinas/Falklands); it is surely the most emblematic example of the case of disputed possession.[51] To this day, Argentina has not renounced its *titulus, so that* the British occupation of this archipelago still remains an invalid occupation:

> [T]he Argentina government has constantly maintained its protests over that occupation at all times to its rights and jurisdiction over the islands.

47 ICTY, Prosecutor v. Dusko Tadic (Judgment), Appeals Chamber, judgment of 3 October 1995, paras. 28–30 (https://www.icty.org).

48 See: UNGA Resolution 2625 (XXV); 3314 (XXIX) as well as the Helsinki Final Act (1975), https://www.osce.org/helsinki-final-act. Also: ICJ, Legality of Nuclear Weapons, Advisory Opinion of 8 July 1996: *ICJ Reports* 1996, § 46.

49 'The delinquent [State] which is in actual possession of the illegal advantage is protected by the Charter against any enforcement action other than that taken by the Security Council', *The Law of the United Nations*, 1950, 269. This marks a fundamental difference from the legal regime of the League of Nations, whose Article 15 § 7 of its Covenant provided that: 'If the Council fails to reach a report which is unanimously agreed to by the members thereof, other than the Representatives of one or more of the parties to the dispute, the Members of the League reserve to themselves the right to take such action as they shall consider necessary for the maintenance of right and justice'. In other words, States concerned were entitled in this case to resort to armed force (retaliation or self-help) in order to enforce their rights.

50 McGibbon (1953), 310 [emphasis added]. One case of disputed possession was precisely at the origin of an armed conflict between Ecuador and Peru (Cordillera del Condor) on 26 January 1995. The border controversy concerned the disputed territorial sovereignty between these two states along the 78 kilometers of their common border. The Peace Treaty of 17 February 1995, signed by the representatives of the two countries and those of the four guarantor states of the Rio Protocol of 26 February 1942 (Argentina, Brazil, Chile and the United States of America) put an end to the armed conflict, whereas it was not until the Treaty of Brasilia ("Acta Presidencial de Brasilia", concluded on 26 October 1998) that the territorial dispute was definitively resolved. See also *infra* Part 3. Chapter 8. Section A.ii.

51 Marcelo Kohen, Facundo Rodriguez, *Las Malvinas entre el Derecho y la Historia*, Buenos Aires, 2000.

> It follows that the islands in question continue to form de jure part of the territory of our State.[52]

As a conclusion to this sub-section, it is legitimate to ask how long the international order will be able to admit this divorce between the two elements of legal title. The question of whether persistent protest (or even lack of acquiescence) can prevent the process of consolidation of title with the occupying state thus remains highly problematic and is shared by the jurisprudence.[53] While stressing that examples of this situation – such as the Argentine-British dispute mentioned above – can be counted on the fingers of one hand, we favour the impossibility of validating legal title in the absence of the consent or assent – however expressed – of the *titular* state.

iii *Usucapio in International Law: a Highly Controversial Concept*

This legal concept reflects – and betrays – the requirement, present in any legal order,[54] to transform *a de facto* situation, initially contrary to the *titulus*, into a valid legal situation, opposable therefore *erga omnes*. In other words, usucapio (in English: "adverse possession") consists of the acquisition of rights, in this case real rights, over *time* and *thanks to* the conducts of the States concerned.[55]

In order to guarantee the certainty of legal relationships, especially with regard to the ownership of rights *in rem*, usucapio is an original means of

52 In Re Carlos Gleadell Watson (Federal Court of Rio Gallegos), judgment of 11 February 1935, 8 *ILR*, 180. The Court thus recognised the validity of the applicant's nationality, which he had acquired *ius soli*; it was therefore necessary to prove beforehand that the islands in question were under Argentine sovereignty.

53 In the Island of Palmas case, arbitrator Max Huber stated: "The principle that continuous and peaceful display of the functions of State within a given region is a constituent element of territorial sovereignty is not only based on the conditions of the formation of independent States and their boundaries (as shown by the experience of political history) as well as on an international jurisprudence and doctrine widely accepted; this principle has further been recognized in more than one federal State, where a jurisdiction is established in order to apply, as need arises, rules of international law to the interstate relations of the States members. This is the more significant, in that it might well be conceived that in a federal State possessing a complete judicial system for interstate matters – far more than in the domain of international relations properly so-called – there should be applied to territorial questions the principle that, failing any specific provision of law to the contrary, a *jus in re* once lawfully acquired shall prevail over *de facto* possession however well established", 840.

54 The prescription mechanism is thus a 'process by which, through the influence of time, possession *without title, ripens* into ownership, and *ownership without possession withers away and dies*', Sir John Salmond, Appendix V, § 105, 406 [emphasis added].

55 "The elements of title by prescription are *open, visible and continuous use under a claim of right, adverse to and with knowledge of owner*", *Black's Law Dictionary*, 1486 [emphasis added].

acquiring ownership in modern civil law. In the wake of Roman law,[56] the requirements are roughly as follows: a) possession of the thing; b) good faith; c) passage of time (prescription period); d) title; e) suitable thing.[57]

It must also be stressed that usucapio is certainly a mode of original acquisition,[58] but it is so because a statute, in this case the civil law code, rules that such a juridical fact may give rise to such effects, in return for possession during a period of time fixed by that same law and, as such, is an integral part of that juridical fact. In this sense, it has an *ope legis* effect, i.e., by effect of the law (in this case civil law).

In the doctrinal panorama of international law[59] one cannot help but notice a *summa divisio* between the opponents (deniers)[60] and the supporters[61] of this institution.

56 According to the famous mnemonic brocade: "Usucapionis requisita sunt: res habilis, titulus, fides, possessio, tempus". See: Codex Book VII, 26–40 [Justinian's Constitution of 531 merging *praescriptio longi temporis* with *usucapio*], D.41.2.6, *Iustiniani Institutiones*.

57 The condition of *res habilis* in Roman law is found, for example, in Article 2260 FCC, according to which: "One cannot prescribe goods or rights which are not in commerce" [our translation]. In international law, and insofar as usucapio is admitted, this condition excludes from its field of operation spaces that are not subject to occupation as sovereign *ope legis* (continental shelf and, in general, maritime spaces where the coastal State exercises sovereign rights) as well as land *res communes* (Antarctica), maritime *res communes* (seabed) and outer space *res communes* (Moon, celestial objects).

58 By the combined action of the extinction of one subjective right and the immediately successive creation of another for the benefit of another legal subject.

59 For an overview of the doctrine, see: Giuliano (1956), 32 (note 2), 134 (note 4).

60 Among the deniers: De Visscher (1967), 109; G Barile (1951), 222–223; PCIJ, Case concerning the Legal Status of Eastern Greenland, Vol. C 66, 2659 [Presentation by M Rasmussen, Denmark]; Alphonse Rivier, *Principes du droit des gens*, Vol. 1, Paris, 1896, 183; Bertha Elena Casados Villanueva, *Tiempo, efectividad y prescripcion en derecho internacional*, Mexico City, 1952, 111–115; ICJ, Island Land Boundary Dispute case, 1992, § 99 (at 678) [individual op. of Judge Torres-Bernardez]: '*bona fide* effective possession during a certain period of time [is] a highly controversial concept which, for my part, I have the greatest difficulty in accepting as an established institution of international law'; Pietro Piovani, *Il significato del principio d'effettività*, Milan, 1953, 83–84; Fedozzi, 438; Cavaglieri (1926), 172–173; Rousseau (1977), Vol. III, 183; Robert Redslob, *Traité de droit des gens*, Paris, 1950, 183; Giuseppe Barile, *Lezioni di diritto internazionale*, Milan, 1983, 222–223; Karl Strupp, *Eléments du droit international public, universel, européen et américain*, 2nd edn, Vol. 1, Paris, 1930, 156; Anzilotti (1955), 286; Brownlie, 154–156; Viejobueno, 9–11; William Hough III, "The annexation of the Baltic States and its effect on the development of law prohibiting forcible seizure of territory", 6 *New York Journal of International and Comparative Law* 1986-II, 469–470; Janusz Symonides, "Acquisitive Prescription in International Law", 3 *PYIL* 1970, 112, 117–118; Rolando Quadri, "L'Ile de Camaran", 13 *Revue Égyptienne de droit international* 1957, 24–26; '[C]onquest and acquisitive prescription have totally disappeared from the new law which has condemned war and proclaimed the inalienability of sovereignty', ICJ, Namibia 1971, 92 [individual op. of Judge Ammoun].

61 Among the authors who support usucapio: Sir Hersch Lauterpacht (1927), 104; Schwarzenberger, 301; Lawrence, § 78 (at 168–169); Brierly (1963), 167–169; Menon (1994),

We have already listed and discussed the conditions required by Roman law and continental civil law for the exercise of usucapio as a 'mode of acquisition of property'. It only remains to establish whether such conditions, which at the same time constitute the distinctive conceptual contours of this institution, are also found in international law.[62] Now, leaving aside the condition of continuous, peaceful, open and effective possession, since this quality is accepted by all jurists,[63] it is appropriate to consider the condition of good faith. It would be useful to point out first of all that most of the advocates of this institution in international law hardly mention it and that only a small number of them dwell on it in order to rule on its necessity. Some, pointing to the difference with the Roman law archetype, argue that the bona *fides* requirement is not necessary in international law,[64] while others maintain that:

> The State that claims to acquire a right must be in good faith; it must be unaware that it is infringing on the rights of its partner.[65]

13–17; Menon (1978), 766–767; McGibbon (1953), 319; Paul Guggenheim, "La validité et la nullité des actes juridiques internationaux", 74 *RCADI* 1949-I, 232–233; Jean Charpentier, *La reconnaissance internationale et l'évolution du droit des gens*, Paris, 1956, 156.

62 In the only case in which the Hague Court had to address the question of the admissibility of usucapio in international law, it mentions precisely these five conditions, except for those requiring "legal title" as well as the "appropriate thing", ICJ, Kasikili Island / Sedudu Case (Botswana / Namibia), 1999, § 94 (at 1103). It should also be noted that the Court speaks of "acquisitive prescription" rather than "usucapio", if only because this is the term known in English language terminology.

63 To such an extent that the concept of effective occupation, the outline of which was outlined above in international law [*supra* Part 1, Chapter 4, Section A], is no longer consciously differentiated from the institution of acquisitive prescription. See e.g., Shaw (1986), 19; Sir Robert Jennings (1963), 23; Munkman, 94 [for whom, precisely, the two cases would be included in the broader category of "consolidation by historical title"].

64 E.g., Raggi, 758; Hill, 156; Michael J Goodman, "Adverse possession of Land: morality and motive", 33 *Modern Law Review* 1970, 288; Johnson (1950), 337–338; Paul Fauchille, *Traité de droit international public*, 8th edn, Vol. 1, 2nd part, Paris, 1922–1926, § 557–7 (at 758): "the basis of usucapion will almost always be an act of violence"; Bowett (1957), 201: '[T]he circumstances in which estoppel is relevant are distinct from those in which acquiescence should be considered as one element in the acquisition of a title by prescription. The confusion of these two notions will only serve to lessen the burden of proving the acquisition of title by prescription and, since no requirement of good faith demands such results, it would seem that the use of doctrine of estoppel in circumstances where prescription ought to be relied on and proved is inadmissible in international law'; Charpentier even specifies that acquisitive prescription in international law is characterised by a "condition of bad faith" (1956), 157 [our translation]. In the case between Botswana and Namibia concerning Kasikili Island / Sedudu (Botswana / Namibia), Namibia invoked the subsequent conduct of the Parties in order to establish the "doctrine of acquisitive prescription". However, the Namibian argument in this regard did not include any reference to good faith as a requirement for usucapio (§ 94).

65 Bentz, 89 [our translation]. In the same vein: Territorial Concessions case, 268.

But the general conclusion is that, according to most internationalists, good faith is not, unlike in Roman law, a requirement of international law.

A slightly different discourse must be made for the so-called "res habilis" condition, because although it cannot be identified as such in international law, its spirit is indeed present. Indeed, usucapio, if it exists at all in international law, cannot be exercised with respect to certain spaces, since occupation by one – or even several – states cannot be carried out in a *sovereign capacity*. International law prohibits a state from deploying the mantle of its sovereignty over certain land areas (such as Antarctica), maritime areas (the High Seas, the Zone) and Outer space areas (the Moon and other celestial objects). In this perspective, the difference between *territory* and *space*, in the light of international law of territory, takes on its full meaning.

The condition of 'title' or *titulus* required by Roman law and by most civil codes of Romanist inspiration need not be discussed at length insofar as, in the light of the binary construction of territorial title, *titulus* is provided precisely by the attitude of abandonment – or renunciation in the broad sense – of the titular State.

Another condition required by Roman law (and the domestic laws that have been inspired by it) is the "*tempus ad prescriptionem*", i.e. the period of time during which possession of the thing must be peaceful and uninterrupted. This period is generally fixed by a law and the civil codes provide for different periods of time depending on the thing that is the subject of the prescription and/or on the absence or defect of title (*iusta causa*) *on* the part of the possessor (long or short prescription respectively). It should also be emphasised that since usucapio is, in modern civil law, a "mode of acquisition" *ope legis*, the *precise* prescription period is in all respects one of the founding elements of this institution.[66] Hence, the need felt by the legislator to determine it accordingly.

Now, most of the doctrine that refutes usucapio in international law bases its denial, among other arguments, on the lack of a fixed period resulting from a treaty or a rule of general international law. It therefore follows that, in the absence of the determination of the limitation period, which operates *ope legis* the extinction and correlative acquisition of (real) rights, there would be, *strictly speaking*, no usucapio in international law. For,

---

66 See precisely in this sense: Luis de Molina, *Tractatus* II (1733), Disputatio LX, § 8, 10, 144. This illustrious Spanish jurist-theologian reproduces the thought of the *Panormitanus* (Abbot Niccolò Tedeschi, 1386–1445) in order to clearly emphasize time as the founding element of usucapio: "Panor. *In rub. De praescr.* Definit praescriptionem. Esse jus quoddam ex tempore congruens legum autoritate vim capiens negligentibus poenam inferens and finem litibus imponens".

> The notion of acquisitive prescription is inseparable from the determination of the time period that leads to the acquisition of territorial sovereignty.[67]

According to the advocators of usucapio, on the other hand, the lack of a precise limitation period in international law would not detract from the basis of this institution:

> In the absence of positive law, it is impossible to determine a priori the limitation period here; it is nevertheless, in many cases, the strongest foundation of States' rights.[68]

However, this is not the case, and it would be going too far to say that the absence of determination of the limitation period does not undermine the solidity and the right of this institution to exist in the international legal order. For the limitation period is *consubstantial* with the very notion of this notion and the latter could not exist without it. The *precise* determination of the *tempus ad praescriptionem* is a fundamental element of this institution and it is precisely in the *precision* of its determination that its justification lies.[69]

In a famous territorial delimitation case, the Arbitration Commission took up this position:

> [T]he very controversial question as to whether the right of prescription invoked by United States is an accepted principle of the law of nations, *in the absence of any convention establishing a term of prescription*, the commissioners are unanimous in coming to the conclusion that the

67 Cavaglieri (1929), 406 [our translation]. Likewise: Cavaglieri (1927), 319; Cavaglieri (1926), 173; De Visscher (1958), 604; De Visscher (1960), 393; Blum, 36; Strupp (1930), Vol. 1, 156.

68 Eugène Audinet, "Annexion, cession et démembrement de territoires", in *Répertoire de droit international*, Vol. I, under the direction of MM. Lapradelle and Niboyet, Paris, Sirey, 1929–1931, § 15 [*passim*; our translation]; Eugène Audinet, "De la prescription acquisitive en droit international public", 3 *RGDIP* 1896, 313; Ortolan, 188–193; James Westlake, *International Law*, 2nd edn, Vol. 1, Cambridge, 1904, 92; Balladore Pallieri (1962), 457–458; ICJ, Minquiers and Ecrehos case, 152 [individual op. by Judge Alvarez]; cf. also diplomatic dispatch by M Olney, US Secretary of State. Olney, US Secretary of State, to the British Ambassador in Washington, Sir Julian Pauncefote, of 22 June 1896, concerning the Venezuelan frontier, cited in *Moore*, 296–297; Johnson (1950), 347–348; Fauchille, Book II, 2nd part, 755.

69 If one recalls the various successive codifications in Roman law concerning the *precise* determination of this time limit, one can realise what is at stake.

> possession of the United States in the present case was not of such as to find a prescriptive title.[70]

Therefore, international law hardly prescribes such a limitation period;[71] moreover, there are arbitration agreements that establish, *by convention,* the limitation period of usucapio for the purpose of the *ad hoc* settlement of the case.[72]

The International Court of Justice is extremely cautious on this point, for in the only case in which it had to deal with, it declared that it:

> Need[s] not to concern itself with the status of acquisitive prescription in international law or with the conditions for acquiring title to territory by prescription [since] the conditions cited by Namibia itself are not satisfied in this case and that Namibia's argument on acquisitive prescription therefore cannot be accepted.[73]

---

70 El Chamizal case, 328 [emphasis added]. It is also important to note in passing the ease and lightness with which the Commissioners speak indifferently of "*right* of prescription" and "prescriptive *title*". See *supra* Part 1. Chapter 4. Section B.iii. for the distinction to be made between the two concepts.

71 In the past, Emer de Vattel (Book II, Ch. XI, § 151, at 338) had stigmatised the absence of such a determination: '[I]t would be very proper that adjoining nations should by treaty adopt some rule on this subject, particularly with respect to the number of years required to found a lawful prescription, since this latter point cannot in general be determined by the law of nature alone. If, in default of treaties, custom has determined any thing in this matter, the nations between whom this custom is in force, ought to conform to it (Prelim. § 26)'. This also confirms the idea that the eminent jurist from Neuchâtel has in mind the concept of undisputed possession accompanied by qualified and characterised attitudes on the part of States, and not necessarily the institution of *usucapio* as it emerges from Roman law, because, as he rightly states, the prescription period for this purpose is lacking.

72 Arbitration agreement between Great Britain and Venezuela signed on 2 February 1897 in Washington which established the arbitration tribunal for the settlement of the territorial controversy between the two countries in the region of Guyana. However, Art. IV of the said compromise provided as follows: "(a) *Adverse holding or prescription during a period of fifty years shall make a good title.* The Arbitrators may deem *exclusive* political control of a district, as well as actual settlement thereof, *sufficient to constitute adverse holding or to make title by prescription*", *Pasicrisie*, 555 [emphasis added; our translation]. Again, Guatemala and Honduras signed an arbitration agreement on 1st March 1895, which established an arbitration tribunal in the event that the two governments concerned were unable to agree on the common boundaries of their respective territories. However, Art. XII of the said treaty set the limitation period at 10 years (*Pasicrisie*, 506).

73 ICJ, Kasikili Island / Sedudu Case (Botswana / Namibia), 1999, para. 97 (at 1105). The conditions enunciated by Namibia, and considered "acceptable" by Botswana, are as follows: "1. the possession of the … State must be exercised *à titre de souverain*; 2. the

However, the Court merely notes that the "Parties agree among themselves that acquisitive prescription is recognised in international law", adding that they also agree on the conditions of application. Can one therefore wonder whether the same applies to the Court? The doubt is all the more legitimate if one thinks that the Court, in the end, does not examine the conditions of application.

It follows that for all these reasons it is impossible for us to conclude that an institution analogous to the Roman law *usucapio* exists in international law.[74] However, it is often invoked and sometimes applied, but not under that name, by international and domestic courts. Indeed, if we look closely, we notice that, when the doctrine, the international and domestic courts have evoked the notion of acquisitive prescription[75] as a mode of acquisition of territorial rights, they have merely limited themselves to borrowing from the privatist paraphernalia of Roman law a "synthetic denomination"[76] by which they would designate any other "fact", in addition to extinction, cession, *debellatio*, capable of founding the territorial transfer in law. It is therefore a 'complex juridical fact' that is alluded to when it is referred to by the term, admittedly more eloquent, of acquisitive prescription. And yet this is not just a simple nominalist quarrel, but there are 'issues' of legal logic behind it that it would be unreasonable not to confront. For, while it is true that this doctrinal dispute is coloured by a nominalist tinge, it is no less true that perpetuating this misguided and unfortunate (in two *ways*) terminology can have unfortunate conceptual repercussions in in the corpus of the international law of territory.

We are therefore pleased to note that the latest edition of *Oppenheim*'s famous textbook represents a significant shift in the position of acquisitive

---

possession must be peaceful and uninterrupted; 3. the possession must be public; 4. The possession must endure for a certain lenght of time" (*ibid.*, para. 94, at 1103).

74 Moreover, and for reasons that still have to do with the embryonic nature of the judicial organisation of the international legal order, usucapio, as it is arranged in domestic law, would not be viable in international law. For, as has been stated: "In private law, the interruption of prescription is effected by a suit, but in dealings between nations this is of course impossible, unless and until an international tribunal is established for such purpose", El Chamizal case, 329. The International Court of Justice does exist, but in fact, in the absence of a judicial body with (general international law) compulsory jurisdiction, the prerogative of the legal qualification of a given territorial situation falls too often to the States directly concerned. The peculiar architecture of the international legal order therefore makes recourse to the institution of usucapio unnecessary and unrealistic.

75 This qualification is *per se* erroneous.

76 Mario Giuliano, Tullio Scovazzi, Tullio Treves, *Diritto internazionale*, vol. II, Milan, 1983, 55 [our translation].

prescription-usucapio in relation to Sir Robert Jennings' earlier work. A change in theoretical position that can only be welcomed:

> In short, prescription is not so much now a singular mode of acquisition, or loss, of territorial sovereignty, *as a convenient term for one group of elements which go together to make or break a title.*[77]

One would thus use the formula "usucapio" as a descriptive – not prescriptive – category, like the "modes of acquisition", which were said above to be "icons", images familiar to jurists who grew up with the Civil Code, but nothing more. At the very least, one could speak, as the Common Law doctrine does, of 'adverse possession'[78] (as opposed to 'straightforward possession'), because it is undoubtedly more successful than 'acquisitive prescription', especially since it hardly includes the conditional elements of Romanist *usucapio* which, as we have just seen, are absent in international law.[79] This "complex juridical fact", characterised by the dissociation between the *titulus* and the *modus adquisitionis*, could be referred to as "undisputed adverse possession".

---

77 *Oppenheim's International Law* (1992), § 270 (at 708) [emphasis added].

78 Johnson (1955), 219–221.

79 This fundamental difference between 'acquisitive prescription' (or 'adverse possession') in Common Law (thus devoid of title and good faith) and *usucapio* (and its civil law descendants) is, it seems to us, at the root of the confusion. For, one may well admit, following the example of Common Law jurists, that there is an acquisitive prescription if it is in fact only an 'undisputed occupation' as we have defined it above. In that case, the confusion would only be terminological, and we would be blinded by misleading designations.

PART 2

Territorial Polemology Territorial Titles in Light of Anomalous, Deviant and Borderline Situations

CHAPTER 5

Title of Territorial Sovereignty and the Threat or Use of Force

As Charles de Visscher lucidly observed, "[n]owhere is effectiveness more brutally expressed than in what has long been called the right of conquest".[1] In contrast to the previous subsection, this section will deal with territorial changes that have been carried out in violation of the prohibition of force (or the threat of its use) in international relations. It is true that we are on a continuum *in crescendo* in the tension between law (legality) and fact (effectiveness), or if you like, between *titulus* and *modus*, but in this chapter, we cross a qualitative threshold from the moment when the prohibition of force emerged and especially when, later, it was enshrined in a norm of *ius cogens*.

However, the tension between (armed) violence and law is hardly specific to the international legal system, as every legal order is confronted with this phenomenon. Even the state legal system is torn between the need to invalidate the effects of violence and its capitulation by establishing a new government or even a new constitutional regime.[2] The international system is no exception, and it too oscillates between the invalidation and the validation (very rarely, though) of territorial effects engendered by the use (or threat) of force. Hence the need to go beyond a static vision of the relationship between law and fact, i.e., between nullity and effectiveness, and to resolutely embrace a dynamic conception between these two poles.

The effectiveness of the international legal order depends on its capacity to react to new factual situations; on its capacity to give fine-tuned responses in relation to the situation; on its capacity to offer remedies where effectiveness and nullity are mixed. For a legal order that obstinately hides behind the fig-leaf of a legality that is no longer effective is no longer a legal order, it is a chimera. But, equally, a legal order that will not withstand the assaults and pressures of new factual situations and that, successively, will not delay in issuing a new legal qualification once the original situation has been re-established, is not a legal order either. In this oscillation between nullity and effectiveness, the

1 De Visscher (1967), 115 [our translation].

2 '[T]he truth is that international law can no more refuse to recognise that a finally successful conquest does change the title to territory than municipal law can a change of régime brought about by a successful revolution', Brierly (1963), 172–173.

 | DOI:10.1163/9789004708594_008

legal order might on one hand note, at first, that the new territorial situation, although illegal at the outset, has been definitively stabilised and consolidated.

On the other hand, and this is by far (and fortunately) the most frequent scenario, the international legal order, under the pressure of social forces contrasting with the new territorial situation, *effectively* resists them. In this scenario, the international legal order *will endorse* the *titulus adquisitionis* of the dispossessed state and add to it the effectiveness of the entire International Community. This is in contrast with the opposing effectiveness, *contra titulum*, of the State that has illegally occupied the territory of the previously sovereign State. The (in-)validity of the new territorial situation, in short its *legality*, will ultimately depend on the capacity of the International Community to effectively withstand the illegal effectiveness. By opposing (legal) effectiveness to (illegal) effectiveness, the International Community will thus prevent the illegal situation from consolidating.[3] In the light of our construction of the concept of legal title, it could be said that the conquering (or annexing) State does have a *modus adquirendi*, but lacks the *titulus adquisitionis*. As long as the International Community *effectively* resists, it will protect the illegally dispossessed State so that it is not only the latter's attitude that is here juridically relevant, but also that of the international legal order embodied by the organised International Community. This contrasts with territorial changes, still *contra titulum adquisitionis*, but carried out without the use of force (or the threat thereof), i.e., those studied in Part 1.Chapter 4. Section B, where the attitude of the State directly concerned is of paramount juridical significance. This is so since the international legal order effectively protects the right to territorial integrity of states, as this is one of the pillars on which the International Community in its current structure was built and is based. The practice of the UN Security Council is constant and uniform, as evidenced by the various resolutions adopted with regard to Israel's annexation of the Golan Heights and East Jerusalem:[4]

> *Decides* that the Israeli decision to impose its laws, jurisdiction and administration in the occupied Syrian Golan Heights is null and void and without international legal effect; 2. *Demands* that Israel, the occupying Power, should rescind forthwith its decision.[5]

---

3 See in this sense: Cassese (1986), para. 10; Michel Virally, *L'Organisation mondiale*, Paris, 1972, 432; Abi-Saab (1987), 312.

4 Resolution 476 (30 June 1980).

5 Resolution 497 (17 December 1981). See also the more recent and highly publicised Resolution 2334 (23 December 2016).

The same is true in the case where territorial change leads to the birth of a puppet state, i.e., a territorial entity that is both illegal and lacking in independence (in the sense of the Island of Palmas paradigm) but created artificially by a state as a result of the use of force against another state and on the territory of the latter.[6] The case of the "Turkish Republic of Northern Cyprus" (TRNC) is emblematic in this respect:

> [The Security Council] 7. *Calls upon* all States not to recognize any Cypriot State than the Republic of Cyprus.[7]

International jurisprudence and the practice of other UN bodies as well as the Council of Europe are at unison in denying statehood to the TRNC; as the European Court of Human Rights affirmed in a landmark judgment:

> In this respect it is evident from international practice and the various, strongly worded resolutions referred to above (see paragraph 42) that the International Community does not regard the "TRNC" as a State under international law and that the Republic of Cyprus has remained the sole legitimate Government of Cyprus.[8]

A Conquest, Forcible Annexation, *debellatio*[9]

The use of force in international relations is synonymous with military occupation, i.e., "the effective, but essentially temporary, installation of the armed

---

6 See *infra* Part 2. Chapter 7. Section A.

7 Resolution 541 (18 November 1983). As a further illustration, it should be noted that EU law (and its *acquis communautaire*), following the accession of the Republic of Cyprus to the EU, does not apply to territories where the Republic of Cyprus does not exercise effective control (Article 1 of the Protocol of Accession, 2003). See also: Emin v. Yeldag (Attorney-General and Secretary of State for Foreign and Commonwealth Affairs intervening), England, High Court, Family Division, 5 October 2001, 148 *ILR*, 50 (the court refers to the judgment of the ECtHR in *Loizidou*).

8 Case of Loizidou v. Turkey (Application no. 15318/89), 18 December 1996, para. 44.

9 'Conquest only operates as a cause of loss of sovereignty when there is war between two States and by reason of the defeat of one of them sovereignty over territory passes from the loser to the victorious State', PCIJ, Case concerning the Legal Status of Eastern Greenland, 47. By the rather outdated term of *debellatio,* the doctrine means the total annexation of the defeated state, thus its disappearance as a subject of public international law. See Ludovico M Bentivoglio, *La "debellatio" nel diritto internazionale*, Pavia, 1948.

forces of a belligerent on all or part of the enemy's territory in time of war".[10] However, even before the rule prohibiting the use of force came into being, the law of nations had always denied that the mere material fact of conquest alone could give rise to a valid *titulus adquisitionis*.[11] For the transfer of territorial sovereignty, and thus the completeness of legal title, modern international law (i.e., from the late Middle Ages onwards) has always required the consent[12] of the defeated state, conveyed by a treaty or by another conclusive act,[13] expressed tacitly or explicitly, but always actually existing and not merely presumed. International humanitarian law takes knowledge downstream of this fundamental rule of general public international law insofar as both treaty instruments and customary international law converge in affirming that military occupation 'does not affect the sovereignty of the occupied State. But the exercise of that sovereignty is suspended'.[14]

It is important to note, therefore, that even at a time when war was not prohibited, the renunciation expressed by the defeated state (*animus derelinquendi*) was required by PIL, in order to legalise simple military occupation by means of the *titulus adquisitionis*. This was justified by the fact that, for the reasons set out above, *occupatio bellica*, like effective occupation without thus the *animus imperii*[15]and the *res nullius* character of the territory, could not in itself transfer the *titulus adquisitionis*.

In the light of the bipartite construction of legal title, it can be stated that the mere material fact of military occupation, or even conquest, does

10 *Dictionnaire de la terminologie de droit international public*, 2001, Brussels, 776 [our translation]. Of course, it is also possible to envisage a forcible cession of territory by the defeated state to the victorious state without the latter occupying any part of the former's territory; or, alternatively, that the territory ceded by the defeated state does not correspond to the territory under military occupation by the victorious state.

11 "The usage of the world is, if a nation be not entirely subdued, to consider the holding of conquered territory as a mere military occupation until its fate shall be determined at the treaty of peace. If it be ceded by treaty, the acquisition is confirmed, and the ceded territory becomes a part of the nation to which it is annexed, either on the terms stipulated in the treaty of cession or on such as its new master shall impose", American Insurance Co. V Canter, Supreme Court of the United States, 1828, *Scott,* 511.

12 "[A] territory conquered by an enemy is not to be considered as incorporated into the dominions of that enemy, without a renunciation in a treaty of peace", U.S. v. Hayward, Supreme Court of the United States, Moore Digest, vol. 1, 291.

13 Thomas Baty, 'The trend of international law', 33 *AJIL* 1939, 658: '[I]t appears to be a fair deduction from the principle, always admitted in theory, that conquest (unless by *debellatio*) requires *to be completed by consent, even though the consent may be under duress*'.

14 L. v. N. (Bulgarian Occupation of Greece), Court of Appeal (Greece), Judgment No. 21 (1947), 14 *ILR*, 231.

15 See *supra* Part 1. Chapter 4. Section A.

not bring about a change of sovereignty, since the corresponding *titulus* still belongs to the vanquished state, whereas the *modus*, the effectiveness of the occupation, resides with the victorious state. As long as the former has not renounced its *titulus*, no valid legal title can be formed with the victorious state in relation to the territory concerned. Before 1945, State practice[16], international[17] and domestic[18] case law as well as the

16 Diplomatic note from the British Ambassador in Constantinople, Mr Liston, to the drogman of the Sublime Porte (9 June 1815), on the legal effects of the occupations that followed the "Napoleonic whirlwind": "The Sublime Porte agreed with the other Powers that a fortunate invasion, a momentary possession, does not confer the rights of legitimate sovereignty", in HA Smith, Vol. 1, 100; intervention by Count Shuvaloff (Russia) at the Congress of Berlin (17 June 1878), in "Protocols of the Congress of Berlin", No. 2, cited in *Bruns*, FB12 para. 626 [which demanded that the "benefits of the war against the Sublime Porte should be returned to her"]; the diplomatic protest of King George V of England of 23 September 1866 concerning the occupation of the Kingdom of Hanover in the war against the Austrian Empire, cited in *Bruns*, FB11 para. 986; the circular sent on 5 November 1911 by the Italian Minister of Foreign Affairs, Marquis of San Giuliano, to all Italian Representatives, following the annexation of Tripolitania and Cyrenaica, cited in *Prassi italiana* (Seconda serie), Vol. 3, para. 2219.

17 Société des Quais de Smyrne v. Hellenic Government, award delivered on 1er August 1929 by the Mixed Turkish-Hellenic Arbitral Tribunal, 37 *RGDIP* 1930, 336; Franco-Hellenic Case of the Lighthouses, judgment of 17 March 1934: *PCIJ Reports* A/B 62, 24–25 [The Court, while pretending not to pronounce itself on the question, responds to it incidentally]; Claim of Silberg and Mogilanski (U.S.-Polish Claims Settlement), 20 December 1961 (Foreign Claims Settlement Commission of the United States), 56 *AJIL* 1962, 545 [with regard to the territories acquired by Poland on its western frontier, in the aftermath of WWII]; Island of Palmas Case, 846; Territorial Sovereignty and Scope of the Dispute (Eritrea and Yemen), 1998, para. 147.

18 Fleming v. Page (1850), in *AILC* (1783–1968, Déak), Vol. 3, 230–231; The Foltina Case (U.S. High Court of Admiralty, 1814), in *Scott*, 186; Disability Pension Case (Case N°9a RV 2/84), Federal Republic of Germany (Federal Social Court (BSG)), award delivered the 6 November 1985, 90 *ILR*, 403, 405 [alleged *occupatio imperii* by the USSR of the GDR territory, rejected by the Court]; "Russian territory occupied by German troops remained foreign territory despite the occupation" (German Supreme Court), 17 February 1924, in *Bruns*, A/II/ I, 7 (Case No. 333; our translation); Samuel Weiss v. Hungary (Final Decision N°HUNG-13), award delivered the 4 April 1957 (Foreign Claims Settlement Commission of the United States), *Foreign Claims Settlement Commission of the United States, Decisions and Annotations*, Washington, 1967, 200; Airline Ray v. Hungary (Proposed Decision N°HUNG-688), award delivered the 7 January 1958, 26 *ILR*, 44 [the last two cases relate to the occupation by Hungary of Slovak territories during WWII]; United States v. Hayward, in *Moore*, 291; Bindels v. Administration des Finances, Cour Militaire de Liège, award delivered the 28 February 1946 (Cour de Cassation, 16 May 1947), 17 *ILR*, 46–48; Auditeur Militaire v. Jutenn, Cour Militaire de Liège, award delivered the 3 August 1948, 15 *ILR*, 527–529; In re Greiser, Poznan, Supreme National Tribunal of Poland, award delivered the 7 July 1946, 13 *ILR*, 388; Huby Frères of Echternach v. Racké (Cantonal Court of Utrecht,

doctrine,[19] are in line in supporting this conclusion, which admits of no discussion:

> Whatever the effects of the occupation of a territory by the adversary before the restoration of peace, it is certain *that* this occupation *alone* could not legally effect the transfer of sovereignty.[20]

Netherlands), 8 September 1941, *ILR*, Vol. 11 (1919–1942), 227 [concerning the illegal annexation by Germany of the Grand Duchy of Luxembourg]; Republic Aviation Corporation v. Lowe, District Court for the Southern District of New York, award delivered the 19 November 1946, 13 *ILR*, 45; Status of Occupied Poland Case (Federal Republic of Germany Superior Provincial Court of Munich), 6 July 1970, 61 *ILR*, 677; Ray Claim (United States Foreign Claims Settlement Commission), 7 January 1958, 26 *ILR*, 700–701; Kling and Others v. Lesser and Rotterdam Bank (Court of Appeal, The Hague), 24 June 1955, 22 *ILR*, 102 [a somewhat tortuous judicial reasoning, but ultimately declaring the illegal Soviet annexation of Lithuania in 1939].

19 Emer de Vattel, Book III, Ch. XIII, paras. 194–195; Andrea Rapisardi-Mirabelli, *Il significato della guerra nel diritto internazionale*, Rome, 1910, 45–61; Charles Rousseau, "Le conflit italo-éthiopien", 43 *RGDIP* 1936, 546–588; and Vol. 44 (1937), 5–42, 162–198, 291–329, 681–728; and Vol. 45 (1938), 53–123; Dionisio Anzilotti, "L'annessione del Congo", 4 *Rivista* 1909, 253; Advisory Opinion on Certain Questions Concerning Settlers of German Origin in the Territories Ceded to Poland: *PCIJ Reports* C 3-III (II), 724 [M. Komarnicki's consultation]; Louis M Bloomfield, *Egypt, Israel and the Gulf of Aqaba in International Law*, Toronto, 1957, 104: "This was under the ancient law the most commonly used way of acquisition. It is now *very limited* both by International Conventions and by Charter of the United Nations ... [art.2 para. 4]" [emphasis added]; Percy Cobbett, *Law and Society in the Relation of States*, London, 1951, 101 [arguing that the Italian annexation of Ethiopia was based on the "material fact" of conquest and not on the subsequent recognition by the International Community]; Lord Arnold McNair, "Municipal Effects of Belligerent Occupation" 33 *LQR* 1941, 54; Sir Hersch Lauterpacht, "General Rules of the Law of Peace", 62 *RCADI* 1937, 336–345; Clyde Eagleton, *International Government*, New York, 1932, 91–93; James Westlake, "The Nature and Extent of Title by Conquest", 17 *LQR* 1901, 392; "[Military occupation] is neither abdicative nor translative of sovereignty [...] The State whose territory is occupied remains the sole legal sovereign of the country and no one can take its place", Rousseau (1977), 55 [our translation]; Gowlland-Debbas (1990), 142; Odile Debbasch, *L'occupation militaire*, Paris, 1962, 87–91; *Oppenheim's International Law*, 1992, para. 265; Keith Highet, 'The Kurils Quandary', in *El derecho internacional en un mundo en transformacion*, Vol. 1, Montevideo, 1994, 625.

20 Ottoman Public Debt (Bulgaria, French Mandate States, Iraq, Palestine, Transjordan, Greece, Italy and Turkey v. Ottoman Public Debt Council), Arbitral Award of 18 April 1925, *RSA*, Vol. 1, 555 [our translation; emphasis added].

In fact, this periodization,[21] like any other, is not entirely fortunate, because as early as 1928,[22] through the Briand-Kellog Pact (or Pact of Paris), the vast majority of states at the time had *definitively* renounced war as a means of settling their disputes.[23] This Pact[24] introduced a major qualitative difference compared to Art. 10 (and 15) of the Covenant of the LoN, which only provided for a three-month moratorium and referred in the following articles to an embryonic collective security mechanism.[25] In the wake of the 1928 Pact, mention should also be made of the Stimson Note of 7 January 1932, which will be discussed below [Part 2. Chapter 5. Section B.iii], Art. 11 of the "Treaty for the Prevention of War (Non-Aggression and Conciliation)" signed in Rio de Janeiro on 10 October 1933 by the American states;[26] Art. 11 of the Montevideo Convention on the Rights and Duties of States adopted by the 7th Conference

21 Giovanni Distefano, 'La longue marche vers l'abrogation du droit d'auto-protection armée: *happy end* ou *remake* en vue?', in *Unity and Diversity of International Law. Ecrits en l'honneur du Professeur Pierre-Marie Dupuy*, Leiden, 2014, 299–319.

22 Treaty Concerning the Renunciation of War as an Instrument of National Policy ("Briand-Kellog" Pact), signed in Paris on 27 August 1928, *NRG*, 3rd series, Vol. 21, 3. It should be mentioned, however, that a similar attempt had already been made, on a regional scale, at the 1st Conference of American States (2 October 1889 to 19 April 1890) where a resolution was adopted to declare null and void all annexations effected by the use or threat of force. However, this resolution was only binding as part of an arbitration treaty that was never ratified. The text of this first official condemnation by the states of the American continent of conquest as a 'mode of acquisition' of territory can be found in *NRG*, 3rd series, Vol. 6, 120. Similarly, mention should be made of the "Mutual Assistance Treaty" project, elaborated within the LoN which was not concluded due to the lack of consensus on the definition of aggression [already a stumbling block], but in which the war of aggression was qualified as an "international crime" [*League of Nations Official Journal*, 4th year, n°12 (December 1923)]. As it has been stated: "No one would dispute that in 1937 the League of Nations Covenant of 1919 and the Briand-Kellogg Pact of 1928 had definitively outlawed war as a method of settling international disputes", oral argument by Mr. David (Qatar) in Maritime Delimitation and Territorial Questions (Qatar v. Bahrain), ICJ, 2001, CR 2000/18 (meeting of 21 June 2000), para. 19.

23 As a counterpoint, these same states signed the Geneva Agreement on the Peaceful Settlement of International Disputes, also known as the "General Act of Arbitration", on 26 September of the same year.

24 Article 1 of which reads: "[The Parties] condemn the use of war for the settlement of international disputes".

25 See Robert Kolb, "Article 15", in *Commentaire sur le Pacte de la Société des Nations*, Brussels, 2014, 598–692; Olivier Corten, Anne Lagerwall, "Article 16", in *ibid*, 693–715.

26 *League of Nations Treaty Series*, Vol. 163 (1935–1936), 404. This provision was so worded: 'They declare that between the High Contracting Parties territorial questions must not be settled by resort to violence and that they shall recognize no territorial arrangement not obtained through pacific means, nor the validity of an occupation or acquisition of territory brought about by armed force'.

of American States on 26 December 1933,[27] followed by the Declaration of Lima (or the "Non-recognition of the Acquisition of Territories by Force"), signed by 19 American States on 22 December 1938, and by the Atlantic Charter of 14 August 1941.[28]

But it was only in 1945, with the entry into force of the UNC (art. 2 para. 4), that the Copernican revolution took place, consisting in the comprehensive and unconditional prohibition of the use of force (and its threat) as well as, as a necessary and complementary condition, in the establishment of a system of collective security (Chapter VII). Since then, normative production (under the aegis of the UN or outside it) in the outlawing of armed force and the invalidation of its legal effects (particularly territorial), has proceeded at a frantic pace and it would be impossible to give an exhaustive list of these texts (that would not make much sense either). Nevertheless, it is sufficient to mention a few of the most significant international instruments: article 9 of the ILC Draft 'Articles on the Rights and Duties of States' (1949);[29] 'Declaration on the Inadmissibility of Intervention in the Domestic Affairs of States and the Protection of Their Independence and Sovereignty' (Resolution 2131 (XX) UNGA) ; 'Declaration on Principles of International Law concerning Friendly Relations and Co-operation among States in accordance with the Charter of the United Nations' (Resolution 2625 (XXV) UNGA); Declaration on the 'Definition of Aggression' (Resolution 3314 (XXIX) UNGA); Art. 1 of the Charter of the Organization of American States (Bogotá, 30 April 1948).[30]

The use (and threat) of armed force is considered as a crime against peace,[31] any territorial benefit that may result is "null and devoid of legal effects".[32] The

---

27 *NRG*, 3rd series, Vol. 40, 454. Through this article, the High Contracting Parties definitively assumed as a "norm of their conduct" the obligation not to recognise territorial changes effected by force, whatever the nature of the latter (from diplomatic pressure to the actual use of military force).

28 Declaration Concerning the Aims of the War with Germany and its Allies, signed 12 August 1941 ('Atlantic Charter'), *NRG*, 3rd series, Vol. 41, 323.

29 https://legal.un.org/ilc/texts/instruments/english/draft_articles/2_1_1949.pdf.

30 *UNTS*, Vol. 119, 3. See also Art.17, which states: 'The territory of a State is inviolable; it may not be the object, even temporarily, of military occupation or of other measures of force taken by another State, directly or indirectly, on any grounds whatever. *No territorial acquisitions or special advantages obtained either by force or by other means of coercion shall be recognized*' [emphasis added]. It is impossible not to detect in this provision the prodrome, almost verbatim, of Principle No. 1 of the UNGA resolution 2625 (XXV).

31 Article 8 bis of the Statute of the International Criminal Court; Article 5 of UNGA resolution 3314 (XXIX); Principle 1 of UNGA resolution 2625 (XXV).

32 According to Rudofl Bindschedler "Annexation", in *Encyclopedia of Public International Law*, Vol.1, Amsterdam, 1992, 171, however, the prohibition of annexation by force of arms would only have a conventional basis. Yet, this position is in stark contrast not only with

rule of international law prohibiting the use of armed force, except in self-defence and in the case of measures authorised by the UNSC under Chapter VII of the UNC, is now part of that limited body of overarching principles of the international legal order known as "ius cogens". In this respect, there is no doubt, and both the doctrine,[33] international and municipal jurisprudence[34] and State practice[35] abound in this sense: the material fact of conquest cannot constitute the "material fact" allowing the extension of a state's territorial sovereignty to the territories of the defeated state.

It remains to be explored the only scenario in which, under certain conditions provided for by general international law and UNC law (Art. 51), a State may lawfully make unilateral use of armed force. This refers to the "inherent right", in the terminology of the Charter, of individual or collective self-defence. We must therefore ask ourselves whether a State, in the exercise of self-defence, may annex the territory (or part of it) of the aggressor State. In order to answer this question, and without going into detail about the conditions that general international law and the Charter lay down for the exercise of this right,[36] we

---

the prevailing doctrine, but also to the numerous statements of the International Court of Justice in the Military and Paramilitary Activities in Nicaragua case, as well as to all those *infra-* (para-) and normative texts whose impact on the fabric of customary law can hardly be overlooked.

33 See: ICJ Namibia 1971, 91–92 [individual op. of Judge Ammoun] and 123 [individual op. of Judge Padilla Nervo]; T Kotani, "A Theoretical Approach to the Problem of the Kurile Islands", 24 Japanese *Annual of International Law* 1981, 10–11; Sir Robert Jennings (1963), 56; Guggenheim (1949), 237, 260; Menon (1994), 22–25, 38; *Oppenheim's International Law* (1992), paras. 268, 703–704; Goldstein, 33. *Contra*: Hill, 161; Brierly (1963), 172; Raggi, 758; Bentivoglio, 25, 46; Francesco Capotorti, *L'occupazione nel diritto di guerra*, Naples, 1949; Giuliano (1949), 80–81; Rolando Quadri, *Diritto internazionale pubblico*, 2nd edn, Palermo, 1949, 293.

34 Re an Application by Ernst Jaakson and Aarand Roos (Great Britain, High Court, Chancery Division), award delivered the 14 December 1990, *ILR*, Vol. 85, 55, 59 [in which the Tribunal refers *only to the de facto* recognition of the forcible annexation of Estonia by the Soviet Union]; In Re Goering and Others (International Military Tribunal, Nuremberg), award delivered the 1st October 1946, *ILR*, Vol. 13, 220; ICJ, Corfu Channel Case (United Kingdom v. Albania), Judgment of 9 April 1949 (Merits): *ICJ Reports* 1949, 35 [inter alia]; Military and Paramilitary Activities in and against Nicaragua case, 1986, paras. 227–238, 250–253.

35 "This unilateral act [i.e., the Israeli annexation of East Jerusalem] has not been *internationally recognised to date*. It is a fundamental principle of international law that a territorial gain obtained by the use of force has no legal effect until a peaceful settlement has been reached", Swiss Federal Council response to a parliamentary interpellation requesting the transfer of the Swiss embassy from Tel Aviv to Jerusalem, in *Revue Suisse de Droit International et Européen*, Vol. 47 (1992), 575 [emphasis added; our translation].

36 See: G Distefano, "Chapter 22. Use of Force", in *The Oxford Handbook of International Law in Armed Conflict*, Oxford, 2014, 545–573.

will limit ourselves to mentioning only one, namely that of "proportionality". Indeed, in addition to the requirement[37] of prior aggression *already launched* or *imminent* (which would exclude "preventive self-defence"), general international law provides that the response of the attacked State must be "proportional" to the attack suffered. What about this 'proportionality' (from the standpoint of ius *contra bellum*) ? Does it refer to the aims or to the means of the armed response by the attacked State exercising its right of self-defence?

As Judge Roberto Ago rightly maintained in his 8th Report to the ILC on the Responsibility of States for Internationally Wrongful Acts, the purpose (and raison d'être of self-defence)[38] is to:

> halt and repel the attack [...] The action needed to halt and repulse the attack may well have to assume dimensions disproportionate to those of the attack suffered. [...] *Its lawfulness cannot be measured except by its capacity for achieving the desired result.*[39]

Indeed, proportionality in the aims (the only one that counts, and which prohibits the State from annexing the occupied territory *bello durante*) must not be confused with proportionality in the means to be used in order to achieve the aim aimed at by the exercise of self-defence and which alone is the basis for it in law: i.e., to *safeguard* the "territorial integrity and the political independence" of the attacked State. The latter could therefore *legitimately* encroach on the territory of the aggressor State if this were to prove necessary and proportional, for military purposes, to definitively repel the attack. But this military occupation, like any *flagranti bello* occupation, can in no way confer a valid *titulus adquisitionis* on the aggressed state, even if the latter, at the end of hostilities, were to display its *animus domini* (for example by declaring its annexation). For, as we have just seen, general international law prohibits the use and/or threat of force as a "material fact" for the purpose of establishing territorial title, regardless of the reason for which the armed conflict was initiated.[40] Moreover, the aforementioned resolution 2625 (XXV) categorically states in its para. 10:

37 To this must be added the "UN" treaty obligation to report to the Security Council, which may at any time take up the dispute under the provisions of Chapter VII.

38 The Rapporteur more accurately prefers to speak of a "situation" rather than a "right" of self-defence.

39 Roberto Ago, "Addendum to the Eighth Report", *YILC*, 1980, Vol. II, Part 1, para. 121 (at 69) [emphasis added].

40 In this sense: Richard R Baxter, 'The Legal Consequences of the Unlawful Use of Force under the Charter', *Proceedings of the ASIL* (April 1968), 69; Sir Robert Jennings (1963), 55;

> The territory of a State shall not be the object of military occupation resulting from the use of force in contravention of the provisions of the Charter. The territory of a State shall not be the object of acquisition by another State resulting from the threat or use of force. No territorial acquisition resulting from the threat or use of force shall be recognized as legal.

This excerpt,[41] after establishing the principle of the inadmissibility of the acquisition of territory by force (3rd sentence),[42] which is the corollary, in international law of territory, of Article 2 (4) of the Charter,[43] distinguishes, quite adamantly and subtly, between two scenarios. On the one hand (first sentence), it admits – implicitly (by a negative turn of phrase) – the possibility for the aggressed State to occupy, during hostilities (*bello durante*), part of the territory of the aggressor State, provided that this occupation obviously satisfies the conditions of proportionality and necessity under the right of self-defence

---

Joe Verhoeven, 'Le droit, le juge et la violence. Les arrêts Nicaragua c. États-Unis', 91 *RGDIP* 1987, 1218; *Oppenheim's International Law* (1992), para. 268 (at 704); Stephen M Schwebel, 'What weight to Conquest?' 74 *AJIL* 1970, 345–346; Cassese (1986), para. 10 (at 27); Louis Henkin, 'Use of Force: Law and U.S. Policy', in *Right vs. Might. International Law and the Use of Force*, Louis Henkin et al (eds), New York, 1989, 50; '[The] victim of aggression may not occupy the territory of the aggressor unless this is strictly necessary to prevent him from continuing the aggression by other means [....Article 51 [of the UNC]] ... prohibits prolonged military occupation, let alone annexation, of territory belonging to the aggressor', A Cassese, "Article 51", in *La Charte des Nations Unies. Commentaire article par article* (under the direction of Jean-Pierre Cot and Alain Pellet), 2nd edn, Paris, 1991, 774, 775 [our translation]; Kohen (1997), 395; Hans Wehberg, "Le Protocole de Genève", 7 *RCADI* 1925-II, 115–116; John Dugard, *Recognition and the United Nations*, Cambridge, 1987, 155; Sharon Korman, *The Right of Conquest*, Oxford, 1996, 256. *Contra*: E Lauterpacht, *Jerusalem and the Holy Places*, London, 1968, 52; Schwarzenberger, 288, 293 [more nuanced]; Bindschedler, 171.

41 This important paragraph of Resolution 2625 stands at the crossroads between the two branches of the old law of war, *ius ad bellum* (armed self-protection) and *ius in bello*, i.e., international humanitarian law (military occupation).

42 Principle reaffirmed by the UNSC in its resolution 2334 (23 December 2016) in relation to the Middle East, including the Palestinian question.

43 See *below* 114 et seq. The *futuristic* – as it was in some respects – Geneva Protocol of 2 October 1924 ("Protocol for the Peaceful Settlement of International Disputes" unanimously adopted by the 48 member states of the LoN at the time, but which never entered into force as it received only one ratification) cannot be ignored, since, a few decades ahead of its time, provided in Article 15 (2): "However, having regard to Article 10 of the Covenant, the territorial integrity or political independence of the aggressor State may in no case be prejudiced as a result of the application of the sanctions referred to in the present Protocol" (*Official Journal*, Special Supplement No. 21 (October 1924), 6).

(*ius contra bellum*).[44] On the other hand (2nd sentence), by the capital deletion of the fragment "contrary to", this passage erects an insurmountable obstacle to the possibility for the aggressed state to annex any part of the territory of the aggressor state. In other words, the *legality of* the use of force under the right of self-defence does not give rise to a *valid titulus adquisitionis* in international law of territory. There is therefore a gap between these two branches of public international law:[45] a lawful title to the use of force (in relation to *ius contra bellum*) does not give birth to a valid title to territorial sovereignty (in relation to the international law of territory).

B Illegal Territorial Situations

We have already highlighted above the shortcomings of the nullity mechanism and, consequently, the need to resort in the international legal order to what Sir Robert Jennings happily called "the whole spectrum of combinations of nullity and effectiveness".[46] In other words, the endless navigation of the legal order between the Scylla of the "fait accompli" and the Charybdis of the "crystalline legality". It is certain that in the case of an occupation of territory by armed force, the renunciation of the dispossessed state, the recognition of third states,[47] the effective character of the occupation and the passage of time are all elements that contribute to the establishment of the territorial title. The international legal order could recognise the latter as legally valid (1st scenario) or as still invalid (2nd scenario). In the first scenario, there would be a reunion of *titulus* and *modus adquisitionis* in the same state, i.e., in the state that had previously perpetrated the act of occupation (with *animus domini*) on a non- *nullius* territory (hence absence of *titulus adquisitionis*). The latter will therefore be conferred by the international legal order, whose various actors,

44 For example, it seems hardly conceivable that the aggressed state could indefinitely occupy part of the territory of the aggressed state by invoking a permanent threat of aggression.

45 See above the examples of the Golan Heights and East Jerusalem illegally annexed by Israel in 1981 and 1980 respectively; even assuming, as yet unproven, that Israel were indeed the attacked state in the 1967 Six-Day War, international law, correctly interpreted by UNGA RES. 2625 (XXV) and applied by the UNSC, would not recognise the validity of territorial acquisition. See *supra* notes 4 and 5.

46 Sir Robert Jennings (1963), 87.

47 Joint dissenting opinion of Judges Bedjaoui, Korova and Ranjeva appended to the judgment of the International Court of Justice in the case concerning Maritime Delimitation and Territorial Questions between Qatar and Bahrain, 2001, pars. 113–122.

by their attitudes, have recognised the validity of the new territorial situation or the factual impossibility of returning to the *status quo ante*.[48] On the other hand, and this is by far the most frequent hypothesis especially since the UNC, the reunion between the *titulus* and the *modus adquisitionis* takes place on the side of the previous legality, the new territorial situation not having sufficient effectiveness or succumbing to the pressure of the International Commnunity. In this scenario, therefore, the legal order secretes an institutional response consisting in the return to the previous legality.[49]

i Recognition and "Adjudication" of Territories before 1945

In the case of the transfer of territorial sovereignty by means of a legal act (unilateral or bilateral), the element that allows this legal fact to be the "efficient cause" is certainly the "free will" of the Parties, whereas, for example, the attitude of the International Community, presumed in this case,[50] plays only a subordinate role and is undoubtedly of lesser weight than other elements such as the "*nemo potest*" principle, *etc. On* the contrary, in other cases where the International Community enjoys a "title" to the territorial change (or situation) resulting either from the presence of an armed conflict, or from the very legal nature of the territory,[51] or from previous commitments, which limit the power of disposition of the territory (*ius disponendi*) by the States Parties to the treaty,[52] the attitude of the International Community represents,

48 Sir Robert Jennings (1963), 77–78; Paul Guggenheim, *Traité de droit international public*, Vol. I, Geneva, 1953, 443; "... the wrongful act of a State, without thereby ceasing to be wrongful, may become the basis of a new legal situation in which *the wrongful act is accepted as a fact*, and in relation to which even the State responsible for it may have certain rights", Sir Gerald Fitzmaurice (1957), 117.

49 We will have the opportunity to deal with this issue at length later [Part 2. Chapter 5. Section B.iii].

50 See *above* Part 1. Chapter 2.

51 See *infra* Part 3. Chapter 9.

52 In this perspective, one can mention certain international agreements or unilateral declarations (which would ultimately make it an implicit and diachronic agreement) by which a State undertakes not to cede part (or even all) of its territory, or, alternatively, to cede it only to the other Contracting Party. This is a serious restriction on one of the salient elements of territorial sovereignty and one might legitimately ask whether, in the end, sovereignty over the territories concerned by this clause would not reside with the other Contracting Party or with the Party that "requested" such a declaration. In short, the State having committed itself in this sense would either only enjoy an *ius fruendi*, i.e., a right of administration of territory (*ius in re aliena*), or would only be recognised conditionally as having sovereignty over these territories, i.e. on condition that it does not cede them to a third State. International practice is indeed full of examples. Suffice it to cite Article II of the Treaty between Persia and Russia (signed 13 February 1729 at Riaschtché, 33 *CTS*, 160): 'H.M. Emp. Of Russia ... content with [Persia] in possession of the Provinces

to varying degrees, one of the predominant elements, without which the territorial change could not validly take place, precisely for lack of a valid *titulus adquisitionis.* It is therefore correct to argue that it is precisely the "sanction" of the International Community at large that allows the crystallisation of the *titulus adquirendi.*[53] While it is true that the renunciation of the ceding State is essential for the purposes of territorial transfer, it is also true that the attitude of the International Community (expressed through its various "centres of qualification") is equally decisive for this purpose. This is all the more true if the International community has to carry out activities that have a directly relevant legal meaning, i.e. if Congresses are convened, if it assumes positions through the adoption of collective notes or the conclusion of treaties, *etc.* It will then truly be a "complex juridical fact" tending to the creation of a legal title, and thus to the validation (or invalidation) of a territorial situation. In this case, only the degree (the proportion) of the "mix" between the attitudes of the States directly affected by the territorial change (renunciation and acquisition) and the attitude of the International Community may vary.[54] State

... on condition nevertheless that these Provinces may in no way be given to any other Power: And in case this should happen, the said Provinces, with all that depends on them, shall return to and remain for ever under the Domination of Russia, and all that has been stipulated to the contrary, shall be declared null and void' [our translation]. As an example of a "solicited" unilateral act, we may mention the: Declaration of the Sultan of Muscat giving assurance not to cede the territories of Muscat and Oman and their dependencies to any power except Great Britain, 20 March 1891 (*NRG*, 3rd series, Vol. 6, 287).

53 See, for example, the territorial transfers – with the intervention of *arbitrators* in the dispute between Czechoslovakia and Hungary – decided by the Four Powers (Great Britain, France, Italy and Germany) at the Munich Conference of 1938, without the consent of the two states affected by the arbitration decision. The case of the Spitzbergen archipelago and the effect of the treaty on third parties (Russia) can also be mentioned, as well as the consequences of the Norwegian occupation that can be configured as an internationally wrongful act. See e.g., ICJ, Case concerning the Legal Status of East Greenland, para. 8 (Dissenting opinion of Judge Anzilotti).

54 Even today, we can identify attitudes of the International Community that could be described as *ex post facto* adjudication. A striking example is the peace plan proposed by the "Contact Group" in Bosnia-Herzegovina, according to which the territorial divisions were carried out and which put an end to a non-international armed conflict, but certainly of *international concern* (which demonstrates *a fortiori* the role of the International Community in international conflicts). This plan was finally endorsed by the Parties involved under the guarantee of the Powers that made up the above-mentioned "Contact Group": the Dayton Agreement of 21 November 1995 (35 *ILM* 1996-I, 170–183) subsequently formally sealed by the Peace Treaty signed in Paris on 14 December 1995 (35 *ILM* 1996-I, 89–119), which thus contains both the international guarantee of the new territorial base (indeed, the Constitution of the new Bosnia and Herzegovina is enshrined in Annex IV of the said Treaty) and the 'renunciation' by the Parties to the conflict of their territorial conquests. See in this sense: Arbitral Dispute over Inter-Entity Boundary in Brcko Area,

practice[55] and the doctrine[56] attest to this adjudication function, considering it as a "mode of acquisition" or a mode of defining territorial regimes.[57]

The conclusion in Paris in 1928 of the Briand-Kellog Pact, whereby the Parties "solemnly" renounced war "as an instrument of national policy", in short outlawing wars of aggression,[58] does not seem to have drastically changed the legal regime applicable to territorial acquisitions by force. While the consent of the defeated state continued to be required, as in the Chaco Boreal conflict between Paraguay and Bolivia (1932–1935),[59] so did the intervention of

para. 66 (at 72). Again, with regard to the unfathomable tragedy of the Palestine question, it is the States or subjects directly concerned that proceed with the territorial settlement, admittedly under the aegis of the International Community and some of its representative States. But the successive agreements (Oslo and Wye Plantation) between Israel and the Palestinian Authority have only partially taken on board the UNSC relevant resolutions (and even less so) those of the UNGA. It is therefore legitimate to ask how Israel and the Palestinian Authority were able to derogate from the normative instruments of the United Nations? In the future, will an international judge (or arbitrator) called upon to settle a territorial dispute between these two states apply the legal acts of the United Nations or the bilateral agreements concluded between Israel and Palestine? We believe that they will look first, for the purposes of finding *titulus adquisitionis,* at the latter.

55 See also the diplomatic note (24 March 1864) of the Ambassador of France in London, Prince de la Tour d'Auvergne, to his MFA, Mr Drouyn de Lhuys, regarding the 'European interests' in the controversy over the Duchies of Schleswig and Holstein, quoted in *Bruns*, FB11 para. 1055; and on the same subject the diplomatic note (6 April 1864) from the German Chancellor, Baron von Bismarck, to the above-mentioned French Foreign Minister, quoted in *ibid*, para. 1063; the salient paragraph of the French Foreign Minister's reply to his ambassador in London deserves to be reproduced here: '[I] have enumerated the occasions on which, since 1815, *Europe has intervened in questions of sovereignty*, political organisation, and the *distribution of populations in countries where the pre-existing order of things had been destroyed*, and I have established that the idea put forward by us was only one more application of a precedent enshrined by a practice of half a century in all analogous circumstances' [our translation]. See also the diplomatic note (17 March 1860) from the French MFA, Mr Thouvenel, to his ambassador in Berne, M Tillos, with respect to the legal status of Upper-Savoy ceded by the Kingdom of Sardinia to France and the interests of the European Concert in maintaining this status, quoted in *Bruns*, FB11 para. 1132. It should not be forgotten that the League of Nations had also proceeded to the territorial delimitation of state entities, namely in the Jaworzina border; and that it had "participated" in the first place in the territorial settlement in the Mosul region dispute.

56 Sir Hersch Lauterpacht (1947, 412) speaks of a 'quasi-legislative measure in the general interest of international society and of international peace'.

57 In this sense: Verzijl, Vol. III, 378; Sir John Fischer Williams (1926), 40.

58 Obviously, self-defence and military actions recommended by the Council of the LoN were excluded from this prohibition; see: Distefano (2014–1), 299–319.

59 It was not until 28 April 2009 that Bolivia and Paraguay concluded a historic agreement in Buenos Aires that fixed the border between the two countries, which was the source of the conflict that caused more than 100,000 deaths between 1932 and 1935. This war for the

the organised International Community, embodied by the LoN, or in a dispersed manner, i.e., third states *uti singuli*. At the same time, territorial changes (annexation of the *Sudetenland* by Germany) were decided in 1938 during the Munich Conferemce by France, Great Britain, Italy and Germany without the consent of the territorial sovereign,[60] Czechoslovakia.[61] At the same time, these four states set up an arbitration tribunal to delimit the border between Czechoslovakia and Hungary without the consent of these two states to the procedure.

A distinction must therefore be made between two scenarios with very different meanings for the matter at hand. On the one hand, there is the situation where the defeated state expresses its consent to the cession of part of its territory, on the other hand, when such consent is absent. In both cases, it is necessary to take into account the attitude of the International Community for the purpose of perfecting the territorial transfer.

Both scenarios are discussed below, using historical examples, starting with the case where there is no consent from at least one of the states concerned (or dispossessed), and ending with the case where consent is lacking.[62]

The term "Concert of Great Powers" has often appeared in the literature of international law. It first appeared in the Treaty of Chaumont (1er March 1814), by which Austria, Great Britain, Prussia and Russia, in forming an alliance against Napoleon, undertook to use all their resources "in perfect concert". The "Concert of the Great Powers" was replaced by the "European Concert",[63] which constituted an advance on the theory of Balance of Powers since it provided for cooperation between states, or at least between the Great Powers, in solving problems of *general interest*.[64] This *de facto* cooperation (also called

---

control of the Chaco region, which was thought to be rich in hydrocarbons at the time, had indirectly opposed the American oil companies Standard Oil and the British-Dutch Royal Dutch Shell (source: AFP).

60 However, this international agreement was considered invalid by many national courts.

61 The text of the 'famous' Munich Agreement of 29 September 1938 can be found in *NRG*, 3rd series, Vol. 36, 24–30 [in German, English and French]. It is worth recalling that, in the First Annex to the said agreement, these same states, once Czechoslovakia had been amputated from the Sudetenland, set themselves up as guarantor powers "of the new borders of the Czechoslovak state against any unprovoked aggression", decision of 2 November 1938, quoted in *NRG*, 3rd series, Vol. 36, 30 [our translation].

62 See *infra* 106–108.

63 See in this respect, in general: Robert B Mowat, *The Concert of Europe*, London, 1930; Maurice Bourquin, "Le Concert européen au XIXème siècle", in *Festschrift für Rudolf Laun*, Göttingen, 1956, 89–100.

64 At the Congress of Châtillon on 5 February 1814, the Austrian, British, Prussian and Russian envoys declared, during armistice talks with Napoleon, that they were not acting as envoys of the four courts by which they had been given full powers, but as being

"de facto international government")[65] took various forms and functions until 1919 when it was supplanted[66] by an even more institutionalised version represented by the League of Nations.[67] This "succession" between centres of qualification of the international legal order is a constant in the recent history of international relations, as can be seen in the advisory opinion rendered by the Permanent Court of International Justice in response to Albania's claim. Indeed, the Court agreed with Albania's claim that the League of Nations 'as successor to the European concert of nations, should possess [the] competence' to delimit its borders'.[68]

The European Concert, faced with the outbreak of crises such as the slow dislocation of the Ottoman Empire, insurrectional movements, the emergence of new state entities, *etc.*, represented the means by which the international legal order of yesteryear tried to provide an effective response to the expectations emanating from the social body. It reconciled the demands of validity with the "effectivités en action" rooted in social reality. It was a form of self-organisation of international society, which had been left without hierarchically ordered authorities following the collapse of the medieval *ordinatio ad unum* (Pope and Emperor). It was also the response to the organisational needs of international society that better suited the latter's new structures and goals. In 1921, one of the "centres" of this self-organisation of the International Community, namely the Conference of Ambassadors of the Principal Allied Powers of the First World War, had to tackle the territorial dispute between Albania and the Serbo-Croatian-Slovenian Kingdom in the region of the Monastery of St. Naoum. The Conference, vested by the International community with the power to settle the dispute between the two states, decided to:

---

responsible for negotiating peace on behalf of the whole of Europe. See: G Distefano, "L'ordre international en quête d'organisation: 1454-(1815), 'Prove d'orchestra' du Concert européen", in *The International Legal Order in the XXIst Century. Essays in Honour of Professor Marcelo Gustavo Kohen*, Brill, 2023, 251-269.

65 See also *infra* Part 3. Chapter 8. Section C.

66 However, the Concert of Europe in its old configuration was still assigned certain functions by the states before WWII, especially in the delimitation of the international borders of Albania. See Articles 3 and 5 of the Peace Treaty between Greece, Bulgaria, Montenegro, Serbia and Turkey, in *NRG*, 3rd series, Vol. VIII, 18. See also *infra* note 95.

67 See: Stanley Windlass, "The League and Territorial Disputes", in *International Regulation of Frontier Disputes*, ed. by E Luard, London, 1970, 31–83; Dugard, 13–40 (Chapter III); Quincy Wright, "The Goa incident", 56 *AJIL* 1962, 632.

68 Monastery of Saint-Naoum (Albanian frontier), advisory opinion of 4 September 1924: *PCIJ Reports* B 9, 10 [emphasis added].

> To inform the Delimitation Commission [which it had entrusted with the task of determining the said boundary on the ground] and the Albanian and Serbian Governments that the Conference has decided to allocate the monastery of St. Naoum to Albania.[69]

Due to Serbia's protests and France's concerns, the Conference decided to refer the matter to the Council of the League of Nations, which, in its turn, submitted it to the Permanent Court of International Justice for an advisory opinion. The latter rendered an advisory opinion on 4 September 1927, in which it recognised the definitive character of *the attribution* by the Conference of Ambassadors of the Monastery of Saint Naoum to Albania.[70] The Court thus reproduced in its advisory opinion the passage of the decision adopted on 6 December 1922 by the Conference of Ambassadors, by virtue of which:

> [i]t was decided to inform the Serbo-Albanian Boundary Commission and the Albanian and Yugo-Slav Governments that the Conference *has agreed to allocate the Saint-Naoum Monastery to Albania.*[71]

We can close this brief parenthesis devoted to the question of the Monastery of Saint-Naoum, which saw the involvement of several "qualification centres" of the time (in turn the Conference of Ambassadors, the League of Nations, the Permanent Court of International Justice), with an extract from the opinion issued by the Conference of Ambassadors in which we read that

> Baron Romano Avezzana [i.e., Ambassador of the Kingdom of Italy to the Conference] wishes [...] to make a proposal concerning the question of Saint-Naoum. The Italian Government is of the opinion that the Conference of Ambassadors is entirely competent to decide. Moreover, it has on several occasions reversed a decision already taken, *because it must be considered not as a court, but as a political body endeavouring to find solutions in accordance with justice.*[72]

Other examples of adjudication of territories by the European Concert concerned the Question of Crete, which is part of the (wider) "Eastern Question".

---

69 Reproduced in: *Prassi italiana*, 3rd series, Vol. V, paras. 1158, 2591 [translated from French].

70 PCIJ, Monastery of Saint-Naoum (Albanian frontier), 14–15.

71 *Ibid.*, 15 [emphasis added].

72 Reproduced in: *Prassi italiana*, 3rd series, Vol. V, para. 1158, 2592 [emphasis added; our translation].

It was discussed by the European Concert in Paris (1856) and Berlin (1877–78), but it took an umpteenth anti-Ottoman rebellion in 1896 for the Great Powers to override the resistance of the Sublime Porte and, after occupying the island, create an "International Government" under Ottoman suzerainty. The intervention was described by the Powers themselves as a "decision".[73] A series of constitutions marked the evolution of the Cretan regime; the *de facto* union with Greece was gradually achieved from 1909 onwards, while in 1913 the Ottoman Empire renounced its suzerainty in favour of the European guarantor powers. In this case, therefore, the consent of the territorial state was sometimes absent at the outset and sometimes subsequently extorted.

The activity of adjudication of territories (or settlement of territorial disputes) carried out by the European Concert extended even to Africa, since Berlin (*Scramble for Africa*), in 1885, was the scene of the distribution of territories, respectively the validation of previous territorial acquisitions, in an entire continent decreed by the same occasion as *res nullius*.

With regard to international waterways, it is worth mentioning the example of the Danube Commission – established in 1856 by the Treaty of Paris – and the *de facto* extension of its competence to Romania. By the Treaty of London of 10 March 1883,[74] concluded by the members of the Concert of Europe, the Commission was able to extend its jurisdiction to Braila, i.e., to Romanian territory. However, Romania was not a party to this treaty, its delegates having been accepted only in an advisory capacity.[75] When asked to rule on this issue, the ICJ did not establish either Romania's acquiescence or a collateral agreement (acceptance of an obligation by a third State) – within the meaning of Article 35 of the VCLT 1969[76] – but merely stated laconically that:

> Roumania did not sign or ratify this Treaty [...] In the long period of time that has elapsed since the conclusion of the Treaty of London, matters

73 Collective note of 2 March 1897; see the submission of the Hellenic Government to the ICJ in the case of the Lighthouses in Crete and Samos, C 82, 62–131.

74 *CTS*, vol. 161, 353.

75 PCIJ, Jurisdiction of the European Danube Commission between Galatz and Braila, advisory Opinion of 8 December 1927, B 14, 11.

76 In this passage, especially in the part relating to the basis ("title") of the Commission's powers, ICJ's reasoning is as thin as its successor's 20 years later in the Reparation case ('had the power, in conformity with international law, to bring into being an entity possessing objective international personality, and not merely personality recognized by them alone, together with capacity to bring international claims', Reparation for Injuries Suffered in the Service of the United Nations, Advisory Opinion of 11 April 1949: *ICJ Reports* 1949, 185). See also *infra* Part 3. Chapter 8. Section C ("objective territorial regimes").

> had continued in a more or less satisfactory way, and no one denied that the European Commission had exercised some powers on the sector from Galatz to Braila, no matter what the legal ground and nature of these powers may have been.[77]

Another example of 'adjudication' that seems to violate both the principle of the relative effect of treaties[78] and that of '*nemo plus iuris transferre quam ipse haberet*',[79] is the famous (and infamous) Munich Agreement of 29 September 1938 ceding the *Sudetenland* to the German Reich.[80] This agreement was in no way different from the territorial arrangements concocted under the aegis of the European Concert, but the times were over and there was no 'communal sense' presiding over this territorial adjudication by the 4 European Great Powers.

Thus, the International Community did not seldom manifest itself in new territorial situations where the consent of the dispossessed state was lacking. Of course, in view of the legality of war as a means of settling disputes, the International Community had no choice but to endorse or condemn such territorial situations. And to this end, it was not uncommon for the 'organ' of the International Community to take coercive measures to restore the *status quo ante* or to force the imposition of a solution previously negotiated in the

77 PCIJ, Jurisdiction of the European Commission, 27. It is difficult to agree with the conclusions of Judge Negulesco, in his dissenting opinion (the only one) attached to this advisory opinion, which lifts the veil on this "title" by, though, challenging it: 'It has been sought to explain that independently of Roumania the Treaty of London possesses legal force as being an application of the system adopted by the Concert of Europe which left to the Great Powers alone the task of deciding the principal affairs of Europe. The Concert of Europe has always been regarded as apolitical system and has never been considered as a legal organization; in other words, the decisions of the Great Powers, met together as the Concert of Europe, have sometimes been able to command respect by reason of the power behind these decisions, but they have never been held to be legally binding upon States not represented in the Concert' (*ibid.*, 95). However, the 'decisions' of the European Concert were binding or, at any rate, were considered binding, regardless of any legitimate doubts about their legal basis. In other words, the effects were legally binding, while the exact nature of the title empowering the Concert of Europe, may remain open to debate.

78 'The Munich Agreement ... was concluded without the Czechoslovaks participating in the matter at all. It was *res inter alios acta*, a typical agreement to the detriment of a third party, such occurs only exceptionally in the realm of international law', Edward Taborsky, "'Munich', the Vienna Arbitration and International Law", 21 *Czechoslovak Yearbook of International Law* 1942, 26.

79 See *supra* Part 1. Chapter 2. Section B.

80 Text in *NRG*, 3rd series, Vol. 36, 24–30 [in German, English and French].

backrooms of the Cabinets. This 'European Concert' was, in short, an organ of territorial validation and invalidation through the function of recognition or non-recognition of the territorial situation. The International Community thus tried to solve *in specie* the temporary divorce between the effectiveness and the validity of the new territorial situation. The post-1945 or contemporary doctrine,[81] international and municipal jurisprudence[82] as well as States practice[83] relating to this period corroborate the position that the attitude of the International Community was *the determining factor for the* validation or invalidation of the territorial change brought about by (threat of) force. The European Great Powers[84] acted as 'representative groups of

81 See: Guggenheim (1949), 232–233; Lord Arnold McNair, "The Stimson Doctrine of Non-Recognition. A Note on its Legal Aspects", 14 *BYIL* 1933, 71; Gaetano Morelli, "L'ordinamento internazionale di fronte alle nuove situazioni di fatto", 1 *Archivio di diritto pubblico* 1936, 198–200; De Visscher (1967), 23–24, 110; Anzilotti (1955), 295; Viktor Bruns, "Völkerrecht als Rechtsordnung", 1 *ZaöRV* 1929, 24; Gabriela Arevalo Blumenkron, *La doctrina del reconocimiento en la teoria y en la practica de los estados*, Mexico City (Thesis), 1954, 123–136; Sir John Fischer Williams (1926), 36; *Oppenheim's International Law*, 8th ed. (by Sir Hersch Lauterpacht), Vol. 1, London, 1955, para. 75c; Cassese (1986), para. 139.

82 See: Nemec v. Etablissements L.A.B. and Others, Tribunal civil de la Seine, award delivered the 22 February 1955, 22 *ILR*, 101 [recognition of the German annexation of Austria]; Kling and Others v. Lesser and Rotterdamscher, 102 [judicial recognition of the Soviet annexation of the Baltic States in 1940]; Arrangement for the Settlement of Differences between the Sultan of Muscat and the Sultan of Zanzibar, and the Independence of their respective States, 111; Bank of Ethiopia v. National Bank of Egypt and Liguori (England, Supreme Court, Chancery Division), award delivered the 11 may 1937, 8 *ILR*, 120; In re Alexandravicus' Estate, Supreme Court of New Jersey, decision of 30 June 1961, 32 *ILR*, 74 [This Court pronounced, as a result of the non-recognition of the US Government – an 'Act of State' – the invalidity of the Soviet annexation of Lithuania from the standpoint of the legal order of the United States of America].

83 See the parliamentary reply (26 June 1882) of the Italian Minister of Foreign Affairs, M Mancini, concerning the international recognition of the "conquest" of the Bay of Assab, quoted in *Prassi italiana*, Prima serie, Vol. II, para. 840; the diplomatic note sent on 23 July 1914 by the Italian MFA, Marquis of San Giuliano, to his Ambassador in Sofia, M Cucchi-Boasso, concerning the legal effects of the Bulgarian annexation of Western Thrace, which had not obtained international recognition, quoted in *Prassi italiana*, Seconda serie, Vol. 3, para. 2222; the diplomatic despatch sent on 18 February 1929 by the British Minister Sir Austen Chamberlain to the Persian Ambassador in London, regarding the Persian-British dispute over the Bahrain Islands, cited in Smith, 71–72; the international recognition of Norwegian sovereignty over the Spitsbergen Archipelago, *Treaty Series*, No. 18 (1924), Cmd. 2092; the recognition in 1920 of Romanian sovereignty over Bessarabia, *Hertslet's Commercial Treaties. A Collection of treaties and Conventions between Great-Britain and the Foreign Powers, ed.* by E Hertslet, London, Vol. 29, 1024.

84 See Pietro Ziccardi, *La costituzione dell'ordinamento internazionale*, Milan, 1943, 262–280; Lord Arnold McNair (1933), 72, according to whom "representative groups of States" would be the *maior et sanior pars of* the International Community.

states'[85] in the creation, modification or extinction of customary rules and subjective legal situations, *etc.*

Just as science proceeds by successive *falsifications*,[86] so the legal order proceeds by successive qualifications of factual situations: *dynamic legality*. As an example, it would be interesting to review the different judicial "qualifications" expressed by international tribunals in relation to the annexation of the Ethiopian Empire by Italy. The Franco-Italian Conciliation Commission, established by the Peace Treaty of 1947 declared that:

> It is not disputed that, on 9 May 1936, the Ethiopian State ceased to exist as a sovereign and independent State, and that its territory was annexed to Italy, whose sovereignty, which gave rise to rights with regard to third parties [*iure* character of the territorial change], was recognised *de jure* by France, which *noted* the de facto state of affairs; that Italy's sovereignty ceased *in fact* to be exercised over Ethiopian territory as from 1941.[87]

However, in an award pronounced 7 years later by the same tribunal, it is stated that there is a "will" to reinstate Ethiopia in its sovereignty *of iure* and absolute despite the Italian parenthesis between 1936 and 1941, but especially notwithstanding the international recognition of the 1936 annexation, and against the previous jurisprudential practice:[88]

> [W]ith particular reference to Ethiopia [alongside Albania], the [1947 Peace] Treaty cannot deny the historical fact that Italy exercised a certain *de facto power* over Ethiopia following its annexation – considered by the Treaty [despite the recognition of the International Community as early as 1936!] – from 9 May 1936 until the *liberation of* Ethiopian territory by

85 Texaco-Calasiatic v. Government of Libya, arbitral award of 17 January 1977, 17 *ILM* 1978, para. 87 (at 30). Within the meaning provided by René-Jean Dupuy (who was the sole arbitrator in the aforesaid case), "Coutume sage et coutume sauvage", *Mélanges offerts à Charles Rousseau*, Paris, 1974, 76, 85, as well as by the ICJ in relation to the process of formation of customary norms (ICJ, North Sea Continental Shelf, 1969, para. 73).

86 Within the meaning of Karl Popper, *The Logic of Scientific Discovery*, New York, 1958, 40–43.

87 Re Interpretation of Article 78, Paragraph 7, of the Peace Treaty with Italy, 1947 (Franco-Ethiopian Railway Company Claim), Franco-Italian Conciliation Commission, award delivered the 16 March 1956, RSA, Vol. XIII, 659 [emphasis added].

88 See Bank of Ethiopia v. National Bank of Egypt and Liguori, 119–123.

> British troops in 1941 – but it [the Treaty] *retroactively* restores Ethiopia's sovereignty.[89]

Ultimately, one can only agree with Brownlie when he affirms that:

> In the years 1919 and 1920 [but even earlier, as we have just seen] decisions were taken by the Supreme Council of Allied and Associate States; in 1943 and 1945 by meetings of leaders at Tehran, Yalta, and Potsdam, and subsequently by meetings of Foreign Ministers ... The existence of this power of disposition or assignment is recognised by jurists, but they find it difficult to suggest, or to agree upon, a satisfactory legal basis for it ... *Much turns on the extent to which recognition and acquiescence may counteract any elements of illegality which may infect such procedures in some cases* [...] for example, the Geneva Conference of 1954, in regard to Indo-China, the express delegation power prior to agreed disposition of territory ensures that a certain number of States are bound to accept the results of the procedure.[90]

It is therefore difficult to contest the existence of a power of adjudication[91] of territories which a small body of the International Community has been

---

89 Comptoirs Dufay et Gigandet et al (France v. Italy), Award rendered by the Franco-Italian Conciliation Commission on 9 July 1962, *RIAA*, Vol. XVI, 211 [our translation; emphasis added].

90 Brownlie (1990), 135–136 [emphasis added]. Similarly: Gidon Gottlieb, 'Nations without States', 73 *Foreign Affairs*, 100, 103. See, however, below for a more nuanced reading of the 1954 'Final Act' in relation to Indochina (*infra* Part 2. Chapter 5. Section B.ii).

91 "There is adjudication if territories are allocated by a community of states (Congress of Vienna, Congress of Berlin, League of Nations) or by an award of an international court of justice or international body", Strupp (1930), Vol. 1, 156 [our translation]. However, according to Verdross, "Règles générales du droit de la paix" 30 *RCADI* 1929-V, 377–378, extra-jurisdictional adjudication could not constitute an autonomous "mode of acquisition" since territorial transfer always finds its legal basis in an agreement, especially a bilateral one (between the States directly concerned). One cannot share the opinion of the eminent Austrian jurist because the conception he defends clashes not only with the data drawn from State practice but also with logico-legal considerations. It is clear (see, for example, the Preliminary Peace Agreements signed in San Stefano in 1876 and the successive concerted territorial reorganisation of the Congress of Berlin in 1878) that territorial changes which have their political origin in decisions of the International Community also have their legal basis in the latter. Thus, very often no further legal act is required to validate the territorial change. And, in case it is required, e.g., a treaty of cession, this is often only the result of a *pactum de contrahendo*.

vested with over the centuries, even in the absence of the consent of all the Parties concerned.

Let us now turn to the more numerous cases where, on the other hand, there is the consent of all the parties (or states) concerned. In more recent times, we have witnessed this function of allocating and (re-)distributing spaces performed by a small group of states, anointed with the *potestas* that was once that of the Pope.[92] One thinks, for example, of the Berlin Conference of 1878, convened by the honest broker Bismarck, for the purpose of dividing up the spoils of Europe's "homme malade" – the Ottoman Empire. Concerted decisions had to be taken, as the European Concert could not leave the decision on the Balkan territory to the conquering and defeated states alone, i.e., Russia and the Sublime Porte.[93] These matters did not fall within their exclusive competence alone, but were of international concern[94] and it was therefore up to the European Concert to decide on them,[95] since it was the highest authority,

92 It is significant to note in passing that the Pope, in this process of validating territorial titles, referred to the effectiveness of the occupation to the detriment of the legality of the 'holder'. One need only think of the preference expressed by Pope Zechariah in favour of Pepin (effective holder of power) at the expense of the Merovingian (legal holder). The pontiff ended up consecrating the first king of the Franks and a Roman patrician. See: Henri Pirenne, *Mahomet et Charlemagne*, 2nd edn, Brussels, 1961, 144ff.

93 In short, the Treaty of San Stefano (1876), honorably obtained by the Russians on the battlefield and by which the Sultan renounced almost all Ottoman territories in Europe [*animus derelinquendi*], was not sufficient to transfer legal title between the two High Parties. It required the *ratification of* the Third Powers, who therefore had an *interest in* the matter. Consequently, the (bilateral) Treaty of San Stefano was 'annulled' by the (multilateral) Treaty of Berlin of 13 July 1878 (see in particular Articles 58–60). As if the *ius tractatus* of Turkey and Russia in this area was circumscribed and limited by the *legal interests* of the European Concert. So much so that Holland (Thomas E, *The European Concert in the Eastern Question*, Oxford, 1885, 2) did not hesitate to speak of a "corpus iuris publici orientalis".

94 For these territorial regimes had been established by multilateral agreements such as the Treaty of Paris of 1856 ("Public Law of Europe"). Therefore, their "international concern" would exclude any unilateral modification (or only between certain Parties to the Treaty).

95 Protocols of the Congress of Berlin, No. 13 [5 July 1878], quoted in *Bruns*, FB12 para. 635. Another example of this conciliatory and adjudicative function can be found in the advisory opinion of the Monastery of St Naoum (10), where Albania claimed that the competence to fix frontiers "belonged to the League of Nations, as the successor of the European concert. However, the Assembly of the League of Nations, by its unanimous vote of October 2, 1921, left to the Principal Powers to fix the Albanian frontiers, recommending Albania to accept already the decision of the Powers in this respect". Thus, one can underline: a) the succession in the "Concertation of adjudication"; b) even in the presence of the LoN, polycentrism in the function of "qualification" of territorial situations was still in place and will still be, albeit to a lesser extent, thereafter. This outline of institutionalisation of the International Community generated by the establishment of the LoN did

the only one empowered to resolve conflicts of any kind, especially territorial ones.[96] Consequently, the Treaty of San Stefano (1876), imposed by the victorious Russia on the defeated Ottoman Empire, was *invalidated* by the decisions taken by the "European Areopagus" meeting in Berlin. It should be stressed in this respect that the consent of the defeated state, necessary for the territorial settlement, was indeed present, but the legal issue at stake would require a confirmation (or reversal, as was finally the case) of the territorial treaty.

The European Concert also proceeded to create states, as was the case for Albania by virtue of the Treaty of London of 1913 that effectuated the detachment of the Turkish provinces of Scutari and Jannina as well as the vilayets of Kosovo and Monastir which had been under Ottoman sovereignty since 1571. After several revolts, local autonomy was granted in 1912, but the question of the status of these territories contributed to the outbreak of the First Balkan War (1912–1913). Thanks to British mediation, the dispute was referred to the Six Powers under Article III of the 1913 Treaty of London:

> His Majesty the Emperor of the Ottomans and their Majesties the Allied Sovereigns declare that they remit to His Majesty the Emperor of Germany; His Majesty the Emperor of Austria, King of Hungary; the President of the French Republic; His Majesty the King of Great Britain and Ireland, Emperor of India; His Majesty the King of Italy; and His Majesty the Emperor of All the Russias the matter of arranging the delimitation of the frontiers of Albania and all other questions concerning Albania.[97]

Accordingly, on 29 July 1913 the Conference of Ambassadors produced an "Organic Statute for the State of Albania", whose Article I reads as follows

> Albania is constituted as an autonomous, sovereign and hereditary principality by order of primogeniture under the guarantee of the six Powers. The Prince shall be designated by the six Powers.[98]

---

not erase completely the structure of the international legal order (as today, perhaps to a lesser extent, by the juxtaposition of the United Nations General Assembly and the other centres of legal qualification).

96 During the Ottoman-Egyptian crisis of 1840–41, Russia, in order to legitimise its intervention in the Dardanelles, declared that it had acted, albeit alone, but as "the representative of Europe" (Tsar's ambassador in London to the English Prime Minister, Mr Palmerston, quoted in Efraim Karsh, Inari Karsh, *Empires of the Sand. The struggle of mastery in the Middle East 1789–1923*, Cambridge (Mass.), 1999, 38).

97 *Major Peace Treaties of Modern History*, 1648–1967, Vol. II, New York, 1967, 245.

98 *NRG*, 3rd series, 650 [our translation].

The principality was thus freed from Ottoman suzerainty (Article 2) and neutralised (Article 3); an international police force was created for the purpose of maintaining order (Articles 8 to 11). The borders were delimited, again by the Conference of Ambassadors, in the Florence Protocol of 17 December 1913.

Not without some vicissitudes during and immediately after WWI, Albania was soon recognised by most states; on 9 November 1921 the Conference of Ambassadors – still vested with the power of disposition by virtue of the 1913 London Treaty – issued a Declaration in which it recognised:

> that the independence of Albania, as well as the territorial integrity and inalienability of its borders, as determined by their decision of 9 November 1921, is a matter of international importance.[99]

Unlike the Cretan example – mentioned above – here the territorial ruler, still the Sublime Porte, gave his consent to allow the European Concert to exercise the power of adjudication over part of its territory. In other words, the Ottoman Empire relied on the arbitration of the Six Powers.

However, the International Community may become even more "involved" in the *erga omnes* characterisation of territorial rights. Diplomatic practice knows, for example, the cases of the guarantee of territories by the International Community (or a smaller Concert). One thinks of the guarantee of Romanian territories during the Russo-Ottoman conflict[100]conflict, the admittedly short-lived guarantee of Czechoslovakian borders following the infamous Munich Agreement of 29 September 1938[101]or the international guarantee of Switzerland's permanent neutrality, sealed by the Final Act of the Congress of Vienna in 1815.[102] In short, the International Community had (and has) reinforced, by its conclusive attitude, the legal title on which the

99 *Ibid.*, 654 [our translation].

100 Subsequently sanctioned by the 1878 Congress of Berlin (*Bruns*, B.1.1., para. 600), in relation to the international recognition of Romanian borders (notably at the mouth of the Danube) given by the 'guarantor' powers under the Protocol of 6 January 1857 (*ibid.*, para. 615).

101 Where, once Czechoslovakia had been amputated from the Sudetenland, France and the United Kingdom (in addition to Germany and Italy), by the First Annex to the said agreement, set themselves up as guarantor Powers "of the new frontiers of the Czechoslovak state against any unprovoked aggression", decision of 2 November 1938, quoted in *NRG*, 3rd series, Vol. 36, 30 [our translation].

102 See the reiteration of the 'international concern' that the status of permanent neutrality implied for the guarantor states in the diplomatic despatch (22 March 1860) from the British Ambassador in Paris, Earl Cowley, to his Foreign Secretary, Lord Russell: 'there could be no doubt that he [the King of Sardinia] *could not dispose of property on which*

territorial situation is based. It thus brings an additional element of effectiveness, and therefore of objectification, to what would be otherwise a matter of simple intersubjectivism between the States directly concerned (*inter partes*).

ii *The Invalidation of Illegal Territorial Situations and the "Adjudication" of Territories under the UN Charter (after 1945)*

Does contemporary international law brought to the baptismal font by the UNC contain enzymes allowing the metabolism of illegal territorial situations? Does it contain the usual triptych: effectiveness (*modus adquirendi*), consent of the affected state and (non-) international recognition (both constituting the *titulus adquirendi*)?[103] We will only examine here territorial changes by partial annexation and refer the reader later in this volume to the case of violent secessions, i.e., without the consent (at least initially) of the parent state.[104]

The general prohibition of the use of force, which is enshrined in the Magna Charta of the International Community as one of the principles by which the Members of the United Nations are to be guided [Art. 2 §4], has engendered two major structural consequences: a) a system of collective security established by Chapter VII;[105] b) an attempt to centralise and institutionalise the legal function of qualification (recognition). The latter requirement was made necessary in particular by the increasing institutionalisation of the International Community as it has taken shape since the end of the Second World War.[106] An indication of this is the emergence of the category of peremptory norms of general international law (*ius cogens*). In other words,

---

Europe had a lien; that such was the condition on neutral districts', quoted in Bruns, FB11 para. 1135 [emphasis added; our translation].

103 We can subsume this triptych under the acronym RER: "Recognition, Effectiveness and Renunciation".

104 See *infra* Part 2. Chapter 6. Section B.i.

105 For, as has been very ably pointed out, it is difficult to 'think of the exceptions to the prohibition of the use of force, and in particular self-defence, outside of any reference to a system of collective security, comparable to that organised today by the United Nations', Verhoeven (1987), 1217 [our translation].

106 See: Roberto Ago, "Third Report to the ILC on the International Responsibility of States", *YILC*, Vol. II, Part I, para. 41 (at 211): 'a trend towards incipient personification of the International Community' (with regard to the determination of "international crime"). *Contra* (erroneously) ICJ, Namibia 1971, para. 33 (at 241) [dissenting opinion of Judge Sir Gerald Fitzmaurice]: 'The notion therefore of such a community as a sort of permanent separate residual source or repository of powers and functions, which are re-absorbed on the extinction of one international organization, and then automatically and without special arrangement, given out to, or taken over by a new one, is quite illusory'; similarly: Lazare Kopelmanas, "La reconnaissance en droit international", 9 *Comunicazioni e Studi* 1957, 13.

"constitutional" rule-principles in the technical sense of the term in domestic public law, i.e., rules that can only be created, amended or repealed by a 'qualified majority' or through longer and more selective procedures than for ordinary laws.[107] As we have already observed above, the prohibition of the use of force is included among these rules and any violation of it could only be remedied by the cooperation of the entire International Community (or its "representative states", the *maior et sanior pars*)[108] in addition, of course, to the consent of the injured state. In this respect, the doctrine often refers to the 1954 Geneva Conference at which the colonial conflict in Indochina was brought to an end and the creation of North and South Vietnam was decided.[109] Article 6 of the "Final Act", however, offers a more nuanced and certainly less extensive reading of the Conference's power to dispose of territory:

> The Conference recognizes that the essential purpose of the agreement relating to Viet-Nam is to settle military questions with a view to ending hostilities and that the military demarcation line is provisional *and should not in any way be interpreted as constituting a political or territorial boundary*.[110]

---

107 "Once again, the realist observer sees the median structure of the juridical, "between" ethics and politics. The law, as has often been observed, mediates an ethical requirement within the political; and, conversely, it infuses something of the constraints of the political into the ethical domain. Thus, for example, it accommodates a majority decision-making procedure (which is certainly not the best ethical criterion), but takes care, in a democratic regime, to ensure both the fundamental rights of the minority and the always provisional and reversible character of the majority", Michel van de Kerchove, François Ost, *Le droit ou les paradoxes du jeu*, Paris, 1992, 231 [our translation].

108 'The attitude of non-recognition may undergo a change by virtue of a collective decision of the International Community. In law, there is a fundamental difference between such a decision and individual acts of recognition. Judge Sir Robert Jennings wrote of "some sort of collectivisation of the process, possibly through the United Nations itself" [1963, 61]. But up till now nothing of the sort has happened with regard to East Timor. Nor is there any consolidation of the Indonesian 'title' through other means', dissenting opinion of Judge Skubiszewski appended to the Judgment of the International Court of Justice in the Case concerning East Timor (Portugal v. Australia), judgment of 30 June 1995: *ICJ Reports* 1995, para. 132 (at 265).

109 The photo of the "Big Four" in front of the main entrance of the European UN headquarters in Geneva is emblematic because one cannot help but see a reverberation of the Yalta and Potsdam summits in 1945. It should be recalled that 19 other countries participated in this conference from 26 April to 21 July 1954, the day the "Final Act and Related Declarations" were adopted.

110 21 July 1954, *Foreign Relations Of The United States, 1952–1954*, The Geneva Conference, Volume XVII (96.1 GE/7–2154), emphasis added. In a similar vein (*ius contra bellum*), it should be pointed out that this provisional line – which was short-lived because of a new

This conference embodies the traditional, non-institutional and non-organic approach, which we have previously dealt with, and which is illustrated in particular by the European Concert. In this sub-section, however, we must ask ourselves whether the UNC has introduced an element of institutional novelty with regard to the "centrality of legal qualification" in the person of the UNSC or whether it has left unchanged the horizontality of this function as it existed in the past.[111] In short, can it be said loud and clear that the Security Council is the only, or the most authorised, centre of qualification of the International Community? Is it the Areopagus?

We posit that the institutional response (legal qualification) to an illegal factual situation can only emanate from an organ (or "Social Body") that enjoys both effectiveness and legitimacy in this sense.[112] While the UNSC (perhaps) satisfies the first of these two conditions by virtue of the powers conferred on it by Chapter VII of the Charter, the same cannot necessarily be said of the second. The validity of the legal characterisation of a situation depends on these two requirements being met. For, as we have seen, only the legal qualification of the International Community can grant or deny the territorial transfer the *titulus adquisitionis* alongside the consent of the injured State.

In the Advisory Opinion on the 'Legal Consequences for States of the Continued Presence of South Africa', the ICJ repeatedly referred to the 'qualifying power' of the Security Council, stating that:

> A binding determination made by a competent organ of the United Nations to the effect that a situation is illegal cannot remain without consequence.[113]

This qualification power of the Security Council, which is not expressly stated in the UNC, has developed from a consistent practice[114] of recognition and

conflict that finally ended in 1975 – was nevertheless protected by Article 2 para. 4. In other words, any violation of this line, however provisional, constituted an unlawful use of force (see UNGA Resolution 2625 and ICJ, Wall in Palestine, 2004, para. 87 (at 171)).

111 Vera Gowlland-Debbas, *Collective Responses to Illegal Acts in International Law. United Nations Action in the Question of Southern Rhodesia,* Leiden, 1990, 143 [hereinafter: (1990–2)], is of the (right) opinion that the UNC and the institutionalisation of legal relations that it engenders has led to a shift from *uti singuli* recognitions to a centralised legitimating function.

112 Effectiveness, it ought to be remembered, corresponds to *modus adquisitionis,* while legality refers to *titulus adquisitionis*.

113 ICJ, Namibia 1971, para. 117 (at 54).

114 See Vincenzo Villani, "Lo status della Repubblica serbo-montenegrina nelle Nazioni Unite", 76 *Rivista* 1993, 31. In general and for further information on this practice: Giuliana

(especially) non-recognition of illegal situations on the basis of Chapter VII of the Charter and its Article 39.[115] When the Security Council, which has the primary competence to determine a breach or threat to the peace or an act of aggression (Art. 39), for the purpose of triggering measures under Chapter VII, finds that the International Community is faced with one or other of these situations, it may, as a first "sanction", declare its illegality.[116] The Security Council thus enjoys, by virtue of and within the limits contained in articles 39 and 41[117] and on the basis of its practice, the prerogative of qualifying certain territorial situations.[118] However, this competence is not exclusive, but primary, as the Security Council must share it with the General Assembly in accordance with the interpretation of the relevant provisions of the UNC given by UNGA resolution 377 (V) (3 November 1950). Moreover, the "dilution" of these institutional competences in the more general and decidedly more representative participation of the International Community through its various "qualification centres" should also be mentioned.

Ziccardi Capaldo, *Le situazioni territoriali illegitime nel diritto internazionale*, Naples, 1977, 99 ff; Conforti (1994), 186–194; Gerhard Zimmer, *Gewaltsame territoriale Veränderungen und ihre völkerrechtliche Legitimation*, Berlin, 1971.

115 See, e.g., Resolutions Nos. 242, 267 (4th OP), 298 (3rd OP), 541, 550 (3rd OP). See, in general, Gowlland-Debbas (1990–2), 145–152.

116 See ICJ, Namibia 1971, para. 111 (at 52); Sir Robert Jennings (1963), 79; Jean Combacau, *Le pouvoir de sanction de l'ONU. Etude théorique de la coercition non militaire*, Paris, 1974, 157; Gowlland-Debbas (1990–2), 153.

117 See Conforti (1994), 194. *Contra*: ICJ, Namibia 1971, para. 115 [at 294; dissenting opinion of Judge Sir Gerald Fitzmaurice].

118 See Cassese (1986), para. 38 (at 69). In this respect, it would be useful to remember that in this "determination/qualification" function, the Security Council not only enjoys an absolutely discretionary margin of maneuver, but also and above all that its judgement (and the ensuing binding decisions) appears to be without appeal. As a result, the power of "qualification" in situations under Art. 39 of the Charter would seem to know no bounds and limitations, and only the consistent practice of that body should prevent abuses (or omissions) in the performance of this essential task, through self-interpretation (and, therefore, self-opposability). In the light of these considerations, we can only share the concerns expressed by the delegate of Zimbabwe in his intervention at the Security Council meeting of 31 March 1992 (S/PV. 3063, 54–55): '[T]his 15-member Council acts on behalf of a total of 175 States Members of the United Nations. This means that 160 States have placed their security, and possibly their very survival, in the hands of the 15. This a solemn and heavy responsibility that each and every member of the Council carries. It is therefore of crucial importance that every decision taken by the Security Council be able to withstand the careful scrutiny of the 160 Member States on whose behalf the Council is expected to act [as per Art. 24 (1) UNC]'.

In the wake of the Security Council's function to validate or invalidate territorial titles, can we also speak of adjudication of territories in the same way as it was done before 1945?[119]

At this stage, one can only sketch out a tentative answer, since, apart from situations of legal qualification, the Security Council has only once been confronted with this kind of problem: UNSC resolution 687 (1991) ending the conflict between Kuwait (and its allies) and Iraq. This resolution, which could be equated, for its aspects, to a peace treaty[120] between Iraq – having violated a rule of *ius cogens* (Article 2 para. 4 UNC) – and the entire International Community acting through UNSC, contained the mandate of the Iraq-Kuwait Boundary Demarcation Commission. The Security Council would thus have the competence under Art. 39 to proceed through a Commission "to demarcate a boundary between two Member States in the context of the maintenance of peace and security".[121] The same could also be said of the Security Council's power to *set* "restrictive conditions on the permanent status of [part of] the territory of [a Member State]" in relation to the Serbian province of Kosovo.[122]

Even more striking is the case of the territories acquired (conquered?) by the State of Israel following the first Arab Israeli war in 1949. This new state, which founded its application for admission to the UN on the 1947 Partition

119 *Contra*: 'There is more. *Even when acting under Chapter VII of the Charter itself*, the Security Council has no power to abrogate or alter territorial rights, whether of sovereignty or administration. Even a war-time occupation of a country or territory cannot operate to do that. It must await the peace settlement. This is a principle of international law that is as well-established as any there can be, – and the Security Council is as much subject to it (for the United Nations is itself a subject of international law) as any of its member States are. The Security Council might, after making the necessary determinations under Article 39 of the Charter, order the occupation of a country or piece of territory *in order to restore peace and security*, but it could not thereby, or as part of that operation, abrogate or alter territorial rights; – and the right to administer a mandated territory is a territorial right without which the territory could not be governed, or the mandate be operated. It was to keep the peace, not to change the world order, that the Security Council was set up', Dissenting Opinion of Judge Sir Gerald Fitzmaurice attached to the ICJ Advisory Opinion in the Namibia case 1971, para. 115 (at 294; italics in the text).

120 Giorgio Gaja, "Reflections on the Role of the Security Council in the New World Order", 97 *RGDIP* 1993, 312.

121 Jean-Pierre Queneudec, "La démarcation de la frontière entre l'Irak et le Koweït", 97 *RGDIP* 1993, 774. Similarly: Maurice H Mendelson, Hulton, SC "The Iraq-Kuwait Boundary", 64 *BYIL* 1993, 146, 147 [who consider, however, that the Security Council, not being an "adjudicative body", could only proceed to delimitation and not to demarcation, 147–148].

122 Accordance with international law of the unilateral declaration of independence in respect of Kosovo, Advisory Opinion of 22 July 2010, *ICJ Reports*, 2010, para. 114 (at 449).

Plan adopted by the General Assembly,[123] was tacitly and subsequently recognised for its territorial conquests in relation to the Partition Plan. Indeed, numerous UN resolutions (both Security Council and General Assembly) require Israel to withdraw within the 1949 armistice lines (the 'Green Line').[124] This means that the UN has ended up recognising (at least since 1967) implicitly the Israeli conquest of those territories that were originally allocated – by the Partition Plan – to the future Arab state of Palestine. In many respects, this acquisition of territory represents, leaving aside the still unresolved case of Crimea – and of the other (four) illegally annexed regions of Ukraine (Donetsk, Luhansk, Kherson and Zaporizhzhia) –, the latest (validated) *conquest* in the history of international law[125] and the only one since the UNC.

Consequently, the adjudication of territorial titles[126] would thus seem to be admitted by this practice which would revive the function once granted to the Concert of Powers and, further still, to the Pope.[127] Moreover, would this not be the meaning to be attributed to one of the two safeguard clauses to the principle of the inadmissibility of the acquisition of territory by force, contained in resolution 2625? The General Assembly, after affirming this paramount principle, which is the cornerstone of the international law of territory, takes care to specify that: '(b) the powers of the Security Council under the Charter'.

Therefore, in the light of this fragment, we may wonder whether the Security Council has succeeded to the "Concert of Great Powers", or, even before that to, Emperor/Pope (pre-1600 century).[128] For the reasons mentioned above and for others that will be explained later in this sub-chapter, it can be argued that the

123 UNGA Resolution 181 (II), adopted on 29 November 1947. See *infra* Part 2. Chapter 6. Section B.iv.

124 ICJ, Wall in Palestine, 2004, paras. 72–78 (at 166).

125 See Giovanni Distefano, "Effectivités et titres territoriaux en Palestine mandataire". G Distefano, "Effectivités et titres territoriaux en Palestine mandataire", in *Les compétences de l'État en droit international*, Paris, 2005, 185–200.

126 For this is what it is all about, since UNSC decided *ratione imperii* that the Iraq-Kuwait agreement was valid, thus making it the (only) legal title on which the definition of the border should be based. This means that, in the final analysis, the Security Council 'validated' a legal title in concrete terms.

127 Not to mention the League of Nations in the cases of Jaworzina and Mosul. With regard to the former, one cannot help but see analogies with the Demarcation Commission in the Iraq-Kuwait boundary (see in this respect PCIJ's advisory opinion on Jaworzina case (Polish-Czechoslovakian Frontier), *Reports of the PCIJ*, advisory opinion of December 6, 1923, B 8, 40).

128 This is the "de facto international government" thesis. See Michel Virally, 'L'O.N.U. devant le droit', in *Le droit international en devenir. Essais écrits au fil des ans*, Paris-Geneva, 1990, 260–261. See also *infra* Part 3. Chapter 8. Section C (in the specific context of "objective territorial regimes").

Security Council alone cannot, in view of the current structure of international society, represent the only "centre of qualification", but that this function must be sought in the International Community at large (General Assembly or "representative states" outside the UN forums). For this structural institutionalisation that has been observed for at least two centuries in the International Community does not necessarily mean the "verticalisation" of legal relations. The "primacy" of the Security Council, established by the UNC and by the joint action of the above-mentioned provisions, has not upset the structure of the international legal order and its qualification "mechanisms", which remains eminently "polycentric". On the other hand, since 1945 and by virtue of the UNC and the normative General Assembly's resolutions, there has been a notable evolution in the "substantive" principles (the "values") that govern the legal relations between States, and from which they draw inspiration in their free legal "qualification" of territorial situations.[129] In this respect, it is worth highlighting the role of 'oracle' that UNGA has played since 1945.[130]

It could be said, then, that the function and power of 'legal qualification' of illegal territorial situations, tending either to their condemnation or to their remediation, remains polycentric. In the sense that the conclusive attitude of international society must be sought not only in the positions of the UN (and the competent regional organisations), but also in the behaviour of third

129 It is worth recalling that the principles of international law relating to the use and threat of force, as well as those relating to forcible annexations (e.g., the right of peoples to self-determination), have evolved radically since at least the UNC. States do not, after all, pose a threat to the survival of international law, nor is it wrong to maintain that their conduct is increasingly inspired by legal considerations, and that this is done in accordance with the governing principle that permeates every area of the legal order and especially the international order, namely the principle of *good faith*. It is therefore ill-considered to demonise States and their attitudes in this respect at all costs, thus sacralising the virginal idea of a law that is as utopian in its content as it is dangerous in its consequences. Moreover, it should not be forgotten that it is the states that 'created' and believed in the rule prohibiting the use of force and in its necessity. As it is true that no state could now seriously argue, and indeed no state does, that such a rule does not exist or that it is not "peremptory". On the other hand, there is still disagreement as to the exact content of this rule, with different hermeneutical readings being proposed by both scientific and state doctrine. This proves, if proof were needed, that the rule exists and that it is surely revolutionary. Indeed, never before has the legal regulation of international relations gone so far. The established and consolidated presence of this rule has stripped states of one of their most effective and best-tested foreign policy tools. This faculty has accompanied, albeit sometimes with various limitations (e.g., the right to just war, *etc.*), the state and international society since its origin (see Distefano (2014)).

130 See: Abi-Saab (1987), 451.

states[131] *uti singuli*.[132] The "polycentrism" in the legal qualification of "facts" reflects the horizontal structure of international society and consequently the "atomization" of international power among the various states.

The identification of these "centres of qualification" is therefore not as easy as it may appear and the determination, in each case, of such a qualification is, in the eyes of the jurist, a painstaking and meticulous task. This difficulty is compounded by the temporal aspect, i.e., that the same States (or groups of States) may issue different legal qualifications throughout time: there is therefore no reason to neglect the diachronic and dynamic character of legality in international law. Because of the "polycentrism" of legal qualification, in order for it to be truly effective and efficient, there must be "assonance", or at least a relative "convergence" among the various "centres". In this perspective, the legal qualification of the International Community for the reorganisation of the territorial situation can be compared to the case of the (constitutive?) recognition[133] of new States resulting from violent secessions, which we will discuss *below* (see Part 2. Chapter 6. Section B.i).[134] As a conclusion to this subsection, we would like to reproduce a passage from an authoritative textbook in which its author acknowledges the ineradicable role of violence in international relations by looking candidly at this reality:

131 See the legitimate perplexities of Dupuy (*Droit international public*, 5th edn, Paris, 2000, para. 42) when he wonders about the legal effects of the "tacit consent" of third States with regard to an illegal territorial situation: 'In other words, in such situations, does effectiveness end up taking precedence over illegality?' [our translation]. In this respect, and we cannot but agree, this author stigmatises the ambiguity of the International Court of Justice in the East Timor case (1995).

132 In this sense: *Oppenheim's International Law*, para. 275 (at 715).

133 In this light, how can one fail to consider the legal significance of the statement of ad hoc Judge Krécka in the case concerning Application of the Convention on the Prevention and Punishment of the Crime of Genocide (Bosnia and Herzegovina v. Yugoslavia), Judgment of 11 July 1996 (Preliminary Objections): ICJ *Reports* 1996, para. 24 (at 683): '*In the light of the foregoing it may be said that the relevant factual and legal status of Bosnia and Herzegovina as a State within the administrative borders of the same ex-federal unit, may be defined as a political project of the organized international community, whose materialization was transformed by the Dayton Agreements into a binding obligation of the Parties to the Agreements*' [italics in the text].

134 This led Starke to speak of an "international quasi-adjudication of territory", John G Starke, "The Acquisition of Title to Territory by Newly Emerged States", 41 BYIL 1965–1966, 413. In the same sense: Sir Robert Jennings (1963), 37; Shaw (1986), 169. *Contra* H Kelsen, *Das Problem der Souveränität und die Theorie des Völkerrechts, beitrag zu einer reinen Rechtslehre*, Tübingen, 1920, para. 54 (at 258); Panayis A Papaligouras, *Théorie de la société internationale*, Geneva, 1941, 223; Hough III, 470–471 (who argues that this quasi-legislative function would conflict with the right of peoples to self-determination).

> New situations are not recognised as legally valid unless they can be seen to rest on a firm and durable display of authority. Rebellions, the splitting up of existing States, the emergence of new entities, and so forth: none of these new situations can claim international legitimacy so long as the 'new men' fail to demonstrate that they have firmly supplanted the former authority [...] The formal 'endorsement' of power tends to legalise and crystallise it.[135]

The effectiveness of the situation *qualified by* the passive or benevolent attitude of the International Community, to say the least, could, together with the consent of the dispossessed State, give rise to a valid *titulus adquisitionis*. In this case, the International Community subsequently, and once the *status quo ante has been* re-established, issues a new qualification, through the fiction of retroactive restoration of sovereignty. We will then speak of 'dormant sovereignty'[136] (as happened to the three Baltic States after 1940 following their annexation by the Soviet Union).[137]

iii *The Principle of the Inadmissibility of the Acquisition of Territory by Force and the Obligation of Non-recognition*

In the wake of the emerging need in the international legal order not to grant legal protection to certain illegal situations, States are henceforth under an obligation not to recognise them. While it is true that the existence of a state, or even a territorial situation, depends on its actual existence, it is also true

135 A Cassese (1986), para. 10 (at 27). Of course, the case referred to in this quotation is in some respects different from the one under consideration. It is nevertheless indicative of a certain (and correct) conception of the relationship between law and fact.

136 On the Soviet annexation of the Polish eastern territories following the infamous 1939 Molotov-Von Ribbentrop agreement and the ensuing armed conflict, see *The Soviet Takeover of the Polish Eastern Provinces, 1939–1941*, Keith Sword (ed.), Basingstoke, 1991. However, the International Community's non-recognition of the Soviet annexation of the Baltic states eventually paid off, as this continued attitude allowed the *covert* existence of the previous sovereignties. This is again a manifestation of the principle of *dynamic legality*.

137 The historian N Davies (737) offers a vivacious description of the extinction/suspension of the sovereignty of the three Baltic States and the 'temporary' annexation by the USSR: 'In 1940, the Soviet takeover of three Baltic States was accompanied by a combination of military invasions, phoney 'referendums' and international perplexity. Handpicked delegates were assembled. Portraits of Stalin were paraded. The public was terrorized. Critics were harassed or physically removed. The result was known in advance, and the world was told that the victimized countries had joyfully petitioned Moscow for admission to the USSR. In the process, the 'bourgeois republics' were liquidated. Suicide by coercion' might also fit'.

that, as the *modus / titulus* dichotomy tells us, this is not sufficient. Besides effectiveness (*modus*), international law requires – first and foremost – validity (*titulus*) for the territorial situation in question to be legally valid and therefore opposable *erga omnes*.

Therefore, a territorial situation that is brought about in defiance of a peremptory norm of international law (*ius cogens*), such as the one prohibiting the use of force and the one guaranteeing the right of peoples to self-determination, lacks the necessary condition of *titulus* and is not only unworthy of legal protection by international law, but also constitutes a violation of it. The international legal order, in order to prevent the entrenchment of these situations, contains the obligation of non-recognition. In other words, the obligation of non-recognition derives from the principle of the inadmissibility of the acquisition of territory by force, an overarching principle of the international law of territory, itself a corollary of the aforementioned norms of *ius cogens*. It is now codified in UNGA resolution 2625 (XXV):

> The territory of a State shall not be the object of acquisition by another State resulting from the threat or use of force.[138]

The seeds[139] of the concept of the doctrine of 'non-recognition' must be sought in the plurilateral agreements between the Latin American states[140]

138 It was more recently reaffirmed by the UNGA in its resolution A/ES-11/L.1. (2 March 2022) condemning the aggression of Ukraine by the Russian Federation (paras. 6,11).

139 'The refusal to recognise certain internationally relevant acts or facts as treaties, agreements or territorial mutations, on the ground that their formation is unlawful, is ab antiquo, a means adopted in the international field', Carlo Cereti, "Il non-riconoscimento come pretesa sanzione", in *Scritti giuridici in onore di Santi Romano*, Vol. III, Padua, 1940, 149; Kotani, 9; Georges Scelle, *Manuel de droit international public*, Paris, 1948, 179–180: this author considers, however, that the effectiveness of the recognition (or non-recognition) function is subject to the existence of an international institutional organisation that provides for compulsory arbitration, jurisdiction and review procedures. Can such an institutionalisation be found in the system provided for by the Charter in Article 33 and Chapter VII?

140 These treaties codify a conspicuous practice of collective refusal to recognise territorial changes effected by force. See, for example: the Declaration of the Diplomatic Corps (of Representatives of Latin American Countries) of 20 April 1864 meeting in Lima which adopted a common position of refusing the Spanish occupation of the Chincha Islands belonging to Peru, quoted in *Bruns*, FB11 para. 1402; '.[The High Contracting Parties] declare that between the High Contracting Parties territorial questions must not be settled by resort to violence and that they shall recognize no territorial arrangement not obtained through pacific means, nor the validity of an occupation or acquisition of territory brought about by armed force', Article II of the Anti-War Treaty (Non-Aggression and Conciliation), signed at Rio de Janeiro on 10 October 1933, *LNTS*, Vol. 163 (1935–1936),

where they found their first normative elaboration.[141] Its *ratio iuris* derives from the Latin maxim: *Quod initio vitiosum est, non potest tractu temporis convalescere.*[142] In other words, time cannot restore that which is contrary to the law from its origin. As has been rightly pointed out, '[t]he object of the policy or the obligation of non-recognition is not to render illegal an otherwise lawful and valid act; its object is to prevent the validation of what is a legal nullity'.[143] In the European continent, and for purposes antipodal to those prevailing in the Latin American continent, the European Concert gave birth to the doctrine of non-recognition based on dynastic legitimacy. Principle 2 of the Protocol of Troppau (19 November 1820) read as follows:

> The Powers undertake to deny recognition to changes effected by illegal means.[144]

Despite its prodromal stages, the doctrine of non-recognition was eventually dubbed the "Stimson Doctrine" after the name of the US Secretary of State

---

405; Resolution concerning the illegality of the Right of Conquest, adopted by the First Conference of American States in Washington on 19 April 1890, *NRG*, 3rd series, Vol. 6, 120; 'The essential content of non-recognition of a territorial transfer is the refusal, of the part of a non-recognizing Power, to regard the sovereignty of the dispossessed Power over the area in question as ended and the sovereignty of the dispossessing Power as established', Robert Langer, *Seizure of Territory. The Stimson Doctrine and Related Principles*, Princeton, 1947, 100. For a history of the diplomatic and legal developments of the institution of non-recognition, see Sir Hersch Lauterpacht (1947), para. 122.

141 However, we can find the harbingers of this doctrine in the Protocol of Troppau, signed at the eponymous Congress (19 November 1820) by Austria, Prussia and Russia. Principle 3 was formulated as follows: 'When the States in which the changes have thus taken place cause other countries to fear an imminent danger["threat to the peace" of Article 39 UNC?] by their proximity["spillover"], and, when the Allied Powers are able to take effective and beneficial action against them, they will employ, in order to bring them back into the alliance, firstly, friendly approaches [today's article 41 UNC?] and secondly coercive force, if the use of force becomes indispensable [today's article 42 UNC]', Georg Friedrich De Martens, *Recueil des traités et conventions conclus par la Russie avec les puissances étrangères*, Tome 4 (I), Saint-Pétersbourg, 1874, 33 [our translation].

142 D.50.17.29 [Paulus lib.8 ad Sabinum]: "Time cannot validate an act which is null in principle".

143 Sir Hersch Lauterpacht (1947), 413.

144 De Martens (1874), 33 [our translation]. Equally eloquent, in a related vein (the maintenance of international peace and security), is the above-mentioned Principle 3 (*supra* note 141).

who sent a diplomatic note dated 7 January 1932 to the Japanese ambassador in Washington,[145] stating that his Government:

> does not intend to recognise any situation, treaty or agreement which may be brought about by means contrary to the covenants and obligations of the Pact of Paris of August 27, 1928, to which treaty both China and Japan, as well as the United States are parties.[146]

After its invasion of Manchuria[147] (a region of the Republic of China), Japan had in fact rushed to create the puppet state of Manchukuo,[148] with a view to disguising its *de facto* annexation. However, Japan was a party to the 1928 Briand-Kellogg Pact and was therefore bound by the obligation not to resort to war as an "instrument of national policy" (Article 1). Consequently, a war of aggression could hardly give rise to a valid title to territorial sovereignty, especially since the consent of the dispossessed state (China), the *sine qua non* of *titulus adquirendi,* was lacking. Of course, in the past, as we have seen, it was not uncommon for the International Community, in its various incarnations, to disregard this requirement in order to recognise the illegal territorial situation and thus finally establish it in law (see Part 2. Chapter 5. Section B.i *above*). The "Stimson Doctrine", however, set an insurmountable limit to this power vested in certain states that were supposed to act as the governing body of the

145 An identical diplomatic note was sent the same day to the Chinese ambassador in Washington.

146 Text in 26 *AJIL* 1932, 342 [emphasis added]. On the Stimson doctrine, see among other references cited above: Hans Wehberg, 'Die Stimson Doktrin', in *Festschrift Spiropoulos*, Bonn, 1957, 433–444; Quincy Wright, "The Stimson Note of January 7, 1932", 26 *AJIL* 1932, 342–348; Sir John Fischer Williams, "The New Doctrine of Recognition", in 18 *Transactions of the Grotius Society* 1932, 109–130, which develops very pertinent considerations on the synergies of the principle of non-recognition with the requirements of legality. An archetype of the Stimson doctrine can be found in the argumentation of the jurist Caramanico in the XIII century [Francesco Calasso, *I glossatori e la teoria della sovranità*, Milan, 1957].

147 See generally on the Manchurian question, Roland H Sharp, *Non-Recognition as a Legal Obligation*, Geneva, 1934, 141–148, who followed the question closely because of his presence in Geneva during the crisis. On the fallacy of the LoN sanctions: the author relates (p.167 and note 1) a personal anecdote, according to which he received, during his stay in Geneva, the official Bulletins of the Ministry of Foreign Affairs of the Government of Manchukuo, despite the non-recognition of this Government and the recognition of the immanence of Chinese sovereignty over this territory. Notwithstanding this, and notwithstanding the fact that Manchukuo was hardly a member of the UPU, its postage stamps were honoured in Switzerland where both the LoN and the Universal Postal Union had their headquarters.

148 On the notion of "puppet State" in International Law, see *infra* Part 2. Chapter 7. Section A.

International Community. The United States of America[149] as well as the other countries of the American continent made non-recognition a pillar of their foreign legal policy.[150] International[151] and domestic courts frequently refer to it and very often based their *ratio decidendi on* it:

> Our Government [of the United States of America] as a national policy has refused recognition of any puppet government of any country which has been the victim of aggression and has refused recognition of de facto control set up by an aggressor.[152]

The Stimson Note also had institutional repercussions, as it was followed first by an 'Appeal' issued by the President of the Council of the League of Nations, reaffirming that:

> No encroachment upon the territorial integrity or political independence of a Member of the League of Nations, committed in disregard of Article 10 [of the Covenant], shall be recognized as valid and effective by the Members of the League.[153]

A month later – the Assembly of the League of Nations solemnly adopted a resolution proclaiming the principle of the refusal of recognition of a territorial acquisition obtained by "illicit" means:

149 "The Stimpson [sic] statement ... shows us the official ideology by which the United States of America tried to justify its 'denial' of *recognition*", Papaligouras, 218 [emphasis added].

150 "The United States has not recognized the annexation by the Soviet Union of the Baltic States ... In most practical respects they [their citizens] will have to be treated as stateless persons", Memorandum (April 29, 1946), in *Selected Opinions*, Vol. III, 47, 49 [Office of Military Government for Germany, U.S. Legal Division, March 1, 1946 – May 15, 1946]. This position was reaffirmed in 1960 on the occasion of the 42nd anniversary of the declarations of independence of the three Baltic States, cf. Department of State press release N°65, Feb.15, 1960, in *Bulletin of State*, Vol. 42, N°1080 (March 7, 1960), 361; In Re Alexandravicus' Estate, Supreme Court of New Jersey, 30 June 1961, 32 *ILR*, 74.

151 Arbitral Tribunal for Dispute over Inter-Entity Boundary in Brcko Area, para. 77 (at 422).

152 In Re Grauds' Estate, 42; similarly: United States ex Rel. Schwarzkopf v. UHL (District Director of Immigration), Circuit Court of Appeals (Second Circuit), award delivered the 18 August 1943, 12 *ILR*, 194.

153 Appeal dated 16 February 1932, addressed to the Japanese Government by the President of the Council of the League of Nations, on behalf of the Members of the Council other than the Representatives of China and Japan, *Official Journal*, 12th year, No. 3 (March 1932), 383. "These collective obligations of non-recognition of consequence of acts contrary to international law constitute a new feature of international practice", Sir Hersch Lauterpacht (1947), 419.

> Members of the League of Nations are obliged not to recognize any situation, treaty or agreement which might be reached by means contrary to the Covenant of the League of Nations or the Paris Pact.[154]

And in this case the Member States were enjoined not to recognise the new territorial situation unilaterally:

> The members of the League will continue to recognize this regime neither *de jure* nor *de facto*. They intend to refrain, with regard to the situation in Manchuria, from any isolated action and to continue to concert their action among themselves, as well as with that of interested States not members of the League.[155]

The vast majority of the LoN member states[156] complied with this obligation and refused to recognise *uti singuli* the state of Manchukuo.[157]

At the same time, another conflict saw the application of the "Stimson Doctrine": the Chaco Boreal or Great Chaco conflict (1932–1935) between Bolivia and Paraguay. Indeed, on 3 August 1932, in the midst of the conflict, the representatives of nineteen Latin American states – meeting in Washington – adopted a collective declaration in which they undertook not to:

> recognise any territorial arrangement which has not been obtained by peaceful means nor the validity of territorial acquisitions through occupation or conquest by force of arms.[158]

154 Resolution adopted by the Assembly of the League of Nations at its fourth plenary meeting on 11 March 1932, *Official Journal*, Special Supplement No. 101, 87.

155 Report under Article 15, paragraph 4, of the Covenant, prepared by the Special Committee of the Assembly in pursuance of Part III (paragraph 5) of the resolution of 11 March 1932, and adopted by the Assembly on 24 February 1933, *Official Journal*, Special Supplement No. 112, Part IV, Section 3, 76.

156 Which were also Contracting Parties to the Treaty concerning the renunciation of war as an instrument of national policy ("Briand-Kellog" Pact), signed in Paris on 27 August 1928, *NRG*, 3rd series, Vol. 21, 3.

157 Each state unilaterally did not recognise the puppet state of Manchukuo, so that one cannot speak in this instance of collective non-recognition, but rather of an obligation arising from the resolution of the N.D.S. and which the states fulfilled individually. The difference with respect to a collective position or qualification is therefore significant and is due to the different institutional structure of the International Community, in comparison with what was happening previously (European Concert) and what is currently taking shape.

158 *Department of State Press Release*, August 3, 1932. The territorial dispute was finally settled by an arbitration submitted to a Tribunal formed by the ambassadors of the American

They wanted to reaffirm the American continent's tradition of refuting the validity of forcible territorial changes.[159] In addition, another crisis had erupted in the South American continent, involving Peru and Colombia. This territorial dispute, which originated in a boundary treaty signed in March 1922, escalated into a full-blown armed conflict when Peruvian irregulars seized the Colombian town of Leticia. They were immediately disavowed by the Peruvian government, but strongly supported and backed by its local authorities. The LoN took up the issue and on 18 March 1933, the Council adopted a resolution establishing an "Advisory Committee to monitor the situation".[160] The recitals preceding the operative part of the resolution list the various normative instruments by which both the LoN and the American States:

> declared ... that they would not recognise the validity of any territorial acquisitions that might be obtained by an occupation of conquest effected by force of arms.[161]

The last case before the UN Charter is represented by the annexation of Ethiopia by Italy following the 1935–36 conflict initiated by the latter. With regard to the said annexation[162] sanctioned by the Decree-Law of the Kingdom of Italy of 9 May 1936 (No. 754), no resolution similar to the one adopted during the Manchukuo crisis was adopted; this made it easier (or, at least, less embarrassing) for Member States to behave as they were left free to recognise or not to

---

states, which was called upon to decide *ex aequo et bono*, but whose arbitration compromise, by restricting the spatial extent of the Tribunal's jurisdiction, ended up by ratifying in advance a considerable part of the Paraguayan acquisitions obtained during the conflict. See in this regard: Distefano (2002), 440–452.

159 This conclusion must be, though, nuanced, because the peace settlement finally imposed on the two belligerent parties by the Organisation of American States (OAS) provided for an arbitration whose special agreement empowered the six Representatives of the American States to rule *ex aequo et bono*, ratifying *ex ante* the territorial conquests of Paraguay. In the end, the arbitrators had to confine themselves to drawing the limits, rather narrow ones at that, of these appropriations made by force of arms.

160 The Leticia issue and its outcome are also examined from the perspective of direct international administration (by the League of Nations), see *infra* Part 3. Chapter 10. Section A.ii.

161 Resolution adopted by the Council of the LoN on 18 March 1933 at its 71st extraordinary meeting convened under Art. 15 of the Pact, at the request of the Government of Colombia, *Official Journal*, 14th session, No. 4 (Part 1), April 1933, 526.

162 On the facts and circumstances of this war and the territorial dispute which sparked it, see in general: Pier Angelo Sereni, *La rappresentanza nel diritto internazionale*, Padua, 1936. For the vicissitudes of this affair within the League of Nations, see *Official Journal*, special supplements no. 145–150 and 164.

recognise the new "fait accompli".[163] Indeed, the new territorial status (leading to the proclamation of the "Impero d'Italia e di Etiopia") was eventually recognised by forty-four states. These forty-four recognitions, which represented a strong majority in 1936 (especially since the European and Western countries were all there), "cleaned up"[164] the wrong perpetrated by Italy in 1935 (armed aggression), and the resulting illegal situation (territorial annexation).[165]

---

163 The implementation of economic sanctions was indeed left to the discretion of individual Member States. See Joachim A Frowein, "Article 39", in *United Nations Charter. A Commentary*, 1st edn, Oxford, 1995, 607.

164 This is notwithstanding the resolution of 11 March 1932 condemning conquest as a means of acquiring territory.

165 It is interesting in this respect to study the reasons that led Switzerland, a neutral country and member of the LoN (which, moreover, had not associated itself with the sanctions policy decided by the LoN against Italy following the conflict), to recognise the new territorial qualification. The reasons for this were political (Italy was a Great Power at the time), "good neighbourliness", but above all necessity, namely the concern to see Swiss interests in Ethiopia protected. But Switzerland also did not want a possible non-recognition to be interpreted as a "condemnation": "The postponement of recognition could, not without reason, be considered as a coercive measure which our country has in no way undertaken to take", *Répertoire de la pratique suisse de droit international public. Documentation concerning the practice of the Confederation in matters of public international law 1914–1939*, Basel, 1975, 457 [our translation]. The concern to see one's own interests protected was expressed by the Swiss Political Department as follows: "[R]ecognition is indispensable if the third State wishes to safeguard its interests in the conquered territory, since this safeguard can only be ensured with the *new holder of sovereignty*" (460; emphasis added; our translation). However, the same department was quick to point out that the 'Federal Council neither recognised nor even sanctioned the "conquest" of Ethiopia, but merely recognised Italian sovereignty over Ethiopia [...] The recognition ... does not affect the legal basis, the "causa", of the territorial acquisition; it focuses only on the fact that the rights of sovereignty have changed' (*loc. cit.*; our translation). This is the quintessence of diplomatic art! Indeed, one may ask where there is any difference from the legal point of view. The position thus assumed by Swiss Government, while irreproachable from a political point of view, leaves us perplexed from the standpoint of strict legal logic. It is nonetheless true that the attitude of the Swiss Federal Council in this instance is indicative of the significance of state attitudes in such cases. For example, in the East Timor case, Australia made it clear that its recognition of Indonesia's annexation of East Timor 'does not alter the opposition which the Government has consistently expressed regarding the manner of incorporation' (1995, para. 17 (at 98)). This subtle distinction is, however, difficult to establish in law, as was ably pointed out by Judges Weeramantry and Skubiszewski in their dissenting opinions attached to the judgment of the International Court of Justice in the above-mentioned case (201 and para. 119–122 respectively). As regards the concern for the protection of one's own interests with the "new holder" of sovereignty, it will not be tired of repeating that this follows from the very structure of the international legal order to which we have already referred. See: Cereti, 153–154; Balladore Pallieri (1962), 40–343; Langer, 147.

The UN Charter will erase the stain of the Abyssinian crisis and root the obligation of non-recognition permanently in the fabric of international law. Its article 2 para. 4 – enshrining the prohibition of force (and its threat) – in international relations between states, as well as Article 1 para. 2 – which brings the principle of the right of peoples to self-determination to the forefront – set insurmountable limits on the behaviour of states in matters of territorial acquisition. Several – important – rules in other areas of general international law shield the principle of territorial acquisition by force of arms. At the outset, mention should be made of resolution 2625 (XXV), which is, in this respect, the "mother" of all UN resolutions in this area. The Security Council, as the body with "primary responsibility for the maintenance of international peace and security" (Article 24 (1) UNC), referred to it in the case of Israel's annexation of East Jerusalem,[166] 'call[ing] upon on all Member states' not to recognise the situation;[167] the same was true of Israel's annexation of the Golan Heights, which it described as 'null and void and without international legal effect'.[168] The Security Council reiterated this principle when Iraq annexed Kuwait following its war of aggression:

> *Calls upon* all States, international organizations and specialized agencies not to recognize that annexation, and to refrain from any action or dealing that might be interpreted as an indirect recognition of the annexation.[169]

With regard to the illegal annexation of Crimea by the Federation of Russia, with the Security Council unable to act because of the threat – wielded by the former – of its veto, the General Assembly called upon

166 Resolution 476 (30 June 1980).

167 Resolution 478 (20 August 1980). See also, more recently, its Resolution 2334 (23 December 2016).

168 Resolution 497 (17 December 1981). The UNGA followed suit with its resolution 37/123 (A) of 16 December 1982. On 28 September 2018, Palestine filed a case against the United States concerning a dispute over alleged violations of the 1961 Vienna Convention on Diplomatic Relations resulting from the respondent State's recognition (on 6 December 2017) of Jerusalem as the capital of Israel and the subsequent "relocation" of the US embassy in Israel from Tel Aviv to Jerusalem. The case is currently pending before the ICJ, with the Respondent having raised preliminary objections to the jurisdiction and admissibility of the application of the State of Palestine.

169 Resolution 662 (9 August 1990).

> all States, international organizations and specialized agencies not to recognize any alteration of the status of the Autonomous Republic of Crimea and the city of Sevastopol on the basis of the above-mentioned referendum and to refrain from any action or dealing that might be interpreted as recognizing any such altered status.[170]

Mored recently, and in the same context, the Security Council, blocked by the veto of the Russian Federation, referred the situation in Ukraine (under Article 11 para. 2 of the UNC) to the General Assembly which adopted on 2 March 2022, at its 11[171] (under Article 11 para. 2 of the UNC) the situation in Ukraine to the General Assembly, which adopted resolution ES-11/1 on 2 March 2022 at its 11th emergency special session. In this resolution, the General Assembly "deplores" the decision by the Russian Federation to recognise the independence of the Ukrainian regions of Donetsk and Luhansk, which 'constitutes a violation of the territorial integrity and sovereignty of Ukraine and [is] inconsistent with the principles of the Charter' (para. 5). In the same vein, on 12 October 2022, the UNGA:

> Condemn[ed] the organization by the Russian Federation of *illegal so-called referendums* in regions within the internationally recognized borders of Ukraine and the *attempted annexation* of the Donetsk, Kherson, Luhansk and Zaporizhzhia regions of Ukraine, following the organization of the above-mentioned referendums.[172]

In the same spirit, Article 52 VCLT 1969 strengthens the principle of the inadmissibility of the acquisition of territory by force by sanctioning the nullity of treaties concluded under 'coercion of a State by the threat or use of [unlawful] force'.[173] This obviously excludes peace treaties[174] where, so to speak, the act of

---

170 Resolution A/68/262 (27 March 2014).

171 Resolution 2623 (27 February 2022): 'Taking into account that the lack of unanimity of its permanent Members at its 8979th meeting has prevented it from exercising its primary responsibility for the maintenance of international peace and security'.

172 Resolution ES-11/4 (12 October 2022), para. 2 [emphasis added].

173 Both the International Court of Justice (Case concerning Fisheries Jurisdiction (United Kingdom v. Iceland), judgment of 25 July 1974 (Merits): *ICJ Reports* 1974, para. 24) and, inter alia, the arbitral tribunal in the Dubai-Sharjah Territorial Dispute case (para. 42), have found that Article 52 of the VCLT 1969 certainly codifies contemporary customary international law on the subject.

174 Paul Reuter, *Introduction au droit des traités*, 2nd edn, Paris, 1985, para. 257; Touscoz, 230. According to Bellini (336–337), the peace treaty ceding territory following an armed conflict provides the victorious state with the *titulus adquisitionis* it lacks, and this is why,

force or violence, whether illicit or not, forms the *causa*, in the civil law sense of the term, of the treaty. It is not external to it, but is the reason for it, it is consubstantial with the treaty itself.[175] But De Visscher is certainly right when he asks the question:

> The question is whether our contemporary international law still recognises the validity in principle of such a treaty.[176]

---

he says, recourse is always had to the treaty in order to legalise the territorial transfer. Otherwise, one would find oneself in the case of an effective occupation [valid *modus adquisitionis*], devoid of *titulus adquisitionis* [the territory not being *res nullius*], the Peace Treaty would therefore transfer the *titulus adquisitionis* [see the analogous situation in this respect in the case of 'voluntary' transfers of territory, *supra* Part 1. Chapter 2]. *Contra* Karl Heimburger, *Der Erwerb der Gebietshoheit: eine staats- und völkerrechtliche Studie*, Berlin, 1888, 127–139; Quadri (1968), 167, for whom *debellatio* would extinguish the State (in case of subjugation) or extinguish its territorial sovereignty over the occupied part of territory, so that it would become *res nullius*. Therefore: Peace treaties 'are often merely fictitious treaties' [in case of *total* occupation of the territory of the defeated state] (our translation), hence the configuration, by some authors, of the peace treaty as a unilateral act. However, as proof of the legal necessity of the treaty for the legitimisation of the territorial transfer, it can be argued that very often the territory to which the treaty relates does not always coincide with the territory occupied *manu militari* by the transferee state. Therefore, the fiction of the *res nullius* qualification of the territory subject to territorial transfer falls apart. It is sufficient for the transferee State to be "satisfied" with a smaller part of the territory than that actually occupied at the end of hostilities; or, conversely, that the simple occupation of a small part of the territory of the other State enables it to bring the latter to its knees and thus obtain a larger part by means of the Treaty (or even a different part). The thesis, therefore, that territory becomes *res nullius*, is hardly convincing in the light of both the concept of legal title and State practice. For a doctrinal overview of the authors who would configure in *debellatio* (or forcible annexation) a situation of *res nullius* following the disappearance of the territorial sovereignty of the defeated State, see M Giuliano (1951), 181 (note 2) and 182 (note 1). In the (Florence Strunsky-)Mergé case, decision (n°55) of 10 June 1955 by the Italian-American Conciliation Commission, *RIAA*, Vol. XIV, 238–239, it is clearly stated that: 'From the juridical point of view, the Treaty of peace is an international convention, not a unilateral act'. It seems to us that this passage reflects contemporary positive law.

175 Moreover, the peace treaty has always constituted a valid legal title for the purposes of territorial changes: "One of the ordinary incidents of a treaty is the cession of territory. It is not too much to say that it is the rule rather than the exception, *that a treaty of peace, following upon a war, provides for a cession of territory to the victorious party*", De Lima v. Bidwell (1901), *AILC* (1783–1968, Deak), Vol. 3, 279 [emphasis added]; Island of Palmas case, 846.

176 De Visscher (1967), 116 [our translation]. Formerly: Fiore (1868), 384. Thus the figure of 'peace treaties' can fall into the category of 'unequal treaties'; in this sense: Gureckas, 111–112. See UNGA Resolution 2625, *a contrario*, where it refers to agreements predating the Charter, and thus to the principle of the inadmissibility of the acquisition of territory by force.

But, despite the validity of this treaty, the consolidation of the new territorial situation it establishes may nevertheless contribute to its successive "validation" by other means[177] than the legal act of disposition of territory. All the more so since, under the terms of the aforementioned Resolution 2625, the principle of the inadmissibility of the acquisition of territory by force 'shall [not] be construed as affecting … (b) the powers of the Security Council under the Charter'. Therefore, because of the peremptory norm character of the prohibition of the threat and use of force, a treaty of territorial cession concluded between an aggressor and an aggressed state could not carry the *titulus adquisitionis*. Moreover, a UNSC resolution under Chapter VII would be required, which would endorse the content ("negotium") of the treaty.[178] This would have a double effect: on the one hand, it would shelter (by virtue of the UNC) the territorial cession, formally removing it from the empire of the law of treaties (and thus from the sanction of Article 52 VCLT 1969); on the other hand, this resolution would contribute to the validation of the territorial transfer under the heading of international institutional *recognition* (the triptych).

In the same vein, another important branch of general international law supports this fundamental principle of international law of territory, insofar as international humanitarian law introduces a safeguard against the possibility for the government of a state whose territory is – partially or even entirely – occupied by the other belligerent power to derogate from the provisions of the Fourth Geneva Convention of 1949 relative to the Protection of Civilian Persons in Time of War. This provision is based on the presumption that one of the parties to the conflict finds itself

> restricted, even temporarily, in its freedom to negotiate with the other Power or its allies by reason of military events, more particularly where the whole, or a substantial part, of the territory of the said Power is occupied.[179]

---

177 Sir Robert Jennings (1963), 77–78.

178 The Security Council has already resorted to this "subterfuge" in the aftermath of the military operations conducted by some NATO members against the Federal Republic of Yugoslavia in 1999. Resolution 1244, adopted on 10 June 1999, paved the way for a possible change in the territorial status of the Serbian province of Kosovo, in agreement with the interested parties (Belgrade and representatives of the Kosovar people). See Giovanni Distefano, "The Security Council and the Validation of Treaties Concluded by the Threat or Use of Force", in *La crise des Balkans de 1999. The Historical, Political and Legal Dimensions of the Kosovo Conflict*, Brussels, 2000, 167–192.

179 Article 11 para. 5 of the IV GE 1949.

In a way, this provision internalises the coercion by one State on another State when concluding a treaty that may derogate from the provisions of the Fourth Geneva Convention to the detriment of the Party temporarily in an unfavourable situation.[180] This factual condition would therefore *ipso iure* fulfil the condition that triggers the application of Article 52 VCLT 1969.

The right of peoples to self-determination, which will be discussed in more detail in the next section (Part 2. Chapter 6. Section A), is not left out insofar as it is guaranteed by the obligation of non-recognition denying any validity to territorial situations that are variance with it. In addition to UNSC resolutions regarding East Jerusalem, which attest to the violation of both the prohibition of the use of force *and* the principle of the right of peoples to self-determination, it is worth mentioning the famous case of Southern Rhodesia[181] ruled by a white minority government in defiance of multiple UN resolutions. The Security Council:

> 1. *Decide[d] to condemn* the unilateral declaration of independence made by a racist minority in Southern Rhodesia; 2. *Decide[d] to call upon* all States not to recognize this illegal racist minority régime in Sothern Rhodesia and to refrain from rendering any assistance to this illegal régime.[182]

We could conspicuously extend the list,[183] but it is more interesting, instead, to investigate the consequences of the non-recognition obligation reflected in this practice.

---

180 In this regard, UNSC Resolution 1546 (8 June 2004) on the situation in Iraq, which 'blessed' the agreement between the Iraqi government and the occupying powers, is at odds with Article 11(5) of the 1949 Geneva Convention. It is as if the New York Law (embodied in UNC) prevailed (or would have prevailed) over the Geneva Law (ICJ, Threat or Use of Nuclear Weapons, para. 75 (at 256)); or in other words, the imperatives of international peace and security prevailed (or would have prevailed) over the requirements of humanity embodied in IHL. By this agreement, in effect, the Iraqi authorities consented to the transformation of a military occupation into an occupation by invitation, while, among other flaws, serious doubts existed as to the representative character of the Iraqi government at that time.

181 See the seminal work on this subject: Gowlland-Debbas (1990–2).

182 UNSC Resolution 216 (16 November 1965).

183 However, we cannot ignore Resolution 541 (of 18 November 1983), in which the Security Council "2. *Considers* the declaration referred to above [of independence of the Turkish Republic of Northern Cyprus] as legally invalid and calls for its withdrawal;". As the Security Council ultimately determined that TRNC was thus a puppet state [supra Part 2. Chapter 5. Section A., 123 it "6. *Calls upon* all States to respect the sovereignty,

At the outset, the following question must be asked: if this obligation exists, as we are inclined to believe, under general international law, then the consequences flow for states independently of any action by the UNSC, the UNGA or, if applicable, a competent organ of a regional organisation.[184] In the latter case, the obligation would only exist by virtue of the decision of any of these bodies. In the latter case, it is important to verify its powers and, consequently, the legal effects of the decision.

Similarly, and irrespective of the answer to the first question, a distinction must be made, in the case of a decision taken by a competent organ, between the legal effects *inside the organisation* and those *outside*, i.e., at the level of general international law.

We believe that the two advisory opinions of the ICJ, in the *Namibia* case and in the *Palestine Wall case* respectively, serve as excellent navigational charts in this regard. It is worth reproducing two long extracts from these two Court pronouncements. First, in the Namibia case, in 1971, the Court observed that:

> With respect to existing bilateral treaties, member States must abstain from invoking or applying those treaties or provisions of treaties concluded by South Africa on behalf of or concerning Namibia which involve active intergovernmental co-operation. With respect to multilateral treaties, however, the same rule cannot be applied to certain general conventions such as those of a humanitarian character, the non-performance of which may adversely affect the people of Namibia. It will be for the competent international organs to take specific measures in this respect [...Member States] are under obligation to abstain from sending diplomatic or special missions to South Africa including in their jurisdiction the Territory of Namibia, to abstain from sending consular agents to Namibia, and to withdraw any such agents already there. They should also make it clear to the South African authorities that the maintenance of diplomatic or consular relations with South Africa does not imply any recognition of its authority with regard to Namibia [...] the termination

---

independence, territorial integrity and non-alignment of the Republic of Cyprus; 7. *Calls upon* all States not to recognize any Cypriot State other than the Republic of Cyprus;".

184 In the same vein: Dissenting opinion of Judge Skubiszewski attached to the ICJ judgment in the East Timor case (1995): 'the rule of non-recognition operates in a self-executory way. To be operative it does not need to be repeated by the United Nations or other international organizations. Consequently, the absence of such direction on the part of the international organization in a particular instance does not relieve any State from the duty of non-recognition. Nor does the absence of "collective sanctions" have that effect' (para. 130 (at 264)).

> of the Mandate and the declaration of the illegality of South Africa's presence in Namibia are opposable to all States in the sense of barring *erga omnes* the legality of a situation which is maintained in violation of international law: in particular, no State which enters into relations with South Africa concerning Namibia may expect the United Nations or its Members to recognize the validity or effects of such relationship, or of the consequences thereof [However,] the non-recognition of South Africa's administration of the Territory should not result in depriving the people of Namibia of any advantages derived from international co-operation [Therefore,] this invalidity cannot be extended to those acts, such as, for instance, the registration of births, deaths and marriages, the effects of which can be ignored only to the detriment of the inhabitants of the Territory.[185]

In the *Palestine Wall* case, the World Court relied on these determinations while at the same time expanding the sphere of application of the consequences of violations of *erga omnes* obligations, such as that protecting the right to self-determination of peoples,[186] through the obligation of non-recognition:

> The obligations *erga omnes* violated by Israel are the obligation to respect the right of the Palestinian people to self-determination, and certain of its obligations under international humanitarian law. [...] Given the character and the importance of the rights and obligations involved, the Court is of the view that all States are under an obligation not to recognize the illegal situation resulting from the construction of the wall in the Occupied Palestinian Territory, including in and around East Jerusalem. They are also under an obligation not to render aid or assistance in maintaining the situation created by such construction. It is also for all States, while respecting the United Nations Charter and international law, to see to it that any impediment, resulting from the construction of the wall, to the exercise by the Palestinian people of its right to self-determination is

185 ICJ, Namibia 1971, paras. 122–126 (at 55–56). Similarly, concerning in particular the exception relating to the recognition of legal effects to acts performed by the illegal occupying State, but for the benefit of the inhabitants of the territory: Emin v. Yeldag (Attorney-General and Secretary of State for Foreign and Commonwealth Affairs intervening), England, High Court, Family Division, 5 October 2001, 148 *ILR*, 50 (the court refers to the judgment of the ECtHR in the *Loizidou* case).

186 In so doing, the Court puts an end to the doubtful ambiguity that it had dangerously left hanging since its judgment in the East Timor case (1995, para. 32 (at 104)).

> brought to an end. [...] Finally, the Court is of the view that the United Nations, and especially the General Assembly and the Security Council, should consider what further action is required to bring to an end the illegal situation resulting from the construction of the wall and the associated régime, taking due account of the present Advisory Opinion.[187]

Not only does the Court extend the application of the obligation of non-recognition to competent international organisations, such as the United Nations, but it also deduces from it a positive obligation on their organs for the purposes of an international settlement of the Israeli-Palestinian conflict. The obligation of non-recognition is thus metamorphosed when applied to international organisations.

The Court's approach is in line with the ILC's works on State responsibility, now recorded in ARSIWA. Indeed, in accordance with its Articles 40 and 41, which govern the consequences of a serious breach of obligations contained in a norm of *ius cogens*, all States have a legal interest in the restoration of legality. To this end, Article 41 – which undoubtedly reflects general international law on the subject – introduces two types of obligations, the first negative, the second positive. *First*, States 'shall cooperate to bring to an end through lawful means' the violation in question (Article 41 para. 1), the choice of means depending on the 'circumstances of the given situation'.[188] *Secondly*, under Article 41 para. 2, States are under an obligation not to 'recognize as lawful situations created by serious breaches in the sense of Article 40' and not to 'render aid or assistance in maintaining that situation'.[189] It is difficult not to hear a distant echo of the pronouncements of the International Court of Justice in the two cases mentioned above.[190]

187 ICJ, Wall in Palestine, 2004, paras. 155, 159, 160 (at 199, 200). See also Security Council resolution 2334 (23 December 2016), in which the Security Council '*calls upon all States* ... to distinguish, in their relevant dealings, between the territory of the State of Israel and the territories occupied since 1967' (OP 5).

188 Paragraph 3 (at 114) of the Commentary to Article 41 ARSIWA (UN DOC. A/56/10).

189 Paragraph 4 (at 114) of the Commentary to Article 41 ARSIWA (UN DOC. A/56/10).

190 It is in this light that the careful considerations of the General Court of the European Union in its judgment of 10 December 2015 in case -T512/12should be read: http://curia.europa.eu/juris/document/document.jsf?docid=172870&%3Bdoclang=EN. In its decision, the Court of First Instance partially annulled a European Union trade treaty with Morocco insofar as it infringed the Saharawi people's right to self-determination, since it included territory under the sovereignty of the latter and not of the Cherifian Kingdom (paras. 226–248).

The declaration of illegality (by the UNSC, the UNGA or the ICJ), which will be joined by the entire International Community, in fulfilment of the obligation of non-recognition,[191] will prevent the illegal situation from being consolidated by the effect of its mere effectiveness.[192] Of course, this dissociation between *titulus* (validity) and *modus adquisitionis* (effectiveness) is and can only be temporary,[193] as the legal order abhors such situations, and *a fortiori* the international legal order, whose current structure is ill-suited to such anomalies. In the event of persistent passivity on the part of the International Community over time, we must ask whether such a situation will not eventually impose itself *erga omnes* as valid in the eyes of international law.[194] As has been bluntly stigmatised in an authoritative textbook on public international law:

---

191 In the absence of other, much more binding measures (e.g., those involving the use of force under Chapter VII) or other "classical" international law mechanisms such as collective self-defence (if applicable) or compulsory enforcement of the injured right (in the past), see countermeasures under the regime of international responsibility for internationally wrongful acts (Articles 22, 49–53 ARSIWA).

192 '[T]he Court considers that the qualification of a situation as illegal does not by itself put an end to it. It can only be the first, necessary step in an endeavor to bring the illegal situation to an end', ICJ, Namibia 1971, para. 111 (at 52).

193 'If non-recognition should leave unchanged the facts of which it marks disapproval, it would result in a discordance between the law and the facts which in the long run would merely advertise the impotence of law', J-L Brierly (1963), 172. The qualification of reorganisation that the International Community issues with regard to an illegal territorial situation does not mean the abdication of law to force, but rather the effectiveness of the legal order, an essential condition of its efficiency. For, if the international legal order has the means and is motivated by the intention to restore the injured right, then the reunion of the *titulus* and the *modus adquisitionis will take* place with the legal sovereign. But if this is not the case, it is highly likely that, since Law is shaped by the pressure of social forces, legal title will be formed with the occupying state.

194 We do not, however, go so far as to assert with Borchard that the doctrine of non-recognition 'is an instrument of that moralistic world which was supposedly built up after 1919, *a world of mechanical devices which has produced more immorality in the world than I think has ever existed before. In the search for moral ends this school has actually undermined much rational thinking concerning the world we live in.* It has been a great enemy of law and of international law. *It has developed a theology.* Its disciples are substituting *theology for law*, and although their theology is defeated on every hand by the unhappy facts of life, they nevertheless continue to postulate a kind of natural law and to condemn positive law, so that they are leaving us in a state of anarchy. I might approve their aspirations, but this does not justify a destruction of the *only legal structure we have for keeping man alive in some semblance of predictable order*', Borchard's speech, quoted in Herbert Briggs, 'Non-Recognition of Title by Conquest Limitations on the Doctrine', *Proceedings of the American Society of International Law*, Vol. 34 (1940), 96 [emphasis added].

> [T]he practice of non-recognition is not a universal remedy; based on a confusion between *the two logics of recognition*, that of recognition and that of approval [which is quite true], it submits to the criterion of legitimacy situations that belong to the order of facts ; *and effectiveness often ends up winning*. At first, third States refuse to take into account the new belonging of the territory to the conquering State, for example by opposing the application to the annexed territory of the treaties that bind them to the annexing State, or by not recognising the validity of the acts made by the latter in order to have effect on that territory, but this sort of inopposability of the consequences of the incorporation of a territory carries little weight, and third States sooner or later come to treat the annexing State as the competent authority to act on the territory.[195]

Non-recognition can therefore sometimes be followed by deferred recognition (*de iure*) which is frequently preceded in turn by *de facto* recognition,[196] which constitutes the prelude to the capitulation of "rigid legal legitimism" or, perhaps, the beginning of the "normalisation" of the relationship between Law and Fact.

However, and fortunately for the health of contemporary international law and the safeguarding of its fundamental principles, the cases in which there have been such restorations have been very rare and have concerned singular and exceptional situations such as certain violent secessions – of which we will speak later.[197] In these cases, we find the current triptych formed by: a) the effectiveness of the situation; b) the consent of the injured State (holder of the right of territorial sovereignty); c) the concomitant (or even earlier or later) recognition of the International Community. Today, and contrary to the

---

195 Combacau, Sur, 429–430 [emphasis added; our translation]. Also: De Visscher (1967), 117; Bentivoglio, 18–19, 25.

196 See: Venturini (1946), 112–116; Bentivoglio, 92 [note 192]. With regard to the subtle distinction, entirely diplomatic and to be framed within the dynamics of the weakening of the position of the International Community, between *de facto* and *de iure* recognition, see the legitimate conceptual perplexities displayed by various domestic tribunals: Bank of Ethiopia v. National Bank of Egypt and Liguori, 122; Re an Application by Ernst Jaakson and Aarand Roos, 59–60; Deutsche Continental Gas-Gesellschaft v. Polish State, Award of 1 August 1929 by the German-Polish Mixed Arbitral Tribunal, in *Recueil des décisions des Tribunaux arbitraux mixtes*, Vol. 9, Paris, 343–344. On the usefulness of this distinction, supported by considerations of international policy, Briggs (82) and Sir Hersch Lauterpacht (1947, 433) have expressed themselves positively, albeit for different reasons. Consider also Australia's *de iure* recognition of Indonesia's incorporation of East Timor, which was preceded by *de facto* recognition: ICJ, East Timor (1995), para. 16.

197 See *infra* Part 2. Chapter 6. Section B.i.

situation before the Charter, the recognition of the International Community is required since the territorial situation was carried out in defiance of a peremptory norm of general international law.[198] Therefore, the legal qualification of reorganisation confers on the illegal but effective territorial situation [*modus adquisitionis*] the *titulus adquisitionis* (i.e., the specific derogation from the norm of *ius cogens* violated such as the prohibition of the use of force and the right of peoples to self-determination) which precisely resides in the entire International Community.

This triptych, which today in UNC law is legitimised by and based on the two *ius cogens* norms mentioned above (prohibition of the use and threat of force; right to self-determination of peoples), had already been prefigured by the Commission of Jurists in the famous Åland Islands case. The Court, after having correctly clarified that the right of a fraction of the people of a State to separate from it is within its reserved domain[199] states that:

> From the point of view of both domestic and international law, the formation, transformation and dismemberment of States as a result of revolutions and wars create situations of fact which, to a large extent, cannot be met by the application of the normal rules of positive law. This amounts to a statement that if the essential basis of these rules, that is to say, territorial sovereignty, is lacking, either because the State is not yet fully formed or because it is undergoing transformation or dissolution, the situation is obscure and uncertain from a legal point of view, and will not become clear until the period of development is completed and a definite new situation, which is normal in respect to territorial sovereignty, has been established. This transition from a *de facto* situation to a normal situation *de jure* cannot be considered as one confined entirely within the domestic jurisdiction of a State. *It tends to lead to readjustments between the members of the international community and to alterations in their territorial and legal status; consequently, this transition interests the community of States very deeply both from political and legal standpoints.*[200]

198 "An illegality cannot, as a rule, become a source of legal right to the wrongdoer. *This does not mean that it cannot produce any legal results at all*", Sir Hersch Lauterpacht (1947), 420 [emphasis added].

199 See *infra* note 55 (at 189).

200 Question of the Åland Islands, decision of 5 September 1920 by the International Committee of Jurists entrusted by the Council of the League of Nations with the task of giving an advisory opinion upon the legal aspects of Åland Islands question, *Official Journal of the League of Nations*, October 1920, para. 3 (at 6).

Hence the need for a position to be taken by third States *uti singuli* and, equally important, by the UN and, possibly, by the competent regional organisation(s). This *third-party* position must, it should be recalled, be accompanied by the verification of the consent of the parent State (two-headed construction of the *titulus*) in order to validate the originally illegal territorial situation.

CHAPTER 6

The Title of Territorial Sovereignty and the Principle of the Right of Peoples to Self-Determination

A As a Basis for the Title of Territorial Sovereignty

Without a doubt, the first of the human rights, as it appears in the first two universal international treaties – the two Covenants of 1966 (Article 1er common) – is the basis for the *titulus* allowing a people to establish itself as a State. However, this is not, or not always, sufficient, as the eternal effectiveness (*modus adquisitionis*) will always be required.

i *The Genesis of the Principle*

Resolution 1514 (XV)[1,2] can rightly be considered the mother of all UNGA resolutions on the right to self-determination and, by extension, of the body of rules on this matter. By reaffirming the *fervent* wish and the necessity 'of bringing to a speedy and unconditional end colonialism in all its forms', Resolution 1514 sets out the first case (or situation) in which a people enjoy the right to self-determination, i.e., colonialism, understood as 'alien subjugation, domination and exploitation', thus constituting 'a denial of fundamental human rights' as well as being 'contrary to the Charter of the United Nations'.[3] Colonial rule is reflected in the existence of a "non-self-governing territory", i.e., 'a territory which is geographically separate and is distinct ethnically and/or culturally from the country administering it'.[4] However, the penultimate paragraph

1 This is hardly the place to discuss the principle of the right to self-determination, but simply to assess its impact on legal title and the validity of a territorial situation.

2 "Declaration on the Granting of Independence to Colonial Countries and Peoples" (14 December 1960).

3 It is important to note that, as a simple literal and teleological interpretation of the Preamble and Article 1 UNC shows, the promotion of human rights, the right of peoples to self-determination, and economic and social progress are considered instrumental in safeguarding the supreme value (at least in 1945) of international peace and security.

4 Principle IV of Resolution 1541 (15 December 1960): "Principles which should guide Members in determining whether or not an obligation exists to transmit the information called for in Article 73(e) *of* the Charter of the United Nations". See Giovanni Distefano, Aymeric Hêche, "Chapter 8. Colonies and Mandates", in *Cambridge History of International Law*, Vol. X (Global International Law in the Era of the League of Nations (1920–1945)), Cambridge, 2023.

 | DOI:10.1163/9789004708594_009

(5) introduced the safeguard clause that the exercise of this right had to be reconciled 'with the national unity and the territorial integrity of a country' member of the United Nations.[5] For, in the end, any state – provided that the right to self-determination is respected – is only the effective outcome of the exercise of the latter. This paragraph, read in conjunction (contextual interpretation) with the other subparagraphs dealing with colonial regimes, makes it clear that the right to self-determination can – according to this resolution – only be exercised in this particular situation of foreign domination. By way of example, one can mention the colonial – and therefore illegal – occupation by the Portuguese military forces of certain parts of the Republic of Guinea-Bissau as well as the acts of aggression committed by them against the people of the Republic of Guinea-Bissau. In its resolution 3061 (XXVIII) of 2 November 1973, the UNGA, welcoming 'the recent accession to independence of the people of Guinea-Bissau', 'strongly condemns the policies of the Government of Portugal in perpetuating its illegal occupation of certain sectors of the Republic of Guinea-Bissau and the repeated acts of aggression committed by its armed forces against the people of Guinea-Bissau and Cape Verde', and 'demands that the Government of Portugal desist forthwith from further violation of the sovereignty and territorial integrity of the Republic of Guinea-Bissau and from all acts of aggression against the people of Guinea-Bissau and Cape Verde by immediately withdrawing its armed forces from those territories'.

The forcible denial by a colonial power of the exercise by the colonised people of their right to self-determination is thus considered to be tantamount to a permanent aggression triggering, for the benefit of that people, the right of self-defence. Furthermore, under UNGA resolution 2625, the colonised people have the right to seek and receive aid, in accordance with the UN Charter, for the purpose of emancipating themselves from the colonial yoke.[6]

---

5 Resolution 1514 (XV), Principle VI. This clause will be quite naturally inserted in resolution 2625 (XXV): 'Nothing in the foregoing paragraphs shall be construed as authorizing or encouraging any action which would dismember or impair, totally or in part, the territorial integrity or political unity of sovereign and independent States conducting themselves in compliance with the principle of equal rights and self-determination of peoples as described above and thus possessed of a government representing the whole people belonging to the territory without distinction as to race, creed, or colour'.

6 However, some states would have liked to see an explicit inclusion in Resolution 2625 of a provision authorising collective self-defence alongside the oppressed people. Instead, we are left with a less bold formulation, which nevertheless leaves the door open to non-forcible assistance, even military supplies, by third states, without the assistance becoming co-belligerece, i.e., without third state(s) intervening directly in the conflict. In the famous Nicaragua case (ICJ, Nicaragua, 1986, para. 206), the Court considers precisely this case in

On 15 December 1960 (the day after the adoption of 1514), the General Assembly adopted another resolution, 1541,[7] which informs us of the three possibilities open to a people legitimately exercising its right to self-determination: a) to become "a sovereign independent State"; b) to 'associate free[ly] with an independent State'; or c) to 'integrat[e] with an independent State' (Principle VI).[8] Any people, in a colonial situation, can therefore freely determine itself for one or the other of these solutions; this will be expressed through the exercise of a referendum consultation (Principle VII), following the example of plebiscites organised in the past.

ii *Strengthening of the Principle and Extension of Its Scope of Application*

Resolution 2625 (XXV) of the UNGA remains unquestionably both the authentic interpretation of the fundamental principles of the UNC (including precisely the right to self-determination) and the faithful reflection of customary international law in this area. It is therefore not surprising that it devotes an entire paragraph, full of clarifications, to the right of peoples to self-determination, but also and above all novelties regarding the regime relating to it and the delimitation of its scope of application. After reaffirming the internal and international dimensions of this right, this resolution, by underlining the peremptory duty to put an end to "colonialism", adds that "subjugation, domination or foreign exploitation constitute a violation" of the right of peoples and are "contrary" to the UN Charter. The simple contextual and systemic interpretation shows that colonialism is only one species of the broader genus represented by these three synonyms. It follows that a people under foreign occupation (or subjugation) is vested with the right to self-determination even if the situation cannot be described as colonial rule.[9] Consequently, the right of peoples to self-determination is not – and historically has not been – exhausted by decolonisation. Any occupation by a State of a territory of which it does not possess a valid title (according to international law) of territorial sovereignty is, therefore, a case of foreign occupation, thus triggering the right

---

the context of decolonisation. International practice – despite a highly contrasted doctrinal panorama – seems to be moving towards this interpretation.

7 Resolution 1541, Principle VI.

8 UNGA Resolution 2625 (see below Part 2. Chapter 6. Section A.ii) similarly envisages these three scenarios in its paragraph on the right of peoples to self-determination.

9 It must be remembered, as pointed out above, that a colonial regime (or situation) is characterised by a different legal status at the territorial level (between metropolis and colony).

to self-determination for the people concerned. Resolution 2625 clearly affirms this concept when it declares that:

> The territory of a colony or other Non-Self-Governing Territory has, under the Charter, a status separate and distinct from the territory of the State administering it; and such separate and distinct status under the Charter shall exist until the people of the colony or Non-Self-Governing Territory have exercised their right of self-determination in accordance with the Charter, and particularly its purposes and principles.

It goes without saying that this right must be exercised *freely* and *validly* by the people, i.e., without coercion or fraud on the part of any State. In its Advisory Opinion on the Chagos Archipelago, 'the Court considers that this detachment was not based on the free and genuine expression of the will of the people concerned'[10] as a result of the coercion exercised by the United Kingdom on the representatives of Mauritius during the talks with the colonial power.[11] This resulted, at the time of Mauritius' independence, in the amputation of its

10 ICJ, Legal Consequences of the Separation of the Chagos Archipelago from Mauritius in 1965, Advisory Opinion of 25 February 2019: *ICJ Reports* 2019, para. 172, at 137. The General Assembly, which had requested this advisory opinion (resolution 71/292 of 22 June 2017), took note of it in its resolution 73/295 (22 May 2019). After noting, in the wake of the ICJ, that 'the detachment of the Chagos Archipelago was not based on the free and genuine expression of the will of the people of Mauritius, the decolonization of Mauritius has not been lawfully completed' (2 (a)), demanded that the United Kingdom 'withdraw its colonial administration from the Chagos Archipelago unconditionally within a period of no more than six months from the adoption' of this resolution (3). To date, however, the former colonial power has not complied with UNGA's request.

11 Judges Kateka and Wolfrum observed in their dissenting and concurring opinion attached to the arbitral award of 18 March 2015 (PCA) in "The Arbitration regarding the Chagos Marine Protected Area between Mauritius and the United Kingdom" (Mauritius v. United Kingdom) that: 'A look at the discussion between Prime Minister Harold Wilson and Premier Sir Seewoosagur Ramgoolam suggests that Wilson's threat that Ramgoolam [Mauritian negotiator] could return home without independence amounts to *harshness*. The Private Secretary of Wilson used the language of "frighten[ing]" the Premier "with hope". The Colonial Secretary equally resorted to the language of intimidation', *RSA*, Vol. XXXI, para. 77, at 602 [emphasis added]. The word *duress* obviously refers to its equivalent "coercion" on the State representative, a cause of absolute nullity codified by Article 51 of the VCLT 1969. Unfortunately, the PCA could not hear this case, and thus the argument of Mauritius, due to lack of jurisdiction in the case. See also: Giovanni Distefano "Article 51. Coercion of a Representative of a State", in *Vienna Conventions on the law of treaties: A Commentary*, 2nd edn, Oxford, 2025, 1178–2000 [forthcoming].

original territorial base and thus in the partial denial of the Mauritian people's right to self-determination.

In a judgment delivered on 21 December 2016 regarding the "Agreement between the European Union and the Kingdom of Morocco concerning liberalisation measures on agricultural and fishery products", the Court of Justice of the European Union stated that:

> In the light of the foregoing, the General Court erred in law in holding, in paragraphs 101 and 103 of the judgment under appeal, that the European Union and the Kingdom of Morocco should be regarded as having tacitly agreed to interpret the words 'territory of the Kingdom of Morocco' in Article 94 of the Association Agreement as meaning that they included the territory of Western Sahara.[12]

Most recently, the General Court (Ninth Chamber, Extended Composition) of the EU found[13] to be invalid and consequently annulled the:

> Council Decision (EU) 2019/441 of 4 March 2019 on the conclusion of the Sustainable Fisheries Partnership Agreement between the European Union and the Kingdom of Morocco, the Implementation Protocol thereto and the Exchange of Letters accompanying the Agreement.[14]

The Court of Justice of the European Union, in order to conclude to the annulment of this decision of the Council, relies extensively on the advisory opinion of the ICJ of 1974 as well as on the normative resolutions of the General Assembly on the right to self-determination of peoples. The agreements concluded by the EU with Morocco undermine the right to self-determination of the Saharawi people, who are the sole holders of the title of territorial sovereignty over the maritime areas concerned. Consequently, without the consent of the latter, represented by its "National Liberation Movement" ("MLN") – Polisario – there can be no granting of exploitation rights to the EU,[15] the agreements in

12 Judgement of the Court (Grand Chamber), Case C-104/16 P, para. 108. See also *supra* note 190.

13 Front populaire pour la libération de la Segui el-Hamra et du Rio de Oro (Front Polisario) v. Council of the European Union, Judgment of 29 September 2021, CJEU, Joint Cases T-344/19 and T-356/19.

14 *Ibid.*, para. 400, Operative 1. See also paras. 142–152.

15 '[T]he breach of the right of the people of that territory to freely dispose of such natural resources constituted a breach of its right to self-determination', *ibid.* para. 216.

question being a *res inter alios acta* vis-à-vis the territorial sovereign.[16] In the light of these jurisprudential pronouncements, it is therefore regrettable that some states have implicitly[17] or even explicitly[18] recognised Morocco's sovereignty over Western Sahara. Such behaviour is both illegal – as it is contrary to the right to self-determination of peoples – and unlawful as it not only contributes little to the validity of Morocco's title to Western Sahara, but is also devoid of legal effects in international relations (*supra* Part 2. Chapter 5. Section B.iii).

The ICJ confirmed this interpretation of the territorial basis for a people's exercise of its right to self-determination in 2004 in its Advisory Opinion on the Wall in Palestine, where it reaffirmed in unequivocal terms that:

> The Wall severs the territorial sphere over which the Palestinian people are entitled to exercise their right of self-determination and constitutes a violation of the legal principle prohibiting the acquisition of territory by use of force [...] As regards the principle of the right of peoples to self-determination, the Court observes that the existence of a 'Palestinian people' is no longer in issue [...] The Court concludes that the Israeli settlements in the Occupied Palestinian Territory (including East Jerusalem) have been established in breach of international law [...] The Court concludes that the Israeli settlements in the Occupied Palestinian Territory (including East Jerusalem) have been established in breach of international law [...] That construction, along with measures taken previously, thus severely impedes the exercise by the Palestinian people of its right

16 *Ibid.*, para. 269.

17 The opening of a consulate (*The National* (Abu Dhabi), 5 November 2020) by the United Arab Emirates of a consulate in Laayoune (Western Sahara), constitutes a clear, albeit implicit, recognition by the United Arab Emirates of Morocco's sovereignty over Western Sahara, as the exequatur was granted by the host country.

18 On 10 December 2020, US President Donald Trump reversed decades of US policy and recognised the sovereignty of the Kingdom of Morocco: "[A]s of today, the United States recognises Moroccan sovereignty over the entire Western Sahara territory and reaffirms its support for Morocco's serious, credible, and realistic autonomy proposal as the only basis for a just and lasting solution to the dispute over the Western Sahara territory. The United States believes that an independent Sahrawi State is not a realistic option for resolving the conflict and that genuine autonomy under Moroccan sovereignty is the only feasible solution", White House Press Release, Proclamation on Recognizing the Sovereignty of the Kingdom of Morocco Over the Western Sahara (Dec. 10, 2020), https://trumpwhitehouse.archives.gov/presidential-actions/proclamation-recognizing-sovereignty-kingdom-morocco-western-sahara.

to self-determination, and is therefore a breach of Israel's obligation to respect that right.[19]

Finally, the last extension of the operative scope of the right to self-determination – which was, however, already alive and kicking in customary international law – is due to an international instrument elaborated in a body of rules of the international order close to that of human rights, namely IHL. We refer to the First Additional Protocol of 1977 to the Four Geneva Conventions. The Diplomatic Conference held in the same city was torn by the question of which conflicts – previously considered non-international – should henceforth be qualified as international and thus benefit from the application of the entire body of IHL. The Protocol, which "supplements" the above-mentioned conventions, will therefore extend the category of international armed conflicts to those 'in which peoples are fighting against colonial domination and alien occupation and *against racist regimes in the exercise of their right to self-determination*' (Article 1 (4)).

This latest expansion of the scope of the right to self-determination – to include regimes based on racial discrimination – stems from the belief that a people so oppressed has the right to determine itself freely both internally and internationally. In other words, if a section of the population is discriminated against on the basis of race, it can fight to free itself from this yoke, which is in every respect comparable to colonial rule or foreign domination. The two dimensions of the right to self-determination are thus merged and confused in the case of the racist regime. The historical situation that dominated the debates within the Geneva Diplomatic Conference in 1975–1977 was certainly the apartheid regime in South Africa and the similar one in Southern Rhodesia, consisting in the systematic denial of the right of peoples

19 ICJ, Wall in Palestine, paras. 115, 120, 121, 122 (at 181, 182–183, 184). See also UNSC resolution 2334 (23 December 2016). Another situation had inspired the drafters of resolution 2625, namely the illegal and invalid occupation of South West Africa (later Namibia) by South Africa, which gave rise to no less than five different cases (four advisory and one contentious with a total of six pronouncements, one of the contentious cases giving rise to two judgments) before the ICJ. In the latest (advisory) episode of this judicial saga, the Hague Court declared that: 'South Africa, being responsible for having created and maintained a situation which the Court has found to have been validly *declared illegal*, has the obligation to put an end to it. It is therefore under obligation to withdraw its administration from the territory of Namibia. By maintaining the present *illegal situation*, and occupying *the Territory without title*, South Africa incurs international responsibilities arising from a continuing violation of an international obligation. It also remains accountable for any violation of its international obligations, or *of the rights of the people of Namibia*', ICJ, Namibia 1971, para. 118 (at 54) [emphasis added].

to self-determination, envisaged as a supreme human right (Common Article 1 to the UN 1966 Covenants). As the ICJ says, referring to the same system set up by that state in Namibia,

> To establish ..., and to enforce, distinctions, exclusions, *restrictions and limitations exclusively based on grounds of race, colour, descent or national or ethnic origin* which constitute a denial of fundamental human rights is a flagrant violation of the purposes and principles of the Charter.[20]

The case of the racist regime violates the right to self-determination insofar as it introduces a different personal status – according to race or ethnicity, for example – between nationals of the same state and, unlike the colonial regime, within the same territory.

iii *The Institutional Dimension: Who Makes the Determination?*

Once the material scope of the right of peoples to self-determination has been established, it is necessary to ask the institutional question, i.e., who determines that a people is in one of these three situations and that it therefore enjoys this right.[21] This is one of the gaping structural wounds of the international order, i.e., what are the organs or centres of determination of legal situations? In this case, the answer is easier: it is the UN General Assembly that has arrogated to itself this power of determination. In order to do so, the General Assembly relied on its general competence to deal with any matter "within the scope of the present Charter" (Article 10 UNC) in order to support its action of "codification and progressive development" of international law on the right of peoples to self-determination. It has done so precisely by means of numerous normative resolutions that have created and then consolidated a substantial body of substantive rules henceforth belong to CIL.[22] It has also, quite logically, given birth to institutional rules on the qualification of the situation as falling within the right of peoples to self-determination. It is therefore the Court, often with the welcome assistance of the ICJ, that has proceeded

---

20 ICJ, Namibia 1971, para. 13 (at 57) [emphasis added].

21 For, as we have just seen, it is not so much the people (its definition, its characteristics) as such that counts, but the specific situation that makes the people the holder of the right to self-determination.

22 '[A] series of [UNGA] resolutions may show the gradual evolution of the *opinio juris* required for the establishment of a new rule', ICJ, *Threat or Use of Nuclear Weapons*, 1996, para. 70 (at 255).

to this qualification, with, consequently, the recognition – in each concrete case – of the representative of the people struggling in the exercise of this right. The wave of decolonisation in the 1960s, in the wake of Resolution 1514, saw the application of this *modus operandi*: the General Assembly qualifies the situation as likely to trigger the right to self-determination and identifies the representative of the people holding this right, thus conferring on him or her the status of observer.[23] The representative of a people is referred to as the 'NLM' and the war ('War of National Liberation')[24] that it wages in the exercise of its right to self-determination is, as we have just seen, an international armed conflict. As such, the people, represented by its MLN, is a subject of international law, functional in nature, enjoying the three capacities that constitute the hard core of international legal personality: a) to conclude treaties; b) to maintain diplomatic relations (admittedly limited and therefore different from those between States or International Organisations); c) to bring and receive international claims.[25]

iv *The Presumptive Contradiction with the Principle of* uti possidetis

This general principle – dispositive in nature[26] – 'logically connected with the phenomenon of the obtaining of independence, wherever it occurs'[27] has given rise to a vast literature,[28] nourished by an impressive States practice and international case law, which it is not necessary to examine here. We will limit

---

23 The issue is less trivial than it might seem, for during the Cold War, the confrontation between the two blocs also manifested itself through the support of different 'representatives' of the people in question, thus provoking a conflict encapsulated in the war of national liberation against the oppressor. For example, in the Namibian situation, the General Assembly declared the South West African People's Organisation ('SWAPO') to be 'the authentic representative of the people of Namibia' (resolution 3111 (XXVIII) adopted on 12 December 1973).

24 Georges Abi-Saab, "Wars of National Liberations in the Geneva Conventions and Protocols", 165 *RCADI* 1979-IV, 353–445.

25 Distefano (2019), 60–68.

26 '[U]*ti possidetis* is of a dispositive character, and the Parties are able to derogate from it by joint agreement [or even by consistent conduct]', dissenting opinion of Judge Bennouna appended to the ICJ judgment in the case of the Frontier Dispute (Benin/Niger), Judgment of 12 July 2005, *ICJ Reports 2005*, para. 6 (at 154).

27 ICJ, Border Dispute (Burkina Faso/Mali), Judgment of 22 December1986, *ICJ Reports 1986*, para. 20 (at 565).

28 See: Giuseppe Nesi, *L'uti possidetis iuris nel diritto internazionale*, Padua, 1996; 'L'uti possidetis hors du contexte de la décolonisation: le cas de l'Europe', 44 *AFDI* 1998, 1–23; Marcelo Kohen, 'L'*uti possidetis* et les délimitations maritimes', in *Le procès international. Liber Amicorum Jean-Pierre Cot*, Brussels, 2009, 155–170; 'L'*uti possidetis* revisité: L'arrêt du 11 septembre 1992 dans l'affaire El Salvador / Honduras', 97 *RGDIP* 1993, 939–973.

ourselves here to showing that *uti possidetis* is hardly irreconcilable with the principle of the right of peoples to self-determination. This principle was born at the beginning of the 19th century when the former Spanish colonies in Latin America gained their independence. In the absence of general rules of international law, this principle was a response to the question of the definition of the borders of the new states, following States succession. According to this principle, the former administrative limits of the Spanish Empire became *ipso iure*[29] the new international borders between these States, which then succeeded the Spanish sovereign in this territorial base. This principle, which was closely linked to state succession (dismemberment of a state),[30] easily solved, at least on paper, the thorny issue of borders between successor states. Colonial law was taken into account for the determination of administrative boundaries but was not the source of the right of territorial sovereignty of the new states. The title-source title was 'the continuous and peaceful display of territorial sovereignty (peaceful in relation to other States)'[31] as a result of successful rebellion against the metropolis; hence, colonial law became the title-proof of the territorial limits of this actual assumption of sovereign power.[32] As the ICJ makes clear:

> The Court observes that the mere invocation of the principle of *uti possidetis juris* does not of itself provide a clear answer as to the sovereignty over the disputed islands. If the islands are not *terra nullius* ... it must be assumed that they had been under the rule of the Spanish Crown [...] The Court recalls that *uti possidetis juris* presupposes the existence of a delimitation of territory between the colonial provinces concerned having been effected by the central colonial authorities. Thus in order to apply the principle of *uti possidetis juris* to the islands in dispute it must be shown that the Spanish Crown had allocated them to one or other of its colonial provinces.[33]

29 '[T]he application of the principle of *uti possidetis* resulted in administrative boundaries being transformed into international frontiers in the full sense of the term', ICJ, Frontier Dispute (Burkina Faso/Mali), 1986, para. 23 (at 566).

30 See *supra* Prolegomena B.3.ii.

31 Island of Palmas case, 839.

32 See Judge Bennouna's dissenting opinion attached to the ICJ judgment in of the Border Dispute (Benin/Niger), 2005, para. 14.

33 ICJ, Territorial and Maritime Dispute between Nicaragua and Honduras in the Caribbean Sea (Nicaragua v. Honduras), Judgment of 8 October 2007, para. 158 (at 707–708).

The definition of these international borders through the principle of *uti possidetis*, served, as the Hague Court said, a dual purpose:

> First, a defensive purpose, towards the rest of the world, in the form of an outright denial that there was any land without a sovereign (or *terra nullius*) in the decolonized territories, even in unexplored areas or those beyond the control of the colonizers; secondly, a preventive purpose: to avoid or at least to minimize conflict occurring in the relationships among the successors, by freezing the carved-up territory in the format it exhibited at the moment of independence.[34]

The jurisprudential refinement resolved the question of whether, for the purposes of establishing the colonial legacy, "colonial effectiveness", i.e., effective administrative boundaries prevailing at the time of independence of the new states, should also be taken into account alongside colonial law.[35] This distinction gave rise to two different formulations of this principle: *uti possidetis iuris* and *uti possidetis de facto*.[36] The inexhaustible dialectic between the two elements of legal title is inevitably found here. International case law, while reaffirming 'the pre-eminence accorded to legal title over effective possession as a basis of sovereignty'[37] is *broadly* oriented towards taking these effectivities into account, insofar as they may help to determine *uti possidetis iuris*, 'i.e., the manner in which those [colonial] titles were interpreted and applied by the competent public authorities of the colonial Power'.[38]

This principle, which quickly acquired a regional customary nature, i.e., a Latin American special law, also ended up being imposed at the universal level, as attested to by the famous judgment of the World Court in 1986 in the case of the border dispute between Burkina Faso and Mali, where the Chamber, after stressing 'its general scope, in view of its exceptional importance for the African continent',[39] observed that

34 Separate opinion of Judge Abi-Saab appended to the ICJ judgment in the Frontier Dispute (Burkina Faso/Mali) case, 1986, para. 13 (at 661–662).

35 See *supra* note 33.

36 See in particular: Honduras Borders Case (Guatemala v. Honduras), Award of 23 January 1933, *RSA*, Vol. II, 1307.

37 ICJ, Border Dispute (Burkina Faso/Mali), 1986, para. 23 (at 566).

38 ICJ, Border Dispute (Benin/Niger), 2005, para. 140 (at 148).

39 ICJ, Border Dispute (Burkina Faso/Mali), 1986, para. 20 (at 565).

> The elements of *uti possidetis* were latent in the many declarations made by African leaders in the dawn of independence. These declarations confirmed the maintenance of the territorial status quo at the time of independence, and stated the principle of respect both for the frontiers deriving from international agreements, and for those resulting from mere internal administrative divisions.[40]

Thus, as the practice in the Latin American continent has shown with regard to the borders between the Portuguese colony (Brazil) and the other neighbouring Spain's colonies, the principle of *uti possidetis* finds, one could say *a fortiori*, application not only between:

> the colony of one State [and] the colony of another State, or indeed [between] a colonial territory [and] the territory of an independent State, or one which was under protectorate, but had retained its international personality.[41]

In the same vein, it is now undisputed that the operating field of the principle of *uti possidetis iuris* extends, *ratione materiae*, to maritime spaces[42] as well as outside decolonisation, as shown by the Badinter Commission at the time of the dismemberment of the Socialist Federal Republic of Yugoslavia in 1992 as well as by the Alma-Ata Declaration (21 December 1991) signifying the cessation of existence of the USSR.

The generality of this principle as well as its universal customary value is reflected in Article 11 VCSS 1978[43] according to which borders established by

---

40 ICJ, Frontier Dispute (Burkina Faso/Mali), 1986, para. 22 (at 565). Similarly: ICJ, Frontier Dispute (Burkina Faso/Niger), judgment of 16 April 2013: *ICJ Reports* 2013, paras. 66, 98 (at 75, 84).

41 *Ibid.,* para. 24. The same applies to treaties establishing borders or territorial regimes in the case of international administration (LON mandates, trust administration and direct administration by the UN Security Council); see: Sâ B Traoré, 'Les régimes d'administration internationale de territoire et la succession en matière de traités', in Distefano, Gaggioli, Hêche, 2016, 1703–1754.

42 Case concerning the delimitation of maritime boundary between Guinea-Bissau and Senegal, 1989, paras. 61–66.

43 See: Jean-Paul Pancracio, 'Article 11. Régimes de frontière', in Distefano, Gaggioli, Hêche, 2016, 373–396. The same principle underlies Article 62 (2) (a) VCLT 1969, according to which a State may not invoke a fundamental change of circumstances as a ground for terminating a treaty establishing a frontier; see in this regard ard: Aymeric Hêche, "Les conditions d'application de la clausula rebus sic stantibus", *RBDI*, 2014/1, 322–354.

treaty are not affected by state succession; the same applies, almost by logical extension, to territorial regimes established by treaty (Article 12 VCSS 1978).[44]

Finally, it remains to be demonstrated why, 'desptite the apparent contradiction', the principle of *uti possidetis* does not 'conflict outright with [the principle of] the right of peoples to self-determination'.[45] There are three main reasons for this, of decreasing importance. *Firstly*, because, as the World Court emphasises, 'it was by deliberate choice that African States selected, among all the classical principles, that of *uti possidetis*. This remains an undeniable fact'.[46] *Secondly*, because, as the same Court would later clarify in 2004, the principle of *uti possidetis* defines the territorial basis within which the people concerned exercise their right to self-determination.[47] *Third*, because, as Judge Abi-Saab noted, the principle of *uti possidetis* 'like any other, is not to be conceived in the absolute; it has always to be interpreted in the light of its function within the international legal order'.[48] Its function is precisely, with regard to the principle of the right to self-determination of peoples, that of circumscribing the territorial scope of application of the latter. Consequently, as the principle of *uti possidetis* is not contained in a norm of *ius cogens*, States can derogate from it by the traditional means recognised by the international law of territory: act and/or legal facts.[49] At the same time, the principle of *uti possidetis* supports (and strengthens) the distinction between the case of the right of peoples to self-determination and that of violent secession. For, as we shall see in the next subsection, in the case of the exercise of the right of peoples to self-determination, the people concerned has *determined itself* within

44 See: Giovanni Distefano, 'Article 12. Other territorial regimes', in Distefano, Gaggioli, Hêche, 2016, 399–458.

45 ICJ, Frontier Dispute (Burkina Faso/Mali), 1986, paras. 26, 25 (at 567).

46 ICJ, Frontier Dispute (Burkina Faso/Mali), 1986, para. 26. 'African countries, for instance, had decided to respect the boundaries imposed on them by the colonial Powers, even though they were conscious of the injustice done to them in the past by the imperialist countries. Thus, if international law was viewed as a whole, it must be concluded that the principle of self-determination and the principle of the inviolability of the territorial integrity of States were not conflicting, but interdependent principles, which should both be equally respected, having regard to all the means available to States under contemporary international law for the settlement of their boundary problems', Sahóvic, 1288th meeting (2 July 1974) of the ILC, Succession of States in respect of treaties, *YILC* 1974, vol. I, para. 59 (at 217).

47 ICJ, Wall in Palestine, 2004, paras. 88, 121, 155 (at 171–172, 184, 199). See also UNSC resolution 2334 (23 December 2016).

48 Separate opinion attached to the ICJ's judgment in the Frontier Dispute (Burkina Faso/Mali) case, 1986, para. 13 (at 661).

49 *Supra* Part 1. ICJ, Sovereignty over Pedra Branca/Pulau Batu Puteh, Middle Rocks and South Ledge (Malaysia/Singapore), 2008, para. 290 (at 99).

its own borders, i.e., those spatially defined in application of the principle of *uti possidetis*.

B Distinguished from Secession

In its external dimension, the right to self-determination of peoples is from time to time amalgamated – in good or bad faith – with a so-called right to unilateral secession in the international legal order. In international law, this term refers to 'any part of the territory of a State' which separates from 'the predecessor State [which] continues to exist … after separation'.[50]

It is thus a specific type of territorial change. For the purposes of this study, it should be stressed at the outset that a right to secession as such does not exist in public international law unless there is consent from the predecessor (parent) state.[51] In other words, in a proven case of the exercise of the right of peoples to self-determination (foreign occupation, colonial regime and racist regime), it is not correct to speak of secession because the people in question is *different* from that of the metropolis or the alien occupation.[52] The existence of

50 Article 35 VCSS 1978. This definition reflects customary international law. See *supra* Prolegomena B.3.i.

51 'It is clear that international law does not specifically grant component parts of sovereign states the legal right to secede unilaterally from their "parent" state', Reference re Secession of Quebec, Judgment of 20 May 1998 (Supreme Court of Canada), 37 *ILM* 1998, para. 111 (at 1368).

52 In other words, there is indeed a "non-self-governing territory" within the meaning of resolution 2625 (XXV), i.e. with a status distinct and separate from the mainland. See *supra* Part 2. Chapter 6. Section A.ii and note 203. Today, with Palau's independence (1994), the Trusteeship Council has suspended its activities, but 16 self-governing territories remain on the UN list under resolution 1514 (XV). The most recently added territory is French Polynesia, which was re-listed in May 2013 despite opposition from France (sovereign power) and representatives of the population living in the territory (A/67/265, 17 May 2013). The Nouméa Accord of 5 May 1998 (https://www.legifrance.gouv.fr/jorf/id/JORFTEXT000000555817/), which gives New Caledonia a high degree of autonomy, provides for a referendum mechanism allowing for self-determination of the Kanak people (point 5). If the response to the first consultation, finally organised on 4 November 2018, is 'negative[then] one third of the members of the Congress can provoke the organisation of a new consultation'. This was indeed the case, and a new referendum was held on 4 October 2020 resulting in another negative vote for independence (53.26%). Again, according to Point 5.4, "a new consultation may be organised according to the same procedure", which finally took place on 12 December 2021, even though a substantial part of the pro-independence organisations had called for non-participation. The no to independence won with 96% of the votes (with a participation rate below 44%). In any case, in accordance with Point 5.5, "As long as the consultations have not resulted in the proposed new

the right of peoples to self-determination, on the other hand, allows the "subjugated" people to determine themselves freely on the international legal scene.

In the absence of a right to secede recognised by international law, only the state concerned, within its domestic jurisdiction, can authorise a part of its territory to secede. This right, which is therefore internal in origin, may be based on the Constitution[53] or, failing that, on an express authorisation by the competent organs of the State (e.g., executive and/or legislative).[54] As the International Committee of Jurists (arbitral tribunal) stated in the Åland Islands case:

> [I]n the absence of express provisions in international treaties, the right of disposing of national territory is essentially an attribute of the sovereignty of every State. Positive International Law does not recognise the right of national groups, as such, to separate themselves from the State of which they form part by the simple expression of a wish, any more than it recognises the right of other States to claim such a separation. Generally speaking, the grant or refusal of the right to a portion of its population of determining its own political fate by plebiscite or by some other method, is, exclusively, an attribute of the sovereignty of every State which is definitively constituted.[55]

Most of the time, secession *roughly* leads to three types of scenarios: a) *De facto* states; b) "Puppet states"; c) New independent states. The first two of these will be discussed later in this section, while the third type will be examined in the next subsection.

---

political organisation, the political organisation set up by the 1998 agreement will remain in force, in its final stage of evolution, with no possibility of going back, this" irreversibility [of the process of self-organisation; Preamble, 5.9] being constitutionally guaranteed" [our translation]. See also "New Caledonia. L'indépendance en VF", *Le Temps* (Geneva), 1 November 2018.

53 There are, not surprisingly, few examples (formerly Article 72 of the USSR Constitution of 19 1); today there is only Ethiopia ("*Every nation, nationality or people in Ethiopia shall have the unrestricted right to self determination up to secession*", Article 39 §1) and St. Kitts and Nevis (which admits the possibility for Nevis to separate from St. Kitts, Article 115).

54 This was the case in the Scottish referendum – which took place on 18 September 2014 – instituted by an agreement, under domestic law, between the UK central government and Scotland (Edinburgh Agreement of 15 October 2012).

55 Åland Islands case, para. 2 (at 5). The legal regime in this respect has not changed, if one refers to a judgment of the Supreme Court of Canada (*supra* note 51).

i Successful Violent Secessions and the Birth of New Independent States: the Exception

In international practice, there are heretofore only three examples where new states have emerged by the mere material fact of separation from the parent state, with little or no consideration of the right to self-determination: Bangladesh (East Pakistan), Eritrea and Southern Sudan. In the first case, the International Community eventually recognised the new state that broke away from West Pakistan, following an armed conflict (1971). The United Nations was surprisingly silent on the emergence of this new state: with the Security Council blocked by cross-veto threats, the General Assembly merely demanded an 'immediate ceasefire' from the 'Governments of India and Pakistan', without taking an official position on the legality of the secession.[56] In the end, third states endorsed *uti singuli* the secession: the vast majority of states (86) of the International Community recognised Bangladesh before Pakistan (the sovereignty holder) had itself renounced its former province. In any case, Bangladesh was admitted as a Member of the UN on 17 September 1974,[57] only a few months after Pakistan's formal recognition on 22 February of the same year.[58] In this respect, and as we shall see immediately, the case of Bangladesh differs substantially from those of Eritrea and South Sudan in that the consent of the parent State will only come after the recognition – by a significant number of states – of the statehood and therefore the effective independence of Bangladesh. The genesis of Bangladesh's *contra titulum* is truly unique in this respect compared to the other two examples. It is truly a violent secession in every respect.

The legal situation of Eritrea and its secession from Ethiopia differed from the other two cases for two main reasons. *First,* Eritrea's legal status could not be amalgamated with that of Ethiopia: it had been an Italian colony for almost 80 years, and it was only in 1952 that it was reunited with Ethiopia

56 Resolution 2793 (XXVI), adopted on 7 December 1971. The Government of India intervened, citing, among other things, humanitarian reasons arising from the influx of refugees caused by the conflict.

57 A/3203 (XXIX). The Security Council adopted the recommendation of the Bangladesh Admissions Committee, without going through the formal voting procedure.

58 "India – Pakistan', Joint Communiqué on the progress of normalization of relations, New Delhi, April 9, 1974, 13 *ILM* 1974, 602–603. The formal recognition was the culmination of a series of bilateral agreements to address the issue of the repatriation of prisoners of war and the return of civilians. It should be noted in passing that the term "normalization" was chosen by Israel and some Persian Gulf states (UAE, Bahrain) to indicate the establishment of diplomatic relations and mutual recognition effected by the so-called Abraham Accords (15–20 December 2020).

as a federated entity, in accordance with a UNGA resolution.[59] Accordingly, Ethiopia integrated Eritrea with this condition, which it was obliged to respect; the (constitutional) maintenance of Eritrea's federal character was one of the conditions for the extension of Ethiopian sovereignty to Eritrea. However, on 20 May 1960, Ethiopia unilaterally abolished this autonomy, which was internationally guaranteed by the UNGA resolution.[60] It then proceeded to simply incorporate Ethiopia – without the UNGA being overly concerned – thus triggering the civil war or war of liberation. *Secondly*, after the fall of Mengistu (28 May 1991), who had in turn deposed the last emperor of Ethiopia Haile Selassie in 1974, the representatives of the Eritrean rebellion participated as observers in the Addis Ababa Conference (1–5 July 1991) leading to the establishment of a transitional government. On this occasion, they obtained the right to organise a referendum on Eritrean independence, which was finally held under the supervision of the United Nations peacekeeping mission (UNOVER) from 23 to 25 April 1993 in the administrative province of Eritrea alone. By an overwhelming majority (99.79% of voters), the Eritreans decided in favour of independence, which was declared on 28 May, the same day as its admission to the UN. Unlike the case of Bangladesh, here the parent States gives his consent to the holding of a referendum and undertakes, under UN supervision, to accept the result. In other words, *titulus* is provided by Ethiopia's express consent plus institutional and third state recognition.

The third case, in chronological order,[61] is Southern Sudan, whose situation would be similar in some respects to that of Eritrea in that the consent of the *titular* state (*titulus*), i.e., Sudan, was expressed after a long civil war outside, at least formally, any context of the right to self-determination. A particularly bloody non-international armed conflict was fought for more than twenty years between the central government (Khartoum) and the "Sudan People's Liberation Army" (SPLA), which represented the predominantly Christian population of Southern Sudan. Finally, thanks to the joint mediation of the US ambassador in Khartoum and the UN special envoy, a peace treaty was signed in Nairobi on 5 January 2005 between the SPLA and the Sudanese government.

59 'The General Assembly recommends that Eritrea shall constitute an autonomous unit federated with Ethiopia under the sovereignty of the Ethiopian Crown', resolution 390 (V) of 22 December 1950.

60 Eritrea thus became a mere administrative province of the Ethiopian Empire.

61 This enumeration is not only chronological in that it highlights the increasing role of the consent of the parent state and the recognition by the International Community (the two elements of *titulus adquisitionis*). Conversely, it reflects the decreasing role of violence, i.e., the effectiveness of the situation, in its legal consolidation.

According to this international agreement,[62] Sudan bestows autonomous rule for Southern Sudan for a period of 6 years, after which a referendum will be held on that part of the country only. The participants in the referendum (9–15 January 2011) overwhelmingly chose independence (98%).[63] Sudan was also the first state to recognise the new state, which surely paved the way for its admission to the UN on 14 July 2011, five days after the official proclamation of its independence. The Security Council, while reaffirming its 'commitment to the sovereignty, independence, unity and territorial integrity of Sudan', welcomed the holding 'of a referendum to determine the future status of the people of Southern Sudan in *exercise of their right to self-determination* […]'.[64] The reference to the right of peoples would seem to be intended to give legitimacy to the results achieved by the South Sudanese people through armed struggle.

The cases of Eritrea and Southern Sudan, unlike Bangladesh, show a more substantial involvement of the organised International Community in this delicate phase of a secession, which is certainly violent, but with the prior consent of the parent state.

Consequently, the metabolisation by the international legal order of the invalidity of secessions takes place through these three "enzymes" which we have subsumed under the acronym "RER":[65] recognition (by third states and the UN/competent regional organisations),[66] effectiveness (of the exercise of governmental authority), renunciation (by the parent state).

ii *Unsuccessful Violent Secessions: the Rule*

1 The So-Called "Remedial Secession"

By this formula, doctrine indicates a situation in which a people whose the exercise of its right to internal self-determination has been denied, would be entitled, as an *extrema ratio,* to exercise it internationally, paving thus the way to secession. This is perhaps what the Supreme Court of Canada referred to in its decision on the right of secession of Quebec: 'when a people is blocked from the meaningful exercise of its right to self-determination internally, it is entitled, *as a last resort,* to exercise it by secession […] such a complete blockage may potentially give rise to a right of secession'.[67] The requirement of the

62 The Comprehensive Peace Agreement (CPA), also known as the Naivasha Agreement, is a set of agreements concluded until January 2005.

63 The voters could choose between the three solutions provided for in Resolution 1541 (see *supra* note 8).

64 Resolution 1945, adopted by the Security Council on 24 October 2010 [emphasis added].

65 See *supra* note 103 (at 147).

66 Åland Islands case, supra note 200 (at 173).

67 Reference re Secession of Quebec, para. 134 (at 1373) [emphasis added].

UN Vienna Declaration (1993)[68] that the government of a state must represent 'the whole people belonging to the territory without distinction of any kind' would, according to some international jurists, support the argument that in case this requirement is not met, the disadvantaged fraction of the population would enjoy a right of secession. Hence the word "remedial" because in this particular context secession would be the only possibility for this group of the state's population to exercise its right to self-determination (in its internal dimension) "as a last resort".

So-called "remedial secession" might be envisaged in the case [where] a people is 'the victim of attacks on its physical existence or integrity, or of a massive violation of its fundamental rights',[69] in short, when it is a question of an oppressed and subjugated people, like the cases already envisaged by the right to self-determination today. This theory therefore emphasises the indissoluble intertwining of the internal and external dimensions of the right of peoples to self-determination. However, the Canadian Supreme Court could only admit that it 'remains unclear whether [this legal situation] actually reflects an established international law standard'.[70]

The same was true for the ICJ in the case concerning the question of the unilateral declaration of independence of Kosovo.[71] In fact, the Court did not dwell upon this question since it was outside ambit of the request for an advisory opinion submitted by the General Assembly and to which it had to respond.[72] The ICJ, noting furthermore the deep dissensions in the doctrine and confronted with a simply non-existent international practice, did not fail to express its perplexities with regard to the doctrine of 'remedial secession'.[73]

68 World Conference on Human Rights, *Declaration and Programme of Action*, A/CONF.157/24 (Part 1), 25 June 1993, Chapter III.

69 Reference re Secession of Quebec, para. 135 (at 1373).

70 *Loc. cit.*

71 See *infra* Part 2. Chapter 6. Section B.iii.1.

72 'Whether, outside the context of non-self-governing territories and peoples subject to alien subjugation, domination or exploitation, the international law on self-determination confers upon part of the population of an existing State a right to separate from that State is, however, a subject on which radically different views were expressed by those taking part in the proceedings and expressing a position on the question. Similar differences existed regarding whether international law provides for a right of "remedial secession" and, if so, in what circumstances. There was also a sharp difference of views as to whether the circumstances which some participants maintained would give rise to a right of "remedial secession" were actually present in Kosovo', ICJ, Accordance with international law of the unilateral declaration of independence in respect of Kosovo, 2010, para. 82 (at 438).

73 ICJ, Accordance with International Law of the Unilateral Declaration of Independence in Respect of Kosovo, 2010, para. 82.

Finally, it is legitimate to be deeply skeptical about the right of remedial secession in the international legal order.

2 The Denial of the Right of Unilateral Secession: Confirmation by International Practice

The practice of states and international organisations – the UN and relevant regional organisations – leaves no doubt that there is no right to secession without the consent of the 'parent' state, which holds territorial sovereignty.

This should not surprise us too much since international law sanctifies the principle of the territorial integrity of states as a corollary of the joint action of paragraphs 1 and 4 of Article 2 of the UNC. To demonstrate this, it is useful to reproduce the text of the famous "territorial integrity safeguard" clause codified in UNGA resolution 2625,[74] where, after reaffirming the right of peoples to self-determination in the contexts we have examined above, the UNGA takes care to specify that:

> Nothing in the foregoing paragraphs shall be construed as authorizing or encouraging any action which would dismember or impair, totally or in part, the territorial integrity or political unity of any sovereign and independent States *conducting itself in compliance with the principle of equal rights and self-determination of peoples* as described above and *thus possessed of a government representing the whole people belonging to the territory without distinction as to race, creed or colour.*[75]

Not surprisingly, international practice reflects this principle. During the crisis of Katanga, this region tried to secede from the Congo (Leopoldville) and effectively controlled a part of the latter's territory, UNSC:

> *Reaffirm*[*ed*] the policies and purposes of the United Nations with respect to the Congo (Leopoldville) … (a) To maintain the territorial integrity and the political independence of the Republic of the Congo; … and *Deplore*[*d*] all armed action in opposition to the authority of the Government of the Republic of the Congo, specifically secessionist activities and armed action now being carried on by the provincial administration of Katanga with the aid of external resources and foreign

74 This principle appeared, albeit in a more concise formulation, in UNGA resolution 1514 (XV) on granting of independence to colonial countries and peoples (para. 6).

75 Emphasis added.

> mercenaries, and *completely rejecting* the claim that Katanga is a "sovereign independent nation".[76]

Similarly, once again on the African continent – the Biafran crisis – the OAU Heads of State and Government:

> Reiterat[e] their condemnation of secession in any Member States, Recogniz[e] that situation as an internal affair, the solution of which is primarily the responsibility of Nigerian themselves.[77]

The International Community's "resistance" to the attempted secession of Somaliland and to its subsequent proclamation of independence[78] is therefore part of this trend confirming the vigour of the principle of territorial integrity and political unity of any state whose creation and existence is in accordance with the principle of the right of peoples to self-determination.

iii *Two (Currently) Controversial Cases: Kosovo and Crimea*

1 Kosovo (1999–2008–Present): the Laborious Gestation of a Secessionist State

The question of Kosovo, and more specifically that of its statehood under international law, can be considered from several angles of international law of territory: secession, the right to self-determination of peoples, remedial secession, direct international administration of territories, *etc.*

We will limit ourselves here to mentioning some of them.[79] At the outset, and without wishing to abuse this formula, the question of Kosovo is, especially in comparison with other cases to which it has been compared, truly *sui generis*, insofar as the direct involvement of the Security Council in the definition of its legal status has a considerable impact in the examination of its statehood. UNSC resolution 1244 (10 June 1999) – which, it should be recalled, is still in force – commits the Parties concerned, the Federal Republic of Yugoslavia (then Serbia-Montenegro and finally Serbia), on the one hand, and the representatives of the Albanian-speaking population of Kosovo (first through the

76 Resolution 161 (21 February 1961).

77 Resolution 51 (IV) of 14 September 1967 (OAU).

78 More recently, the 'Mouvement national de libération de l'Azawad (MNLA)' declared its secession – and independence – from Mali (6 April 2012). On Somaliland as a "*de facto* state", see *infra* Part 2. Chapter 7. Section B.

79 Kosovo will be discussed below as an example of direct international administration by the UN (see Part 3. Chapter 10. Section B).

KLA and then through the Provisional Institutions), on the other, to negotiate a final agreement. This agreement should contain a:

> political solution to the Kosovo crisis [which] shall be based on the general principles in Annex 1 and as further elaborated in the principles and other required elements in Annex 2.[80]

These principles include, first and foremost:

> A political process towards the establishment of an interim political framework agreement providing for substantial self-government for Kosovo, taking full account of the Rambouillet accords and the *principles of the sovereignty and territorial integrity of the Federal Republic of Yugoslavia and the other countries of the region.*[81]

Therefore, the Security Council was careful to reaffirm that no political solution to the legal status of Kosovo could prejudice the territorial sovereignty, belonging to the Federal Republic of Yugoslavia, without the consent of the latter (holder of the *titulus adquirendi*). In other words, Resolution 1244 does not depart from the principle that the consent of the parent state is required for separation, which can only be thus consensual.

The advisory opinion of the International Court of Justice, rendered at the request of the UNGA, does not change this conclusion. ICJ found that:

> [T]he interim administration in Kosovo was designed to *suspend temporarily Serbia's exercise authority flowing from its continuing sovereignty over the territory of Kosovo*. The purpose of the legal regime established under resolution 1244 (1999) was to establish, organize and oversee the development of local institutions of self-government in Kosovo under the aegis of the interim international presence.[82]

Moreover, the UN's principal judicial organ was called upon to determine the conformity of the "unilateral declaration of independence of the Provisional

80 Para. 1 of UNSC Resolution 1244 (10 June 1999).

81 Para. 8 of Annex 2 to UNSC Resolution 1244 [emphasis added]. See also ICJ, Accordance with International Law of the Unilateral Declaration of Independence in Respect of Kosovo, 2010, para. 114 (at 449).

82 *Ibid.* para. 98 (at 444) [emphasis added].

Institutions of Self-Government of Kosovo" with international law as well as with UNSC resolution 1244. Therefore, the ICJ was not required:

> by the question it has been asked to take a position on whether international law conferred a positive entitlement on Kosovo unilaterally to declare its independence or, *a fortiori*, on whether international law generally confers an entitlement on entities situated within a State unilaterally to break away from it. Indeed, it is entirely possible for a particular act – such as a unilateral declaration of independence – not to be in violation of international law without necessarily constituting the exercise of a right conferred by it. The Court has been asked for an opinion on the first point, not the second.[83]

Accordingly, no conclusion as to the statehood of Kosovo can be inferred either implicitly or, even less explicitly, from the Court's findings in this Advisory Opinion, that declarations of independence do not generally violate general international law[84] unless they are prohibited by special obligations (conveyed by competent UN bodies or established by international treaties) and/or peremptory norms of general international law. The Court was therefore not called upon to address either the legality of a declaration of independence or an alleged right to secession by a fraction of the people of its parent state without its consent. Moreover, the Court would seem to be saying, by implication, that while a declaration of independence is not *per se* illegal, the acts that would give effect to it, especially if they involve the threat and use of force, would be unlawful and illegal, as it affirmed, explicitly, in the Namibia case in relation to the occupation by South Africa.

In the same vein, the Court was careful not to discuss in the 2010 opinion the status in the international legal order of the so-called "remedial secession". This question did not fall within the scope of the question put to it by the

83 *Ibid.*, para. 56 (at 426).

84 'During the eighteenth, nineteenth and early twentieth centuries, there were numerous instances of declarations of independence, often strenuously opposed by the State from which independence was being declared. Sometimes a declaration resulted in the creation of a new State, at others it did not. In no case, however, does the practice of States as a whole suggest that the act of promulgating the declaration was regarded as contrary to international law. On the contrary, State practice during this period points clearly to the conclusion that international law contained no prohibition of declarations of independence', ICJ, Accordance with international law of the unilateral declaration of independence in respect of Kosovo, 2010, para. 79 (at 436).

General Assembly. Consequently, the alleged right to "remedial secession" can hardly support the legality of the creation of Kosovo as a state.

Thus, the statehood of Kosovo must be assessed against the backdrop of the traditional instruments of the internationalist's toolbox, namely international recognition by third States, membership in international organisations, especially universal ones, effectiveness of the exercise of governmental authority *to the exclusion* of another State (Island of Palmas' paradigm). Since international legal personality is universal, i.e., *erga omnes*, it is crucial that the entity in question enjoys very broad recognition by the International Community. Not to mention, and this is hardly a detail, that in the case of Kosovo, we are faced with a situation of (attempted) secession, hence the decisive role of the consent of the dispossessed state, Serbia, as in the case of the secession of Bangladesh from West Pakistan. However, Serbia's consent is currently lacking, which probably prevents Kosovo from obtaining more than the individual 117 State recognitions to date, as states fear that this could become a dangerous precedent overriding the territorial safeguard clause codified in general international law by UNGA resolution 2625.

This does not mean that state recognition generates constitutive legal effects, but that the greater or lesser number of recognitions that a territorially organised entity may or may not enjoy is certainly an important indicator of its effective existence as a state. Therefore, this aggregate of recognitions, which does not alter their declarative legal character, is a powerful indicator of both the effectiveness and the validity of the creation, especially in fluctuating situations,[85] i.e. of transition from one legal status to another. This process seems to be furiously reminiscent, obviously *mutatis mutandis*, of the evolution of customary international law as depicted by the International Court of Justice in the Nicaragua case.[86] Today, therefore, in the absence of

85 'From the point of view of both domestic and international law, the formation, transformation and dismemberment of States as a result of revolutions and wars create situations of fact which, to a large extent, cannot be met by the application of the normal rules of positive law. This amounts to a statement that if the essential basis of these rules, that is to say, territorial sovereignty, is lacking, either because the State is not yet fully formed or because it is undergoing transformation or dissolution, the situation is obscure and uncertain from a legal point of view, and will not become clear until the period of development is completed and a definite new situation, which is normal in respect to territorial sovereignty, has been established', Åland Islands Case, para. 3 (at 6) [emphasis added].

86 'In order to deduce the existence of customary rules, the Court deems it sufficient that the conduct of States should, in general, be consistent with such rules, and that instances of State conduct inconsistent with a given rule should generally have been treated as

Serbia's relinquishment of its legal title and in the face of a insufficient aggregate of international recognitions, by other states, it is difficult to conclude that Kosovo exists objectively[87] (*erga omnes*) as a state, i.e., opposable even to those states which do not recognise it.

On the other hand, if we take into account only the dimension of individual recognitions, there is no doubt that in the eyes of the states that have recognised it, Kosovo does exist as a state. On the contrary, it does not exist as such in the eyes of the states that do not recognise it, with easily imaginable practical consequences. In other words, the legal personality of a state, in principle enforceable *erga omnes*, is fragmented into as many bilateral relations linking Kosovo to each of the states of the International Community.

Furthermore, no decisive clue can be deduced from Kosovo's membership in international organisations,[88] especially universal ones, or in the specialised agencies of the United Nations. Its application to UNESCO in November 2015 was rejected (92 yes, 50 against and 28 abstentions). On the other hand, it was admitted to the IMF and the World Bank,[89] where, it should nonetheless be noted that the vote is weighted by economic criteria, which has allowed most of the Western countries, which have largely recognised Kosovo, to carry its full weight. Again, on 14 June 2016 the Permanent Court of Arbitration (PCA) decided, by a majority vote of its members (120), to revise its decision of 4 January of the same year, and to admit Kosovo as its 121st member.

With regard to the dynamic between the recognition of a state (by states) and its admission to an international organisation, it is important to stress that the rights and obligations that arise from the participation of a state in an international organisation are enforceable even between states that do not

breaches of that rule, not as indications of the recognition of a new rule', ICJ, Nicaragua, 1986, para. 186 (at 98). See: Distefano (2019), 365–369.

87 ICJ, Reparation for Injuries Suffered in the Service of the United Nations, 185 (the Court alluded to the 'the vast majority of the members of the International Community'). This is not to mention the absence of consent by the parent state, the only case in which this renunciation occurred *after the* admission of the new state to the United Nations, which is really a solitary exception, probably destined to remain so in view of the other two cases of secession, Eritrea and Southern Sudan.

88 Kosovo's admission to international sport bodies such as UEFA and FIFA in 2016 is of no internationally juridical relevance for the purposes of assessing its statehood. These are sports NGOs that are not subjects of international law and are therefore not qualified to scrutinize the statehood of Kosovo. This is especially true if one considers that among FIFA's 216 members there also are entities which are not independent states.

89 This implies the emergence of treaty links (rights and obligations), within these two UN specialised agencies, even vis-à-vis states that do not recognise Kosovo.

recognise each other bilaterally. International practice in this sense is constant, general and uniform, as the example of Israel and most Arab and Muslim States shows.

2 Crimea (from 2014 to Present Day)

In view of the purposes of this book, we will only deal with certain aspects of international law of territory. Under public international law, the current legal status of Crimea would be akin to that of a military occupation, according to Common Article 2 (2) GE 1949, even if the 'said occupation meets [and has met] with no [or almost no] armed resistance'. Article 6 of the Fourth Geneva Convention 1949 – which requires the effectiveness of the occupation – as well as Article 42 (1) of the Regulations Respecting the Laws and Customs of War on Land (annexed to the Fourth Hague Convention 1907) converge to corroborate the characterisation of the Crimean Peninsula (with Sevastopol) as a military occupation by the Russian Federation. The ICC Chief Prosecutor – Fatou Bensouda – was not wrong in this respect when she observed that:

> The available information suggests that the situation within the territory of Crimea and Sevastopol constitutes an international armed conflict between Ukraine and the Russian Federation which began on or before 26 February, when the Russian Federation deployed its armed forces to take control of parts of Ukrainian territory without the consent of the Government of Ukraine. The law of international armed conflict would continue to apply after 18 March 2014 to the extent that the situation on the territory of Crimea and Sevastopol relates, in effect, to an ongoing state of occupation [...] For the purposes of the Rome Statute, an armed conflict may be international in character if one or more States occupy the territory of another State in whole or in part, whether or not the occupation meets with armed resistance.[90]

The question of attribution (under the Law of State responsibility codified by ARSIWA) of the initial military acts of occupation – was the latter carried on by organs of the Russian Federation? – has no bearing on the legal regime of the occupation from the moment that Russia (illegally) annexed and (still) effectively occupies the Crimean Peninsula. As we have shown, this annexation has no legal effects in the international order (see *supra* Part 2. Chapter 5. Section

90 Report on preliminary examination activities in 2016, 14 November 2016, para. 158 (at 36–37): https://www.icc-cpi.int/sites/default/files/iccdocs/otp/161114-otp-rep-PE_ENG.pdf.

A) – apart from constituting an internationally wrongful act – and hardly changes the legal characterisation of military occupation.

On 11 March 2014, the regional parliament of Crimea proclaimed Crimea's independence and thus its detachment from Ukraine. It is curious to note that it refers in its proclamation to the 2010 ICJ advisory opinion on the declaration of independence of Kosovo:

> The parliament of the Autonomous Republic of Crimea has adopted an independence declaration from Ukraine which is necessary for holding a March 16 referendum: "We, the members of the parliament of the Autonomous Republic of Crimea and the Sevastopol City Council, with regard to the charter of the United Nations and a whole range of other international documents and taking into consideration the confirmation of the status of Kosovo by the United Nations International Court of Justice on July, 22, 2010, which says that unilateral declaration of independence by a part of the country doesn't violate any international norms, make this decision".[91]

In addition to the fact that the parliament relied on a highly questionable, if not outright erroneous, interpretation of the 2010 advisory opinion, it is important to stress that it did not have the power to transfer territorial sovereignty to the Russian Federation, as it had no such title under the Ukrainian Constitution. Moreover, the Crimean regional parliament did not represent a people in the sense of international law, and therefore entitled to exercise its right to self-determination in the international legal arena.[92] Furthermore, the argument that Crimea constitutes a *sui generis* situation is not tenable, as is often the case when, lacking legal titles, one relies on the exceptionality of circumstances. Indeed, it has been recalled that Crimea, formerly a region of the Russian Federation (within the USSR), was "granted" in 1954 to Ukraine by Nikita Khrushchev (at that time First Secretary of the Central Committee of the Communist Party of the Soviet Union) as a tribute to commemorate the 300th anniversary of the attachment of "Cossack Hetmanate" to the Russian Empire.[93] Whatever (USSR) constitutional flaws may affect the (internal)

---

91 The text was adopted at an extraordinary session of the Crimean regional parliament by an affirmative vote of 78 of its 100 members [italics in text].

92 Crimea was not a "non-self-governing territory" within the Ukrainian legal order under UNGA resolutions 1514 (XV) and 2625 (XXV).

93 Treaty of Pereiaslav (April 1654): https://ia801300.us.archive.org/15/items/traitdeproolaus/traitdeproolaus.pdf.

validity of this donation, they cannot change the legal status of Crimea within the independent Republic of Ukraine since 1991 following the dissolution of the USSR. Moreover, this status as an autonomous republic within Ukraine was recognised by the Russian Federation itself in 1997.[94] Much more decisive are the explicit and implicit recognitions by Russia of Ukrainian sovereignty over Crimea since the break-up of the USSR: i) Belovzeh Agreements (8 December 1991)[95] (i) Belovzeh Agreements (8 December 1991) in conjunction with the Alma-Ata Agreements (Declaration) (21 December 1991); (ii) Budapest Memorandum (5 December 1994);[96] (iii) Kharkov Agreement (21 April 2010);[97] (iv) Agreement on Cooperation in the Sea of Azov and the Kerch Strait (24 December 2003);[98] (v) Treaty on Friendshiṕ, Cooperation

94 Treaty on Friendship, Cooperation and Partnership between Ukraine and the Russian Federation (31 May 1997), *UNTS*, vol. 3007, n° 52240, 117–166.

95 Concluded by the three founding (existing) republics of the USSR (Russian Federal Socialist Republic, Belarus and Ukraine), https://www.cvce.eu/content/publication/2005/4/15/d1eb7a8c-4868-4da6-9098-3175c172b9bc/publishable_fr.pdf. The other (12) republics were invited to join this act of dissolution of the USSR and creation of the Commonwealth of Independent States (CIS). All except the three Baltic States (Estonia, Latvia, Lithuania) joined through the Alma-Ata (https://www.cvce.eu/content/publication/2002/9/17/ffcd1505-481e-42f5-8293-c8089b125eb0/publishable_fr.pdf).

96 Memorandum on Security Assurances in Connection with Ukraine's Accession to the Treaty on the Non-Proliferation of Nuclear Weapons (*UNTS*, Vol. 3007, n° 52241, 167–182), Article 2 of which is worded in the following terms: 'The Russian Federation, the United Kingdom of Great Britain and Northern Ireland and the United States of America reaffirm their obligation to refrain from the use of nuclear weapons and to take all necessary measures to prevent the proliferation of nuclear weapons (167–182), Article 2 of which reads: 'The Russian Federation, the United Kingdom of Great Britain and Northern Ireland and the United States of America reaffirm their obligation to refrain from the threat or use of force against the territorial integrity or political independence of Ukraine, and that none of their weapons will ever be used against Ukraine except in self-defense or otherwise in accordance with the Charter of the United Nations' (at 169).

97 "The Agreement between Ukraine and the Russian Federation on the Stay of the Black Sea Fleet of the Russian Federation on the Territory of Ukraine", Article 1 of which provides for the extension of the lease of the Russian military base on the territory of Crimea under Ukrainian sovereignty from 2017 for a period of 25 years from the entry into force (i.e., until 2042), extendable for further periods of 5 years. Article 2 sets out the terms of payment for the lease through financial and energy benefits. The Kharkov Agreement (https://zakon.rada.gov.ua/laws/show/643_359#Text) renews and extends the Treaty of Sharing on the Status and Conditions of the Black Sea Fleet (actually three bilateral treaties concluded on 28 May 1997). None of these international treaties have been registered with the UN Secretariat in accordance with Article 102 UNC (*International Newspapers*, Vol. 16 (15 August 1997), 577–582).

98 "Agreement between the Russian Federation and the Ukraine on cooperation in the use of the sea of Azov and the strait of Kerch" (https://faolex.fao.org/docs/pdf/bi-45795.pdf),

and Partnership between Ukraine and the Russian Federation (31 May 1997).[99]

Consequently, this proclamation of independence, which precedes the request for incorporation into Russia, has no legal effect in the international order. The legal regime of Crimea remains that of military occupation – a qualification made in the light of IHL – of a territory whose annexation has been contested both by Ukraine, the depositary of the *titulus*, and by the majority of states in the International Community. Furthermore, the UN General Assembly adopted a resolution on 24 March, the relevant passages of which are reproduced below:

> The General Assembly, [...]
>
> 5. *Underscores* that the referendum held in the Autonomous Republic of Crimea and the city of Sevastopol on 16 March 2014, having no validity, cannot form the basis for any alteration of the status of the Autonomous Republic or the city of Sevastopol;
>
> 6. *Calls upon* all States, international organizations and specialized agencies not to recognize any alteration of the status of the Autonomous Republic of Crimea and the city of Sevastopol on the basis of the above-mentioned referendum and to refrain from any action or dealing that might be interpreted as recognizing any such altered status.[100]

It is not surprising to see the usual triptych (*à la Namibie 1971*) at work here: invalidity, condemnation and non-recognition.

The question then is how this dissociation between *titulus* – with which Ukraine is clothed – and *modus* (effectiveness of Russian possession) will be reconciled. We have already discussed at length above the different scenarios that can be envisaged (see above Part 2. Chapter 5. Section B.ii).

---

whose Article 1 reads: 'The Sea of Azov and the Kerch Strait are historically internal waters of the Russian Federation and Ukraine. The Sea of Azov is delimited by the State border line, in accordance with the agreement between the parties' [our translation from Russian].

99 (*UNTS*, No. 52240, Vol. 3007, 117–166). Article 2 reads: 'The High Contracting Parties, in accordance with the provisions of the Charter of the United Nations and their obligations under the Final Act of the Conference on Security and Co-operation in Europe, shall respect each other's territorial integrity and confirm the inviolability of their common borders'. In the same vein, Article 29: 'The High Contracting Parties, as Black Sea States'.

100 Resolution 68/262 of 27 March 2014. This resolution is a good example of the application of Article 41 para. 2 and 3 ARSIWA.

C A (Truly) *sui generis* Case: Palestine (1998–2012–Present Day)

The birth of the Arab State of Palestine, contemplated by the UNGA Partition Plan in 1947,[101] wonderfully illustrates all the difficulties of a gestation hampered by – illegal – contrary effectiveness. In short, we find here, not surprisingly, the violation of the Palestinian people's right to self-determination[102] as well as, downstream, the inevitable violation of the obligation to use force.[103]

Of course, it is hardly a question here of retracing the path of the calvary leading to the birth of the State of Palestine, nor even less of examining the Israeli-Palestinian conflict,[104] but more simply of indicating the metamorphoses that preceded this birth.[105]

After the failure of the Partition Plan of 29 November 1947 recommended by the UNGA and the end of the British mandate over Palestine[106] In the night between 14 and 15 May 1948, the Jewish State of Palestine, i.e., Israel, was proclaimed. This was followed by no less than three Arab-Israeli conflicts, the first in 1948–1949, the second in 1967, the Six-Day War, and the third and last in 1973, the Yom Kippur War. In the wake of this last conflict, UNGA, by virtue of its powers[107] regarding the right of peoples to self-determination:

> *Invites* the Palestine Liberation Organization to participate in the sessions and the work of the General Assembly in the capacity of observer.[108]

According to the constant, general and uniform practice of the General Assembly, the granting of this status, a true constitutive recognition of a people enjoying the right to self-determination, implies that UNGA has identified the PLO as the true and sole representative of the Palestinian people. In 2004, the Court, after reaffirming the principle of the right to self-determination of

---

101 Resolution 181 (II) of 29 November 1947. It is worth recalling that Israel relied, among other bases, on the Partition Plan as the legal basis for its existence as a State, for the purposes of its admission to the UN (see *supra* Part 2. Chapter 5. Section B.ii).

102 ICJ, Wall in Palestine, 2004, para. 88 (at 171–172).

103 ICJ, Wall in Palestine, 2004, para. 87 (at 171).

104 In this regard, the monumental work of: Henry Laurens, *La Question de Palestine*, 5 volumes, Paris, 1999–2015.

105 See also: Distefano (2006), 185–200.

106 This resolution declares the *titulus adquisitionis* of the Jewish *and* Arab States of Palestine in the territories allocated by the Partition Plan. At the same time, it establishes the character of Jerusalem as an international city. See *infra* Part 3. Chapter 9. Section C.

107 See *supra* Part 2. Chapter 6. Section A.i.

108 Resolution 3237 (XXIX) of 29 November 1974.

peoples and noting its application to the Palestinian people, reproduced an excerpt from resolution 2625 (XXV) according to which '[e]very State has the duty to refrain from any forcible action which deprives [a people] of [its] right to self-determination'.[109] The Oslo Accords, concluded between Israel and the PLO in 1993, corroborate the former's recognition of the existence of this right in chief to the Palestinian people represented by the PLO. As the Court states in its 2004 Advisory Opinion:

> as regards the principle of the right of peoples to self-determination, the Court observes that the existence of a "Palestinian people" is no longer in issue.[110]

The same is true, accordingly, of the territorial base that spatially delimits the exercise of this right by the Palestinian people, namely the "Green Line" of the 1949 armistice in addition to the Gaza Strip.[111] Of course, this does not prevent the Parties[112] to freely conclude territorial adjustments or cessions.[113]

In 1998, UNGA took a further step to facilitate the implementation by the Palestinian people of its right to self-determination by adopting a resolution, the salient paragraphs of which are as follows:

> *Recalling* its resolution 181 (II) of 29 November 1947, in which, *inter alia,* it recommended the partition of Palestine into a Jewish State and an Arab State, with Jerusalem as a *corpus separatum,*
>
> *Recalling also* its resolution 3237 (XXIX) of 22 November 1974, by which it granted observer status to the Palestine Liberation Organization, [...]
>
> *Recalling* its resolution 43/177 of 15 December 1988, in which it acknowledged the proclamation of the State of Palestine by the Palestinian National Council on 15 November 1988 and decided that the designation "Palestine" should be used in place of the designation "Palestine Liberation Organization" in the United Nations system, [...]

109 ICJ, Wall in Palestine, 2004, para. 88 (at 172).
110 *Ibid.,* para. 118 (at 183).
111 *Ibid.,* para. 121 (at 184).
112 The wall in question, the result of unilateral action on the part of Israel, where it extends beyond the "Green Line", 'thus severely impedes the exercise by the Palestinian people of its right to self-determination, and is therefore a breach of Israel's obligation to respect that right', ICJ, Wall in Palestine, 2004, para. 122 (at 184).
113 As indeed the Security Council rightly stated in its resolution 2334 (23 December 2016).

1. *Decides* to confer upon Palestine, in its capacity as observer, and as contained in the annex to the present resolution, additional rights and privileges of participation in the sessions and work of the General Assembly and the international conferences convened under the auspices of the Assembly or other organs of the United Nations, as well as in United Nations conferences, [...]

7. Seating for Palestine shall be arranged immediately after non-member States and before the other observers; and with the allocation of six seats in the General Assembly Hall.[114]

Therefore, UNGA created an unprecedented status of a "super-observer", halfway between non-member state status and NLM status. In other words, Palestine became more than a mere NLM while not yet reaching the threshold of statehood, mainly due to the lack of effectiveness of the occupation (the *modus*). Indeed, despite the Oslo Accords, Palestine had not (and still has not) succeeded in exercising, even on a substantial part of the occupied territories, all State functions *to the exclusion of* any other state, according to the Island of Palmas' paradigm. A sort of a State *in statu nascendi*,[115] with the *titulus*, represented by the right of peoples to self-determination, enhanced by a very large number of international recognitions (today 146). Thus, for nearly 14 years, the legal status of Palestine was defined within the UN, a hybrid specimen of an international legal person that was half-state/half-NLM, bearing witness both to the right of the Palestinian people to constitute a state (*titulus*) and to the Israeli obstacles and *faits accomplis* (adverse *modus*).

However, this unprecedented, and necessarily transitional, status was replaced in 2012 by that of "non-member state" decided by the UNGA in the following terms:

The General Assembly,

Guided by the purposes and principles of the Charter of the United Nations, and stressing in this regard the principle of equal rights and self-determination of peoples,

Recalling its resolution 2625 (XXV) of 24 October 1970, by which it affirmed, inter alia, the duty of every State to promote, through joint and separate action, the realization of the principle of equal rights and self-determination of peoples,

114 Resolution 52/250 of 13 July 1998.

115 Like the "nascent *opinio juris*" the Court refers to in relation to the customary prohibition of nuclear weapons (ICJ, Threat or Use of Nuclear Weapons, 1996, para. 73, at 255).

Stressing the importance of maintaining and strengthening international peace founded on freedom, equality, justice and respect for fundamental human rights,

Recalling its resolution 181 (II) of 29 November 1947,

Reaffirming the principle, set out in the Charter, of the inadmissibility of the acquisition of territory by force, [...]

Recalling the advisory opinion of the International Court of Justice of 9 July 2004, [...]

Recalling its resolution 52/250 of 7 July 1998, by which additional rights and privileges were accorded to Palestine in its capacity as observer, [...]

Reaffirming the principle of universality of membership of the United Nations,

1. *Reaffirms* the right of the Palestinian people to self-determination and independence in their State of Palestine on the Palestinian territory occupied since 1967;
2. *Decides* to accord to Palestine non-member observer State status in the United Nations, without prejudice to the acquired rights, privileges and the role of the Palestine Liberation Organization in the United Nations as the representative of the Palestinian people, in accordance with the relevant resolutions and practice;
3. *Expresses the hope* that the Security Council will consider favourably the application submitted on 23 September 2011 by the State of Palestine for admission to full membership in the United Nations.[116]

Palestine is henceforth party to numerous multilateral conventions, including the four Geneva Conventions of 1949 and its two Protocols of 1977 (in addition to P/III of 2005). It is, inter alia, a member of the ICC and a party to the 1948 Convention on the Prevention and Punishment of the Crime of Genocide and the 1961 Vienna Convention on Diplomatic Relations (and its Optional Protocol concerning the Compulsory Settlement of Disputes).[117] It is also a Member State of UNESCO.

In the light of the foregoing, the statehood of Palestine is therefore difficult to dispute; it follows that its *status* is enforceable even against States that do not recognise it with regard to the application of general international law

116 UNGA Resolution 67/19 (4 December 2012).

117 See UNSC Resolution 497 (17 December 1981). See also the more recent and highly publicised UNSC Resolution 2334 (23 December 2016) and UNGA Resolution A/RES/ES-10/23 (14 May 2024).

and multilateral conventions to which Palestine and those States are parties. Admittedly, it is ultimately a state whose territory is almost entirely under military occupation.[118] But the uniqueness does not lie in this, but rather in the fact that Palestine, as a state, has been in this situation since its birth.[119] This is the *sui generis* character of Palestine as a state under international law, the territorial basis of which was nevertheless noted by the ICJ in its 2004 Advisory Opinion on the Wall in Palestine.[120]

118 ICJ, Wall in Palestine, 2004, para. 78 (at 126–127).
119 Para. 1 of Resolution 67/19 (4 December 2012).
120 ICJ, Wall in Palestine, paras. 121–122 (at 59–60).

CHAPTER 7

"The State in All Its States"

Although the prodromes can be traced back to the inter-war period, the creation of a state is, under the UNC, no longer a simple primary fact, an absolute triumph of effectiveness, mixed with the consent of the states concerned, but it must now satisfy certain peremptory rules of general international law, including the prohibition of the threat or use of force as well as the right to self-determination of peoples, as well, if applicable, UNSC or UNGA resolutions.[1]

The scenarios scrutinized in this section illustrate not only the tension between effectiveness (*modus*) and validity (*titulus*) in the creation of a state, but above all the way in which public international law deals with these situations. It should be noted that some of these situations, puppet states, *de facto* states and failed states, share at least one common feature: they fall nowadays within the compass of "New York Law", i.e., of collective security, and therefore represent a challenge for international peace and security.

A Puppet States

The term "puppet State" implies that behind this ectoplasm of a State there is another State, this time a real one, which *manipulates* the first one on the international legal scene. Most of them were created by violence at the expense of another state (Manchukuo, TRNC, South Ossetia, Abkhazia, Transnistria, *etc.*).

Having in mind the Island of Palmas' paradigm, a puppet State lacks both fullness and exclusiveness in the exercise governmental authority. Rather, another State (the "puppeteer", following the theatrical metaphor) wields these governmental functions, so that the puppet State has no exclusiveness in the exercise of state functions, both internally and, above all, externally – in its relations with other States and subjects of the international legal order.[2]

---

1 We have paraphrased – and translated into English – the title of a famous article by Prof. Georges Abi-Saab ("La coutume dans tous ses états", in *Etudes en l'honneur de Roberto Ago*, Vol. 1, Milan, 1987, 53–65).

2 'A puppet State is not a State at all according to international law. It is the occupant's creation and its instrument, and to this extent the position is relatively *clear, as the puppeteer State does not pretend to be related to, or act on the behalf of, the occupied State*', Krystyna Marek, *Identity and Continuity of States in Public International Law*, Geneva, 1968, 113.

 | DOI:10.1163/9789004708594_010

Thus, the negation of the statehood of a puppet state must be sought in the absence of "independence", i.e., *the* lack of *exclusiveness in the actual exercise of the fullness of state functions*, according to the famous *dictum* of M Huber in the Island of Palmas case. In other words, the "suprema potestas" according to Judge Dionisio Anzilotti:

> Independence as thus understood is really no more than the normal condition of States according to international law; it may also be described as *sovereignty* (*suprema potestas*) or *external sovereignty*, by which is meant that *the State has over it no authority than that of international law.*[3]

Indeed, the immediacy of a (true) state's subjection to public international law is the genuine mark of its statehood. Many authors have linked international legal personality to the immediate submission of the entity concerned to public international law, which reveals its anchorage in the international legal order. It has thus been observed that:

> German theory rightly accepts the distinguishing feature of this qualification: a community of law (*Rechtsgemeinschaft*) is as a subject of international law that it can be in immediate and direct relation and connection with the international order (*völkerrechtsunmittelbare Gemeischaft*).[4]

This passage resonates like a vibrant echo of the paradigm of the Island of Palmas or, later still, of the assertions of the Federal Constitutional Court of Germany, which identifies in the "Kompetenz-Kompetenz"[5] the ultimate competence of a state without which it would lose its statehood.

3 PCIJ, Austro-German Customs Regime, advisory opinion of 5 November 1931: *PCIJ Reports* A/B 41, 57 (individual opinion; emphasis added to the last sentence).

4 The Free City of Danzig and the International Labour Organisation, ICJ Reports, C 18-II, 41 [our translation].
(Speech by Mr Rundstein (Poland)). See also: James Westlake, *Chapters on the Principles of International Law*, Cambridge, 1894, 78; Thomas Lawrence, *Principles of International Law*, London, 1911, para. 34, at 54; *Hall's International Law*, ed. by Pearce Higgins, 8th edn, Oxford, 1924, para. 2, 20; Verdross (1929), para. 21, at 321; Hans Kelsen, "General Theory of International Law, Public. Selected Problems", 42 *RCADI* 1932-IV, 89; Guggenheim (1953), 83.

5 In its decision delivered on 30 June 2009, the German Federal Constitutional Court so declared (as to the ratification of the Lisbon Treaty on the European Union): 'The Basic Law does not authorise the German state bodies to transfer sovereign powers in such a way that their exercise can independently establish other competences for the European Union. It prohibits the transfer of competence to decide on its own competence (Kompetenz-Kompetenz) (see BVerfGE 89, 155 <187–188, 192, 199>; see also BVerfGE 58, 1 <37>; 104, 151 <210>). Even

In this respect, it is important to differentiate the case of the puppet state from the sometimes erroneously related case of the "Quisling Government". This term, coined after the name of the Norwegian Prime Minister (1942–1945) appointed by Nazi Germany – the occupying power for a large part of the Second World War – refers to a puppet government of a (real) state that is *in fact* run by another state. In contrast to a puppet state, in this case the state's statehood is not contested, but rather one of its elements, i.e. the political organisation that is supposed to maintain order and security within it and represent it on the international legal stage, is missing. This is where the finesse of the distinction between the state (its independence) and the government (its independence) and the consubstantiality between the two lies. While it is true that every puppet state is characterised – to varying degrees – by a "Quisling government",[6] the reverse is not true, as the example of Norway rightly shows.

Similarly, a distinction must be made between the case of the puppet state and that of the protectorate, which will be discussed below.[7] *Firstly,* the protected State was not created from scratch by the protecting State, as it existed before the protectorate link was established.[8] *Secondly,* and the two differences are intertwined, the protectorate is established by the consent of the protected State, normally conveyed by an international treaty, which precisely presupposes the international legal personality of the latter. The protected state retains internal sovereignty and its exercise (*summa potestas*), while the exercise of its external sovereignty (*suprema potestas*) is entrusted, by treaty, to the protecting State.

a far-reaching process of independence of political rule for the European Union brought about by granting it steadily increased competences and, by gradually overcoming existing unanimity requirements or so far as prevailing rules of State equality can, from the perspective of German constitutional law, only occur as a result of the freedom of action of the self-determined people. According to the constitution, such integrational steps must be factually limited by the act of transfer and must, in principle, be revocable. For this reason, withdrawal from the European union of integration (Integrationsverband) may, regardless of a commitment for an unlimited period under an agreement, not be prevented by other Member States or by the autonomous authority of the Union. This is not a secession from a State union (Staatsverband), which is problematical under international law (Tomuschat, 'Secession and Self-Determination', in: Kohen, Secession – International Law Perspectives, 2006, 23 et seq.), but merely the withdrawal from an association of sovereign States (Staatenverbund) which is based on the principle of reversible self-commitment' (para. 233, http://www.bundesverfassungsgericht.de/entscheidungen/ es20090630_2bve000208en.html).

6 The coevals "Quisling government" of Monsignor Tiso in Slovakia must be noted in this respect.

7 See *infra* Part 3. Chapter 8. Section G.

8 The existence as an independent state of the protected state is the very raison d'être of the protectorate.

Finally, it is important to explore the issue of verification, but more importantly, the tools that international law provides us with for the purpose of verifying and thus the existence of a puppet state. To this end, the body of rules on the international responsibility of the State perfectly fulfils this mission insofar as at least three provisions of the ARSIWA can be taken into account: articles 4, 8 and, by ricochet, 17. The notion of control is obviously central to each of these rules of attribution of conduct to a State, but while the last provision presupposes the existence of two States, a hypothesis which by definition must be ruled out here, the first two envisage cases where one State controls a more or less organised group of individuals. There is obviously no question here of sifting through the concepts underlying Articles 4 and 8, and even less of examining the refinement of case law by the ICJ, the ICTY and the ECtHR.[9]

While Article 4 ARSIWA requires,[10] for the purposes of attributing the conduct of a group of persons to a State, the former's "complete dependence" to the latter, Article 8 ARSIWA requires that the State concerned exercises "effective control" over the group of persons. As the ICJ had to repeat in 2007,[11] these two types of control are not the same and cannot be interchangeable, otherwise we would not need two different titles of imputability. In one case, the one envisaged by the "new wave" Article 4, as interpreted by the World Court in 2007, private individuals are "equated" to the *de iure* organs; in the second scenario, governed by Article 8, private individuals are *de facto* organ, even if sometimes the legal criterion shares the same name (i.e., "control"), albeit differently qualified.[12] Almost instinctively, it seems to us that the 'new wave'

9 We refer the reader to: Distefano, Hêche, 3–33.

10 It should be noted, however, that the situation generally governed by Article 4 is where the conduct of a person, group of persons or entity which "has the status of an organ" under the domestic law of a State is attributable to that State. In its 2007 judgment in the Genocide case, the Court was keen to emphasise that in exceptional circumstances, this provision may also cover the situation where this juridical link, bestowed by domestic law, is lacking.

11 ICJ, Application of the Convention on the Prevention and Punishment of the Crime of Genocide (Bosnia and Herzegovina v. Serbia and Montenegro), Judgement of 26 February 2007 (Merits): *ICJ Reports* 2007, paras. 379–407 (at 199–211).

12 This pre-eminence of control in both articles is explained by the criteria used to apprehend "complete dependence" in the *Nicaragua* case, namely "control" and "dependence". The criterion of control subsequently reached such proportions (with the *Tadic* judgment) that it became the spearhead of the attribution to bodies not formally recognised as such by domestic law. More generally, the question of attribution has mainly arisen in the context of armed groups (*Nicaragua* case; ICJ, *Armed Activities on the Territory of the Congo*, judgment of 19 December 2005, *ICJ Reports*, 2005; *Tadic* case and *Genocide* case). This centrality of armed groups as organs necessarily shaped the response to the Article 8 criteria and the residual Article 4 case. The violation at issue in the *Nicaragua*

Article 4 is better suited than Article 8 to pierce the veil, artificially erected by the controlling state in order to hide these misdeeds and to support, as far as possible, the statehood of the puppet state.

In the "complete dependence" scenario under Article 4, it must be shown that the State exercises a "particularly high degree of State control" (or, alternatively, "such strict control") over such persons or entity. If this is the case, the group of persons or entity is *equated* to a *de iure* State organ for the purposes of its international responsibility.[13]

As it has been rightly pointed out, Article 4 allows for the identification of cases where the state would "attempt to use this right [domestic law] in a fraudulent manner"[14] or to "deceive the International Community".[15] Effectiveness is therefore the key word thanks to which PIL triumphs over the attempt of states to "mask reality"[16] and thus avoid the wrath of international responsibility. The fictitious creation of a puppet state meets precisely this requirement: in addition to pretending that a real state has come into being, the controlling state escapes international responsibility for the actions of the organs of the puppet state.[17] In this context, it is worth recalling what the ICJ stated in a different context:

> Physical control of a territory, and not sovereignty or legitimacy of title, is the basis of State liability for acts affecting other states.[18]

---

case (use of force *through* armed groups; Article 2(4) of the UN Charter; see ICJ, Pleadings and Documents, *Military and Paramilitary Activities in and against Nicaragua (Nicaragua v. United States of America)*, vol. IV, 70 et seq., paras. 252 et seq.) has permeated the law of international responsibility in this area.

13 ICJ, Application of the Convention on the Prevention and Punishment of the Crime of Genocide, 2007, paras. 391–393 (at 204–205). It should be pointed out that the verb *equated* does not mean that these persons or this entity become organs of that State, since only the internal law of the State can make this qualification (it falls within its domestic jurisdiction). On the other hand, under the rules of international responsibility, the conduct of such persons or entity is attributable to the State in question in the same *way* as its *de iure* organs.

14 Public Hearing in the Genocide Case (ICJ, 2007), Official Report, CR 2006/10 (6 March 2006), 17.

15 *Loc.cit.*

16 *Ibid.*, 26.

17 '[A]ny other solution would allow States to escape their international responsibility by choosing to act through persons or entities whose supposed independence would be purely fictitious', ICJ, Application of the Convention on the Prevention and Punishment of the Crime of Genocide, 2007, para. 392 (at 205).

18 ICJ, Namibia 1971, para. 118 (at 54).

New wave Article 4 is therefore perfectly appropriate, it seems to us, to apprehend in the *Genocide* case the real and effective relations between the Republic of *Srpska* and Serbia, as in the case of puppet states, where what Professor Luigi Condorelli wisely calls "intégration organique" [organic integration] is manifested. In this light, the words of the ECtHR in the *Loizidou* case are strikingly eloquent:

> The Commission [of the ECHR] found that the applicant has been and continues to be denied access to the northern part of Cyprus as a result of the presence of Turkish forces in Cyprus which exercise an overall control in the border area [...] It is obvious from the large number of troops engaged in active duties in Northern Cyprus that her army exercises effective overall control over that part of the island. Such control, according to the relevant test and in the circumstances of the case, entails her responsibility for the policies and actions of the "TRNC".[19]

It is this lack of independence on the part of the puppet state that characterises its legal relationship with the puppeteer state and its impact not only in terms of international responsibility but also and above all on the statehood the former.

Indirectly, international humanitarian law also envisages the situation where, following – or during – an international armed conflict, the occupying power, instead of annexing *sic et simpliciter* the territory (or part of it) of the defeated state, proceeds to create a puppet state by concluding, for example, agreements with representatives of the population. Article 47 of IV GE 1949, which seems to harmoniously mix the "Geneva law" (*ius in bello*) and the "New York Law" (*ius contra bellum*), provides that:

> Protected persons who are in occupied territory shall not be deprived, in any case or in any manner whatsoever, of the benefits of the present Convention by any change introduced, as the result of the occupation of a territory, into the institutions or government of the said territory, nor by any agreement concluded between the authorities of the occupied territories and the Occupying Power, nor by any annexation by the latter of the whole or part of the occupied territory.

---

19 ECtHR, Case of Loizidou v. Turkey (Application no. 15318/89), Judgment of 18 December 1996, para. 56 (at 18).

Since one of the Powers finds itself:

> restricted, even temporarily, in its freedom to negotiate with the other Power or its allies by reason of military events, more particularly where the whole, or a substantial part, of the territory of the said Power is occupied.[20]

It is difficult not to discern in these two provisions the powerful resonance of Article 52 VCLT 1969, according to which "[a] treaty is void if its conclusion has been procured by the threat or use of force in violation of the principles embodied in the Charter of the United Nations". For, in the case of military occupation, violence by the victorious (and occupying) state on the vanquished state is built into the factual situation and the very reason for the agreement, hence its invalidity.

International practice abounds with situations, albeit with their own specificities, where the puppeteer state proceeded to create puppet states on part of the territory of the defeated state: Manchukuo (by Japan in 1932), Croatia and Slovakia (by Nazi Germany during WWII), the TRNC (by Turkey in 1983),[21] Abkhazia and South Ossetia (supported by the Russian Federation in 1993 and 1992 respectively), Transnistria (in 1991)[22] or the infamous "homelands"[23] and other "self-governing territories"[24] set up by South Africa on its own territory in order to solve, in its own way, the *apartheid* problem.

---

20 Article 11 (5) IV GE 1949. This is so unless the UNSC gets involved, as it did during the military occupation of Iraq in 2004 with its resolution 1546 (8 June 2004). See on this subject the brilliant reflections of: Luigi Condorelli, 'Le Conseil de sécurité entre autorisation de la légitime défense et substitution de la sécurité collective: remarques au sujet de la Résolution 1546 (2004)', in *Société française pour le droit international. Les métamorphoses de la sécurité collective – droit, pratique et enjeux stratégiques: actes des journées d'études franco-tunisiennes*, Paris, 2005, 231–239.

21 By its Resolution 541 (18 November 1983), UNSC '(2) *Considers* the declaration [of independence issued by the Turkish Cypriot authorities] as legally invalid and calls for its withdrawal' (para. 2) and therefore '(7) *Calls* upon all States not to recognize any Cypriot State other than the Republic of Cyprus;'.

22 Although in 2014, in the wake of Crimea's illegal occupation, Transnistria expressed its intention to join the Russian Federation.

23 Transkei, Ciskei, Bophuthatswana and Venda.

24 KwaZulu, KaNgwane, Gazankulu, Lebowa, KwaNdebele and Qwaqwa.

B *De facto* States

Being in turns tagged as "anomalies of the international system, oddities of public international law",[25] *de facto* states, despite their excessively small number, give grist to the mill of internationalists[26] as well as to the chancelleries of states, without forgetting, of course, the international organisations, which are sometimes solicited by their requests for recognition or even admission.

In nuce, while puppet states lack both effectiveness (*modus*) and validity (*titulus*), *de facto* states fulfil by definition the first condition, i.e., the effectiveness of their existence as territorially organised political entities.

In other words, unlike puppet states, which do not possess independence, *de facto* states are characterised by their *factual independence*. The *ius excludendi alios*, i.e., the exclusiveness in the exercise of State functions, according to the Island of Palmas' paradigm, is indeed present.[27] The four traditional elements for verifying the existence of a State in the sense of international law are present. Of course, sovereignty is present only *de facto*, since other States and international organisations are reluctant to recognise the "legal capacity to enter into relations" with them, as required by the definition enshrined in Article 1 of the 1933 Montevideo Convention.[28]

Indeed, there is a flaw in the genesis of *de facto* states, since their birth took place in defiance of one or more peremptory norms of general international law and/or (possibly) of a UNSC and/or UNGA resolution, or, failing that, of an organ of the competent regional organisation. Indeed, *de facto* states are almost always secessionist entities, parts of a state that secede from it outside the right of self-determination of peoples, and without the consent of the parent state.

The category of *de facto* states is necessarily the offspring of the new law that the UN Charter brings to the baptismal font; the introduction by the latter of norms prohibiting the threat and use of force or of the one erecting the right to self-determination of peoples as the architrave of the international system: mere effective independence is no longer sufficient for the purposes of

25 Maurice Bonnot, *Des États de facto*, Paris, 2014, 9.

26 See the fine thesis by Frank G Somé, *Les États de facto en droit international. Le cas du Somaliland*, Basel, 2020 (Collection Neuchâteloise).

27 They have been described as 'functioning reality with effective territorial control of a given area that is denied legitimacy by the rest of international society', Scott Pegg, *De Facto States in the International System*, Institute of International Relations, The University of British Columbia, working paper no. 21, February 1998, abstract.

28 See *supra* Prolegomena A.

creating a state. Hence, as we have just seen, the obligation of non-recognition, a guarantee of the international legal order. However, even if they are rare, precisely because of the safeguards that international law sets for them, *de facto* states have existed and continue to exist.

In the same vein, a distinction must be made between *de facto* states and rebels (or insurgents or insurgent movements) which 'exercise such control over a part of its territory as to enable them to carry out sustained and concerted military operations and to implement this Protocol', according to Article 1 (1) of the 1977 AP/II to the GE 1949. While it is true that in both cases there is control over territory, which is a matter of state sovereignty, it is also true that the situation of a *de facto* state is characterised by a certain degree of stability (*status*) both within and outside its 'borders'.[29] In other words, whereas in the case of rebels (or armed non-state actors) there is an ongoing non-international armed conflict (even latent and even with pauses), in the case of the *de facto* state, the conflict has factually ceased to exist, with the territorially organised political group exercising State functions more or less peacefully. It can even be argued that the *de facto* state can constitute the successive stage of a non-international armed conflict that sees the appearance of a subject of international law claiming recognition, constitutive in this case, of its statehood.

These *deviating* cases are necessarily temporary, transitory, as international law abhors a prolonged split between the effectiveness and validity of a territorial situation, or *a fortiori*, of a state.[30] Consequently, the two usual scenarios must be considered. International recognition (collective, institutional and *uti singuli*) and the consent of the parent state (sometimes one precedes the other, but both are cumulatively necessary, as in the case of successful secessions) eventually reconcile law and fact (*titulus* and *modus*). Otherwise, the reunification of the two elements of territorial title will take place with the sovereign, so that the *de facto* state will return within the ambit of the parent state. From this point of view, it should be emphasised that, as in the case of puppet states, the case under consideration is also at the crossroads between the

29 'Territorial sovereignty is, in general, a situation recognised and delimited in space', Island of Palmas case, 838 [emphasis added].

30 This temporary situation is nevertheless accompanied by an indisputable effectiveness, so that private international law, a long-standing companion of our science, envisages the possibility that third States might recognise the validity, or at least the applicability, of decisions given by the courts of the non-recognised State. See: Henry Battifol, Paul Lagarde, *Traité de droit international privé*, 8th edn, Paris, 1993, vol. 1, 430–433.

"New York Law" (international peace and security) [31] and the international law of territory. Finally, the existence of a *de facto* state constitutes a permanent challenge to international peace and security and as such is dealt with first, with the international law of territory coming later to define its legal status.

In conclusion, both *de facto* states and puppet states carry out and constitute international violations, but for different reasons that are precisely due to the specificities of their nature and genesis. The former are distinguished by the effectiveness of the exercise of state functions, but they lack the legal basis of this power, in short the validity; hence the illegal and illicit nature of their existence. In contrast, puppet States lack both effectiveness and validity, the former because it belongs to the controlling state, the latter to the dispossessed state, i.e., the state holding territorial sovereignty.

The exceptionality of *de facto* states is reflected in their rarity; indeed, on a strict interpretation of the definition, there is currently only one genuine example: Somaliland.[32]

It is worth tracing, if only briefly, some of the salient stages of its emergence as a *de facto* state, in order to illustrate its exceptionality. Formerly a British protectorate, it merged – 4 days after becoming independent on 26 June 1960[33] – with Somalia, which had just emerged from the Italian trust administration (Act of Union, 18 January 1961),[34] formerly a colony of that state. The

31 '[I]nternational society has traditionally chosen to respond to the existence of the de facto States in three main ways: actively opposing them through the use of embargoes and sanctions; generally ignoring them and having no dealings with them; and coming to some sort of limited acceptance and acknowledgment of their presence', Pegg, 4. Similarly: Michael Rywkin, "The Phenomenon of Quasi-States", *Diogenes*, 53(2), 23–28.

32 *The de facto* statehood of the secessionist territory of Nagorno-Karabakh (from Azerbaijan) is highly controversial. Its proclamation of independence (2 September 1991) has only been recognised by other puppet states (South Ossetia, Abkhazia and Transnistria), while Armenia has only *de facto* recognised its separation from Azerbaijan. In addition to a 1995 Security Council Presidential Statement (S/PRST/1995/21), the issue of the independence of Nagorno-Karabakh has not escaped the attention of this body, which has reaffirmed the principle of the territorial integrity of Azerbaijan as well as the inadmissibility of the acquisition of territory by force: resolution 884 of 12 November 1993, as well as its previous resolutions: 874 (14 October 1993); 853 (29 July 1993); 822 (30 April 1993).

33 That Somaliland was, at the time of its union with Somalia, an independent state is confirmed by the "Act of Union" with Somalia, Article 11 para. 4 of which provides that "all rights lawfully vested in or obligations incurred by the *independent Governments of Somaliland and Somalia* ... shall be deemed to have been transferred to and accepted by the Somali Republic upon its establishment" [emphasis added].

34 On the vicissitudes of this union, see Paolo Contini, *The Somali Republic: An Experiment in Legal Integration*, London, 1969. Indeed, the union between these two states – to be achieved by international treaty – had been approved by Somaliland on 27 June 1960, but not by Somali representatives. Another "Act of Union" (*Atto d'unione*) was drafted by the

attachment of Somaliland did not, however, erase the profound differences between these two former colonies: at the tribal level (different clan structures) as well as in terms of legal cultures imported from the metropolis (British and Italian, respectively). The lack of communication infrastructure between the two parts of the new state and a major territorial dispute with Ethiopia in the Ogaden region certainly did not help. In addition, repeated famines and droughts precipitated the end of the Siad Barre dictatorship in early 1991 and plunged the country into an unprecedented crisis.[35] While the former territory of Italian Somalia fell prey to the various Warlords,[36] on 17 May 1991, following an assembly of the former Somaliland clans, independence was declared in the territory of the former British colony. A first (provisional) constitution was adopted in February 1997, which was replaced by the constitution of 31 May 2001, following a plebiscite. Its Article 1 (1) reads as follows:

> The country which gained its independence from the United Kingdom of Great Britain and Northern Ireland on 26th June 1960 and was known as the Somaliland Protectorate and which joined Somalia on 1st July 1960 so as to form the Somali Republic and then regained its independence by the Declaration of the Conference of the Somaliland communities held in Burao between 27th April 1991 and 15th May 1991 shall hereby and in accordance with this Constitution become a sovereign and independent country known as "The Republic of Somaliland".

Although the OAU and the League of Arab States remain committed to the principle of Somalia's territorial integrity,[37] the UN noted that:

> "Somaliland" ... has maintained a high degree of autonomy for six years. The Transitional National Government and most of the other authorities have instituted varying degrees of stability and administrative order within their respective areas, allowing civilians to resume economic, social and, in some instances, political activities. Traditional rulers and civil society also play a greater role.[38]

Legislative Assembly of the Somali Trust Administration as a single text and later submitted to the National Assembly of that state.

35 Somalia holds the sad distinction of being the prime example in the category of 'failed states' discussed in the next section.

36 Minister for Immigration v. Haji Ibrahim, Australia, High Court, 26 October 2000, 131 *ILR*, para. 11.

37 See Report of the UN Secretary-General, S/2001/963 (11 October 2001), paras. 16 ff.

38 Report of the UN Secretary-General, S/2002/189 (21 February 2002), para. 28 (at 5).

Despite fairly vigorous diplomatic activity, no state has so far recognised Somaliland. Somaliland has unofficial, and therefore unrecognised, representations to the world's major powers, which it somewhat pompously describes on its website as "Embassies". International jurisprudence is, to say the least, absent, while domestic jurisprudence is not very significant:

> In May 1991, the breakaway Somaliland Republic was declared in the northwest within the pre-independence borders of the former British Somaliland. It is separately administered by a provisional government but it is not internationally recognized.[39]

An exception should perhaps be made for a decision of the European Court of Auditors:

> In Somalia, support was given to new structures that would generate revenue (e.g., import duties), the most important being the port in Berbera. Although the Commission supported the introduction of financial control systems, there are still doubts about transparency and accountability. The Commission should have been more cautious before committing itself to revenue-generating projects under the present conditions as Somaliland, where the port is located, has not been internationally recognized as an autonomous [sic!] State.[40]

Due to the absence of renunciation by the parent state, Somalia, the *titulus* still belongs to the latter, so it is appropriate to define Somaliland as a *de facto* secessionist state from its parent state. As long as Somalia's consent (renunciation) is lacking, and in the absence of recognition by International Community at large and by States *uti singuli* (two elements of the 'triptych'), it is impossible to consider Somaliland as a State in the sense of international law with all the consequences that flow from it. It would therefore be inappropriate for a third State to enter into legal relations with Somaliland. Consequently, international treaties with, for example, the United Arab Emirates (hereinafter: UAE) providing for the establishment of a military base in the strategic port of Berbera with

---

39 Minister for Immigration v. Haji Ibrahim, para. 112.

40 Special Report No 4/2000 on rehabilitation operations in favour of ACP States as a preparation for normal development aid, together with the Commission's replies, C 113/1, 19 April 2000, para. 83 (at 14). The adjective "autonomous" is rather unfortunate for it would have been more accurate to replace it by "independent", according to PIL tenets.

a related lease agreement, must be considered as violations – by these states – of the territorial integrity and political independence of Somalia.[41]

In conclusion, it is worth mentioning here some of the aspects that make Somaliland a true *de facto* state, if only to set aside, in its light, the other false examples, among which is Taiwan (or Taipei). Not only has the latter never proclaimed its independence from the People's Republic of China, but it has always claimed, at least initially, to be the real government representing the whole of China. Here we are faced with a situation where, following a civil war in which the (Maoist) rebels triumphed, the (Nationalist) government had to take refuge in 1949 precisely on the island of Taiwan. Until 1971, the government of Chiang Kai-shek continued to claim exclusive representation of the whole of China and as such was considered by the majority of states (except, of course, the communist states and in particular the USSR) and by the UN, where it occupied the seat of a permanent member of the Security Council (under the denomination "Republic of China"), as the representative of the whole of China (including the mainland). It was only in 1971 that UNGA adopted resolution 2758 (XXVI)[42] recognising – this recognition engendering constitutive legal effects – that:

> the representatives of the Government of the People's Republic of China are the only lawful representatives of China to the United Nations and that the People's Republic of China is one of the five permanent members of the Security Council.[43]

41 The agreement in question, concluded on 14 February 2017 (the date is uncertain, however), is entitled "Seven-Point Economic and Military Pact". According to its Article 1, this agreement '*is an agreement in line with international standards* [*sic!*] *and proves that Somaliland is indeed the sole legitimate authority of its territory and people*'. According to its Article 2, the Republic of Somaliland 'will lease' Berbera International Airport (and its adjoining naval base) to the UAE for a period of 25 years in exchange for projects funded by the UAE to the tune of US$1 billion. However, it is Article 6 (and incidentally 7) of this agreement that puts the UAE in serious trouble with international law and the obligation to neither recognise nor aid and abet a separatist entity: "The [UAE] promises to protect the Republic of Somaliland from all external threats and to protect Somaliland's sovereignty and territorial integrity (land and maritime boundaries) [sic!]". The text of this agreement, which has not been registered with the UN Secretariat (in accordance with Article 102 of the UNC), was found by the author in the *National* (Abu-Dhabi), 21 March 2017.

42 Resolution of 25 October 1971.

43 This recognition included the immediate expulsion 'the representatives of Chiang Kaishek from which they unlawfully occupy at the United Nations and in all the organizations related to it'.

Republic of China ("Taiwan") is today a subject of international law *sui generis*, party to treaties and member of certain universal international organisations, such as the WTO (as "separate customs territory", Taipei Chinese, since 2002).[44] It is therefore not a state, even if it exercises the full and exclusive sovereign functions over a given territory; it has not declared its independence from the People's Republic of China, even if from time to time it has brandished the threat, considered by Beijing as a real *casus belli*. It is currently recognised as a state by only 13 states,[45] but this does not prevent the other states from maintaining (sometimes very close) trade relations,[46] governed by international treaties. To conclude briefly, the case of Taiwan raises issues of representativeness, of government, of a single state and this by the very claims of Taiwan and Beijing.[47]

C Failed or "Failing" States

This label was coined by Helman and Ratner, in an article that could be described as 'seminal':[48]

44 It is important to note that it was admitted simultaneously with the People's Republic of China (as a Member State).

45 The People's Republic of China quite logically demands that a third state cannot recognise both Taiwan and Beijing at the same time, which proves, in Beijing's eyes at least, that it is indeed a single state *de iure*.

46 In the form of "Economic and Cultural Representative Offices" or "Economic and Trade Offices". In addition, the national airline "Eva" serves numerous stopovers in countries which nevertheless recognise the People's Republic of China. As Taiwan is not a party to, for example, the Warsaw Convention of 12 October 1929 – subsequently amended and supplemented by the Hague Protocol of 28 September 1955 – matters governed by these treaties are regulated by bilateral treaties between Taiwan and the states concerned. In this respect, it should be noted that the People's Republic of China attached to its instrument of accession of 16 June 1997 the following notification: "The Government of the People's Republic of China is the sole legal government representing the Chinese people. The [Warsaw] Convention to which the Government of the People's Republic of China adheres shall of course apply to the entire Chinese territory including Taiwan". Beijing saw fit to issue this notification because Taiwan (or more correctly the "Nationalist Republic of China") had been a party to it since 20 July 1958.

47 Taiwan 'would appear to be a non-State territorial entity which is capable of acting independently on the international scene, but is most probably *de jure* part of China', Malcolm Shaw, *International Law*, 7th edn, Cambridge, 2014, 170.

48 As has been very correctly observed, the denomination *failed State* is 'clearly a misnomer, since the bodies concerned, though infirm, have still not reached the international graveyard. They should be called "Failing States" and are said to be "in danger of disintegration"', Davies, 731.

> The idea, then, that states could fail – that they could be simply unable to function as independent entities – was anathema to the raison d'etre of decolonization and offensive to the notion of self-determination. New states might be poor, it was thought, but they would hold their own by virtue of being independent. While it lasted, the Cold War prolonged the viability of some of the newly independent and other Third World states. Countries with seriously underdeveloped economies and governments received hefty infusions of aid from their former colonial masters as well as from the two superpowers. The systemic corruption that characterized many of the new states did not stop the superpowers from sending foreign aid as they sought to buttress a potential ally in the Cold War.[49]

However, from the point of view of international law, the term is highly mistaken and misleading[50]since in this recent phenomenon, what has failed is not the state as such, but rather its *government* in the sense of international law, or rather the inability of a political organisation to exercise "State functions", as Max Huber stated in the Island of Palmas case.[51] Consequently, the case under consideration ("failed States") highlights a question of "(good) governance"[52] and not of statehood. As a matter of fact, in the first historical example that has been identified, that of Somalia (since 1991),[53] the international legal personality of the latter, or rather its existence as a state, has never been contested.[54] What was lacking, however, was the existence of a single government – over and above the cacophony determined by the warlords infesting

49 Gerald Helman, Steven Ratner, 'Saving Failed States', 89 *Foreign Policy* 1992–3, 4. Similarly: Steven Ratner, 'The Cambodia Settlement Agreements', 87 *AJIL* 1993, 1–41. See also: Ashraf Ghani, Clare Lockhart, *Fixing Failed States*, Oxford, 2009 (the first author is a former President of the Islamic Republic of Afghanistan).

50 Despite domestic and international jurisprudence that is sometimes not very meticulous in this regard: "Where the State has disintegrated, as appears to have been the case in Somalia", Minister for Immigration v. Haji Ibrahim, Australia, para. 69; Al-Dahas v. Attorney-General and Others, Kenya High Court, 1er March 2007, 143 *ILR*, 343. See also the dissenting opinion of Judge Kateka attached to the ICJ judgment in Armed Activities on the Territory of the Congo (DRC v. Uganda), judgment of 19 December 2005: *ICJ Reports* 2005, para. 37 (at 372).

51 Island of Palmas case, 838.

52 "Fixing Fragile Nations. Conquering Chaos", *The Economist*, 7 January 2017.

53 "The brutal term 'failed state' was almost invented for Somalia. Since 1991, when its military dictator was overthrown, it has had no government that fully controls the country and no election worthy of the name", "Hope among Terror", *The Economist*, 19 November 2016.

54 The same has been true in all other examples that are rightly or wrongly cited as 'failed states', such as Liberia and the DRC.

the country – which was able to exercise the regalian functions over the whole (or almost the whole) Somali territory (law and order). As a result, it was one of the constitutive elements of the state, i.e., the government as a political organisation with territorial control, that was missing, not the state. The difficulty, or even the inability, of a government to fulfil its mission[55] is certainly one of the conditions for its existence under international law,[56] but it cannot extinguish its statehood.[57]

As a result, at the international level, the representativeness[58] of Somalia was suspended (e.g., within the UN and its specialised agencies). In this context, the recognition (or lack thereof) of the government as the legitimate representative of the Somali population by the UN and/or the relevant regional organisation(s) plays a crucial role, as was the case recently in Libya, where UNSC:

> Endorses the Rome Communiqué of 13 December 2015 to support the Government of National Accord *as the sole legitimate government of Libya*, stresses that a Government of National Accord that should be based in the capital Tripoli is urgently needed to provide Libya *with the means to maintain governance*, promote stability and economic development, and expresses its determination in this regard to support the Government of National Accord.[59]

The issue of "failed States" becomes even more complicated and the analysis is often "polluted" because this topic is at the crossroads of other branches of PID: The use of force (and international security and peace), the so-called right of (humanitarian) intervention, the right to development, the right to

55 What we call *governance today* and what Machiavelli once called the "Buongoverno" (see the allegory – a set of frescoes – painted by Ambrogio Lorenzetti in the "Palazzo Pubblico" in Siena, 1338–1339).

56 '[I]ts ability to maintain itself, and discharge its internal duties and its external obligations', Tinoco case, 378.

57 *Contra*: 'The essence of State failure … is a lack of capacity or factual power pure and simple … State failure is the inability to run a modern State as a going concern. Within the failed State there is an inability per se to uphold a minimum level of normative institutional order that statehood requires. Hence the overall situation of disorder and anarchy that characterizes State failure', Gerard Kreijen, *State Failure, Sovereignty and Effectiveness: Legal Lessons from the Decolonization of Sub-Saharan Africa*, Leiden, 2004, 96.

58 'So far its international obligations are concerned, it [the government] represents the state', Tinoco case, 378.

59 Resolution 2259 (23 December 2015), para. 3 [emphasis added].

self-determination of peoples, IHL (there is – or has been – necessarily a CANI, or even an IAC), often with the intervention of one or more third-party states, the issue of rebels or even secessionist entities and, as in the paradigmatic example of Somalia, the presence of a *de facto* state (Somaliland).

D Drowning States: Looming Deterritorialisation of Sovereignty?

In view of the purpose of this book, we will limit ourselves to a brief discussion of some of the aspects and consequences of partial or complete drowning of a state's territory.[60] Unsurprisingly, these different dimensions of the same problem are intimately linked and, as we shall see, the solutions that the International Community will have to find through international law arise from taking this uniqueness into account. Moreover, the fact that this phenomenon is still in its infancy "invites us not only to an exercise in international law by anticipation",[61] but also offers the organised International Community a rare opportunity for preventive settlement of the problems it raises.

First, the effects of drowning on the *status of* a state,[62] in other words its statehood. In the case of partial recovery of a state's territory, the statehood of the latter, despite the reduction of its original territorial base, cannot be affected. The same cannot be said of the drowning of most of its territory, or even of the complete recovery of the state's land territory. Can we still speak of a state within the meaning of international law? Would it not lack one of its constituent elements, making it impossible, under these circumstances, for another constituent element to exist, namely its population? In the ubiquitous Island of Palmas case, the sole arbitrator rightly insisted on the consubstantiality[63] between the State and its territory, particularly in the context

60 In 2019, the ILC has started its work on this issue by establishing a working group on "Sea-level rise under international law". This will be examined from three perspectives: (i) the law of the sea; (b) "the situation of the State whose territory and population disappear"; and (c) "what protection do people directly affected by sea-level rise enjoy under international law?" (UN Doc. A/73/10, 352).

61 Julien Jeanneney, 'L'Atlantide. Remarques sur la submersion de l'intégralité du territoire d'un Etat', 118 *RGDIP* 2014, 97 [our translation].

62 "Second issues paper by Patrícia Galvão Teles and Juan José Ruda Santolaria", ILC, 31 March 2022, A/CN.4/752. See also: Additional paper to the first issues paper (2020) by Bogdan Aurescu and Nilüfer Oral (74th session of the ILC (2023)).

63 "It seems therefore natural that an element [the territory] which is essential for the constitution of sovereignty should not be lacking in its continuation", Island of Palmas Case, 839.

of the territorial sovereignty that the former exercises over land areas and which uniquely distinguishes it from other subjects of the international legal order. The independence of a state is *concretely* based on the enjoyment of *ius excludendi alios* over part of the land surface.[64] It is therefore difficult,[65] if not impossible, for contemporary international law to accommodate a state without territory,[66] a situation that must obviously be distinguished from that of a government[67] in exile. In this case, it would be an absurd hypothesis that it would be a "State in climatic exile".

Consequently, and without prejudice to the aspects of international responsibility (especially in terms of compensation or even restoration of the situation), we should conclude that a State has disappeared due to a natural event, albeit determined by human activities. Moreover, according to current international law, the natural extinction of a state as a result of the complete drowning of its territory would also have the consequence of rendering its nationals' *ipso iure* stateless. In effect, we would be faced with the extinction of a state *without* state succession, precisely because of the drowning of the earth's soil, the very ground of its territorial base.

From this perspective, it is easy to understand the cry of alarm launched by the delegate of the Republic of Palau at the annual session of the UNGA in 2008:

> Never before in all history has the disappearance of whole nations been such a real possibility.[68]

Or the highly publicised meeting of the Maldives Council of Ministers on 17 October 2009 at a depth of 5 metres in a wetsuit.[69]

---

64 Island of Palmas case, 838.

65 In this sense: Jeanneney, 2014, 126.

66 This situation is different, of course, from that of a State whose entire territory is under military occupation, including from the very beginning of its existence as a State, as in the case of Palestine (see *above* Part 2. Chapter 6. Section B.iv).

67 The doctrine has always considered the government as the distinctive element, among the four (see *supra* Prolegomena A). But even this assertion must be qualified, insofar as the temporary disappearance of an effective government has not prevented the survival of a "failed State" such as Somalia (see *supra* Part 2. Chapter 7. Section C).

68 UNGA 63rd session (25 September 2008) – UN General Assembly resolution on "Climate Change and Its Possible Security Implications" – UN doc A/63/PV.9, Mr Chin (Palau), 9.

69 Courrier international, 18 October 2009.

In a related register, that of maritime spaces,[70] while it is true that State is an amphibious animal, it is no less true that it needs land territory in order to be recognised under international law to be vested with rights over maritime spaces which are generated by territorial sovereignty. Thus, still considering the two above-mentioned scenarios, even in the case of partial drowning, there will be several consequences: the shrinking of maritime spaces (including EEZ) and the transformation of the legal status of some of them. Indeed, the rise in sea level will lead to the withdrawal of the baselines (straight or not) from which the width of all maritime areas is measured and, as a consequence, the shrinking of maritime areas. The same applies to the delimitation of the outer edge of the continental shelf, since even in the absence of another State's continental shelf (facing or adjacent), the withdrawal of the baseline will result in the retreat of the continental shelf, while leaving its extent unchanged, since the criterion used by general international law, codified in the Convention on the Law of the Sea of 1982 (hereinafter referred to as UNCLOS), is that of the distance from the coast (Article 76 para. 4 UNCLOS)

Of course, one solution would be, still in the case of partial drowning, to ensure that the width of maritime areas and their outer limits remain unchanged despite the rise of sea level. On 6 August 2021, the Pacific Island Forum (PIF)[71] adopted the "Declaration on Preserving Maritime Zones in the Face of Climate Change-Related Sea-Level Rise", the third paragraph of which reads

> *Declare* that once having, in accordance with the Convention, established and notified our maritime zones to the Secretary-General of the United Nations, we intend to maintain these zones without reduction, notwithstanding climate change-related sea-level rise.[72]

---

70 "First Issues Note by Bogdan Aurescu and Nilüfer Oral, Co-Chairs of the Study Group on Sea Level Rise under International Law", ILC, 28 February 2020, A/CN.4/740, 23–84.

71 The "Pacific Islands Forum" is an international organisation (Article 1 er) created in 1971, although it was formally established by the eponymous Treaty concluded on 27 October 2005 in Port Moresby (https://forumsec.org/sites/default/files/2024-03/Agreement-Establishing-the-Pacific-Islands-Forum-Secretariat-2005-1.pdf). It comprises 16 States in addition to French Polynesia and New Caledonia, which are also members despite not being States.

72 https://forumsec.org/publications/declaration-preserving-maritime-zones-face-climate-change-related-sea-level-rise. The following paragraph follows the same logic and deserves to be reproduced here: "*Further declare* that we do not intend to review and update the baselines and outer limits of our maritime zones as a consequence of climate change-related sea-level rise'.

This solution would be dictated by analogy[73] with the legal regime of international river boundaries in the case of gradual natural changes, as evidenced by both international jurisprudence[74] and doctrine.[75] Moreover, it would meet the requirements of equity and justice that otherwise permeate the law of the sea in relation to the EEZ and the continental shelf where reference is made to the "equitable solution" (in Articles 74 and 83 UNCLOS respectively). More specifically, considering the human causes of sea-level rise, this solution would fit perfectly with the principles of international state responsibility governing the consequences of an internationally wrongful act, i.e., restitution and/or compensation. More on this later.

This same solution could be adopted, in a perspective of progressive development of international law (Article 13 UNC), in the case of the total drowning of some parts of the territory of a State, i.e., certain islands of which it is composed. There would then be continuance of the maritime boundaries determined by the islands now submerged. In this hypothesis too, the same considerations of equity and justice as those mentioned above in the situation of partial drowning apply. In this context, it should be noted that the change in the characteristics of the islands, due to the rise in sea level, might have consequences, by virtue of the principle of "the Land dominates the Sea", on the legal status of the bordering maritime areas. If, for example, an island becomes a 'rock which cannot sustain human habitation or economic life', then this 'naturally formed area of land' (121(1)) 'shall have no exclusive economic zone or continental shelf', in accordance with Article 121(3) of UNCLOS, although it will continue to generate its territorial sea (2). This is of little consolation, as the State would lose in one fell swoop huge areas of water, soil and subsoil of the sea as well as the exclusive right to exploit their natural resources. In order to maintain its economic and sovereign rights over *its* EEZ and even *its* continental shelf, Japan has artificially consolidated the island of Okinotorishima[76] and

73 *Oppenheim's International Law* (1992), vol. I, 717–719.

74 El Chamizal case, 320.

75 Dionisio Anzilotti, 'Intorno agli effetti delle modificazioni del corso di un fiume sul confine fra due Stati', 3 *Rivista* 1914, reprinted in *Scritti di diritto internazionale pubblico*, vol. 1, Padua, 1956, 687–705; Lucius Caflisch, "Règles générales du droit des cours d'eau internationaux", 219 *RCADI*, 1989-VII, 62–103.

76 The Commission on the Limits of the Continental Shelf, established by Article 76 of UNCLOS, to which Japan referred the question of whether this "tract" of land territory is an island or a rock, suspended its judgment in 2012 pending the prior resolution of disputes on this issue between Japan, China and Taiwan. See also Andrew L Silverstein, "Okinotorishima: Artificial Preservation of a Speck of Sovereignty", 16 *Brooklyn Journal of International Law* 1990-II, 414.

Venezuela is reportedly preparing to do the same for the island of Aves in the Caribbean Sea. But can we imagine a state doing the same for its entire territory? Leaving aside the astronomical costs – especially for states without sufficient financial resources – the question of the compatibility of this work with the requirement of the Law of the Sea of the 'naturally formed area of land' arises with acuity. In other words, it is difficult to acknowledge the statehood of a state whose entire territory is submerged by the sea, unless, of course, exceptions are made for island states 'in the process of drwoning'.

On the other hand, in the case of the *total* drowning of a State, or at least of a very substantial part of its territory, the limits of the *equitable* solution proposed here would be reached. Applying it to this extreme situation would run the risk of offending both the very logic that underlies it and would not meet the practical needs that underlie the rights and competences recognised to riparian States over these maritime spaces: protection, applying and enforcing international law, exercising criminal action, etc. Moreover, how can we imagine that the land territory generating sovereign and economic rights over adjoining maritime spaces would disappear without the latter sharing the same fate? Furthermore, from what territory could the State – now drwoned – exercise its governmental authority over these maritime spaces? Some of the answers can be found in the broader question of the survival of the state – with its land territory – at all.

This naturally brings us to the very basis of the State's rights over its maritime spaces, i.e., its land territory, particularly in the case of the scenario of total drowning feared by certain island States in the Pacific and the Indian Ocean. Is it possible to imagine a state without land territory? If not, would leasing a parcel of the latter's land territory from another state be sufficient to maintain the fiction of land territory as a *fons and origo of the* tenant state's rights over maritime spaces no longer adjoining that territory? Not to mention, upstream, the absence of real sovereignty since the territory is only *leased* in ownership or *administration*, with the lessor state retaining the right of sovereignty.[77] Even in the most favourable case of administration, where the lessee state would exercise State functions, we would be qualitatively far from the notion of sovereignty. The solution of merging a drowning State with another State[78] has also been mentioned; however, this would be a short-lived ploy, as if the process of sea-level rise continues, the problem will simply be pushed further back in time.[79]

77 On these concepts, see below Part 3. Chapter 8. Section A.

78 Alfred H Soons, "The Effects of a Rising Sea Level on Maritime Limits and Boundaries", 37 *Netherlands International Law Review* 1990-II, 230.

79 See: "Second issue paper" (supra note 62), 49–60.

These extreme scenarios are likely to occur in the near future[80] and states and international organisations will have to draw on the toolbox of international law to devise innovative solutions to phenomena unprecedented in the history of international relations.

In the same vein, it is worth touching on one of the possible consequences of the drowning of states, namely that of 'climate refugees',[81] also known as 'climate stateless people'.[82] There is no need to go into this at length here, as the discussion must be conducted within another branch of international law, refugee law. However, since the material cause that drives some inhabitants (nationals) of drowning States falls within the scope of international law of territory, it is worth devoting a few lines to it.

In the light of the regime enshrined in the 1951 Geneva Convention on refugees, the right to be received in a country other than that of residence or nationality ("the principle of non-refoulement") must be sought in discrimination based on any of the five grounds listed, in a restrictive manner, by the 1951 Geneva Convention in Article 1 §2: 'for reasons of race, religion, nationality, membership of a particular social group or political opinion'. There must therefore be discrimination, which is apparently absent in this case, if one follows the considerations of the New Zealand Court of Appeal:

> These claims had all been dismissed because the indiscriminate nature of these environmental events did not point to any nexus with a Convention ground.[83]

In other words, the rise in sea level forcing the inhabitants of certain at-risk islands to flee these territories does not discriminate on the basis of one of these five elements, but affects all inhabitants equally. Discrimination does exist and concerns the inhabitants of certain territories that are below the sea

80 Faced with a rising Pacific, Kiribati is buying 20 km² of refuge land from Fiji. Mostly covered in lush forests, the area was given by the Anglican Church for AU$9.3 million (€6.4 million). "I hope we wouldn't have to send anyone there, but if it became absolutely necessary, then we could do it", said Mr Tong (President of Kiribati), *Le Monde*, 14 June 2014 [our translation].

81 See: Sheila C McAnaney, "Sinking Islands? Formulating a Realistic Solution to Climate Change Displacement", 87 *New York Law Review* 2012, 1172–1209. See, e.g., especially the ILC's thorough and articulate study ("Second issue paper", *supra* note 62, 61–83).

82 See: Etienne Piguet, "Des apatrides du climat?", *Annales de Géographie*, n°683 (2012), 86–100.

83 Teitiota v. Chief Executive of the Ministry of Business, Innovation and Employment, High Court, Court of Appeal, 26 November 2013/8 May 2014, 158 *ILR*, para. 28.

level than others in the world, but it cannot constitute a valid reason for refuge within the meaning of the 1951 Geneva Convention. Consequently, pending, if ever, an evolution of the latter or even of the underlying general international law, we are left to turn to another branch of international law, namely the law of international state responsibility.

Is it possible to conceive of international state responsibility[84] for activities that are not prohibited by international law but which, a few decades later, cause damage to the environment and indirectly to drowning States?[85] This brings us to the other branch of international state responsibility, the one that does not require an internationally wrongful act, but does require material damage caused by a dangerous activity. The ILC has dealt with the issue of 'International liability for injurious consequences arising out of acts not prohibited by international law' and in 2001 and 2006 respectively adopted two texts of articles entitled: (a) 'Prevention of transboundary damage from hazardous activities'; and (b) 'International liability in case of loss from transboundary harm arising out of hazardous activities'. Principle 4 of the latter text reads "prompt and adequate compensation",[86] which could possibly include, in the event of failure to *return* the territory now submerged, the obligation for States to *sell* or *lease* parts of their land territories, or to grant them in administration or ownership. Or, in the event of partial drowning, that they recognise the same amount of maritime space to the States affected by the rise in sea level, despite the disappearance of the land areas generating it. In a word, the states responsible, through their industrial or other activities, for the rise in sea level would not be able to avoid their liability, in accordance with the well known principle: *nemo ex suo delicto meliorem suam condicionem facere potest* (Ulpien).[87]

Whether or not international law will fail will depend in part on the effectiveness of the International Community's responses to the issue of drowning States.

---

84 See, inter alia: Roda Verheyen, *Climate Change Damage and International Law. Prevention Duties and State Responsibility*, Leiden, 2005; Lilian Yamamoto, Miguel Esteban, *Atoll Island States and International Law. Climate Change, Displacement and Sovereignty*, Heidelberg, 2014.

85 The ILC, in its work on "Sea Level Rise under International Law" (supra note 60), will not dwell on this crucial and highly sensitive issue.

86 A/61/10: https://legal.un.org/ilc/texts/instruments/english/draft_articles/9_10_2006.pdf.

87 Regula 134.

PART 3

Territorial Irenicism: Specific Territorial Situations and Regimes

CHAPTER 8

The Pertinacious Sovereignty: Traditional Territorial Regimes

A Divorce between *ius nudum* and *exercitium iuris*, as well as between Sovereignty and Ownership

An unbiased analysis of state practice leads to the conclusion that in certain circumstances one state exercises sovereign competences in the territory of another state.[1] This territorial situation is normally governed by an agreement between the two states so that the exercise of these competences takes place peacefully and with the consent of the state in whose territory they are wielded.[2]

In the same vein, there are other territorial situations where one of the two states has both sovereignty and its exercise, but another state is the *owner of* the resources in the territory in question, like a *usufructuary*. We will review these two categories of situations while emphasising the differences between them.

i *Divorce between Sovereignty and Its Exercise*

A doctrinal trend maintains that these are merely 'disguised cessions'[3] concocted in order not to offend the territorial state or to upset the balance of powers.

1 It is important to stress that the divorce between *ius nudum* and *exercitium iuris* is hardly comparable to the one we have studied above between *titulus* and *modus adquisitionis* (see *above* Part 1. Chapter 1. Section B). Indeed, all the territorial regimes analysed in this section presuppose the undisputed union in one and only one state of *titulus* and *modus adquisitionis*. Consequently, the exercise of certain territorial competences by another state is based on an international agreement with the state that retains *ius nudum* or *nuda potestas*. The two divorces thus occur at completely different logical and temporal stages.

2 It should be noted, however, that the suspension of the exercise of sovereignty can also be brought about by a binding decision of the Security Council, as is further evidenced by General Assembly resolution 2625 (XXV) (1 (b)). The ICJ's 2010 Advisory Opinion (Compliance with International Law of the Unilateral Declaration of Independence in Respect of Kosovo, para. 98, at 444) provides a good illustration of this situation: 'The interim administration in Kosovo *was designed to suspend temporarily Serbia's exercise of its authority flowing from its continuing sovereignty over the territory of Kosovo*' [emphasis added].

3 See Jean Perrinjaquet, "Des annexions déguisées de territoires", 16 *RGDIP* 1909, 316–367; Louis Gerard, *Des cessions déguisées de territoire en droit international public*, Paris, 1904; Quadri (1968), 718–719; Kelsen (1920), para. 19, 81–82; De Louter, 369–371; Liszt, 108; Giulio Diena,

 DOI:10.1163/9789004708594_011

On the other hand, a vast doctrinal current,[4] to which we adhere, leans towards the admissibility of a dissociation between the titularity of territorial sovereignty and its exercise. Indeed, the conception of territorial sovereignty that we have just stated above[5] allows to effectively grasp those particular territorial situations where the titularity[6] of *dominium* (sovereignty) is disjointed from that *of imperium* (exercise of sovereignty). Now, by qualifying the territory both as a thing and as the spatial extent of state sovereignty, specific legal statuses can be attributed to these territorial situations. Acts performed by the state that are not accompanied by *animus domini* will be considered as purely factual acts, akin to possession under domestic law. The absence of such intent is provided for in certain specific situations by general international law, such as in the case of wartime occupation. In other cases, treaty norms between the Parties regulate the legal relations between the two States and define the contours of the legal status of the territory concerned.[7] Leaving aside the scenario

---

"Die Erwerbung Tripolitaniens durch Italien und deren völkerrechtlichen Charakter", 23 *Niemeyers Zeitschrift für Internationales Recht* 1913, 9; Cobbett, Vol. 1, 113; Brierly (1963), 190; Aug Ribère, *Les occupations fictives dans les rapports internationaux*, Bordeaux, 1897; Redslob (1950), 182–183.

4 Cavaglieri (1909), 387–402; *id.* (1929), 484; Erik Suy, "Reflections on the Distinction between Sovereignty and Territorial Jurisdiction", in *Internationale Festschrift für Alfred Verdross*, München-Salzburg, 1971, 498–499; Combacau, Sur, 423; Bentivoglio, 40; Diena (1930), 223; Blackstone, Vol. II, 197; Lawrence, para. 83 (at 183); Gilbert Gidel, *Des effets des annexions sur les concessions*, Paris, 1904, who was the first, in the doctrine, to have clearly traced the conceptual contours of *animus derelinquendi* in international law [See *supra* Part 1. Chapter 3. Section A.]; Woodbury Willoughby, *Types of Restricted Sovereignty and of CoLoNial Autonomy*, Washington, 1919; Fedozzi (1938), 425–427; Benedetto Conforti, "Sovranità sui paesi in amministrazione fiduciaria e rapporti tra gli ordinamenti dell'amministrante e dell'amministrato", 38 *Rivista* 1955, 21; Pierre Michel Eisemman, 'Le statut d'Okinawa: de la souveraineté résiduelle à la restitution au Japon', 17 *AFDI* 1971, 255–280; Carlo Ghirardini, "Delle cosidette occupazioni qualificate in diritto internazionale", 34 *Rivista* 1942–1943, 193–223; Alessandro Marazzi, *I territori internazionalizzati,* Torino, 1959; Francis B Sayre, "Legal problems arising from the United Nations Trusteeship System", 42 *AJIL* 1948, 263–288; Georges Scelle, "La situation juridique de Vilna et de son territoire", 35 *RGDIP* 1928, 730–780; Kohen (1997), 75 et seq.; Romano (1933), 184–186; PCIJ, S.S. Wimbledon : *PCIJ Reports* C 3, 278 [Intervention by M Pilotti].

5 See *above* Prolegomena B.2.iv.

6 By this term we refer to the *quality* (fact), for the benefit of a subject of law, *of being the holder of* a right, a benefit, a privilege, in short *a subjective right.* Titularity is therefore this legal expression relating to the attribution (imputation) of a subjective right to a subject of law.

7 "It is well known that a territory belongs to a State when it is inherently subject to the sovereignty of that State. The close ties between the two juridical situations – the link between the territory and the State to which it belongs, on the one hand, and the State's subjective right, on the other – allows us to speak of 'nominal sovereignty' or 'naked sovereignty' whenever the first situation exists but the second does not, owing to the exercise of rights of another

of military occupation, which is largely defined (and governed) by customary and conventional IHL, it is appropriate to review certain situations established by States by means of treaties – most often – or by special customs.

These cases, where one state has full and undisputed title to sovereignty over territory while another state exercises sovereign functions therein, are characterised by the continuity of *nudum ius* revealed by the obligation to pay tribute[8] (personal right) to the foreign state for the benefit of the first state.[9] The refusal to pay may constitute, in these cases, proof of *interversio possessionis*. Moreover, one of the arguments put forward by those who consider

---

[State] over the territory such as to render impossible any effectiveness of the territory by the sovereign". Cernorograz and Zudich v. INPS (Italy, Court of Cassation), award delivered the 6 June 1978, 77 *ILR*, 628. This case [Italian text, in 63 *Rivista* 1980, 506–510] is part of the extensive jurisprudence developed by the Italian Courts on the status of the City and Free Territory of Trieste before and after the 1954 London Memorandum between the Italian Republic and the Yugoslav Federation (Memorandum of Understanding, signed in London on 5 October 1954 by Italy and the Federative People's Republic of Yugoslavia and co-signed by Great Britain and the United States of America, *Relazioni internazionali*, No. 41 (October 1954), 1158). In the same sense: Società Teatro Puccini v. Commissioner General of the Government for the Territory of Trieste (Council of State, Plenary session), award delivered the 20 December 1961, 40 *ILR*, 45; C.E.A.T. v. Società Hungaria (Court of Cassation), award delivered the 15 March 1951, 18 *ILR*, 83.

8 See Article 14 of the Treaty of 18 November 1903 between the United States of America and the Republic of Panama concerning the lease of the Canal territory and the statement of the US Deputy Under-Secretary (Mr. Merchant) of 24 November 1959: 'During the course of our discussions, in response to a question by the President of Panama, I assured him that the policy of the United States Government with respect to the status of the Canal Zone remains as it had been stated more than 50 years ago to the effect that the United States recognizes the *titular sovereignty* over the Canal Zone remains in the Government of Panama', in *Digest of International Law*, Vol. 3, 1147 [emphasis added]. See the legal status of the US military base at Guantanamo (Cuba), "under lease" since 1903, *ibid*, Vol. 2, 1216–1217.

9 There are, however, rare cases where this divorce occurs without the payment of tribute, either in money or in kind. On 17 January 1950, the King of Saudi Arabia – Ibn Saud – sent a telegram to the King of Egypt – Farouk – with the following content: "At the entrance of the Gulf of Aqaba, there exist[s] two islands about which there had been negotiations between us of old. It's not important now if the two islands belong to us or to Egypt. What's important now is to take quick action to prevent the Jewish advance towards those two islands" (Askar H Enazy, *The Legal Status of Tiran and Sanafir Islands*, Ryadh, 2017, 19–20. Egypt proceeded with the occupation not without first sending an aide-memoire to the US embassy in Cairo: 'The Government of Egypt, acting in full accord with the Government of Saudi Arabia, has given orders to occupy effectively these two islands" (*ibid.*, 23). In other words, this divorce between sovereignty and its exercise – which lasted until 2016 (see *infra* note 251) – was only possible thanks to the consent of the sovereign (or at least of one of the two contenders, the other being precisely Egypt). We could also call this situation a *modus vivendi* (see *above* Part 1. Chapter 3. Section A).

such territorial situations to be 'disguised cessions' has to do precisely with their duration in time. For, according to some jurists,[10] a possession of territory for an indefinite period of time, devoid of any limitation and without any right allowing the territorial State to recover its territory, could be a mere abstraction, due to the disappearance of the *animus res sibi habendi* in the latter. However, the practice of the states[11] runs counter to this argument. We take the liberty of

10 The thesis of a camouflaged cession was argued in these terms by Lammasch in relation to Bosnia-Herzegovina (*Times*, 10 November 1908, quoted in Cavaglieri (1909), 387 et seq.). The annexation of Bosnia-Herzegovina was justified, according to the Austrian jurist, by the fact that it had already been effectively achieved in 1878, when it was ceded to Austria-Hungary "under occupation and administration" [see Art. 25 of the Berlin Treaty, in *NRG*, 2nd series, Vol. 3, 449; and the Diplomatic Note concerning the abrogation of Art. XXV of the Berlin Treaty of 1878, of 7 April 1909, sent by Austria-Hungary to Germany, *NRG*, 3rd series, Vol. 2, 665]. This formula was therefore adopted, it is claimed, only in order not to offend the susceptibility of the Ottoman state and to conceal the actual cession. This is contrary to Cavaglieri (1909), who notes instead that Turkey's *ius nudum* was not as 'bare' as it is made out to be. Indeed, the Sultan retained certain important regalian prerogatives, such as the circulation of the Turkish currency, the Turkish flag was to continue to be hoisted on minarets, and prayers to the Sultan remained obligatory. Moreover, it is necessary to study the preparatory work of the above-mentioned treaty [see in this respect *Bruns*, B.1.2, para. 630 for the reasons which led the European Concert to propose the concession in administration of Bosnia and Herzegovina] to realise that there was no intention on the part of the Contracting States to make a 'disguised transfer'. Therefore, the absence of a temporal clause relating to the duration of the Austro-Hungarian occupation did not detract from the conclusion that it was an exercise of *ius in re aliena*. Similarly, the waiver by the other (European) powers of their rights under the capitulations does not in any way indicate an implicit recognition of Austro-Hungarian sovereignty, but reveals, at most, their confidence in the Austro-Hungarian judicial administration. See in this sense: Arrigo Cavaglieri, "La questione cretese", 7 *Rivista* 1912, 244 et seq. and 407 et seq. (more nuanced on the subsistence of Turkish *ius nudum* on the island of Crete); Jan Blocislewski, "L'annexion de la Bosnie-Herzégovine", 17 *RGDIP* 1910, 417–449; Marc Vesnitch, "L'annexion de la Bosnie-Herzégovine et le droit international", 11*RDILC* 1909, 123–141; PCIJ, Legal Status of Eastern Greenland, Vol. C 74, 252 (Presentation by M Basdevant, France). Austria-Hungary hastened in 1908 to seek the *post festum* consent of the Ottoman Empire, but also of the States parties to the 1878 Berlin Treaty ! *Contra*: Enrico Catellani, 'Le sentenze civili pronunciate nel Dodecaneso durante l'occupazione italiana', 3 *Rivista* 1914, 22–31, which, on the one hand, maintains the thesis of a disguised cession in the species of Bosnia-Herzegovina and Cyprus, administered by England following the Anglo-Turkish Convention of 4 June 1878, and, on the other hand, asserts that the Italian occupation of the Dodecanese was, on the contrary, only a *pledge for the* execution of the Lausanne Peace Treaty (1912). See *infra* Part 3. Chapter 8. Section F.

11 See also, among other references: *Prassi italiana*, 753 (on Bosnia-Herzegovina), para. 2219 and para. 2223, at 1182 and 1186 (on the alleged 'shadow of nominal sovereignty' of the Porte over Tripolitania and Cyrenaica following the Lausanne Peace Treaty with Italy). See also: Foltina case (USA, High Court of Admiralty, 1814), in *Scott*, 186: 'shadowy right'. In relation to the leasing of Guantanamo Bay by Cuba to the United States, it was stated

reproducing two passages from the dispatch of Lord Cairns (Lord Chancellor) to Lord Salisbury on the question of the extent of English rights in Cyprus:

> I do not think that we can look on Cyprus as in any sense acquired by conquest, ... we acquired it deliberately and for obvious reasons by an arrangement which was described to be the reverse of alienation, and still more of forcible alienation. [Therefore:] We must take the arrangement then as it really is. The Porte has given us every power in and over Cyprus which it possessed, but we have got nothing more than the Porte had give [sic]. And we have this for a limited time, the Porte retaining the reversion.[12]

In a similar vein, one might quote Lord Salisbury's statement to Lord Lyons in Paris on 16 January 1879:

> If Cyprus had passed to England by absolute cession there can be no doubt that none of the liabilities imposed by the Capitulations or by any other engagements of the Sultan would have been taken over with it by England. The Sultan has not ceded Cyprus absolutely to her Majesty, for it remains within the limits of the Ottoman Empire, and he has reserved the reversion of actual rule in a certain specified contingency.[13]

In other words, the Sublime Porte continued to hold the (naked) right of sovereignty over Cyprus, despite the exercise of sovereignty by England, allowing

---

by the United States that: "While the United States undoubtedly exercises a certain jurisdiction and control over the United States Naval Station at Guantanamo Bay, it is the view of this Department that this locality has never been incorporated into or become a part of the United States", Assistant Secretary of State (Carr) to the Secretary of the Navy (Adams), 1932, *Hackworth*, vol. III, 9.

12 Smith, 400 [emphasis added].

13 *Ibid.*, 402–403 [emphasis added]. In order to support the English interpretation of the territorial regime of Cyprus, it is important to recall that both by the Treaty of Sevres (10 August 1920) – which never came into force – and by the final Treaty of Lausanne (24 July 1923), Turkey renounced all rights and titles over the said island and thus recognised the British annexation of 5 November 1914. The Treaty of Sèvres, in fact, provided in its Article 115 that: 'The High Contracting Parties recognise the annexation of Cyprus proclaimed by the British Government on November 5, 1914' (*The Treaties of Peace 1919–1923*, Vol. II, Carnegie Endowment for International Peace, New York, 1924). This corroborates the assertion that the Ottoman Empire had not, in 1878, relinquished its sovereignty over Cyprus but had retained, until 1914, the *ius nudum*. There was therefore no transfer of sovereignty at that time (1878).

it to recover its exercise in accordance with the 1878 Berlin Treaty. The latter, therefore, did not transfer the title of sovereignty to England, which therefore did not acquire the *ius disponendi*.

In the same vein, Article 69 of the 1920 Treaty of Sèvres – which however never came into force – provided for the divorce between the sovereignty of Turkey (the defeated state) and the 'the exercise of her [Turkey] rights of sovereignty' by Greece (the victorious state) over Smyrna and adjacent territories.[14] Subsequent events vindicated this article.

A slightly more recent example, but one that has made headlines in both the general and specialised press, is the US base in Guantanamo, Cuba.[15] Following the war between the United States and Spain, Cuba gained independence in 1902. As a token of gratitude for the support offered by the United States and 'to enable the United States to maintain the independence of Cuba, and to protect the people thereof', Cuba 'leases to the United States, for the time required for the purposes of coaling and naval stations, the following described areas of land and water situated in the Island of Cuba'.[16]

It should be noted in this regard that under a second treaty (concluded on 2 July of the same year),[17] the United States, as lessor, undertook to pay an 'annual sum of two thousand dollars, in gold coin of the United States' (Article 1).[18] Neither of these two treaties, which govern the Guantanamo concession, establishes its duration in time or contains denunciation clauses. On the contrary, by a third treaty, concluded on 29 May 1934, the two parties agreed that the provisions contained in the two treaties would remain in force "[u]ntil the

14 'The city of Smyrna and the territory defined in Article 66 remain under Turkish sovereignty. Turkey, however, transfers to the Greek Government the exercise of her rights of sovereignty over the city of Smyrna and the said territory. In witness of such sovereignty the Turkish flag shall remain permanently hoisted over an outer fort in the town of Smyrna. The fort will be designated by the Principal Allied Powers' (*The Treaties of Peace 1919–1923*, Vol. II, Carnegie Endowment for International Peace, New York, 1924).

15 As well as 'Bahia Honda'.

16 Article 1 of the Treaty of 16/23 February 1903 between Cuba and the United States of America ("Agreement Between the United States and Cuba for the Lease of Lands for Coaling and Naval stations").

17 "Lease to the United States by the Government of Cuba of Certain Areas of Land and Water for Naval or Coaling Stations in Guantanamo and Bahia Honda".

18 Since 1959, however, the Cuban government has always refused to cash the annual fee: 'The United States pays Cuba $4,085 a month in rent for the controversial Guantanamo naval base, but Cuba has only once cashed a check in almost half a century and then only by mistake, Fidel Castro wrote in an essay published on Friday,' Reuters, 17 August 2007.

two contracting parties agree to the[ir] modification or abrogation" (Article III).[19]

United States has always recognised 'the continuance of the ultimate sovereignty of the Republic of Cuba over the above described areas of land and water',[20] while exercising 'complete jurisdiction and control' over these territories in accordance with the aforementioned agreements.[21] The question of Guantánamo, as a military base, may raise problems as to its permanence over time, precisely because this kind of treaties are concluded *intuitu personae.* The Parties share thus certain common defence interests, of which the military base is one of the embodiments of this alliance. In its commentary on Article 56 para. 1 b) VCLT 1969, the ILC rightly mentions treaties of military alliance – of which the treaty establishing a military base is an example – among the international agreements whose nature would allow for a right of unilateral denunciation.[22] In the same vein, Article 12(3) VCSS 1978 excludes the automatic transmission of territorial treaties for international agreements establishing foreign military bases in the case of state succession.[23]

Apart from the specific situation of military bases (see, inter alia, the case of the Russian Federation's military base in the Crimea),[24] State practice, as evidenced by international case law[25] and domestic case

19 Furthermore, the final sentence of this provision reads: 'So long as the United States of America shall not abandon the said naval station of Guantanamo or the two Governments shall not agree to a modification of its present limits, the station shall continue to have the territorial area that it now has, with the limits that it has on the date of the signature of the present Treaty'. This provision corroborates the indefinite duration of the lease of the territory of Guantanamo Bay.

20 One of the proofs that the territory of the base is not subject to US sovereignty is represented by the inapplicability of the *ius soli* (under the 14th amendment to the Constitution): The Assistant Secretary of State (Carr) to the Secretary of the Navy (Adams), 26 March 1932, quoted in *Hackworth*, vol. III, para. 221, 9.

21 Article III of the Treaty of 16/23 February 1903.

22 Second Report of Sir Humphrey Waldock on the Law of Treaties, A/CN.4/156 and Add. 1–3, *YILC*, 1963, vol. II, 71.

23 Giovanni Distefano, "Article 12. Other territorial regimes", in Distefano, Gaggioli, Hêche, 2016, 445–448.

24 See *supra* Part 2. Chapter 6. Section B.iii.2 (note 287) as well as the Emirati military base in the port of Berbera (Somaliland), see *supra* Part 2. Chapter 7. Section B (note 41).

25 In the same sense: "[I]n modern practice, the exercise by a foreign state of the rights of full ownership to large portions of land is not considered as an encroachment on the sovereignty of the territorial state", Italy v. United Kingdom of Great Britain and Northern Ireland and United Kingdom of Libya, General List No. 1 (Merits), United Nations Tribunal for Libya, award delivered on 31 January 1953, *RIAA*, Vol. 12, 368; ICJ, Lighthouses in Crete and Samos (France v. Greece), judgment of 8 October 1937: *PCIJ Reports* A/B 71, 103: 'Even though the Sultan had been obliged to accept *important restrictions on the exercise of his*

law,[26] is decidedly biased, despite rare exceptions,[27] in favour of the admissibility in the international legal order of the divorce of territorial sovereignty between sovereignty and its exercise.

A rather exotic – and now obsolete – territorial situation is that known as "settlements". This term of juridical art refers to the municipal concessions that China made to the European powers during the 19th and 20th centuries. Jurists have often disputed whether these concessions were in fact colonial empires. State practice at the time,[28] but above all the new diplomatic and territorial

---

rights of sovereignty in Crete, that sovereignty had not ceased to belong to him, however it might be qualified from a juridical point of view' [emphasis added]; Territorial Sovereignty and Scope of the Dispute (Eritrea and Yemen), 1998, para. 442.

26 "Transfer of jurisdiction over a portion of territory from one State to another does not imply a cession of territory or the abandonment of sovereignty by the transferor of the jurisdiction", State of Madras v. Cochin Coal Company (India, High Court of Kerala), award delivered the 9 October 1957, 26 *ILR*, 116. In the same sense: Burna v. District Court (Eastern District, Virginia, US), award delivered the 13 August 1956 (Court of Appeals, Fourth Circuit, the 7 January 1957), 24 *ILR*, 89, 91: 'the fact that Japan retained *residual sovereignty* over the Ryuky Islands under Article 3 of the Japanese Peace Treaty meant that Okinawa was a 'foreign country' within the meaning of the Federal Tort Claims Act [...] the transfer temporarily of a measure of sovereignty here [in this case] is not sufficient to dissolve Okinawa's status as a foreign country'. Porter v. Court of Claims, 107–108; Bank of Ethiopia v. National Bank of Egypt and Liguori, 122 (regarding the Italian annexation of Ethiopia in 1936 and *nuda proprietas for the* benefit of the Emperor of Ethiopia); United States v. Ushi Shiroma (District Court, District of Hawaii), award delivered the 12 August 1954, 21 *ILR*, 84, 85, 86: 'The "residue" or "residual sovereignty" retained by Japan is the traditional "de jure sovereignty"'.

27 PCIJ, Lighthouses in Crete and Samos Case, A/B 71, 127: 'If it can be said that a theoretical sovereignty remained in the Sultan after 1899, it was a sovereignty shorn of the last vestige of power. He could neither terminate nor modify the autonomy with which Crete had been endowed against his will and with the sanction of the four European States. A juristic conception must not be stretched to the breaking-point, and a ghost of a hollow sovereignty cannot be permitted to obscure the realities of this situation' (separate opinion of Judge Hudson).

28 See the opinion of the Legal Office of the Italian Ministry of Foreign Affairs on the legal status of the Tientsin settlement: 'The legal nature of the Tianjin concession is still the subject of differing opinions. In order to clarify the most important ones, it is appropriate to note that the Honorable Fusinato has to define 'settlements' as completely new legal forms, the qualities of which can hardly be identified in the concepts and terminology of the laws in force in the Kingdom. [...] These are new relations for which the government must be left to act swiftly and easily [...] More than by the domestic laws of individual states, this matter is regulated by international law. The Ministry of Foreign Affairs, in its turn, in the management of that concession to date, recognising *a contradiction between the title of ownership by the Italian State and the obligation to pay the annual fee to the Chinese government*, has considered that the State administers that concession, through this Ministry, but with only powers of protection, in the interest and on behalf of that

arrangements that followed, lead us to believe that this was merely an exercise of sovereignty on the part of the European states,[29] with China retaining *the ius nudum*. In short, the Celestial Empire retained the right of *interversio possessionis*.[30] Domestic jurisprudence, in the absence of known pronouncements by international tribunals, is adamant in this regard:

> The British Municipal area at Tientsin was part of Chinese territory within which Great Britain exercised certain jurisdictional rights. It had never been acquired by settlement or otherwise and had never been recognized as, and was not claimed to be, part of the King's dominions. British courts in China had no jurisdiction to try Chinese subjects for crimes committed within British Municipal areas.[31]

Obsessed by the analogy with private law, internationalists are tempted to see it as a territory ceded by way of lease; while it is true that the payment of rent is a characteristic that makes it possible to bring the situation under consideration closer to that of private law, it is no less true that the exercise of sovereign powers (in international law) irreparably undermines this analogy.[32] Here we reach the irreducible differences between sovereignty in international law and ownership in private law, because in the case of the divorce between the right of sovereignty and its exercise, the latter naturally includes the enjoyment of the resources of the territory concerned.

ii Sovereignty and Ownership Rights

Let us now turn, as stated at the beginning of this sub-section, to situations where, despite the absence of a separation between the right of sovereignty and its exercise, a foreign State enjoys ownership rights in the territory of another State, without exercising competences relating to the Public Power.

future body, not yet constituted (municipality), for the benefit of which the settlement was requested and obtained by China and which must therefore be considered the true owner of that land', in *Prassi italiana*, para. 2321 (at 1327–1328) [emphasis added ; our translation].

29 See Jean Escarra, "Le régime des concessions étrangères en Chine", 27 RCADI 1929-II, 1–140.

30 "There was neither a transfer of territorial sovereignty nor the creation of a new subject. It is not, therefore, a question of a cession of the imperium, conceived *as the totality of political powers belonging to a certain state*, but of a substitution of authority and administrative activity", Cavaglieri (1929), 487, 488 [our translation; emphasis added].

31 In re Ning Yi-Ching and Others, England, Vacation Court, 23 August 1939, 9 *ILR*, 116.

32 In this sense: ICJ, Sovereignty over Pedra Branca/Pulau Batu Puteh, Middle Rocks and South Ledge (Malaysia/Singapore), 2008, paras. 137 (at 56), 139 (at 57), 222–223 (at 80).

In short, it enjoys the resources of that territory, whereas the territorial State holds both the right of sovereignty and its exercise. We are dealing here to a still lower stage in the transfer of sovereign rights by one State to another State in relation to a given territory. Similarly, the conception of state territory as a "thing" (*res*), which can be disposed of, rather than as "space", the dimension of the exercise of territorial sovereignty, is highlighted here.

State practice, even in recent times, is not short of examples.[33] Israel and the Hashemite Kingdom of Jordan agreed in two annexes attached to the Peace Treaty of 26 October 1994[34] on a special regime for the Naharayim/Baqura area (Annex 1b) as well as for the Zofar/Al-Ghamfr area, for a period of 25 years, automatically renewable unless notice to the contrary is given at least 12 months in advance.[35] Jordanian sovereignty is thus formally recognised, while "Israeli private land ownership rights and property interests" remain intact (Article 2). Jordanian law applied, but Israel exercised certain functions inherent in the governmental authority, such as the judicial function, police investigation *exclusively* with regard to its own nationals, owners of the aforementioned plots. Similarly, Article 4 provided for the extra-territorial application of Israeli law to its own nationals, while Jordanian law continued to apply throughout the territory in question. This is not far from the Capitulations concluded between the Ottoman Empire and certain European powers in the Near and Middle East.

33 Some cases are extremely curious, such as the one concerning Turkey's ownership of the tomb 'of Suleiman Shah, the grandfather of the Sultan Osman, founder of the Ottoman dynasty (the tomb known under the name of Turk Mézari), situated at Jaber-Kalesi, shall remain, with its appurtenances, the property of Turkey, who may appoint guardians for it and may hoist the Turkish flag there' located at Djaber-Kalessi [river island in Syrian territory at that time under French mandate], Article 9 of the Treaty between France and Turkey, signed in Ankara on 20 October 1921 (*LNTS*, Vol. 54, 181). Following the installation of a dam in the Euphrates River, Syria moved the mausoleum upstream, some 25 kilometres south of the Turkish-Syrian border. On 21 February, Turkey, using the situation in Syria as an excuse and fearing for the integrity of the mausoleum and the security of the garrison in charge of its protection, launched a military operation to *repatriate* the remains of Suleiman Shah" ('Incursion militaire turque en Syrie pour évacuer un mausolée ottoman', *Le Monde*, 22 February 2015). Since then, the divorce between ownership and sovereignty has thus been resolved.

34 See the text in 34 *ILM* 1995-I, 43–66.

35 According to Art. 6 for the first and second zones. A few days before the one-year deadline, King Abdullah II of Jordan declared that he did not want to renew the agreement, thus ending this special territorial regime ("Jordan Reclaims Land Israelis Used Under '94 Peace Accord", *NYT*, 10 November 2019).

A similar territorial regime was established in the Treaty between Ecuador and Peru (arts. 4 and 5) in the so-called "Tiwintza" sector, putting an end to the "Cordillera del Cóndor" or "Cenepa" war (1995). According to these provisions:

> The Government of Ecuador, in its capacity of owner, will have the real rights conferred by Peruvian national law, except for the right to transfer [...] The Government of Ecuador will not keep police or military personnel within the area of its property.[36]

However, whereas Israel exercised sovereign powers – on foreign territory – over its own nationals, here it does not. Ecuador enjoys the right of ownership over the territory in question, it benefits from its fruits and resources, but does not exercise governmental auhority. Despite these differences, these two territorial regimes, established by peace treaties, provide a good example of the possibilities offered by international law to defuse a territorial dispute and reach a settlement that takes into account conflicting interests. Territory and its status are no longer a problem, but become part of the solution.[37]

B Servitudes in International Law (Article 12 (1) VCSS 1978)

In this sub-section, the *vexata quaestio* of servitudes in the international legal order will be addressed. Since we have already seen the possibility of a divorce between the ownership and the exercise of sovereignty, one would be tempted to conclude that servitudes enjoy a well-established status through the same concept of territorial sovereignty. However, unlike the problem dealt with above, the doctrine is largely divided[38] and neither international case law nor

36 "Brasilia Presidential Act" (Brasilia Accords), signed in Brasilia on November 26, 1998.

37 In 1993, a solution consisting of Syrian sovereignty over the Golan against a leasehold concession for Israel (largely modelled on the model with Jordan in 1994) was proposed to Syrian President Hafez El-Assad (Samuel Segev, *Crossing the Jordan*, New York, 1998, 152–153). The same solution was rejected by the Egyptian President Anwar Sadat regarding the Sinai Peninsula.

38 Vattel, Book III, Ch. XIII, para. 199; Romano (1933), 183–184; Brierly (1963), who, by a tortuous reasoning, ends up acknowledging their existence: 'It seems probable that the notion of servitude has been introduced into the terminology of international law owing to the fact that the international rules relating to territory were in the main originally taken from the Roman rules relating to the ownership of land. Thus, the word can be used loosely to denote merely rights held by one state over the territory of another. But if a right over territory does not have the character of being a right *in rem*, it is merely confusing to call it a servitude, for in legal analysis it does not differ from any other right created

State practice provide us with decisive indications on this subject. In view of the purpose of our study, we will limit ourselves by setting out a few milestones.

One of the "famous cases" in this regard is the North Atlantic Fisheries case. Subsequent doctrine has engaged in pointed hermeneutical discussions in order to discern the true meaning of the Permanent Court of Arbitration's statements on the US argument for the existence of this institution in international law. It is worth reproducing the passage in question:

> c) Because a servitude in International law predicates an express grant of a sovereign right and involves an analogy to the relation of a *praedium dominans* and a *praedium serviens*; [...] d) because the doctrine of international servitude in the sense which is now sought to be attributed to it originated in the peculiar and now obsolete conditions prevailing in the Holy Roman Empire of which the domini terrae were not fully sovereigns ... their right being, moreover, rather of a civil than of a public nature, partaking more of the character of dominium than of imperium, and therefore certainly not a complete sovereignty ... [and because] the modern State, and particularly Great Britain, has never admitted partition of sovereignty, owing to the constitution of a modern State requiring essential sovereignty and independence; [... because] e) this doctrine ... has found little, if any, support from modern publicists. It could therefore in the general interest of the Community of Nations, and of the Parties to this Treaty, be affirmed by this Tribunal only on the express evidence of an International Contract.[39]

This is the PCA's *ratio decidendi* with respect to the merits of the US argument for judicial recognition of a servitude right. It is therefore necessary to examine the points on which the PCA based its reasoning.

Firstly [c], the notion of a tenement servitude in Roman law requires a dominant and a servient tenement ("Prædium dominans" and "Prædium serviens").[40] Now, while it is true that in international law one can hardly speak

by a treaty'; Menon (1994), 28; Joint Dissenting Opinion of Judges Bedjaoui, Korova and Ranjeva appended to the Judgment of the International Court of Justice in the Case concerning Maritime Delimitation and Territorial Questions between Qatar and Bahrain, 2001, 172.

39 North Atlantic Coast Fisheries case (USA v. Great Britain), award delivered by the Permanent Court of Arbitration the 7 September 1910, *RIAA*, Vol. XI, 182.

40 These two terms, instrumental for the operation of servitudes, are referred to by the International Committee of Jurists in the Åland Island case (19).

of a dominant territory and a servient territory,[41] it is nonetheless true that the so-called servitudes of international law are indeed real rights, i.e., enforceable *erga omnes*. The first argument therefore does not seem insurmountable.

Secondly [d], we have observed that in certain specific circumstances international law contemplates a divorce between the right of territorial sovereignty and its exercise. The Court's demonstration based on this argument therefore falls apart.

Finally, [e] the Court states that while it cannot be accepted that there is a customary rule of international law providing for servitudes, it is not excluded that the parties may lay down such a standard in their contractual relations. It follows that States may create servitudes by agreement. These will thus be real rights arising from personal obligations; State practice provides us with a large number of precedents in this regard.[42]

The question of servitudes is not only interesting in its own right but is also of crucial importance in the context of the succession of states with treaty-based servitude regimes.[43] In other words, do the so-called "servitudes" survive the change of sovereign over the territory concerned, according to the famous adage "res transit cum onere suo" [A thing passes away with its burden]? The answer must be sought in Article 12 (1) VCSS 1978.

This provision is subdivided into two subparagraphs respectively for obligations and rights which form the territorial regime established by the treaty. Subparagraph (*a*) covers restrictions or obligations on the use of territory which are "established by a treaty *specifically for* the benefit of a *particular territory* of a foreign State *and considered as attaching to the territories in question*".[44]

---

41 Balladore-Pallieri (1962), 470–471. See George Crusen, "Les servitudes internationales", 22 *RCADI* 1928-II, 42–44; Helen D Reid, "Les servitudes internationales", 45 *RCADI* 1933-I, 27.

42 Convention concerning the Boundary between the Philippine Archipelago and the State of North Borneo, signed in Washington on 2 January 1930, in *NRG*, 3rd series, Vol. 27, 61 (Art. IV), by which the Contracting Parties agreed that this servitude would remain applicable in the event of succession between States. On the border between the Netherlands and Prussia (Limburg), Dutch mines surreptitiously extended into Prussian territory, thereby creating sovereign (minor) rights in the subsoil of the land territory. This bizarre territorial situation was finally confirmed, and the servitude ratified, by the treaty of 18 January 1852.

43 Some, not without a touch of exaggeration, have asserted that "the whole problem of state succession, conceived as succession to the international rights and obligations of a state (in the sense of the rights and obligations of a state arising from a treaty), *is identified with the so-called problem of international servitudes*", Kelsen (1932), 340 [emphasis added; our translation].

44 ILC Commentary to Article 30, *YILC*, 1972, vol. II, 298 [the adverb "specifically" will be eventually deleted].

Subparagraph (*b*) is identical in all respects with one exception, namely, that it is not a question of obligations but of *rights*.

Immediately obvious are the local element (rootedness) as well as the "operative" element, i.e., the intention of the parties to the treaty to regulate a territorial situation. These two elements are certainly the distinctive lineaments of this category of territorial treaties. However, it remains to identify the *ratio iuris* of the principle generating the permanence of this territorial regime despite the succession of states over the territory concerned.

Some authors[45] and States[46] base precisely the continuity of the regime (or the succession to the localised treaty) on the notion of servitude in international law or on a legal situation "analogous to the servitudes or easements of private law".[47] In short, from this point of view, they would be minor territorial rights – compared to the major territorial right of sovereignty – which are not affected by either territorial changes or fundamental change of circumstances; in short, "iura in re aliena".

The authors who refute the notion of servitude in international law concede, however, that there can be "universal succession" provided that the "international relations [are] located with *absolute effectiveness in the territory*".[48] Indeed, these authors affirm that the mere transposition of a private law principle is not sufficient to justify the succession of a territorial regulation

45 Among them: Sir Robert Phillimore, *Commentaries upon International Law*, vol. I (Part II), London, 1879, 392, para. 283; Emer de Vattel, Book II, Ch. 13, 410–411, para. 203; Andrea G Mochi Onory, *La succession d'Etats aux traités*, Milan, 1968, 134; Quadri (1968), 504; Pitman B Potter, "The Doctrine of Servitudes in International Law", 9 *AJIL* 1915, 627–641; Lord Arnold McNair, "So-Called State Servitudes", 6 *BYIL* 1925, 111–122; Crusen, 1–79; Claude Mercier, *Les servitudes internationales*, Lausanne, 1939; Ferenc A Váli, *Servitudes of International Law*, New York / London, 1958; Monaco / Curti Gialdino, 530. Jurisprudence trickles down and changes course: "Because of this fact, a sort of international servitude has arisen by which Holland is as a State entitled, now as previously, in the matter of this mine, to exercise its own legislative authority and police supervision; that is, it has real sovereign rights with respect to the object situated within the territory of the foreign state" (Dutch State Servitude, Supreme Court of Cologne, 21 April 1914, *AJIL*, 1914, 909).

46 "When called upon to apply the principles of international law, national courts have, in various countries, accepted the existence of international easements. It seems that they have never ruled against the principle of this institution" (note by the Swiss Government on International Easements submitted to the P.C.I.J. in the *Free Zones of Upper Savoy and the District of Gex*, P.C.I.J., *Series C*, No. 19 I (IV), 2036).

47 Brierly (1963), 154.

48 Liszt, 192, para. 23 [emphasis added; our translation]. Similarly: Sereni (1966), vol. II (I), 395–396; dissenting opinion of Judge Chagla appended to the judgment of 26 November 1957 (Jurisdiction and Admissibility of the Application) of the ICJ in the Right of Passage into Indian Territory (Portugal v. India): *ICJ Reports* 1957, 176–178.

established by treaty. In other words, they identify, like the ILC, a customary international rule providing for this legal continuity.[49]

Still others consider that the notion of servitude is not indispensable[50] for the purposes of the succession of localised territorial regimes, while admitting however that 'the jurisprudential problem of rationalising the category is not thereby in any way simplified'.[51]

In its first contentious case ("Wimbledon"), the PCIJ sidestepped the 'very controversial nature, whether in the domain of international law, there really exist servitudes analogous to the servitudes of private law'.[52] More recently, its successor (the ICJ) touched on the notion without, though, expressly naming it:

> On 5 August 1914, Nicaragua signed a treaty with the United States (the Chamorro-Bryan Treaty) which granted the United States perpetual and "exclusive proprietary rights" for the construction and maintenance of an inter-oceanic canal through the San Juan River. On 24 March 1916, Costa Rica filed a case against Nicaragua before the Central American Court of Justice claiming that Nicaragua had breached its obligation to consult with Costa Rica prior to entering into any canalization project in accordance with Article VIII of the 1858 Treaty. On 30 September 1916, the Central American Court of Justice ruled that, by not consulting Costa Rica, Nicaragua had violated the rights guaranteed to the latter by the 1858 Treaty of Limits and the 1888 Cleveland Award.[53]

Arbitral jurisprudence is even richer as there have been many occasions when it has had to address the issue. For example, in the case of *British Claims in the Spanish Zone of Morocco*, the sole arbitrator Max Huber declared that Spain had succeeded as protecting State 'to the obligations resulting for the Maghzen from the above-mentioned British rights',[54] relating to the exchange of houses for the British consul.

49 Kelsen (1932), 220; Manlio Udina, "La succession internationale quant aux obligations internationales autres que les dettes publiques", 44 *RCADI* 1933-II, 715–716.

50 Lord Arnold McNair, *The Law of Treaties*, Oxford, 1961, 656.

51 Daniel P O'Connell, "Independence and Succession to Treaties", 38 *BYIL*, vol. 38, 1962, 151.

52 PCIJ, S.S. Wimbledon Case (United Kingdom, France, Italy, Japan v. German Empire; Poland intervening), judgment of 17 August 1923: *PCIJ Reports* A 1, 24.

53 Dispute concerning navigation and related rights (Costa Rica v. Nicaragua), judgment of 13 July 2009: *ICJ Reports* 2009, para. 22 (at 230).

54 British Claims in the Spanish Zone of Morocco (Great Britain v. Spain), arbitral award of 1 May 1925, *RIAA*, vol. II, 725 [our translation].

It follows from this very brief sampling of case law that, whatever the doctrinal approach to servitudes, the fact remains that certain categories of territorial treaties, or at least their effects, survive state succession.

State practice[55] and international courts indeed seem to indicate – and the list is not exhaustive but rather illustrative – that Article 12 (1) VCSS 1978 encompasses the following categories of territorial treaties: concerning rights over maritime spaces[56] or river navigation[57] – which the ILC also includes in the category of "treaties creating objective regimes";[58] relating to the operation of a river dam[59] and the maintenance of the banks;[60] granting fishing rights;[61] establishing a right of passage (over land territory);[62] granting concessions to foreign States over railway lines (the cases of Prussia over Luxembourg[63] and

55 See e.g., Article 3 of the Treaty of 14 August 1947 on the Independence of British India (and its partition): "3. (*a*) Rights and obligations under international agreements having an exclusive territorial application to an area comprised in the Dominion of India will devolve upon that Dominion. (*b*) Rights and obligations under international agreements having an exclusive territorial application to an area comprised in the Dominion of Pakistan will devolve upon that Dominion", quoted in the Study prepared by the UN Secretariat on membership (A/CN.4/149, 102).

56 The recognition by Egypt (and Israel) – in the Washington Peace Treaty of 26 March 1979 (*UNTS*, vol. 1136, 116–205) – that "the Strait of Tiran and the Gulf Aqaba to be international waterways" (Article 5 para. 2) has territorial consequences insofar as, at the time of its conclusion, it was the sovereign of the islands of Tiran and Safir located precisely at the entrance to the Strait. However, following the transfer by treaty (8 April 2016) of the Tiran and Safir Islands to Saudi Arabia – a third party to the aforementioned treaty – it is indisputable that the regime of a "strait used for international navigation" applies to the new territorial sovereign, notwithstanding Israel's apprehensions ("Israelis Ask Egyptians to Redraw Border a Bit", *NYT*, 19 January 1982, A3). Saudi Arabia is also bound by UNCLOS, Articles 17 and 37–44 of which enshrine and govern the right of innocent passage through the territorial sea and straits used for international navigation. A different issue is that of Egypt's obligations under the same 1979 Peace Treaty regarding multinational observation forces following the withdrawal of the Israeli army from the occupied territories after the Six-Day War (1967). See *infra* Part 3. Chapter 8. Section H.i.2.

57 Mochi Onory, 131.

58 ILC Commentary to Article 12, *YILC*, 1974, vol. II (Part I), 210, para. 30.

59 I.C.J., Gabčíkovo-Nagymaros Project (Hungary v. Slovakia), Judgment of 25 September 1997 (Merits): ICJ *Reports* 1997, para. 123 (at 172).

60 Arthur B Keith, *The Theory of State Succession with Special Reference to English and Colonial Law*, London, 1907, 20.

61 Mochi Onory, 135.

62 McNair (1961), 658.

63 Prussia's ownership of the Vennbahn railway line, partly in Luxembourg territory, was invoked by Imperial Germany to justify the transport of its troops through the territory of the Grand Duchy – on 2 August 1914 – in the direction of the stronghold of Liège, in defiance of the country's neutrality.

Japan in Chinese Manchuria).[64]

C Objective Territorial Régimes (Article 12 (2) VCSS 1978)

The regimes envisaged by Article 12 (1) VCSS 1978 are not established 'for reasons of general interest, but only for the benefit of one of the contracting parties in synallagmatic treaties, or possibly for the benefit of several specific States – with the exception of the one on which the obligation falls – in other treaties, and never for the direct, immediate interest of all the contracting parties, and even less so of third States'.[65] Instead, the territorial regulations here under scrutiny establish an objective status, hence opposable *erga omnes*. It follows that 'third States may, as subjects interested in the maintenance of the regulation in question, claim respect for the stipulations from which it results'.[66] The juridical interest to act lies, depending on what the treaty in question provides, with "a group of States or all States" (Article 12 (2) VCSS 1978).

The structure of this paragraph is absolutely identical to that of paragraph 1 of Article 12 of the VCSS 1978. The difference lies in the characteristics of the treaties envisaged by this provision. Indeed, unlike Article 12 para. 1, where the decisive element was represented by the attachment of rights and obligations to a specific territory or territories (and specified in the treaty) for the benefit of another State, here we are confronted with a legal regulation which was intended by the Contracting States "for the benefit of a group of States or of all States" and not for the benefit of a particular territory (State).

Of course, the territorial element is present since the rights and obligations enjoyed by third States (in relation to the treaty subject to succession) are, as Article 12 provides, "attaching to that territory", but the idea of a political status remains decisive in the configuration of this category of territorial treaties. In the same vein, treaties should be carefully distinguished according to whether they affect 'the international status of the ceded territory or of any river, canal, etc., within it, or whether it is merely one creating personal obligations for a given country in respect of that territory of things in it'.[67]

64 Under Article 6 of the Peace Treaty (of Portsmouth, 23 August 1905) with Russia, Japan received from the latter, with the consent of China (territorial state), all rights of ownership and exploitation of the "South Manchuria Railway Zone" (text of the treaty in *New York Times*, 17 October 1905, 6).

65 Udina (1933), 717 [our translation].

66 *Ibid.*, 718 [our translation].

67 Sir Gerald Fitzmaurice, "The Juridical Clause of the Peace Treaties", 73 *RCADI* 1948-II, 292. In this sense, Liszt, according to whom "it is the *real* character, the right to a thing, that

The treaties contemplated by Article 12 (2) VCSS 1978 fall precisely into the first scenario described in this doctrinal extract. The ICJ had the merit of making this clear in its judgment in the *Gabčíkovo-Nagymaros Project* case:

> The Treaty also established the navigational regime for an important section of an international waterway, in particular the relocation of the main international shipping lane to the bypass canal. *In so doing, it inescapably created a situation in which the interests of other users of the Danube were affected. Furthermore, the interests of third States were expressly acknowledged in Article 18.*[68]

Once the contours of the category of treaties envisaged by Article 12 para. 2 have been determined, it should be pointed out that this category has often been compared, to the point of misunderstanding, with that of treaties creating objective regimes. This question, which has been widely debated, had already occupied the ILC during the codification of the law of treaties. The (last) Special Rapporteur for the draft of the future VCLT 1969 (Sir Humphrey Waldock) had proposed an article 63 ("Treaties providing for objective regimes") in order to envisage those treaties by which 'the parties intend *in the general interest to create a regime of general obligations and rights for a region, territory or locality which is subject to the treaty-making competence of one or more of them*'.[69] Even though the principle underlying this provision had finally gained a certain consensus among the members of the ILC, the latter decided not to include it in the draft codification.[70]

Consequently, as Sir Humphrey Waldock had observed[71] and as has been glossed over by the most authoritative doctrine,

---

is lacking in these legal situations" (at 81, para. 8; our translation). In this case, it would rather be a matter of international liability law, since – he adds – the State that cedes a burdened territory is obliged, if the beneficiary State (a third party in relation to the succession) does not renounce it, to compensate it, since the succession of States affects precisely the continuity of this type of (personal) treaty.

68 ICJ, Gabčíkovo-Nagymaros Project, 1997, para. 123 (at 71-72) [emphasis added].

69 Third Report of Sir Humphrey Waldock, *YILC*, 1964, vol. II, para. 13 (at 31) [italics in text].

70 Report of the Commission to the General Assembly, *YILC*, 1964, vol. II, 194. According to some – and not wrongly – this case is surreptitiously envisaged by the interplay of Articles 34–37 and 38 VCLT 1969. In this sense: Susanne Bastid, *Les traités dans la vie internationale*, Paris, 1985, 153.

71 '[A]ny general regime that may result is to be regarded as essentially a *customary* régime built around the treaty', Third Report of Sir Humphrey Waldock, *YILC*, 1964, vol. II, para. 8 (at 29), [italics in text].

> [T]he silence of the Vienna Convention with regard to treaties establishing an objective regime implies that treaties may produce effects for a third State only on the basis of Articles 35 to 37 [VCLT 1969] and thus with the acceptance or acquiescence on the part of that State. A further possibility is that a customary rule is formed with a content corresponding to a rule stated in a treaty.[72]

This approach seems to have been espoused by the ILC in its draft codification of the future VCSS 1978.[73] In this sense, other authors have envisaged a "process that the implementation of the treaty triggers and is concretised by the *conclusion of collateral agreements* [Articles 34–37 VCLT 1969] *and by the formation of customary rules that are grafted onto the treaty*".[74]

Whatever the relationship between territorial treaties, governed by Article 12 (1) VCSS 1978, and treaties providing for objective territorial régimes, it has been customary to refer to international agreements whose 'characteristic ... is that they attach obligations to a particular territory, river, canal, etc., for the benefit either of a group of States (e.g., riparian States of a particular river) or of all States generally'.[75] Article 12(2) therefore envisages "treaties the legal effect of which is to confer on a territory a status which is intended to be permanent and which is independent of the personality of the State exercising sovereignty",[76] in short, to entrench in the territory a general and objectively enforceable regulation.[77]

As Justice Sir Arnold McNair observed in his famous dissenting opinion in the *International Status of South-West Africa* case in 1950

72 Giogio Gaja, "Article 38 – 1969 Convention", in: *The Vienna Conventions on the Law of Treaties. A Commentary* (ed. by Olivier Corten and Pierre Klein), vol. I, Oxford, 2011, 958. This hypothesis of creation of customary rules was considered by the ICJ in the *North Sea Continental Shelf* cases and thus illustrates a well-established (secondary) rule on the production of international customary rules (ICJ, North Sea Continental Shelf, 1969, para. 73 (at 43)).

73 ILC Commentary to Article 12, *YILC*, 1974, vol. II, Part I, para. 30 (at 210).

74 Mustafa K Yasseen, "La Convention de Vienne sur la succession d'Etats en matière de traités", 24 *AFDI* 1978, 87 [our translation; emphasis added].

75 See *supra* note 73.

76 Siev (Ireland), 21st session (20 April 1977), *Official acts of the Vienna Conference*, para. 6 (at 134).

77 As has been very clearly stated by a member of the ILC and an authority on the law of treaties: "a status based on considerations of logic, utility and humanity", Yasseen, *YILC*, vol. I, 1195th meeting, para. 22 (at 286).

> From time to time, it happens that a group of great Powers, or a large number of States both great and small, assume a power to create by a multipartite treaty some new international régime or status, which soon acquires a degree of acceptance and durability extending beyond the limits of the actual contracting parties, and giving it an objective existence.[78]

The common characteristics of this category of treaties can be summarised as follows: a) a multilateral treaty (although a bilateral treaty is also conceivable); b) concerning a specific part of the territory of a State (or even several States) party to the treaty;[79] c) bearing or enshrining a general interest,[80] hence its *erga omnes* effect; d) establishing a status[81] or "territorial or objective regulation".[82] This is where the fundamental difference lies compared to the case governed by Article 12 (1) and which obviously has an impact on the legal interest vested with third States, present in Article 12 (2), but absent in Article 12 (1).[83] As Udina brightly remarked, the decisive, but not the only, element lies in the establishment, by treaty, of "obligations which refer expressly to the condition of a given territory and which have been established in the interest of all the contracting parties to a collective agreement, and possibly in the general interest of all States".[84] In this respect, one may dare to speak of a local custom as

---

78 ICJ, International Status of South-West Africa, 153.

79 According to Udina (1933, 708), 'The absence of the condition of general interest would not necessarily entail the non-transferability of the obligations envisaged; whereas the absence of a specific location would have this effect even if the required condition of general interest were fulfilled' [our translation]. On the other hand, the ILC and the majority doctrine would seem to identify the general interest as the salient feature of the case governed by Article 12 (2) VCSS 1978. On the other hand, it may well be, and here we agree with the above-mentioned author, that the territorial regulation can be included in Article 12 (1), provided that the other conditions for its application are met.

80 See: Fiore, Article 138 para. 2, 139; De Visscher, 215; Mochi Onory, 131; Brigitte Stern, "State succession", 262 *RCADI* 1996, 168; Udina (1933), 705; Åland Islands case, 17.

81 Sereni (1966), vol. II (I), 391; Wilfred Jenks, "State Succession in respect of Law-Making Treaties", 29 *BYIL* 1952, 105. It is no coincidence that one of the most authoritative German-language textbooks calls them "Statusverträgen"; Verdross, Simma, 616, para. 998. See also the excellent monograph by: Eckart Klein, *Statusverträge im Völkerrecht. Rechtsfragen territoriale Sonderregime*, Berlin, 1980.

82 Udina (1933), 705 [our translation].

83 The Special Rapporteur, Sir Humphrey Waldock, cites in this regard the right of free passage enshrined in the 1888 Convention between the United Kingdom and Egypt concerning the Suez Canal, and confirmed by the latter in 1957: 'whether by virtue of the treaty or of the customary regime which developed from it, this right was recognized', Fifth Report, *YILC*, 1972, vol. II, 64, §44. It remains to be seen, however, whether States that are not parties to the treaty enjoyed a right to maintain and not modify the regime of free navigation.

84 Udina (1933), 705 [our translation].

well, even if limited *ratione loci*, but generating *erga omnes* effects by virtue of its regime and object. From this perspective, it is precisely the general principles that 'armour' treaties and put them beyond the reach of state succession. In the same way, it may be argued, a multilateral treaty cannot be modified, or even extinguished, by certain States parties only.[85]

International jurisprudence has vastly contributed to shaping the idea of a community of interest[86] established by a multilateral treaty for the benefit of third states. PCIJ, in the wake of the Åland Islands case, which will be discussed at length at the end of this section, referred *expressly to* a "community of interest" of all the riparian states of the river, creating a community of law:

> This community of interest in a navigable river becomes the basis of a common legal right, the essential features of which are the perfect equality of all riparian States in the user of the whole course of the river and the exclusion of any preferential privilege of any one riparian State in relation to the others.[87]

In the "Wimbledon" case, the ICJ, while not ruling, as we have just seen, on the existence of servitudes in public international law, concluded that an 'an international waterway intended to provide easier access to the Baltic for the benefit of all nations of the world' could be placed 'under treaty guarantee'[88] the effects of which were enjoyed even by third States, including Poland.

Similarly, in another case, *Oscar Chinn*, the same Court ascertained Belgium's succession to the regime (including obligations) established by the General Act of the Berlin Conference of 1885 establishing a regime of free navigation on the Congo River.[89]

Its successor, the ICJ, recalled in the Gabčíkovo-Nagymaros Project Case, this principle of community of law between riparian States, and corroborated

85 A structural principle of the law of nations, enshrined in the London Protocol of 17 January 1871; see in this regard: Giovanni Distefano, "Le Protocole de Londres du 17 janvier 1871: miroir du droit international", 6 *Journal of the History of International Law* 2004, 79–142.

86 On this important concept of the international law of territory in relation to the enjoyment of the attributes of sovereignty, see below Part 3. Chapter 8. Section D.

87 PCIJ, Territorial Jurisdiction of the International Commission of the River Oder, Judgement of 10 September 1929: *PCIJ Reports*, A 23, 27.

88 PCIJ, S.S. Wimbledon, 22.

89 PCIJ, Oscar Chinn case, 80.

it by citing the "Convention on the Law of the Non-navigational Uses of International Watercourses" (1997),[90] which has recently entered into force.[91]

The idea of community – and of its interests being asserted by a group of states (which some authors have called "de facto international governments")[92] through the establishment of a territorial status[93] – is often evoked in this respect, in particular, in the matter of the internationalisation of international waterways for the benefit of any state (and therefore precisely *erga omnes*).[94] Referring more specifically to the regime of freedom of navigation on international rivers – and as a consequence of their internationalisation – Judge Jonkheer van Eysinga attributes the genesis of this right to Talleyrand, which he considers to be an "element of international trade" exercised by certain states.[95] The latter would thus act as 'tacitly recognised organs of the International Community'.[96]

This community aspect is one of the elements that differentiate para. 2 of Article 12 VCSS 1978 from the previous paragraph, which is based on the – not necessarily legally correct – concept of servitude, referring to the idea of servient and dominant land. In fact, whereas article 12 (1) is based on reciprocity and the subordination of one territory to another, 12 (2) is inspired by the idea

90 *UNTS*, No. 52106, vol. 2999. This Convention illustrates the overcoming of the Island of Palmas paradigm of "territorial exclusiveness", according to which each watercourse state can do whatever it wants on "its" section of an international river. This paradigm is now undermined by Articles 5, 7 and 8, which refer respectively to equitable use and participation, the obligation not to cause – through use – "significant harm" to other states in their equal right of use, while at the same time establishing the obligation to cooperate.

91 ICJ, Gabčíkovo-Nagymaros Project, 1997, para. 85.

92 These are generally the Great Powers, if not all "particularly interested States", to use the formula resorted to by the ICJ in the *North Sea Continental Shelf* cases, 1969, para. 73 (at 43).

93 "[A] régime based on considerations of logic, utility and humanity", Yasseen, *YILC*, vol. I, 1195th session, para. 22 (at 264).

94 Internationalisation "must be conceived [...] as a concrete and active manifestation of the economic solidarity of States united in society for their common benefit" (Report of the Commission of Inquiry into the *Dispute Relating to the Application of the Articles of the Treaty of Peace Concerning the Oder*, International Oder Commission: PCIJ, *Series C*, No. 17-II, 348); similarly: "community of interests of nations in general" (*ibid.*, 290, Memorandum of the Six Governments).

95 Dissenting opinion appended to the judgment of the P.C.I.J. in the *Oscar Chinn* case, judgment of 12 December 1934, *PCIJ Reports* A/B 63, 139–140.

96 Udina (1933), 705. As it has been aptly observed: "the right in question has been created at the instance and with the concurrence of a group of leading Powers and has come to be regarded as a *permanent part of the public law of Europe or of the world, capable of discharge only by the same kind of machinery*", Lord A McNair (1961), 659 [emphasis added].

of a common good dictated by Nature, independently of any synallagmatic relationship.

In the *Free Zones* case, the PCIJ seems to have differentiated the legal regimes governed by these two paragraphs of Article 12 VCSS 1978. Indeed, for the Saint-Gingolph region (Upper Savoy), the Court states that:

> The concord of wills thus represented by the Manifesto confers on the delimitation of the zone of Saint-Gingolph the character of a treaty stipulation which France must respect as Sardinia's successor in the sovereignty over the territory in question.[97]

It would therefore be appropriate to speak of a servitude – or real rights attached to a territory (or localised) – limited (unlike Article 12 (2)) *ratione personarum* to the sovereign States concerned by the two territories: the servient and the dominant.

For the Gex District area, on the other hand, the Court speaks of "territorial stipulations", provided for by the various treaties and other international normative acts that punctuated the European peace settlement of that time, for the community of European states and in their interest, namely: the neutrality of Switzerland, the "arrondissement" (enlargement) of the territory of Geneva as well as the '[t]he withdrawal of the French customs line from the political frontier in the areas constituting the free zones of the Gex District'.[98] While the legal effects are ultimately similar, i.e., the transmission (or permanence) of territorial rights and obligations, the means and legal basis are different. In this context, it is worth recalling that in Vienna in 1815, France was the defeated power, unlike the Kingdom of Sardinia which was among the allied states of the victorious coalition.

The PCIJ, confirming previous States practice, therefore ended up finding that, at the time of the annexation of Savoy, France had indeed, by Article 2 of the Treaty of Turin of 24 March 1860, assumed all the obligations hitherto incumbent on Sardinia by virtue of the neutralisation of part of Savoy, under a treaty (of 16 March 1816), to which it was not a party: hence the succession of real rights attached to the Savoy territory in question.

No investigation of the issue would be complete without looking at a famous case, probably the jurisprudential precursor in this area, namely the "Question of the Åland Islands", to which we referred at the beginning of this subsection.

---

97 PCIJ, Free Zones of Upper Savoy and the District of Gex (France / Switzerland), judgment of 7 June 1932: *PCIJ Reports* A/B 46, 145.

98 *Ibid.*, 168.

The International Committee of Jurists, directly faced to the question of the existence of servitudes in international law, noted that the demilitarisation regime (demolition of fortifications on the archipelago),[99] established by the Treaty of Paris of 1856 at the *expense of* Russia – the sovereign of the archipelago – and for the benefit of the States benefiting from the "Droit public de l'Europe", had survived the succession of States, as the archipelago of the Åland Islands was thenceforth under Finnish sovereignty.[100]

The International Committee of Jurists, declared, in an oft-cited passage, that:

> Indeed the Powers have, on many occasions since 1815, and especially at the conclusion of peace treaties, tried to create true objective law, a real political status the effects of which are felt outside the immediate circle of contracting parties. In the case in point, the permanent international interests which require the maintenance of the situation created in 1856, showed themselves once again after the constitution of Finland as an independent State ; as evidence of this there is the agreement entered into on 30th December, 1918, concerning the demolition of fortifications erected on the Åland Islands by Russia, by those of the Powers most directly interested on account of their geographical position, namely Sweden, Finland and Germany.[101]

Therefore, even if Sweden is not a party to the 1856 Treaty – and is therefore a third state with respect to these stipulations – it still vested with a legal interest in Finland's compliance with them. Because of the objective nature of the settlement of the Åland Islands question by the Treaty of 1856, 'Sweden may, as a Power directly interested, insist upon compliance with the provisions of this Treaty in so far as the contracting parties have not cancelled it. This is all the more true owing to the fact as Sweden has always made use of it and has never been called in question by the signatory Powers'.[102] If, on the contrary, the Commission had – in this case erroneously – configured the legal situation as one of real servitudes – i.e., in accordance with Article 12 (1) VCSS 1978 – Sweden would have had no legal title to demand that Finland maintain the obligation not to maintain fortification on the archipelago.

---

99 With regard to the question of the Åland Islands from the point of view of demilitarised or neutralised territories, see *infra* Part 3. Chapter 8. Section H.i.

100 Åland Islands Case, 1920, 16.

101 *Ibid.*, 17.

102 *Ibid.*, 18–19.

Indeed, the International Committee of Jurists had very clearly and correctly ruled out the construction based on servitude – thus the case governed by Article 12 para. 1 – where it said: 'It is certain that the provisions agreed upon at Paris between the Powers and Russia went beyond *purely Swedish interests*'.[103] The arbitration tribunal took care to specify that:

> A similar conclusion would also be reached if the point of view enunciated above were adopted, according to which the question is one of *a definite settlement of European interests and not a question of mere individual and subjective political obligations.*[104]

Some have criticised – albeit somewhat naively – the basis of the Committee of Jurists' decision, claiming that, in the end, the 'general interest' was in fact 'the unilateral defence of the interests of the victorious powers in 1815 [sic! it is rather 1856]'.[105] In reality, however, while it is true that this status was imposed (as a punishment) on Russia, it is also true that the circle of beneficiaries extended beyond the contracting parties of the 1856 Treaty of Paris to include all states, and especially the states of the region.

In the light of case law and State practice[106] it can be said that Article 12 (2) is intended to apply to the following categories of international treaties: establishing régimes for international river[107] and international canals (as for example for the Suez Canal);[108] granting 'free access to border territories for grazing

103 *Ibid.*, 17 [emphasis added].

104 *Ibid.*, 18 [emphasis added].

105 Marco Marcoff, *Accession à l'indépendance et succession d'Etats aux traités internationaux*, Fribourg, 1969, 210 [our translation].

106 Nile Waters Agreement of 1929 between the UK and Egypt; Agreements (of 1923 and 1926) between France and the UK (as Mandatory Powers for Syria and Palestine respectively) concerning the use of the waters of the Jordan.

107 Oppenheim, at 128, para.82; Udina (1933), 707; ICJ, Gabčíkovo-Nagymaros Project, 1997, para. 123 (at 72); in this judgment the ICJ does not hesitate to reproduce the text of Article 12 (2) VCSS 1978 and to refer to it as an expression of general international law on the subject.

108 The British Foreign Secretary thus annotated following the merger between Egypt and Syria giving rise to the "United Arab Republic" (UAR): 'It is too early to forecast what effect the union of Egypt and Syria might have on the operation of the Canal. I note, however, that one of the seventeen principles announced by Colonel Nasser as the basis of the union is that: "provisions of international treaties and agreements concluded by Syria and Egypt with other States shall remain in force with regard to the *territorial spheres* stipulated at the time of their conclusion, in accordance with the provisions of international law"', quoted in Elihu Lauterpacht, "The Contemporary Practice of the United Kingdom in the Field of International Law. Survey and Comment", 7 *ICLQ* 1958, 531.

purposes, on the basis of which the States concerned laid down the details of a particular regime';[109] relating, more generally, to international lines of communication;[110] establishing status of neutrality as is the case of Switzerland or, formerly, of Belgium and Luxembourg.

D *Condominium* and *coimperium*

We have already emphasised that the notion of territorial sovereignty encompasses two absolutely *distinct* relationships: on the one hand, a relationship of real right having as its object the territory,[111] on the other hand a relationship of exclusiveness, of *imperium* exercised within the framework of a well-defined territorial base. As stated by an arbitration tribunal:

> To state that in a given matter jurisdiction can only be exercised on the condition of or by agreement between two States is to place an essential restriction on the sovereignty of a State, and this can only be accepted if it is clearly demonstrated. International practice undoubtedly reveals some particular cases in which this hypothesis is verified; thus, sometimes two States jointly exercise State competences over certain territories (joint ownership, *coimperium* or *condominium*).[112]

---

109 Yasseen, *YILC*, vol. I, 1195th session, para. 22 (at 286).

110 'A succession of States cannot affect treaties which are based on 'general principles governing [for example] the right of free passage through certain straits', Intervention (*YILC*, 1972, vol. I, 1195th meeting, para. 32 (at 287)).

111 '[A] *condominium* is a territory over which responsibility is shared by two administering powers (e.g., the New Hebrides)', Douglas Williams, Colonial Attaché, British Embassy, Washington, January 6, 1959, in Digest of International Law, vol. 1, 538.

112 Lac Lanoux Case, Award (Franco-Spanish Arbitral Tribunal), 16 November 1957, *RIAA*, Vol. XII, 306 [our translation]. More recently, the ICJ correctly observed: 'there seems no reason in principle why a succession should not create a joint sovereignty where a single and undivided maritime area passes to two or more new States', Land, Island and Maritime Frontier Dispute, 1992, para. 399 (at 598). See also Island of Palmas Case, 838; Independent Union of Officials of the New Hebrides Condominium (Conseil d'Etat, France), award delivered the 2 December 1970, 57 *ILR*, 116–117, where the Anglo-French *condominium*, instituted by the London Protocol of 6 August 1914, is confirmed. See in this regard the still classic studies of Nicolas Politis, "La condition internationale des Nouvelles Hébrides", 8 *RGDIP* 1901, 121–152, 230–271; *id.*, *Le Condominium franco-anglais des Nouvelles Hébrides*, Paris, 1908. In 1980, the *condominium* ended, paving the way to the birth of the Republic of Vanuatu.

This distinction between *dominium* (sovereignty) and *imperium* (exercise of sovereignty or territorial jurisdiction)[113] which has been already touched upon[114] becomes particularly clear in situations of *condominium* and *coimperium*.[115] The common holding of a (real sovereignty) right over a territory constitutes *condominium*, whereas the common exercise of exclusive territorial sovereignty (*ius excludendi alios*) as a public power constitutes *coimperium*.[116] Situations of *condominium* can therefore arise without there being a *coimperium*, and vice versa.[117]

The first situation may arise in cases of *condominium* over completely uninhabited territories.[118] It can also occur when the exercise of sovereignty over the *condominium* territory (*imperium*) is entrusted to only one of the co-tenants (or to each of them in separate parts of the territories or even on a rotating basis over time).[119] For example, the Anglo-Egyptian *condominium* over Sudan

113 See in this sense: Verdross (1929), 396 ff; Giuseppe Sperduti, "L'individu et le droit international", 90 *RCADI* 1956-I, 752–757; Giorgio Balladore Pallieri (1962), 469; Walter Rudolf, "Das deutsch-luxemburgische Kondominium", 24 *Archiv des Völkerrechts* 1986, 301–313; Alain Coret, *Le condominium*, Paris, 1960, 52–57.

114 See *supra* Prolegomena B.2.

115 See also the legal status of the Gulf of Fonseca between Nicaragua, Honduras and El Salvador and the statements of the Central American Court of Justice (1916 and 1917; see *infra* note 133) and the Chamber of the International Court of Justice in 1992. The latter reiterated the distinction between *condominium* and *coimperium* (in this case) and the possibility that common sovereignty could be established, by treaty, even over maritime spaces (Land, Island and Maritime Frontier Dispute, 1992, paras. 399, 401). The Arbitration Commission in the Continental Shelf case in the area between Iceland and Jan Mayen (Award of 19–20 May 1981, *ILR*, Vol. 62, 126) proposed to the Parties (Iceland and Denmark) a *condominium* for the purposes of joint exploitation of resources.

116 This term is also used in diplomatic practice: "There is no doubt that none of the Allied countries has the right to liquidate the German property in Danzig, although Danzig was ceded by Germany to all the Principal Allied Powers and is now under the undivided co-sovereignty[*coimperium*] of the said Powers" (Note of the Drafting Committee of the Paris Peace Conference, 14 October 1920), in *Prassi italiana*, 3rd series, Vol. V, para. 1185, at 2667 [emphasis added].

117 See, although nuanced, Bruno Aglietti, *Il governo di alcuni condominî. Sudan anglo-egiziano – Nuove Ebridi – Tangeri*, Firenze, 1939, 123 ff; Strupp, Vol. 1, 157; Abdalla A El Arian, *Condominium and Related Situations in International Law; With Special Reference to the Dual Administration of the Sudan and the Legal Problems Arising Out of It*, Cairo, 1952, 87–95; Hans Aufricht, "On Relative Sovereignty", 30 *Cornell Law Quarterly* (1944), 153.

118 See e.g., the Franco-Spanish *condominium* on the Isle of Pheasants (or Conference Island), established by the Treaty of the Pyrenees of 1659, subsequently confirmed by the Treaty of Bayonne of 2 December 1856 and the Franco-Spanish Convention of 27 March 1901.

119 See in this respect the letter of 7 February 1866 from Von Mansdorff to Karoly on the subject of the administration of the Duchy of Holstein, in which it is stated that Prussia, as sole administrator, "ist nicht die alleinige *Eigenthümerin* der holsteinschen

(until its independence on 1er January 1956) was a *condominium* without a *coimperium*,[120] as Britain alone exercised the *imperium*, through its governor in Khartoum.[121] Conversely, in the case of the New Hebrides,[122] France and Britain were both co-sovereigns (*dominium*) and jointly exercised sovereignty (*imperium*)[123] through their commissioners.[124] As for the nationality of the natives, they did not become nationals of both sovereigns, but enjoyed a:

> [S]pecial status and the two Powers may not consider them as under the jurisdiction of one of their Governments or grant to them British or French nationality.[125]

On the other hand, cases of *coimperia* without *condominium* may arise where there is a joint exercise of sovereignty, while leaving open the question of the holding of the (real) right on the territory. This may occur when sovereignty is disputed between the states concerned.[126] This category also includes cases of

Souverainitätsrechte", quoted in *Bruns*, F.B.1.1, para. 1196. The case of the Anglo-Egyptian *condominium* is interesting in that Egypt (under British protectorate but formally under Ottoman sovereignty) and Britain had a *condominium* over Sudan between 1899 and 1956, when independence was achieved. According to Article 2 of the Anglo-Egyptian Treaty of January 1899, 'the supreme military and civil command in Sudan shall be vested in one officer, termed the Governor-General of Sudan. He shall be appointed by Khedival Decree on the recommendation of Her Britannic Majesty's Government and shall be removed only by Khedival Decree with the consent of Her Britannic Majesty's Government'. The administration of the *condominium* by the Governor-General, who reported only to the Foreign Office through the British Resident in Cairo, came to resemble that of a colony. Egypt's independence (14 September 1936) did not affect the permanence of the *condominium* over the Sudan.

120 It should be noted that the treaty establishing the *condominium* did not 'regulate [not] the right of the contracting parties to cede the territory of Sudan', Aufricht, 154 [our translation].

121 Of course, it should be noted that the Governor of the Sudan was appointed by a Khedivial (Egyptian) decree on the recommendation of the British Government (Article III of the Treaty of 19 January 1899).

122 The archipelago gained independence as Vanuatu on 30 July 1980 and became a member of the UN on 15 September 1981.

123 Another example of a *condominium* with *coimperium was* the British-American condominium of the Canton and Enderbury Islands in the Pacific between 1938 and 1979, under the Exchange of Letters of 6 April 1939 (*Hackworth*, vol. 1, 509–510). These islands are now under the sovereignty of Kiribati.

124 Article 1 of the Treaty of 9 August 1914.

125 UN Doc. A/4088/Add. 11, 4 (14 April 1959).

126 For example, in the case of the territory of Moresnet, whose sovereignty was claimed by both Prussia and the Netherlands, and which was finally placed first under joint Dutch and Prussian administration (Treaty of 26 June 1816) and, following Belgian

the joint exercise of 'exclusive territorial jurisdiction in a territory belonging to a *third* power',[127] as was the case between 1878 and 1908 between Austria and Hungary over Bosnia-Herzegovina, which was under Ottoman sovereignty.[128] Similar situations still exist when, following occupation by several co-belligerents, the latter have not yet proceeded to the definitive allocation of the "spoils of war".[129] Of course, in contemporary international law of territory, which is unsurprisingly impacted by the UNC, territorial arrangements (cessions and the like) must comply with the latter's principles, such as the inadmissibility of the acquisition of territory by force and the right of peoples to self-determination. Consequently, at present, this scenario is no longer possible due to the principle of the inadmissibility of the acquisition of territory by forcc [*supra* Part 2.Chapter 5. Section B.iii].

The *condominium* can exist over any space subject to the territorial jurisdiction of a state, which excludes the High seas, the EEZ and other *res omnium* and *communis* spaces (unless there is a historical title of course), but which includes not only land spaces but also bays, lakes[130] and rivers[131] ("community of interests").[132] One of the most famous cases in this area was a *condominium*

---

independence, under Prussian and Belgian administration. The same applies to the situation that arose in the "Vallée des Dappes" from the Treaty of Paris (1815) until the Treaty of Berne of 8 December 1862, through which France and Switzerland proceeded to partition the disputed territory. These cases were erroneously considered as *condominium* cases by Nicolas Politis, "Condition internationale du territoire de Moresnet", 11 *RGDIP* 1904, 84–87. See also the case of the Partition of the Samoan Archipelago (Germany v. Great Britain and the United States of America), deliberation of the Mixed Commission of 8 November 1899, in 8 *RGDIP* 1901, 2–73.

127 Verdross (1929), 396 [our translation].

128 "While in the case of a *condominium* a community of States has sovereignty over a territory belonging to them jointly, a *co-imperium* exists, if several States jointly exercise jurisdiction or governmental functions and powers in territory belonging to another State; the administration by Austria-Hungary of Bosnia and Herzegovina from 1878 to 1908, while the territory belonged to Turkey, is usually given as an example of such a co-imperium", Frederick A Mann, "The Present Legal Status of Germany", in 33 *Transactions of the Grotius Society* 1947, 138–139.

129 This situation is of course transitory, e.g., the territories ceded by the Central Empires as a result of the 1914–1918 war and up to the successive Peace Treaties.

130 The existence of a *condominium* on Lake Constance (Switzerland/Germany/Austria) was refuted in this case by a German criminal court, which nevertheless admitted its possibility in international law: *Hackworth*, vol. 1, 615–616.

131 "The Agreement of 1816 created a joint ownership under international law, a so-called *condominium*, according to which both contracting States exercised a joint jurisdiction over frontier streams", Dutch-Prussian Condominium (1816) Case, Germany, Supreme Administrative Court, 24 November 1932, 6 ILR, 50.

132 PCIJ, Territorial Jurisdiction of the International Oder Commission, 1929, A 23, 27.

over a bay ascertained by the World Court, and one of the most important passages of its judgement deserves to be reproduced in full:

> It is true that condominium as a term of art in international law usually indicates just such a structured system for the joint exercise of sovereign governmental powers over a territory; a situation that might more aptly be called co-imperium. But this was not what the Central American Court of Justice had in mind. By a condominium, they clearly meant to indicate the existence of joint sovereignty arising as a juridical consequence of the succession of 1821. A State succession is one of the ways in which territorial sovereignty passes from one State to another; and there seems no reason in principle why a succession should not create a joint sovereignty where a single undivided maritime area passes to two or more new States. The Chamber, accordingly, sees the Judgment of 1917 as using the term condominium or "co-ownership", to describe what it regards as the legal result where three States jointly inherited by succession waters which for nearly three centuries had been under the single sway of the State from which they were the heirs [...] Certainly there is no reason why a joint sovereignty should not exist over a maritime territory. An instance of a condominium over the waters of a bay is the Baie du Figuier at the Atlantic boundary between France and Spain: by a "Declaration" of 1879, the bay was said, for purposes of jurisdiction to be in three parts, "la troisième formant des eaux communes" [...] a condominium is almost an ideal juridical embodiment of the community of interest's requirements of perfect equality of user of the waters and of common legal rights and the "exclusion of any preferential privilege". [I]t is interesting to note how the language of common interest, with its emphasis on a community comes so near to the language employed by the Central American Court of Justice in its 1917 Judgment.[133]

The International Court of Justice took the opportunity to underline the well-established difference between condominium and *coimperium* while specifying that the former means "joint sovereignty" of the States concerned, i.e., that 'the waters at the central portion of the closing line of the Gulf [of Fonseca] are subject to the joint entitlement of all three States of the Gulf'.[134]

---

133 ICJ, Land, Island and Maritime Frontier Dispute, 1992, paras. 399, 400, 401, 407 (at 597–598, 600, 602). The *condominium* may also concern lake areas, as was admitted by a German criminal court in relation to Lake Constance (see *supra* note 130).

134 *Ibid.*, para. 432 (at 616–617) (Dispositif 1 of the Judgment).

Finally, it should be stressed that this "community of interest" – referred to in another context – is embodied in the condominium and constitutes the true archetype (or prodrome) of territorial irenicism in international law of territory.

E Spheres of Influence

International case law traces back one of the first acts establishing "spheres of influence" (or interests, or friendship[135]) to the Treaty of Alcaçovas (Portugal) of 4 September 1479 between the two Iberian powers. In fact, by virtue of art. 8 of this treaty, the areas of reciprocal expansion were delimited, and future conquests were recognised in advance on both sides.[136] Unlike the other territorial situations analysed in this section, "spheres of influence" do not involve a divorce between the holding of sovereignty and its exercise, nor do they convey real rights over the territory, nor do they transfer sovereign rights or competences.[137] Their sole purpose is to allocate, in advance, the territories to be explored and acquired.[138] They must therefore, by definition, relate to territories considered *nullius*,[139] even though in international practice there are

135 Pasquale Fiore, "Du protectorat colonial et de la sphère d'influence (Hinterland)", 14 *RGDIP* 1907, 148–159; Hans P Neuhold, "Spheres of Influence", in *Encyclopedia of Public International Law*, Vol. 9, Amsterdam, 1986, 357–359 [*passim*].

136 Text in: *Fontes Historiae Iuris Gentium*, ed. by Walter Grewe, Berlin, 1995, Vol. 1, 685.

137 It is therefore an exaggeration to claim that such figures have no legal value and scope at all, as has sometimes been argued: "It can not be irrelevant to remark that 'spheres of influence' and the theory or practice of the 'Hinterland' idea are things unknown to international law and do not as yet rest upon any recognized principles of either international or municipal law", Dispatch from the US Secretary of State, N Olney, to the British Ambassador in Washington, Sir Julian Pauncefote, quoted in *Moore*, 268. State practice and international tribunals abound in examples: the agreement between Germany and Great Britain, signed in Berlin on 1st July 1890, concerning Zanzibar and Heligoland, in *Pasicrisie*, 602; Arbitral Award for the determination of the question relating to the western limits of the territory of the Kingdom of Barotse (Great Britain v. Portugal), rendered in Rome on 30 May 1905 by His Majesty King Victor Emmanuel III of Italy, *RIAA*, Vol. XI, 67–69, in which the tribunal's task was precisely to 'define the question which has arisen between the two States in relation to the *boundary of their respective spheres of influence* in Central Africa' (preamble; emphasis added).

138 In the light of the concept of legal title (see *supra* Part 1. Chapter 1. Section B.), the so-called spheres of influence agreements do not concern the *modus adquisitionis* (because there is, by definition, no actual occupation), but merely delimit the *titulus adquisitionis* territorially and between the contracting parties.

139 In this respect, therefore, such agreements are particularly different from territorial delimitation agreements and, in the event of a territorial dispute, give way to them in

political forms (thus not involving the acquisition of sovereignty) of spheres of influence over sovereign states.[140] As Judge Weeramantry aptly stated in his dissenting opinion appended to the judgment of the International Court of Justice, treaties establishing spheres of influence were characterised by their provisional and programmatic connotations. Indeed,

> [A] sphere of influence did not necessarily mean that the power claiming it [viz. the area] already had control and possession of it [precisely not, by definition], but this was clearly the objective towards which it intended to move.[141]

The treaty relationship thus established obviously creates rights and obligations for the contracting States, but what about extra-conventional effects? Are third States bound by such stipulations? By virtue of the principle of the relative effect of treaties,[142] third States are not affected in their "titles" and "rights" over the territories concerned. However,

> When both States have notified the third powers of their agreement and the latter have expressly or tacitly declared their adherence, or when any claims they may have been overcome by the granting of other advantages, the conventional delimitation of spheres of influence becomes effective

terms of legal value. Diplomatic practice is particularly attentive to this aspect if one believes the statements of the Italian Ambassador in London, Della Torretta, contained in the note of 22 February 1925 sent to the head of British diplomacy, M MacDonald (regarding the territorial dispute between the two Powers). MacDonald (concerning the territorial dispute between the two Powers over the sovereignty of the Jarabub oasis): 'If it were not necessary to add some new elements to demonstrate even better the groundlessness of the British assertion that the 1919 Convention does not modify the provisions of the Declaration of March 1899, I should remind Your Excellency of the fact that, whereas the Declaration of 1899 constitutes a division of spheres of influence over unoccupied and partly unexplored regions, the 1919 Convention represents a true delimitation of the frontier between permanently occupied territories', in *Prassi italiana*, 3rd series, Vol. V, para. 1203 (at 2724).

140 This was notably the case at Yalta (1945) between the United States and Great Britain on the one hand and the USSR on the other with regard to the European continent.

141 ICJ, Kasikili Island / Sedudu Case (Botswana / Namibia), 1999, para. 95 of the dissenting opinion of Judge Weeramantry (at 1185).

142 Balladore Pallieri (1962), 455–456 ("*res inter alios acta*"). See *supra* Part 1. Chapter 2. Section C.

> *erga omnes* and the contracting States are free to act as they wish in the respective reserved area.[143]

It seems to us to be a typical case of an obligation for a third State[144] (in this case, the International Community of States as a whole), whether one wants to configure it as a "stipulation pour autrui" or as a collateral agreement (the hypothesis which we prefer).[145] It is important here to stress that, apart from any extra-conventional obligation, the so-called spheres of influence agreement do not, on its own, produce legal effects for third parties. Only the occupation of these territories *sans maître* renders this situation *erga omnes*. Within the treaty framework, on the other hand, such agreements generally give rise to a particular form of legal title, namely *inchoate title*.[146] The so-called "spheres of influence" agreements, while not transferring real rights between the Contracting Parties, are certainly of negative origin but they may become, through the subsequent conduct of the said Parties, positive.[147] Indeed, as the ICJ has observed:

> While the treaty in question is not a boundary treaty proper but a treaty delimiting spheres of influence, the Parties nonetheless accept it as the treaty determining the boundary between their territories.[148]

143 Cavaglieri (1929), 411–412 [our translation]. Also: Quincy Wright, "Territorial Propinquity", 12 *AJIL* 1918, 522.

144 *Contra:* Cobbett, 117, for whom "such arrangements confer *no territorial rights* and impose no responsibility on the State in whose favour they are created ... Nor can such compacts, *even if acquiesced* in by States, give rise to any prescriptive right" [emphasis added]. We cannot agree with this assertion for the following reason: if an extra-conventional obligation arises and a third power, notwithstanding its acquiescence, breaches it by occupying the territory concerned, this will certainly result in an internationally wrongful act. However, if the occupation, in breach of the obligation, remains effective, it will accordingly be opposable *erga omnes*. For, as we have noted [see *supra* Part 1. Chapter 2. Section B], the collateral agreement gives rise only to a *titulus adquisitionis*, but only the effective extension of the State Power will effect the transfer of territorial sovereignty. These observations also apply to treaty relations between the Parties to the said "spheres of influence" agreements.

145 Distefano (2019), 453–461.

146 On this concept, see *supra* Part 1. Chapter 1. Section C.

147 See: Diena (1913), 5, 7. Diplomatic practice is consonant: the dispatch of the Italian Ambassador in London, the Marquis of San Giuliano, sent on 2 October to the Italian MFA, M Tittoni, quoted in *Prassi italiana*, 2nd series (1887–1918), Vol. II, para. 2329.

148 ICJ, Kasikili Island / Sedudu Case (Botswana / Namibia), 1999, para. 43 (at 1073).

In other words, the subsequent behaviour in the application of the spheres of influence treaty ends up *completing* the legal title on which the delimitation of their respective territories was based.[149]

Finally, it should be emphasised that such agreements are nowadays useless if they concern *res nullius*, as there is no longer any, or contrary to international law if they concern the territories of existing states, as they conflict with the principle of the sovereign equality of states (Article 2 (1) UNC).

F Peaceful Occupation

It is necessary to understand this juridical concept[150] by distinguishing it from other similar institutions. The occupation in question here must be distinguished from the occupation of a *nullius* territory, because it concerns a territory under the sovereignty of another state. It must also be distinguished from the military occupation (*occupatio bellica*)[151] because the latter presupposes the existence of a contemporary or previous state of war 'even if the said occupation meets with no armed resistance'.[152] It must further be distinguished from *condominia*, *coimperia* and various forms of protectorate since they all presuppose an international agreement.

By way of exclusion, therefore, peaceful occupation occurs in the case of occupation of the territory of a defeated state as a reprisal, and not by virtue of an agreement enshrined in a peace treaty; in the case of occupation due

149 See *above* Part 1. Chapter 1. Section C.

150 The reader is invited to consult a conspicuous literature (in addition to that on military occupation), of which the following are some of the highlights: Raymond Robin, *Des occupations militaires en dehors des occupations de guerre*, Paris, Sirey, 1923; Carl L Heyland, *Die Rechtsstellung der besetzten Rheinlande nach dem Versailler Friedensvertrag und dem Rheinlandabkommen, zugleich ein Beitrag zur Lehre von der Besetzung fremden Staatsgebietes*, Berlin, 1923; Sigmund Cybichowski, "Das völkerrechtliche Okkupationsrecht", 18 *Zeitschrift für ausländisches öffentliches Recht und Völkerrecht* 1934, 295–322; Erich Bruel, "Militärische Besetzung", 21 *Zeitschrift für öffentliches Recht* 1941, 145–165; Ernst Fraenkel, *Military Occupation and the rule of Law, Occupation Government in the Rhineland*, London, 1944; Georges Sauser-Hall, "L'occupation de guerre et les droits privés", 1 *Annuaire suisse de droit international* 1944, 58–125; Peter Haggenmacher, "L'occupation militaire en droit international. Genèse et profil d'une institution juridique", 79 *Relations internationales* 1994, 285–301.

151 As has been rightly observed, the institution of military occupation and that of peaceful occupation are intimately linked in their genesis and in some of their legal contours, see in this sense: Haggenmacher (1994), 298.

152 The condition of common Article 2 (2) GE 1949 is therefore not met.

to the non-fulfilment of treaty clauses;[153] in the case of occupation, during a conflict, of the territory of a neutral state;[154] in the case of occupation of the territories of an allied state by one of the co-belligerents;[155] or in the case of peacetime occupation of the territory of a state without its prior consent, as for example the occupation of Haiti by American troops from 1915 until 1934 for the purpose of protecting the interests of foreign states imperilled by internal disturbances;[156] or in the case of occupation by way of *pledge* for the purpose of enforcing a treaty;[157] or as a means of pressure to obtain reparation for an internationally wrongful act.[158]

Like the other territorial situations analysed in this chapter, peaceful occupation, as briefly described here, hardly involves any transfer of territorial sovereignty (due to the lack of both *animus occupandi* and *animus derelinquendi*). On the contrary, it highlights the divorce between the titularity of territorial sovereignty and its exercise (for a temporary period of time). The figure of peaceful occupation is one of the instruments available to the state for its own protection or the protection of its own vital interests (*self-help, autotutela,*

153 See the occupation of the Ruhr by French and Belgian troops in 1925. Emer de Vattel once wrote: '[I]f the treaty be not fulfilled, what has been given in security, may be retained and appropriated … at least until the debt be discharged, or a just compensation made', Book II, Chapter XII, para. 244 (at 399).

154 See the occupation of Iran by Anglo-Soviet troops in 1941.

155 See the occupation of the French colonies in North Africa by Anglo-American troops from 8 November 1942 until early 1945.

156 "[T]he landing [at Haiti] was entirely *friendly and for the preservation of order and protection of legations*", *Hackworth*, vol. 2, 330 [emphasis added].

157 In this respect, the occupation of the Dodecanese islands by Italy in order to ensure the implementation of the 1912 Treaty of Ouchy concerning the cession of Tripolitania and Cyrenaica by Turkey to Italy (*Prassi italiana*, 1887–1918, vol. I, para. 1336, at 38). These islands were then definitively transferred to Italy by the 1923 Treaty of Lausanne with Turkey.

158 In this respect, mention may be made of the occupation of Corfu by Italy in 1923 following the murder of General Tellini, pending the *satisfaction* by Greece of Italian requests. The occupation of this island was legitimised by the Italian delegate, Salandra, in these words, in reply to the criticisms of his Swedish counterpart in the Council of the League of Nations: 'It must not be thought that the Covenant of the League of Nations forbid peaceful means of repression. They are not forbidden by any of its articles. I may add that in its Preamble the principles of international law are expressly recognized. Among these principles is the right of peaceful reprisals and of occupation as a measure of guarantee. These reprisals are therefore legitimate. It should be noted that such eminent authorities on international law as Professors Schücking and Wehberg (*Die Satzung des Völkerbundes*, 1921, page 293), who have studied in detail the Covenant of the League of Nations in depth, state most explicitly that reprisals and retorsions are not forbidden', 18 September 1923 (14th Meeting), *Official Journal*, 1923 (November), 1314.

Selbsthilfe, etc.). State practice is singularly opulent regarding peaceful occupation, as they have made use of this foreign policy tool. This has been open to abuse, in particular hiding otherwise politically unacceptable annexations in the past.

However, as a general rule, states have used peaceful occupation, among other things, to put pressure on a state that has not yet fulfilled its obligations, or even before it has been able to fulfil them (this is also known as "guarantee occupation"):

> Señor Pacheco, however, adds that the Chincha Islands will be occupied, not as a possession of Spain, but as a measure of coercion upon Peru, until full satisfaction shall be obtained, not only for the grievances, the redress of which was the object of Señor Salazar's mission, but for the insults and outrages to which that Commissioner was subjected on leaving Peru for Spain.[159]

Finally, it should be noted that, unless the State on whose territory the occupation is carried out consents,[160] it is now unlawful because it conflicts with Article 2 para. 1 and para. 4 of the UNC, as can be seen, for example, from the fragment of the quote above ("as a measure of coercion"). It would even be an aggression, i.e., 'the most serious and dangerous form of the illegal use of force' and it constitutes "a crime against international peace".[161]

Finally, some of the purposes formerly pursued by peaceful occupation could be achieved today within the framework of the "New York Law", i.e., through the system of collective security, according to the contextual interpretation of Articles 2 (4), 24, 39 and 51 of the UNC. To this end, particular mention should be made of Chapter VII and especially of peacekeeping operations

159 Dispatch from the British Ambassador in Madrid, Sir J Crampton, to Earl Russell, 22 June 1864, in *Bruns*, B.1.1 (1856–1871), para. 1404.

160 In accordance with Article 20 ARSIWA of which "Invitation upon a request" is an illustration. See in this regard: Giovanni Distefano, Etienne Henry, *International Law and the Use of Force: Enchaining Ares* (Leiden 2025).

161 Respectively Preamble 5 and Article 5 para. 2 of UNGA Res. 3314. It is also worth mentioning, if only in passing, that the crime of aggression was the first article in the now defunct Article 19 of the Draft on State Responsibility provisionally adopted by the International Law Commission (UN Doc. A/51/10, 1996, 154). As is well known, the distinction between international State's delicts and crimes disappeared, and with it the latter category of international violations, from ARSIWA. Nevertheless, the crime of aggression is now part of the international crimes that can be prosecuted by the ICC against individuals under article 8 bis of the 1998 Rome Statute.

(which always require the consent of the territorial State), but even more so of peace enforcement operations under Article 42 of the UNC, which precisely do not require the consent of the State on whose territory they are deployed.[162]

G International Protectorates

i *Notion*

As in the two juridical situations reviewed earlier, the regime of international protectorate is at variance with contemporary international law, reflected by the UNC. The legal form of protectorate is patently at variance with the principle of the sovereign equality of States (Article 2 (1) UNC), which prohibits intervention in the internal affairs of a State, as well as with the right to self-determination of peoples (Article 1 (2) and UNGA resolutions 1514 (XV) and 2625 (XXV)). Therefore, cases of protectorate, now completely absent from international legal reality, have disappeared first in Europe and then in the other continents.

As a result, some of the purposes once pursued by this legal figure can now be achieved by direct international administration or by the trust administration discussed below.

Before outlining the conceptual contours of international protectorate, it is important to recall that the '[i]ndependence is really no more than the normal condition of States according to international law'[163] and that this, as Max Huber put it in the Island of Palmas case, entails *plenitude* and *exclusiveness* in the exercise of State functions.[164] Or, if one wants to read these concepts in the context of Huber's definition of "independence" in Island of Palmas: *suprema postestas* emphasises *independence* (i.e., "external sovereignty"[165]) while *summa potestas* refers to the exercise of the regalian activities comprised by sovereignty. This distinction – and dissociation – between sovereignty and its exercise in the international legal arena is the fundamental characteristic of the international protectorate. The raison d'être of the protectorate is to be found in the conception that European – and more generally Western – states

162 Giovanni Distefano, Etienne Henry, *International Law and the Use of Force: Enchaining Ares* (Leiden 2025).

163 Individual opinion of Judge Anzilotti appended to the opinion of the PCIJ in the case concerning the Customs Regime between Germany and Austria, A/B 41, 57.

164 See *above* Prolegomena A.

165 Individual opinion of Judge Anzilotti (*supra* note 163).

had of their legal relations with *non-civilised peoples or entities with a civilisation considered inferior*: 'semi-barbarous'.[166]

Despite the variety of individual situations,[167] the juridical notion of protectorate – which 'is [however] rather vague in international law'[168] – presupposes the presence of two independent states,[169] one of which accepts the intervention, to a very variable extent, or control of the other:

> An arrangement may be entered into whereby one state, while retaining to some extent its separate identity as a state, is subject to a kind of guardianship by another state.[170] The circumstances in which this occur and the consequences which result vary from case to case, and depend upon the particular provisions of the arrangement between the two states concerned.[171]

Under a treaty, a bilateral legal relationship is established through a treaty whereby a state assumes *protection*[172] and therefore undertakes to assist

166 Home Frontier and Foreign Missionary Society of the United Brethren in Christ (United States) v. Great Britain), 22 January 1926), *RIAA*, vol. 6, 43.

167 "Protectorate is ... a conception which lacks exact legal precision, as its real meaning depends very much upon the special case", *Oppenheim's International Law*, 1992, vol. 1, para. 81, 268.

168 Case of Pablo Najera (France) v. Mexico, Award of 19 October 1928, RIAA, vol. 5, 495 [our translation].

169 Article 13 of the London Convention of 29 July 1913 by which both parties recognised the independence of Bahrain, formerly under the sovereignty of the Sublime Porte and now under the protection of Great Britain. This treaty never entered into force for lack of ratification, but ICJ was quick to note in this regard that: 'signed but unratified treaties may constitute an accurate expression of the understanding of the parties at the time of signature' (Maritime Delimitation and Territorial Questions (Qatar v. Bahrain), 2001, para. 89 (at 68)).

170 The idea of "guardianship" would later resonate in the institution of the LoN Mandates; it evokes, admittedly with profound differences that we shall not fail to note (see *infra* Part 3. Chapter 9. Section A.), a relationship of "protection" in the broad sense. In one case, the one under consideration here, to ultimately serve the interests of the protecting State, in the other, that of the Mandates, of the people benefiting from the "sacred mission of civilisation" entrusted to the Mandatory Power.

171 *Oppenheim's International Law*, 1992, para. 81 (at 267).

172 'The term 'protectorate' has been broadly used by writers on international law to apply to cases wherein a comparatively powerful state assumes the duty of protecting a weaker state with the essential feature that the conduct of the external affairs of the protectorate are placed in the hands of the protecting state', Robert Robbins, "The legal status of Aden colony and Aden Protectorate", 33 *AJIL* 1939, 700. Similarly: William E Hall, *A Treatise on International Law*, 8th edn, Oxford, 1924, 28.

it militarily against any external threat and/or to 'conduct [its] foreign relations'.[173] At the same time, the protected state consents to the former state exercising control or intervention – to varying degrees defined in the treaty – in the internal administration and especially in the conduct of its external relations vis-à-vis third states. Normally, the authority of the protecting State is represented and exercised by its *Resident* (or *Agent*) in the protected State.[174]

This "intervention"[175] is explained and justified by the obligation the protecting state assumes to defend the protected state against external threats and perils.[176] Indeed, the protecting state could not perform this task if it had not been previously authorised to exercise control over the protected state and within its legal order.[177] In a nutshell, one can speak of "capitis deminutio", i.e., a limitation of the "traditional legal capacity to enter into international commitments (*internationale Handlungsfahigkeit*)".[178]

This protection must be manifested *erga omnes*, so international law requires that 'the protected state should exhibit a sign on its flag denoting the protective connection ("as a mark of the protection")'.[179]

This intervention can take two different forms. Sometimes, the protecting state assumes *in toto* the external relations of the protected state, i.e., it fully ensures the international representation of the latter.[180] Therefore, the protecting state acts in its own name and on its own behalf,[181] concludes treaties

173 ICJ, Temple of Preah Vihear, 1962, 16. Domestic jurisprudence is unsurprisingly in unison: "[T]he control, for instance, of foreign affairs may be completely in the hands of a protecting Power, and there may be agreements or treaties which limit the powers of the sovereign even in internal affairs without entailing a loss of the position of a sovereign Power", Duff Development Co, Ltd v. Government of Kelantan and Another, House of Lords, 10 April 1924, 2 *ILR*, 127.

174 For example, Article III of the Treaty of 17 November 1905 between Korea and Japan, establishing the latter's protectorate over the former state.

175 Case of Pablo Najera (France) v. Mexico, 507.

176 The requirement of protection is based on the fact that the protected state is considered a "minor" and prefigures a key element of the institution of LoN Mandates where reference is made to "peoples not yet capable of self-government under the particularly difficult conditions of the modern world" (Article 22 para. 1 LoN Covenant).

177 See: Frederick J Lugard, *Dual Mandate in British Tropical Africa*, Oxford, 1932, 35.

178 Case of Pablo Najera (France) v. Mexico, 472.

179 Arbitral Award on the Interpretation of the Treaty of Managua between the United Kingdom and Nicaragua, decision of 2 July 1881, *RIAA*, vol. 28, 178.

180 On the notion of representation, see: Pier Angelo Sereni, "La représentation en droit international", 73 *RCADI* 1948-II, 3–67.

181 The protecting State guarantees consular protection for nationals of the protected State vis-à-vis third States, as was the case for Great Britain and Bahrain (Article 15 of the London Convention of 29 July 1913).

and performs any act on the international scene (this was often the case in the French protectorates). Sometimes the protected state also acts in the international legal arena, but these acts, or at least some of them, must be endorsed by the protecting state, or, failing that, the latter enjoys a veto power over these acts.[182]

From the point of view of international responsibility, it is important to stress in this respect that the relationship between the protecting State and the protected State, established and governed by an international treaty (the protectorate treaty) – which remains *res inter alios acta* vis-a-vis third States – falls within the exclusive jurisdiction of these two States:

> The relationship between the protecting and the protected is therefore to be regarded as an internal affair between these two powers; vis-à-vis the foreigner, the responsibilities of the protecting and the protected States, while legally distinct, merge into one, to be borne by the Protecting Power.[183]

It is important to emphasize that the protectorate treaty hardly extinguishes the international legal subjectivity of the protected State, or even its *status*; on the contrary, this is the *sine qua non* for its establishment and survives the termination of the protectorate.[184] The protected state must therefore be a sovereign state under international law for a treaty relationship of protection to arise under international law:

182 This was notably the case of the British protectorate over the Transvaal before its annexation: treaties concluded by this entity with third states were only final and came into force on condition that Great Britain did not exercise its veto within six months. Likewise, in respect to Bahrain: 'The present status of Bahrain is based on the Agreement of December 22, 1880, wherein the Ruler of Bahrain bound himself and his successors 'to abstain from entering into negotiations or making treaties of any sort with any State or Government other than the British without the consent of the said British Government, and to refuse permission to any other Government than the British to establish diplomatic or consular agencies or coaling depots in our territory, unless with the consent of the British Government' CU Aitchison, *A Collection of Treaties, Engagements and Sanads*, Calcutta, 1933, Vol. XI, 237. However, it has been observed that "[n]o decision of an international tribunal has been found which declares that a treaty is invalid for lack of capacity of a party which had previously placed itself under obligation to another State agreeing not to enter into such a treaty", *Draft Convention on the Law of Treaties*, Harvard Law School, Comment, *AJIL* Suppl. 29 (1935), 709.

183 British Claims in the Spanish Zone of Morocco, 648 [our translation].

184 The Indo-Pakistan Western Boundary (Rann of Kutch) between India and Pakistan, 502.

> The position within the International Community of a state under protection is defined by the treaty of protection which enumerates the reciprocal rights and duties of the protecting and protected States. Each case must therefore be treated according to its own merits [...] But it is characteristic of a protectorate that the protected state always has, and retains, for some purposes, a position of its own as an international person and a subject of international law.[185]

It should be recalled, however, that the protectorate treaty *is* only *law* between these two States and is *res inter alios acta* vis-à-vis third States. For this reason, and in order for the treaty to have effect on the international legal scene, the protecting State must *notify* the protectorate to third states and thus the content of the legal relationship established between it and the protected state.[186] In this respect, the PCIJ insisted in its advisory opinion on the *Nationality Decrees in Tunisia and Morocco* that the recognition of third States is indispensable for the protectorate treaty to have effect in their regard.[187]

This was a constant practice in international relations. Sometimes it was even obligatory by virtue of a treaty, as was the case under Article 34 of the General Act of the Berlin Conference of 1885, relating to the colonial protectorate.[188] Notification thus allowed the protecting States to assert their rights and claims in respect of the protectorate. Consequently, accession – express or tacit (by conclusive behaviour) – by third states had the effect of recognising the protectorate and assuming its legal consequences, i.e., of having legal relations with the protected state only through the protecting State. From this

185 *Oppenheim's International Law*, 1992, para. 82 (at 269).

186 This condition is necessary, as is shown by constant, general and uniform diplomatic practice. See, for example, the notification made by Italy in accordance with the disputed provision of Article 17 contained in the Treaty of Uccialli (Wuhale) of 2 May 1889 (*Prassi italiana*, seconda serie, vol. II, paras. 1438–1440, at 152–157).

187 "The extent of the powers of a protecting State depends, on the one hand, on the treaties of protectorate between the protecting State and the protected State and, on the other hand, on the *conditions under which the protectorate has been recognised by third Powers vis-à-vis which it is intended to avail itself of the provisions of these treaties*", Nationality Decrees Issued in Tunis and Morocco, Advisory opinion of 7 February 1923: *PCIJ Reports* B 4, 27.

188 'Any Power which henceforth takes possession of a tract of land on the coasts of the African continent outside of its present possessions, or which, being hitherto without such possessions, shall acquire them, as well as the Power which assumes a Protectorate there, shall accompany the respective act with a notification thereof, addressed to the other Signatory Powers of the present Act, in order to enable them, if need be, to make good any claims of their own'.

perspective, we are inclined to configure this legal relationship as a treaty creating obligations *for* third States in the sense of Article 35 VCLT 1969, i.e., by means of a collateral agreement.

ii Forms

As usual, whether in law or in any other scientific discipline, a single concept and name can hide different forms. The PCIJ did not fail to note the protean and evolving nature of the international protectorate in the following terms:

> The extent of the powers of a protecting State in the territory of a protected State depends, first, upon the Treaties between the protecting State and the protected State establishing the Protectorate, and, secondly, upon the conditions under which the Protectorate has been recognised by third Powers as against whom there is an intention to rely on the provisions of these Treaties. In spite of common features possessed by Protectorates under international law, they have individual legal characteristics resulting from the special conditions under which they were created, and the stage of their development.[189]

Protectorates can be both individual and collective, depending on whether they are exercised by one or more states jointly. While examples of individual protectorates are much more numerous,[190] a few historical examples of collective protectorates are worth noting: a) that of Russia, Austria and Prussia over the Republic of Krakow between 1815–1846;[191] b) of England, Germany and the United States over the Samoan Islands between 1889 and 1899.[192]

In a similar vein, a distinction must be made between true international protectorates and "special treaty relations",[193] in British practice, where the

189 PCIJ, Nationality decrees issued in Tunis and Morocco, 27.

190 For example, the British protectorate over the "United States of the Ionian Islands" between 1815 and 1863 when they were annexed to Greece. This situation will also be examined from another angle as they were "neutralised" at the time of their cession (reunion) to the Kingdom of Greece (see *infra* Part 3. Chapter 8. Section H.ii).

191 See *infra* Part 3. Chapter 9. Section C ("internationalised territories").

192 This collective protectorate was established by the Treaty of Berlin of 14 June 1889 (*NRG*, vol. 15, second series, 571–590) and was extinguished by the Tripartite Convention of 2 December 1899 (*Treaties and Other International Agreements of the United States of America 1776–1949*, Vol. 1, compiled by Charles I. Bevans for the State Department, Washington, 1968–1976, 276–290).

193 On the differences between the different statuses that emerge from British practice in the Arabian Peninsula, see: Gholam-Reza Tadjbakhche, *La question des îles Bahreïn*, Paris, 1960, 171–179.

protected state enjoyed a much wider exercise of sovereignty in the international legal arena than its neighbours in the Persian Gulf emirates placed under British protectorate. The case of the Sultanate of Oman illustrates this specific form of international régime.[194] In contrast, the 'protected states' of Bahrain and Qatar vis-à-vis Great Britain in 1861 and 1913 respectively enjoyed a much more circumscribed margin of manoeuvre on the international legal scene.

In the same vein, international practice, especially in the United States, identifies provisional situations, such as those of *client States,* which, beyond an ectoplasm of independence, do not, however, satisfy the Palmas test consisting of the full and exclusive exercise of State functions. They are indeed states, but their sovereignty is exercised, both internationally and internally, to varying degrees, by the United States of America. These include Cuba (between 1899 and 1902), which was successively modified by the 1903 treaty with the USA;[195] Santo Domingo, from 1907 (by virtue of the convention of the same year) until 1924.[196] In all these cases, the US had ensured that these states did not enter into treaties with third states that might jeopardise their (these states') independence or incur debts disproportionate to their resources.

Finally, in order to *distinguish* it *carefully* (at least in the spirit of the time), mention should be made of the colonial protectorate, i.e., the cases in which Western powers entered into agreements with the indigenous chiefs. Indeed, it was not uncommon for European states in their colonial expansion[197] to prefer to conclude a protectorate treaty (or a more or less disguised treaty of cession)[198] instead of waging war against an entity considered to be *inferior.* In this way, states indirectly obtained, sometimes without a fight, the same

194 After the entry into force of the treaty establishing these 'special treaty relations' between Great Britain and Oman (1839), Oman was able to conclude friendship and trade treaties with France, the United States and the Netherlands, among others. Furthermore, '[t]he status of Muscat as an independent sultanate was affirmed by The Hague Court of Arbitration in its decision in the Muscat Dhow Case in 1905. Britain itself has indicated that it does not put Muscat into the same category as the other Persian Gulf sheikhdoms by giving, for example, the Political Agent in Muscat the official title of consul', Herbert J Liebesny, 'International Relations of Arabia: The Dependent Areas', 1 *The Middle East Journal* 1947, 163.

195 See *supra* Part 3 Chapter 8. Section A.i, notes 15-16.

196 Under the terms of this treaty, the consent of the United States was required 'for the modification of the import duties of the Dominican Government', *Hackworth,* Vol. 5, 360. Between 1916 and 1924, US administration became a straightforward occupation of the island.

197 Thence the requirement of notification under Article 34 of the General Act of the Berlin Conference of 26 February 1885.

198 See *supra* Part 1. Chapter 2. Section D.

benefits they would have gained by waging a more expensive colonial war leading to conquest.[199] In still other cases, the state in question was not yet able or willing to proceed to the effective occupation[200] of the territories governed by the indigenous chiefs and thus resorted to the 'colonial protectorate'[201] which would require for its validity the notification under Article 34 of the aforementioned General Act of the 1885 Berlin Conference.[202] International jurisprudence has sometimes considered these colonial protectorate treaties as a relationship of *suzerainty*, from lord to vassal, thus excluding any equality between the contracting parties.[203]

By virtue of the colonial protectorate, the protecting State is thus vested with the power not only to manage the external relations[204] of the protected state but also to administer it internally by virtue of the right of interference: to control its finances, to occupy certain strategic locations militarily, to institute its own tribunals responsible for administering justice with regard to its own nationals (a prerogative that historically dates back to the Capitulations),[205] etc.

This includes the French protectorates over Tonkin, over Annam, over Tunisia, over the allotted area of Morocco; the British protectorates over Egypt (1914–1922),[206] over the Sultanate of Zanzibar, over the three states of the

199 '[D]uring the era of the Berlin Conference the European Powers entered into many treaties with local rulers. Britain concluded some 350 treaties with the local chiefs of the Niger Delta', ICJ, Land and Maritime Boundary (Cameroon v Nigeria, Equatorial Guinea Intervening), 2002, para. 203 (at 404).

200 Required by Article 35 of the General Act of the Berlin Conference of 1885 (in relation to the African continent) and more generally by customary international law (Palmas, Clipperton, Legal Status of Eastern Greenland).

201 'To be sure, treaties of protection were sometimes a first step towards the development of full colonial title, or, as they have been described, "a legal lever for acquiring an inchoate title to territory: a title capable of being perfected more or less at leisure" (DJ Latham Brown, 'The Ethiopia-Somaliland Frontier Dispute', 5 *ICLQ* 1956, 254–255) but until that happened and in the absence of provisions which may be interpreted as conveying title, they remained a lever and no more', ICJ, Land and Maritime Boundary (Cameroon v. Nigeria, Equatorial Guinea Intervening), 2002, separate opinion of Judge Al-Khasawneh, para. 7 (at 497).

202 See, for example, Italy's notification of the establishment of its protectorate over Zula (Eritrea): *Prassi italiana*, seconda serie, vol. II, paras. 1550, 397.

203 Island of Palmas case, 858.

204 This includes, for example, the right of diplomatic protection exercised by the Protecting Power for the benefit of the nationals of the protected state: Franco-Moroccan Protectorate Treaty of 1912.

205 The establishment of a dual justice system is one of the hallmarks of the colonial regime (see *supra* Part 2. Chapter 6. Section A.i).

206 Taba case (Egypt/Israel), paras. 64–69 (at 23–24).

Island of Borneo, over the Malay States, over the Sultanate of Johor, over the Tonga Islands, over the feudal princes (maharajas) of India, over Nepal, over Somaliland; Spanish protectorate over the allotted area of Morocco; Indian protectorate over Sikkim; Japanese protectorate over Korea (1905–1910).[207]

The ICJ was confronted with the issue of colonial protectorate in the case of Cameroon v. Nigeria, in which it examined the Treaty of 10 September 1884 between Great Britain and the Kings and Chiefs of Old Calabar, Article II of which reads as follows:

> The Kings and Chiefs of Old Calabar agree[d] and promise[d] to refrain from entering into any correspondence, Agreement, or Treaty with any foreign nation or Power, except with the knowledge and sanction of Her Britannic Majesty's Government.[208]

The Court observes that a distinction must be made between treaties of colonial protection in which the sovereignty of the protected State is "retained" (French protectorate over Morocco, Tunisia and Madagascar in 1885, 1895 and 1912 respectively for France) and those, particularly in sub-Saharan Africa, concluded 'not with States, but rather with important indigenous rulers exercising local rule over identifiable areas of territory'.[209] In order to differentiate between these two categories of situations, the Court rightly refers to the award in the *Island of Palmas* case, where Max Huber stresses that: 'it is not an agreement between equals'.[210] In the same vein, the Court, citing its own advisory opinion in the Western Sahara case, states that this is a derivative mode of acquisition[211] and that '[t]he choice of a protectorate treaty by Great Britain was a question of the preferred manner of rule'.[212] The Court therefore concluded

207 Under Articles I and II respectively of the Treaty of 17 November 1905, Japan was in charge of Korea's subjects and interests in relation to third states, as well as the execution (including therefore responsibility for breach) of treaties in force between Korea and other powers.

208 ICJ, Land and Maritime Boundary (Cameroon v. Nigeria, Equatorial Guinea Intervening), 2002, para. 203 (at 404).

209 *Ibid.*, para. 205 (at 405).

210 Island of Palmas case, 858.

211 ICJ, Western Sahara, 1974, para. 80 (at 39).

212 ICJ, Land and Maritime Boundary (Cameroon v. Nigeria, Equatorial Guinea Intervening), 2002, para. 206 (at 405).

that the treaty between Britain and the chiefs of Old Calabar did not establish a true international protectorate, but merely a colonial protectorate.[213]

How then can such treaties (establishing a colonial protectorate) be distinguished from a treaty establishing a genuine international protectorate? The Court, relying on its judgment in the 2001 Qatar/Bahrain case, '[n]otes that a characteristic of an international protectorate is that of an ongoing meetings and discussions between the Protecting Power and the Rulers of the Protectorate'.[214] This is not necessarily the case in the colonial protectorate.[215]

With a view to distinguishing between these two types of protectorate, some have argued that the colonial protectorate is nothing more than a disguised occupation of a masterless territory; others, not without reason, have seen in these treaties the proof of an indirect administration of these territories, and thus ultimately the effectiveness of the occupation by the "protector" state.[216]

Unless one considers these entities of political organisation (on a territorial basis) as real States, endowed with *treaty-making power*, and consequently these agreements as real international treaties conveying *the titulus*,[217] one can *in any case* consider them as creating territorial subjective rights. In other words, the protecting state obtains, once notified and after having received the adherence of the third states, a conventional *ius excludendi alios*[218] over these territories so that the latter must refrain from proceeding to their effective occupation under penalty of engaging their international responsibility (because of the violation of the express or tacit acceptance of the notification)[219] with the

213 *Oppenheim's International Law*, 9th ed, para. 81 (at 269). *Contra* dissenting opinion of Judge Koroma, ICJ, Land and Maritime Boundary (Cameroon v. Nigeria, Equatorial Guinea Intervening), 2002, paras. 12–17 (at 478–482).

214 *Ibid*, para. 207 (at 406).

215 Other authors (Robbins (1939), 714) identify the differences between the traditional protectorate and the colonial protectorate in the fact that the latter is characterised by the fact that 'government in the colonial protectorate had experienced little development beyond the tribal state at the time of the protection agreement'. Indirectly, however, it can be argued that the absence of 'regular meetings and discussions' is evidence of a lower degree of state development of the protected entity as Robbins claims.

216 Island of Palmas case, 858–859. Also: Hall (1924), para. 38a (at 150).

217 Hebié (2015), 515 ff.

218 In this respect, it is worth highlighting the affinities of this system with that of the "spheres of influence", whose concerns and raison d'être it shares (see *above* Part 3. Chapter 8. Section E.).

219 *Mutatis mutandis*, it is important to stress, as Anzilotti does in his dissenting opinion in the Legal Status of Eastern Greenland case (para. 8), that if a (third) State, in disregard of a commitment with another State not to proceed with the actual occupation of a territory, carries out the occupation, it violates the commitment with the first State, but this violation does not render the occupation "null and void", as the PCIJ claimed in that case.

usual consequences of the time that could go as far as armed reprisals, or even war (before 1928).[220]

iii Some Specific Features

1 Nationality

In principle, the protecting State does not grant its nationality to nationals of the protected state who retain the nationality of the latter but who become "protected" in the international legal arena by virtue of the protectorate treaty.[221] The doctrine[222] as well as national and international jurisprudence converge in this sense.

2 International Responsibility

Because of the presence of two distinct international legal personalities – the protecting state and the protected state – there are two basic situations to be considered. In the first situation, if the two States are bound by the same obligation,[223] the protecting State will engage its own responsibility and that of the protected State, but it is the protecting State that will represent the protected State in the international legal arena, for example by receiving or bringing the international claim. If, on the other hand, the obligation breached concerns only the protected State, it is therefore only the protected State that is responsible – or, alternatively, that engages the responsibility of the third State – even if the protecting State acts in its representation on the international scene. As arbitrator Max Huber has magisterially observed:

> The relationship between the protecting and the protected is therefore to be regarded as an internal matter between these two Powers; vis-à-vis the foreigner, the responsibilities of the protecting and the protected, while legally distinct, are merged into one, to be borne by the Protecting Power.[224]

Of course, there are differences between the Greenland case and the case of notifications in the context of the colonial protectorate, but for the aspects that concern us here (*ius ad rem, i.e.*, exclusionary rights of a conventional nature by way of notification), the conclusions of the Italian Master of public international law remain valid.

220 See *supra* Part 2. Chapter 5. Section A.

221 Case of Pablo Najera (France) v. Mexico, 473.

222 Hall (1924), 28.

223 PCIJ, Moroccan Phosphate Cases, A/B 74, 25–27 (where the PCIJ repeatedly refers to "the international obligations of France and Morocco").

224 British Claims in the Spanish Zone of Morocco, 648 [our translation]. The arbitrator immediately adds: "The responsibility of the protecting State – a responsibility whose scope strictly coincides with that resulting from the general rules governing this

For example, in the case of a violation of the law related to the treatment of aliens, only the municipal courts of the protected State will have to be approached by the rightful claimants before the foreign (third) State will take up the case of its injured nationals.[225]

3 Succession to Treaties

Under the customary rule now codified in Article 29 VCLT 1969, treaties concluded by the protecting State which do not relate to the protected State,[226] are not binding on the latter, 'unless it expressly stipulated in its capacity of protecting power'.[227] This clarification being made, two scenarios can be envisaged, depending on whether the treaty was concluded by the protected State or by the protecting State. In the first situation, if the treaty was concluded before the protected State was placed under the protectorate regime, then it remains applicable, and the protecting State ensures its respect on the international legal scene for the benefit of the protected State. At the end of the protectorate (see *infra* Part 3. Chapter 8. Section G.iii), the treaty will obviously continue to bind the protected State with full legal capacity. The same applies if the treaty was concluded by the protecting State on *behalf of and in representation of* the protected State. On the other hand, with regard to treaties concluded by the protecting State, it should be noted that the VCSS 1978 does not directly govern the issue,[228] but if one refers to its article 16, which enshrines the clean slate principle for newly independent States, then there will be no succession of the protected State to treaties concluded by the protecting State.[229] This is all the more true in the case of colonial protectorates, whose character irrefutably

---

matter – derives ... from the fact that the protecting State alone represents the protected territory in its international relations" (649; our translation). Similarly, PCIJ, Phosphates in Morocco (Italy v. France), judgment of 14 June 1938: *ICJ Reports* A/B 74, 20.

225 British Claims in the Spanish Zone of Morocco, 634–636.

226 In general, extradition treaties, unless otherwise stipulated, did not apply to the territory of the protected State, *Hackworth*, vol. 4, 10.

227 Hall (1924), 29. See the practice of the United States vis-à-vis Puerto Rico before it became an "associated state" (*Hackworth*, vol. 5, 173) as well as the practice of Great Britain in relation to the Federation of Malay States, *ibid*, 406–407.

228 Benjamin Sâ Traoré, "Les régimes d'administration internationale de territoire et la succession en matière de traités", in: Distefano, Gaggioli, Hêche, 2016, vol. 2, 1703–1754. In the case of Maritime Delimitation and Territorial Questions (Qatar v. Bahrain), the International Court of Justice did not address this issue, although raised by Qatar (ICJ, 2001, para. 105, at 73).

229 Etienne Henry, "Article 16. Position with respect to predecessor State treaties", in: Distefano, Gaggioli, Hêche, 2016, Vol. 1, 561–612.

testifies to the fact that they are newly independent states, and therefore a non-self-governing territory[230] at the time the treaty was concluded by the colonial state.[231]

4 Delimitation of the Boundaries of the Protected State by the Protecting State

Given that the protecting State represents the protected state in the international arena and that the delimitation of international borders pertains to the exclusive joint competence of the states concerned, the question arises as to whether, and if so under what conditions, the protecting State can exercise this power. However, if one has in mind the conceptual contours and purposes of the international protectorate, it is not surprising to find that, unless a different intention emerges from the treaty, the consent of the protected state is necessary for the protecting State to proceed to the delimitation of boundaries or to recourse to arbitration to this effect.[232] This was also the view of the International Court of Justice in the 2001 Qatar/Bahrain case:

> The jurisdiction of the British Government to take the decision concerning the Hawar Islands derived from these two [i.e., the two "protected" States'] consents [...] The 1939 decision must therefore be regarded as a decision that was binding from the outset on both States and continued to be binding on those same States after 1971, when they ceased to be British protected States.[233]

230 See *supra* Part 2. Chapter 6. Section A.i.

231 Exceptions to the clean slate principle are treaties establishing borders (Article 11 VCSS 1978) and those creating territorial regimes (Article 12 VCSS 1978), see *supra* respectively Part 3. Chapter 8. Section B and Part 3. Chapter 8. Section C.

232 ICJ, Temple of Preah Vihear, 1962, 16; similarly, ICJ, Request for Interpretation of the Judgment of 15 June 1962 in the Case Concerning the Temple of Preah Vihear (Cambodia v. Thailand), Judgment of 11 November 2013: *ICJ Reports* 2013, para. 15 (at 291).

233 ICJ, Maritime Delimitation and Territorial Questions, 2001, para. 137, 139 (at 83) as well as for the maritime and island boundary (paras. 239–240, at 113–114). On the legal nature of this decision, see: Giovanni Distefano, "L'arrêt de la C.I.J. du 16 mars 2001 dans l'affaire de la délimitation entre Qatar et Bahreïn", *RBDI* 2001/2, 376–383. See also the arbitral decision in the Dubai-Sharjah delimitation case (at 577), where it was also a question of discerning the nature and legal effects of certain decisions taken by the protecting state (Great Britain) vis-à-vis those protected states on the Trucial Coast (the future United Arab Emirates).

5 Cession of the Territory of the Protected State by the Protecting State

By analogy with the previous subsection, and I would say *a fortiori*, the power of the protecting State to cede part of the territory of the protected State, or even to acquire it on its behalf, must derive from the protectorate treaty. In case of silence, i.e., most of the time, it is difficult to support a power – implicit in the (common) protectorate regime – vested with the protecting State to *dispose* (*ius disponendi*) of parts (or even the whole) of the territory of the protected State without the consent of the latter.

6 Belligerence

The answer to this question must be sought in the intention of the belligerents and in the effectiveness of the military activities: if the territory of the protected state is not occupied by the enemy, it is not a belligerent, and the rules of neutrality apply to it. The cases of San Marino and Andorra during World War II reflect the state of general international law.

7 Termination of Protectorate

As the protectorate is a treaty-based arrangement, it may be terminated by mutual agreement, in accordance with the law of treaties, and results in the recovery of the exercise of State functions in the international juridical arena (Kuwait, Tunisia, Morocco, Maldives, Brunei, *etc.*):

> In 1971 Qatar and Bahrain ceased to be British protected States, following an Exchange of Notes between the United Kingdom of Great Britain and Northern Ireland and Bahrain on 15 August 1971, and an Exchange of Notes between the United Kingdom of Great Britain and Northern Ireland and Qatar on 3 September 1971. On 21 September 1971, Qatar and Bahrain were both admitted to the United Nations.[234]

H Neutralised or Demilitarised Territories

From the outset, it is important to distinguish between neutralisation and demilitarisation, terms that are often and wrongly lumped together, but which convey very different concepts.

---

234 ICJ, Maritime Delimitation and Territorial Questions (Qatar v. Bahrain), 2001, para. 65 (at 62).

Demilitarisation is a situation opposable to all states or to a defined state or group of states, whereby the state whose territory is demilitarised undertakes not to station its armed forces there, move its armed forces there and/or erect fortifications or other military installations there. Demilitarization thus represents a restriction, a burden on the exercise by the state concerned of its sovereign powers and, correspondingly, an advantage for the benefit, as the case may be, of all states or of a single state or defined group of states.

The effect of neutralisation, on the other hand, is to render the territory concerned "inviolable"; consequently, crossing it or stationing armed forces there during an armed conflict constitutes a violation of this regime. As was the case with Belgium and Luxembourg by the German Reich in 1914 during the First World War.[235] Neutralisation therefore represents an advantage for the State whose territory is neutralised *and* a burden for the other States, which are therefore obliged to respect it.

It is therefore not surprising that, in the ubiquitous Åland Islands case, the Committee of Jurists was careful to distinguish between demilitarisation, which had been established for the Åland Islands, and neutralisation, for which it cited the example of the Ionian Islands, which will be discussed below.[236]

i *Demilitarisation of Territories*

A distinction must be made between two situations and corresponding juridical regimes: demilitarisation for the benefit of all states (or an indeterminate group of states) and demilitarisation for the benefit of a single state or a defined and limited group of states. This differentiation must be read in conjunction with the notion of territorial regime and the succession of States in international treaties establishing them. It is precisely Article 12 VCSS 1978, discussed above, which governs these two scenarios in order to regulate the question of States succession. We shall therefore examine, with the help of concrete examples, first the case of demilitarisation *erga omnes* (envisaged by Article 12 (2) (a) VCSS 1978) and then that of demilitarisation restricted in terms of the number of beneficiaries (envisaged by Article 12 (1) (a) VCSS 1978).

1 *Erga omnes* Demilitarisation

For the sake of brevity and coherence, we would like to examine this type of demilitarisation, the benefits of which accrue to all states, in the light of the

235 See also *supra* note 63.

236 International Committee of Jurists, decision of 5 September 1920, 16.

example of Åland Islands archipelago, which we have already discussed above in terms of objective territorial regimes (*infra* Part 3. Chapter 8. Section C).

The 1856 Treaty of Paris ended one of the countless episodes of the Eastern Question, a constant and paradigm of Euro-Mediterranean international relations for centuries. One of the parameters of this Question is the Russian quest for the warm seas (the Baltic but above all the Mediterranean). The Russo-Ottoman conflict, which saw three (England, France and Sardinia) and half (Austria, which participated diplomatically) Christian powers[237] ally themselves with the Sublime Porte against Russia, arose precisely from St Petersburg's desire to increase its presence in the Black Sea and, above all, to obtain from Constantinople free passage for its warships in the Straits of the Bosporus and Dardanelles.

This attempt was not successful and Russia, defeated in the Crimean War (1853–1856), was not only locked out of the Black Sea (South) but also prevented from passing through the Baltic Sea (North) precisely by the provisions of the Treaty of Paris of 1856, which imposed the demilitarisation of the Åland Islands. This geographical parallelism is reflected in the legal regime finally ordered by this treaty,[238] which was intended to lay the foundations of the "public law of Europe".[239]

Article 1 of the Convention of 30 March 1856, concluded between France and Great Britain, on the one hand, and Russia, on the other, reads as follows:

> His Majesty the Emperor of all the Russias, in answer to the desire expressed to him by their Majesties the Queen of the United Kingdom of Great Britain and Ireland and the Emperor of the French, declares that the Åland Islands shall not be fortified and that no military or naval establishment shall be maintained or created there.[240]

---

237 Prussia maintained a benevolent neutrality towards Russia.

238 Preamble to the Convention (on the demilitarisation of the Åland Islands) of 30 March 1856: "The High Contracting Parties, desiring to extend to the Baltic Sea the agreement so happily restored between them in the East, and thereby to consolidate the blessings of peace, have resolved" (quoted in the Decision (at17).

239 Article 15 of the "General Treaty of Peace and Friendship", concluded on 30 March 1856 in Paris; the formula was taken up by the Committee of Jurists in its Decision of 5 September 1920, para. 2, at 17.

240 *CTS*, vol. 114, 407 [our translation]. This Convention was annexed to the General Treaty of Peace and Friendship between Austria, France, Great Britain, Prussia, Russia, Sardinia and the Ottoman Porte, signed in Paris on 30 March 1856. Article 33 of this Treaty, the ratifications of which were exchanged in Paris, expressly provides that 'The Convention this day concluded between their Majesties the Emperor of the French and the Queen of the United Kingdom of Great Britain and Ireland, on the one hand, and His Majesty the

The importance and the European, i.e., ultimately universal, character[241] of demilitarisation can be seen most clearly in this passage from the International Committee of Jurists' Decision of 5 September 1920:

> Further, it was by reason of the European interest involved in the question, that the Congress declared, in Article 33 of the Treaty of Peace, that the Convention relating to the demilitarisation of the Åland Islands "is and shall remain annexed to the present Treaty and shall have the same force and effect as if it formed part of the said Treaty". Owing to Article 33, and in spite of the opposition of Russia, Powers intervened which "had not taken part in the acts of war which had taken place in the Baltic". The intention was to make the Convention concerning the demilitarisation of the Åland Islands into "European law" just as other provisions did in the case of the Treaty of 1856. Lord Clarendon, on his return from the Peace Congress, made a definite statement on this point in the House of Lords.[242]

2 Demilitarisation Restricted *ratione personarum*

This subsection deals with demilitarisation that affects a given territory for the benefit of a particular state or a defined group of states. Unlike the situation discussed above, here the interest in territorial demilitarisation is not universal, but rather bilateral or, at most, plurilateral. This differentiation in the ownership of the right or the interest in respecting and maintaining demilitarisation can again be analysed in the light of the notion of territorial rights referred to in Article 12 (1) of the VCSS 1978. This provision, as we have already pointed out (Part 3. Chapter 8. Section B), nods to the notion of servitude which presupposes a relationship of dominance between two territories. In short, the restriction on the exercise by a state of one of its sovereign powers (militarisation) over part of its territory serves the interest of a particular state (or group of states) and is explained by this distinction between dominant territory (beneficiary state) and servient territory (state at whose expense the

Emperor of all the Russias, on the other, with reference to the Åland Islands is and shall remain attached to the present Treaty and shall have the same force and effect as if it formed part of the said Treaty' (quoted in: Decision of 5 September 1920, 15).

241 The International Committee of Jurists rightly speaks of a "permanent international interest" requiring the dismantling of fortifications and the obligation to erect no more (Decision of 5 September 1920, 17).

242 *Loc.cit.*

servitude is created). If such a separation were to disappear, then the very concept of servitude would lose its raison d'être and would follow the same fate.

Here, then, lies the differentiation between the demilitarisation through servitude referred to here and *erga omnes* (or universal) demilitarisation. The Committee of Jurists, in the aforementioned Åland Islands case, described this difference in the following terms

> In the event of Sweden herself becoming possessed of the Åland Islands, she would still be bound by the provisions of 1856, for exactly the same reasons which now permit her to rely on these provisions. Though Sweden was the Power most directly interested in the prohibition of the fortification of the Åland Islands at the time of the enactment of this prohibition, it is quite inadmissible to suppose that this prohibition would cease to be necessary by taking as an analogy the rule concerning the extinction of real servitude following upon the fusion of the "*prœdium dominans*" and the "*prœdium serviens*". In the eventuality under consideration, Finland would acquire an interest in the demilitarisation of the Islands quite as great as that which Sweden can now show. The main reason upon which the provisions of 1856 were based is the wish to prevent the Power possessing the very important strategic position of the Åland archipelago from acquiring too great an influence. This reason retains its full weight, no matter what territorial changes may take place.[243]

In order to illustrate restricted *ratione personarum* demilitarisation, we have chosen another example: the Sinai Peninsula. As the historical background of this issue shows (the three Arab-Israeli wars in addition to the Franco-British-Israeli military operations in the Suez Canal), the demilitarisation of this region under Egyptian sovereignty was introduced for the benefit of Israel, which had occupied it in 1967 following the Six-Day War. However, in accordance with the Peace Treaty of 26 March 1979 signed in Washington, the withdrawal of Israeli armed forces from the Sinai and the initial establishment of the zones were placed under the aerial surveillance of the United States, in accordance with Article VII of the Protocol concerning Israeli Withdrawal and Security Arrangements (Appendix to Annex I).[244] The territory was divided, following

243 *Ibid.*, 19.

244 "Both Parties request the United States to continue airborne surveillance flights in accordance with previous agreements until the completion of final Israeli withdrawal.

this phased withdrawal,[245] into three zones, again specified by Annex I (A, B, C).[246]

Through Article VI of Annex I to the Peace Treaty, the two parties entrusted the United Nations Forces (UNEF II, responsible for peacekeeping operations) with the task of monitoring compliance with these "arrangements".[247] The withdrawal of Israeli military forces (and civilians) thus marked the end of the Israeli military occupation of Sinai and Egypt could once again exercise[248] its sovereignty over this territory.[249] In the Peace Treaty, however, Egypt committed itself to certain obligations *vis-à-vis* Israel regarding the demilitarisation of the Sinai Peninsula. Herein lies the condition of reciprocity enshrined in this treaty: the end of the Israeli military occupation *contra* the demilitarisation of Sinai. Article II para. 1 of Annex I to the Peace Treaty clearly states the Israeli "concept of withdrawal" from the area:

> In order to provide maximum security for both Parties after the final withdrawal, the lines and the Zones delineated on Map I are established and organized as follows ... [follows detailed description of the Zones and their characteristics in terms of Egyptian military strength and capabilities].[250]

This annex establishes a variable geometry demilitarisation, describing a movement from West to East, with an Egyptian military presence decreasing in both numbers and military capabilities (equipment) as one approaches the border with Israel. Four Zones, three of which (A-C) are on Egyptian territory and one (D) on Israeli territory, are accordingly established; from the furthest from the Arab-Israeli border (A) to the closest (C)[251] Egypt can only maintain

245 The implementation of this annex was placed under the supervision of UN forces; to this end, both parties agreed to the redeployment of UNEF II (Article III of the Appendix to Annex I), "up to the time of completion of final Israeli withdrawal".

246 Articles 2 to 7 of Annex I detail the Zones and establish the Security Arrangements, the cornerstone of the 1979 Peace Treaty.

247 Distefano, Henry (2025).

248 'Egypt will resume the exercise of its full sovereignty over evacuated parts of the Sinai upon Israeli withdrawal as provided for in article I of this Treaty', Article VIII of the Appendix to Annex I of the 1979 Peace Treaty.

249 It should be recalled that Egyptian sovereignty over the Sinai Peninsula was never affected by the Israeli military occupation, but was merely suspended in its exercise as a result of the latter (see *supra* Part 2. Chapter 5. Section A.).

250 Emphasis added.

251 It should be noted that the Tiran and Safir Islands (see supra note 56), located at the entrance of the Gulf of Aqaba and under Egyptian sovereignty at the time of the conclusion of the 1979 Peace Treaty, were placed by the latter in Area C. However, on 8

smaller and smaller military forces until C where "[o]nly United Nations [in fact: FMO] forces and Egyptian civil police"[252] are present. In other words, the prohibition on the maintenance of Egyptian military forces near the border is accompanied by the presence of the multinational force. Conversely, in Zone D, i.e., in Israeli territory, 'there will be an Israeli limited force of four infantry battalions, their military installations, and field fortifications, and United Nations [in fact: FMO] observers'.[253]

The monitoring of compliance with these demilitarisation obligations had originally been entrusted to an international force created by the Security Council, but on 18 May 1981, its President declared that such a mission could not be decided upon owing to USSR's veto. Instead of this international force, the parties concerned (Egypt, Israel and the United States) concluded on 3 August 1981 a Protocol to the 1979 Peace Treaty for the establishment of a multinational peace force, the MFO (Multinational Observer Force in Sinai), which became operational on 25 April 1982 (www.mfo.org). This non-UN international security organisation is financed by these three states, while the contingents, scattered through 35 checkpoints and towers[254] and observation posts along a narrow strip on the eastern side of the Sinai territory, are provided on a voluntary basis by more than a dozen countries.

ii *Neutralisation of States or Parts of Their Territories*

Neutralisation – which is also governed by the law of armed conflict[255] – must be understood, as emphasised above, in its passive sense, i.e., as a territorial

April 2016, Egypt ceded them to Saudi Arabia by treaty ("Maritime Boundary Limitation Agreement"). The validity of this treaty, in the light of Article 46 of the 1969 VCLT, was finally established by the Constitutional Court (on 3 March 2018), which overturned a decision of the Supreme Administrative Court, of 16 January 2017, invalidating the treaty due to the violation of Article 151 of the Egyptian Constitution of 2014 ("Egypt court upholds Tiran, Sanafir transfer to Saudi Arabia", *Al Jazeera*, 3 March 2018, https://www.aljazeera.com/news/2018/3/3/egypt-court-upholds-tiran-sanafir-transfer-to-saudi-arabia). However, since the demilitarisation of these islands and the presence of an observation force were established for the benefit of Israel (as opposed to an objective territorial regime), and the new sovereign of these islands is not a party to the above-mentioned stipulations of the 1979 Peace Treaty, Saudi Arabia cannot be bound by them.

252 Article II (1) (c) of Annex I to the 1979 Peace Treaty.

253 Article II (1) (d) of Annex I to the 1979 Peace Treaty.

254 Mention should also be made in passing of the introduction of an innovative means of "confidence building", namely the system of a "liaison officer" between the Parties provided for in Article VII of the Annex, which complements the "early warning system" introduced in Zones A and D by Article V.

255 See for example: Article I of The Hague Convention (V) of 18 October 1907 concerning the rights and duties of Neutral Powers and Persons in case of War on Land; Article I

situation which all States may be required to respect. This territorial regime, opposable (most of the time) *erga omnes*, consists in the *immunisation of* the State – or of a part of its territory – from the effects of an armed conflict. In other words, the State or part of its territory is inviolable and protected against any hostile act by the belligerent parties. Thus, the neutralised state or the state whose territory is neutralised is the beneficiary of an advantage guaranteed by a correlative obligation on the part of any other state.

International practice identifies neutral states such as Switzerland, Belgium and Luxembourg before WWI.[256] The status of neutrality of the former, established by the Acts of the Congress of Vienna in 1815, is a real success insofar as it was respected during the two world conflicts of the 20th century;[257] Switzerland itself made its neutrality the pillar of its foreign policy to such an extent that it made it an express condition of its participation in the League of Nations, whose headquarters was hosted in Geneva.[258]

The fate of the other two states was less fortunate. Belgium, whose neutrality had been established at the time of its creation (Article 7 of the Treaty of London of 15 November 1831),[259] and Luxembourg (Article II of the Treaty of London of 11 May 1867) were both invaded by the German Reich during the First World War. While Belgium's neutrality was abrogated by the Treaty of Versailles of 1919 (Article 31),[260] Luxembourg's neutrality was first tacitly abrogated by the latter and finally recognised by the contracting parties to the

of The Hague (XII) Convention concerning the Rights and Duties of Neutral Powers in Naval War.

256 Mention may also be made of the neutralisation of: "Independent State of the Congo" – under the sovereignty of the King of the Belgians (Leopold II) – between 1885 and 1908, pursuant to Article 10 of the General Act of the Berlin Conference of 26 February 1885; Honduras, in accordance with Article III of the Treaty of Washington of 20 December 1907, concluded between all the Mesoamerican states.

257 For Belgium, see *Hackworth*, vol. VII, 354–355.

258 In 2002, when Switzerland finally became a member of the UN, this condition was not restated. The experience, albeit in some respects different, of Austria, which was also neutralised after the Second World War but soon became a member of the UN, made such a reference superfluous. In other words, neutrality, even permanent neutrality, and participation in the UN are not, rightly so, considered incompatible.

259 Provided for by the Protocol of 20 January 1831, it was subsequently guaranteed by the Great Powers and recognised by the Netherlands (former sovereign) by the Treaty of London of 19 April 1839. See Edoaurd E Descamps, *La neutralité de la Belgique*, Brussels, 1902.

260 Although this treaty only expressed Germany's consent to the abrogation of Belgium's neutrality clauses, other international agreements were added to complete the extinction of this regime: see Judge Negulesco's individual op. cit. appended to the judgment of the PCIJ in the Free Zones case, A/22, 31–32.

1867 Treaty.[261] The neutralisation of the Vatican State through Article 24 of the Lateran Agreement (11 February 1929) should also be mentioned.

There are, however, many more examples of partial neutralisation, i.e., of defined parts of the territory of states. Suffice it to mention here the neutralisation of the territories of Chablais and Faucigny (in France) decided at the Congress of Vienna in 1815 and finally abrogated by Article 435 of the Treaty of Versailles of 1919; the islands of Corfu and Paxos (from the Treaty of 14 November 1863 until 1920), which will be discussed below; and the aforementioned International Zone of Tangiers (by virtue of Article 3 of the Convention of 18 December 1923).[262] Other original solutions such as the creation of buffer zones or the neutralisation of the left bank of the Rhine, in French territory, must be mentioned in this respect (Articles 42–43 of the 1919 Treaty of Versailles).

Other examples of neutralisation concern or have concerned major international communication routes, such as canals (Suez,[263] Panama,[264] Kiel[265]), straits (Bosporus and the Dardanelles,[266] the Strait of Magellan[267]), and even lighthouses (Cape Spartel).[268]

With a view to illustrating this juridical situation, we would like to take a closer look at the case of the neutralisation of the Ionian Islands[269] as it presents aspects that have been discussed in other sections of this book.

---

261 It is interesting to note that Luxembourg was finally admitted to the League of Nations, after a first unsuccessful attempt, only after having removed the reservation on its neutralisation that accompanied its application for admission. See in this regard Albert Wehrer, 'Le statut international du Luxembourg et la Société des Nations', 31 *RGDIP* 1924, 169–202.

262 See also *infra* Part 3. Chapter 9. Section C.ii. Neutrality naturally followed the same fate as the international status of the Zone and was abrogated as a result of the extinction of the latter.

263 Articles I and IV of the Constantinople Convention of 29 October 1888.

264 See: Richard Perruchoud, *Le régime de neutralité du Canal de Panama*, Geneva-Paris, 1983.

265 Article 380 of the Treaty of Versailles; see also PCIJ, S.S. Wimbledon, A 1, 23–24.

266 Sections I and II of the Montreux Convention of 20 July 1936 (recently revived following its closure to Russian military vessels, in accordance with its Article 19 para. 1, by Turkey on the occasion of the conflict in Ukraine), 19 *Foreign Policy Chronicle*, 1966 (November), 706–713.

267 Article 5 of the Border Treaty (between Argentina and Chile) of 23 July 1881 (3 *AJIL* 1909 (supplement), 121–122) subsequently confirmed by Article 10 of the 1984 Treaty of Peace and Friendship (24 *ILM* 1985, 11–16).

268 Convention of 31 March 1865.

269 This group of seven islands, which had been part of the Serenissima Republic until the 1797 Treaty of Campoformio between Austria and France sealed the end of Venice's independence, had been alternately annexed by the French, occupied by Russian-Ottoman

These islands, "neutralised by the Treaties of 14 November 1863 and 29 March 1864",[270] had previously been placed under British protectorate by the Treaty of 5 November 1815 (between Great Britain, Austria, Prussia and Russia)[271] and became known as the "Republic of the Ionian Islands".

Their neutralisation precedes, and is unsurprisingly the condition for, their cession to Greece, which annexed them on 2 June 1864. Indeed, Article II of the Treaty of 14 November 1863, whose Parties are the same as that establishing the British protectorate in 1815,[272] provides that:

> The Ionian Islands, after their Union to Greece, shall enjoy the advantages of a perpetual Neutrality; consequently no armed force, either naval or military, shall at any time be assembled or stationed upon the territory or in the waters of those Islands, beyond the number that may be strictly necessary for the maintenance of public order, and to secure the collection of the public revenue.[273]

The Treaty of 29 March 1864, intended to implement the previous agreement,[274] merely states in Article II that 'the Islands of Corfu and Paxo ... shall, after their Union to Hellenic Kingdom of Greece, enjoy the advantages of perpetual neutrality'.[275]

It should be noted in passing that the reaffirmation by the interested parties of the *transmission of* this territorial regime of neutralisation to Greece probably means that the customary rule – now codified in Article 12 of the VCSS 1978 – had probably not yet emerged.[276] In this sense, the presence of Greece among the contracting parties is explained, as this State expressed its consent to the continued neutralisation of these islands, which it acquired by cession. In other words, the obligation to maintain the neutralization is made

forces, placed under a *de facto* Russian protectorate, retroceded to France, then placed under British protectorate in 1815, and eventually ceded to Greece in 1864.

270 Åland Islands case, 16.

271 Sir Edward Hertslet, *The Map of Europe by Treaty*, vol. II, London, 1875, No. 39: under Articles I and II, the Ionian Islands "shall form a single, Free and Independent State, under the denomination of the United States of the Ionian Islands" and placed "under the immediate Protection" of Great Britain, which was represented there by a "Lord High Commissioner" (Article III).

272 They are the Guarantor Powers of the Kingdom of Greece.

273 Sir Edward Hertslet, 1571 (no. 355). Article III provided for the demolition of the existing fortifications by Great Britain before and as a condition of the cession.

274 One cannot help but notice the disappearance of Prussia among the contracting parties.

275 Sir Edward Hertslet (1875), 1597 (no. 357).

276 See *supra* Part 3. Chapter 8. Section C.

by express acceptance, by the new sovereign (Greece), in the treaty of cession of these islands by Great Britain and not through the succession of states to treaties in the case of territorial regimes. If, on the other hand, the rule codified in Article 12 VCSS 1978 had existed at the time, Article II of the Treaty of 1863, providing for the neutralisation of the Islands and to which Greece was not a party, would have sufficed to bind Greece by succession.

CHAPTER 9

The Deterritorialisation of Space: Indirect and Direct International Administrations

We would like to introduce this vast theme, of which we will see only a few fragments, by quoting a statement by a British diplomat whose name has been consigned to posterity:

> Imperialism, annexation, military triumph, Whiteman's burden have been expunged from the popular political vocabulary … Consequently, Protectorates, spheres of influence, annexations, bases, etc. have to be consigned to the Diplomatic lumber-room.[1]

So exclaimed Sir Mark Sykes on the occasion of the entry of the United States into the war and the Bolshevik revolution (events that took place almost simultaneously, in 1917).

The leitmotif that underlies this last section unfolds from the institution of the international protectorate to progressively embody the internationalisation of spaces as the physical concretisation of the "community of interest". From the LoN mandates to the direct international administration by the UN, through a wide variety of territorial statutes that reflect both the demands of *Realpolitik* and the need to take into account heterogeneous realities.

This part of the course marks the transcendence of space as a territory wherein a State exercises its sovereignty. To different degrees, we will be dealing with territorial regimes where state sovereignty is, if not evanescent, at least suspended in its exercise; or in a less drastic way, with the restriction of a state in the use of its territory (demilitarisation, neutralisation); or with sovereignty residing jointly with an international organisation and a people (mandates, trust administration); or with a new entity coming into being, sometimes with strong links to a pre-existing state, all under direct international control (Danzig, and to varying degrees, the other free cities actually created or remained on paper); or, the true summit of the internationalisation of

1 Quoted in Toby Dodge, *Inventing Iraq: The Failure of Nation Building and a History Denied*, New York, 2003, 12–13.

 | DOI:10.1163/9789004708594_012

space, with direct international administration by the UN, or formerly by the LoN.[2] From this standpoint, territory becomes a means to peace after having been for centuries the bone of contention between states.

We will first review indirect international administrations, which are characterised by the presence of a State (or group of States) wielding governmental authority under the control – and on behalf – of an international organisation (Mandates and Trusteeship), to then address direct international administrations where an international organisation exercises these State powers without intermediary (International Cities and Territories).[3]

A The League of Nations Mandate System

i *Origins, Concepts and Purposes*

There is an immense bibliography[4] on the mandates of the League of Nations, perhaps second only to that on the League itself. In some respects, because of the breadth of rights and obligations established by Article 22 (of the LoN Covenant),[5] which can be considered a fully-fledged treaty establishing a

2 See: Ivan Ingravallo, "L'administration directe de territoires dans la pratique de la Société des Nations", in *Commentaire sur le Pacte de la Société des Nations* (ed. R Kolb), Brussels, 2015, 1207–1246.

3 See on direct international administration by the United Nations the resolution adopted by the IDI in 2021 ("Territorial administration by the United Nations and other international institutions authorised by the United Nations"), https://www.idi-iil.org/app/uploads/2021/09/2021_online_13_fr.pdf.

4 See Jacob Stoyanovsky, *La théorie des mandats internationaux*, Paris, 1925 [*passim*].

5 '1. To those colonies and territories which as a consequence of the late war have ceased to be under the sovereignty of the States which formerly governed them and which are inhabited by peoples not yet able to stand by themselves under the strenuous conditions of the modern world, there should be applied the principle that the well-being and development of such peoples form a sacred trust of civilisation and that securities for the performance of this trust should be embodied in this Covenant.

2. The best method of giving practical effect to this principle is that the tutelage of such peoples should be entrusted to advanced nations who by reason of their resources, their experience or their geographical position can best undertake this responsibility, and who are willing to accept it, and that this tutelage should be exercised by them as Mandatories on behalf of the League.

3. The character of the mandate must differ according to the stage of the development of the people, the geographical situation of the territory, its economic conditions and other similar circumstances.

4. Certain communities formerly belonging to the Turkish Empire have reached a stage of development where their existence as independent nations can be provisionally recognized subject to the rendering of administrative advice and assistance by a Mandatory until such

particularly complex regime and institutional mechanisms. This is evidenced by the fact that, at the 1919 Paris Peace Conference, it was envisaged that mandates would be included in the peace treaties themselves.

It is customary to trace the original idea of mandates back to President Wilson's speeches in which he set the conditions for the United States to enter the war alongside the Allies. Reference is made in particular to his speech of 8 January 1918, containing the famous Fourteen Points, as well as to his earlier speech of 27 May 1916 to the Senate: 'The fundamental idea would be that the *world* was acting as trustee through a Mandatory'.[6]

These points were innovative, even revolutionary, insofar as they enshrined the application of the principle of nationalities (Mazzini) – the precursor of the principle of the right of peoples to self-determination – to colonial territories,

---

time as they are able to stand alone. The wishes of these communities must be a principal consideration in the selection of the Mandatory.

5. Other peoples, especially those of Central Africa, are at such a stage that the Mandatory must be responsible for the administration of the territory under conditions which will guarantee freedom of conscience and religion, subject only to the maintenance of public order and morals, the prohibition of abuses such as the slave trade, the arms traffic and the liquor traffic, and the prevention of the establishment of fortifications or military and naval bases and of military training of the natives for other than police purposes and the defence of territory, and will also secure equal opportunities for the trade and commerce of other Members of the League.

6. There are territories, such as South-West Africa and certain of the South Pacific Islands, which, owing to the sparseness of their population, or their small size, or their remoteness from the centres of civilisation, or their geographical contiguity to the territory of the Mandatory, and other circumstances, can be best administered under the laws of the Mandatory as integral portions of its territory, subject to the safeguards above mentioned in the interests of the indigenous population.

7. In every case of mandate, the Mandatory shall render to the Council an annual report in reference to the territory committed to its charge.

8. The degree of authority, control, or administration to be exercised by the Mandatory shall, if not previously agreed upon by the Members of the League, be explicitly defined in each case by the Council.

9. A permanent Commission shall be constituted to receive and examine the annual reports of the Mandatories and to advise the Council on all matters relating to the observance of the mandates'.

6 Quoted in Judge Koretsky's dissenting opinion appended to the I.C.J. judgment in the South West Africa Statute Cases (Ethiopia v. South Africa; Liberia v. South Africa), judgment of 18 July 1966 (second phase): *ICJ Reports* 1966, 245. This formula was repeated by the President of the United States of America at the 1919 Paris Peace Conference: "The fundamental idea would be that the world was acting as trustee through a mandatory, and would be in charge of the whole administration until the day when the true wishes of the inhabitants could be ascertained", *1919 Foreign Relations of the United States*, Volume 3, Paris Peace Conference, Washington, 1946, 740–741.

which was not necessarily self-evident.[7] The idea that colonial administration (or even protectorate) was beneficial to the indigenous population – as stated in Articles 6 and 9 of the 1878 Berlin General Act was strongly anchored in the minds of the rulers and thus underpinned the mandate approach.

The task of defining the mandate of the LoN and understanding the concept 'defies easy analysis',[8] and although some would argue that the tackling of this issue is not necessarily of practical significance,[9] it is worth giving some thought to it.

At the outset, a distinction must be made between the *mandate system*,[10] established by Article 22, and the implementing agreements, i.e., the *mandates*, or *mandate agreements*: the institution of mandate and the mandates themselves.[11] The mandate as a legal figure obviously refers to civil law.[12] In the wake of Roman law, the term is used to refer to both the (mandate) contract and the institution itself, which is realised by the former.[13] But the analogy is mainly terminological, because the institution constitutes indeed a novelty[14]

7 "The mandate constitutes a transitional form in its very definition. Taking note of the exhaustion of the colonial phenomenon, those in charge of the peace conference had wanted to prolong as much as to signify the end of Europe's colonial expansion", Henry Laurens, *La Question de Palestine*, vol. II, Paris, 2002, 150 [our translation].

8 ICJ, Namibia 1971, 157 (separate opinion of Judge Dillard).

9 See Quincy Wright, "Sovereignty of the Mandates", 17 *AJIL* 1923, 692. That this notion was not immediately assimilated by diplomats unaccustomed to Western, even Roman-inspired, legal scholarship is revealed by the astonishment of a Chinese delegate to the Peace Conference, who, on learning that the German possessions in China were to be administered by a Mandatory, asked, with dismay: "*Who* is Mandatory?", quoted in Margaret MacMillan, *Paris 1919*, London, 2001, 99.

10 In this sense, one can agree with the statement that the mandate is "a social function of international order", Louis Comisetti, *Mandats et souveraineté. La notion de souveraineté au sein du système mandataire international. Critique de l'article 22 du Pacte de la Société des Nations*, Paris-Genève, 1934, 130 [our translation].

11 As an example, it is worth mentioning the case of Mesopotamia (or Iraq), where there was never a mandate agreement, even though the mandate institution had been established.

12 ICJ, South West Africa Cases, 1966, 267 (dissenting opinion of Judge Tanaka).

13 'Nearly every legal system possesses some institution whereby the property (and sometimes the persons) of those who are not *sui juris*, such as a minor or a lunatic, can be entrusted to some responsible person, as trustee, or *tuteur* or *curateur*', International Status of South-West Africa, Advisory Opinion of 11 July 1950: *ICJ Reports* 1950, 149 (separate opinion of Judge Lord Arnold McNair; italics in the text).

14 '[T]he question is an entirely new one and comes under the *new international law*', International Status of South-West Africa, 175 (dissenting opinion of Judge Alvarez; emphasis added); 'The institution of agency is quite original in that it creates a public function in the international plane which is exercised in the general universal interest', Comisetti, 153 [our translation].

in the panorama of international juridical relations. At the same time, certain similarities with other legal concepts of domestic law must be noted:[15] the trust or trusteeship[16] of Anglo-Saxon law and the trusteeship of continental law. The notion of guardianship[17] is not alien to that of the LoN mandate, because 'guardianship is not a contract, it is a *public function* entrusted to a capable person which consists in taking care of the person of an incapable person and administering his property as a good *pater familias*'.[18] In this respect, the term "guardians", often used,[19] seems appropriate. The fact that it is a real guardianship is also supported by the fact that the other States, on whose behalf the mandate is exercised, could have recourse to various bodies, both administrative (LoN Council and Permanent Mandates Commission) and judicial (Permanent Court of International Justice) for the purpose of supervising the management of the mandate. The mandate is therefore a guardianship exercised on behalf of the LoN.

The Mandate has both a conventional (by its origin) and a constitutional nature[20] (by its function);[21] the Mandate represents in many respects the constitution of the mandated country.[22] But, above all, the Mandate embodies

15 See Sir Hersch Lauterpacht, "The Mandate in the Covenant", in *International Law being the Collected Papers of Hersch Lauterpacht*, vol. 3, Cambridge, 1977, 59–60. *Contra*: Giulio Diena, "Les mandats internationaux", 5 *RCADI* 1924-IV, 237.

16 In both languages, this was the name finally adopted by the UN Charter to designate territories formerly under mandate; Società A.B.C. v. Fontana and Della Rocca, Italy, Corte di Cassazione (Sezioni riunite), 10 August 1954, 22 *ILR*, 78–79; The Administration of the Territory of Papua and New Guinea v. Blasius Tirupia and Others (*In re* Vunapaladig and Japalik Land), Papua and New Guinea, Supreme Court, 1 July 1971, 55 *ILR*, 60.

17 One of the I.C.J. judges spoke of guardianship in English and *tutelle* in French (South West Africa Cases, 1966, 217 (dissenting opinion of Judge Wellington Koo)).

18 Comisetti, 138 [our translation]. "[B]y the Mandate the British Government is charged as Agent for the League of Nations with the tutelage of the Palestine Administration, and no doubt it is to be held responsible for any breach by that country of that article", Speech of Sir Douglas Hogg (Great Britain), in the Mavrommatis case (Greece v. United Kingdom, *PCIJ Reports* C 7-II, 101).

19 See: Susan Pedersen, *The Guardians. The League of Nations and the crisis of Empire*, Oxford, 2015.

20 'The Mandate … is an international instrument of an institutional character', ICJ, South West Africa Cases, 1962, 332.

21 This is reminiscent, *mutatis mutandis*, of what the ICJ would later say about treaties establishing international organisations: Legality of the Use by a State of Nuclear Weapons in Armed Conflict, Advisory Opinion of 8 July 1996: *ICJ Reports* 1996, para. 19 (at 74–75).

22 The Mandatory's Courts were therefore required to review the acts of the Mandatory Power in the light of their compliance with the mandate.

a "work of civilisation"[23] and gives concrete expression to the principles of humanity and solidarity (represented by the control exercised by the LoN over the Mandate regime).[24] As the ICJ has repeatedly stated: 'As the Court recalled in its 1950 Advisory Opinion on the *International Status of South-West Africa,* in the setting-up of the mandates system "two principles were considered to be of paramount importance: the principle of non-annexation and the principle that the well-being and development of such peoples form 'a sacred trust of civilization' " (*I.C.J. Reports 1950,* p. 131)'.[25]

The purposes of the mandates, which transcend their tripartite typology – to be discussed later – are clearly stated in Art. 22 (1); the "trusteeship" that is created for the benefit of the people, aims at their "well-being and development" and constitutes a "sacred trust of civilisation".[26] To this end, the Covenant *embodies* "securities for the performance of this trust".

ii *Typology of Mandates and Supervisory System*

Article 22(3) establishes the taxonomy of mandates "according to the stage of the development of the people, the geographical situation of the territory, its economic conditions and other similar circumstances".[27] The terminology used to designate the three classes of mandates clearly betrays the decreasing degree of "development": "communities" (which translates into social and political organisation); "peoples" (absence of such organisation); "territories" (the human aspect, present in the first two classes, is absent here, only the "portion of the globe"[28] being juridically relevant).

The Type A Mandate will be applied to certain "communities"[29] of the Ottoman Empire, endowed with an existence of their own and with the

---

23 Italian PM, Mr. Vittorio-Emanuele Orlando (intervention of 28 January 1919 at the Peace Conference in Paris), in *Prassi italiana*, 3rd series, vol. IV, Rome, 1995, 2317 [our translation].

24 "[I]f the words "a sacred trust of civilization" are to be ignored then the mandatory system is a fraud from the beginning to the end, merely a new word of imposing imperialistic will upon subject people", Duncan C Lee, *The Mandate for Mesopotamia and the principle of trusteeship in English Law*, London, 1921, 17.

25 ICJ, Namibia 1971, para. 45 (at 28).

26 'Whatever its practical deformations may be, the mandates institution represents the most daring attempt to date for the international protection of less advanced peoples', Anzilotti, 1955, 119 [our translation].

27 General Smuts' Project foresaw a bipartite typology: on the one hand the metropolitan territories of the four defeated empires, and on the other the German colonial possessions in Africa and the Pacific.

28 Island of Palmas, 838.

29 'By tradition, which plays so important a part in Eastern countries, the "community" is a group of persons living in a given country or locality, having a race, religion, language and traditions of their own and united by this identity of race, religion, language and

capacity to acquire independence;[30] this paragraph refers to Articles 94 and 95 of the Treaty of Sevres.[31] Syria and Lebanon, under the French mandate as well as Palestine, Transjordan and Mesopotamia (Iraq), under the British mandate, were eventually included in this category. However, these mandates, especially those under British administration, were organised differently from one another and had different fates.

The Type B Mandate concerned certain "peoples" of Central Africa, in other words all the German colonies in that continent, except for South West Africa which was ascribed to Type C. Under the terms of these mandate agreements, the Mandatory Power took over the administration of the territory on condition that it complied with certain obligations[32] and that it respected certain guarantees of a general nature (obligation to prohibit the slave trade and the trade in alcohol – applicable only to the natives, however – and arms, and to ensure freedom of conscience and religion). This regime was applied to the former German colonies of Togo (divided into two mandates, French and British) and Cameroon (divided into two mandates, French and British), Tanganyika (under British mandate), Ruanda-Urundi (under Belgian mandate). Type B mandates, while not as detailed as Type A, are much more articulate than Type C; they contain clauses that are also found in Type C, but add substantial obligations.

The Mandate of type C, concerned certain "territories" in South West Africa and certain islands in the Pacific which, by reason of the smallness of their population, their extent, their distance from the centres of "civilization" as well as their contiguity to the territories of the Mandatory Power, could not be better administered than by the latter directly *as if they were an integral*

---

traditions in a sentiment of solidarity, with a view to preserving their traditions, maintaining their form of worship, ensuring the instruction and upbringing of their children in accordance with the spirit and traditions of their race and rendering mutual assistance to each other', The Greco-Bulgarian "Communities", Advisory Opinion of 31 July 1930, *PCIJ Reports*, B 17, 21.

30 Armenia, having been recognised in the Treaty of Sèvres "as a free and independent state" (Article 88), was not established as a mandate of the LoN. USSR did not bother too much with this provision and Armenia ended up being annexed in 1922 and remained so until 1991.

31 The Treaty of Lausanne of 24 July 1923, which was concluded after the LoN mandates, does not contain any clause corresponding to the above-mentioned provisions of the Treaty of Sèvres, except for Article 16, which provides for a generic renunciation by Turkey of the territories situated outside the borders fixed by the Treaty, their fate having been sealed by other international acts.

32 Rex v Christian, South Africa (Union of), Supreme Court, Appellate Division, 30 November 1923, 2 *ILR*, 30.

part of it: 'The words in Art. 2 of the Mandate, "as an integral portion of the Commonwealth" are found, with the necessary substitution of the mandatory, in the other mandates of the same class [C], namely those for Samoa to New Zealand, for German South-West Africa to the Union of South Africa, and for Nauru to the British Government. The words in the Australian Mandate appear to mean, not that the mandated territory is deemed to be physically part of the continent of Australia, but as territory belonging to the King in right of the Commonwealth of Australia'.[33]

This type of mandate was applied to the former German colony of South West Africa (entrusted to the Union of South Africa) as well as to the former German Pacific island possessions: Samoa Islands (mandate exercised by the Dominion of New Zealand, but conferred on the British Empire), Nauru (conferred on the British Empire), New Guinea and other German Pacific possessions south of the Equator (conferred on the British Empire, but exercised by Australia), the Carolinas, Marianas and Marshall Islands (conferred on Japan). The Type C mandate agreements were all almost identical and were characterised by their relative simplicity and brevity.

All the "communities", all the peoples and territories subject to the LoN Mandates system will – at different times – eventually gain independence, the latest being Palestine.[34]

The LoN Covenant established a system of control over the activity of the Mandatory Power. While it is true that the Society was duly left out of the designation of the territory/mandate pairing, the definition of the territorial limits of the mandate and the choice of the type of mandate,[35] it is also true that it was given a role of the first order in *controlling* the acts of the Mandatory in the accomplishment of its institutional task.[36] It can be said that the "right of control belonging to [the principal Allied and Associated Powers] as principals, has passed automatically to the League of Nations".[37] The control established by Art. 22 (7) strengthens the nexus between the Mandate and the League

33 Mainka v. Custodian of Expropriated Property, Australia, High Court, 10 June 1924, 7 *ILR*, 52.

34 See *supra* Part 2. Chapter 6. Section C (State of Palestine).

35 These tasks were carried out with zeal by the major victorious powers outside the League's system.

36 'The administrative supervision by the League constituted a normal security to ensure the full performance by the Mandatory of the "sacred trust" toward the inhabitants of the mandated territory', ICJ, South West Africa Cases, 1962, 336. *Contra*: ICJ, South West Africa Cases, 1962, 454, 457–458 (dissenting opinion of Judge Winiarski).

37 Report by Mr Van Rees on the system of property ownership in the Mandate Territories B and C (PMC, P.V., 3rd session (1923), 222 (annexed to the Procès-verbaux)).

and increases the institutional character of the former. Control, as a "supervisory element", "is an integral part of the Mandate"[38] and is in many ways "the truly original feature of the new institution".[39] Already at the 1919 Paris Peace Conference, the need for "trusteeship" control by the LoN was emphasised. In its 1971 Advisory Opinion, the ICJ stated: 'the reply to the essential question, *quis custodiet ipsos custodes?*, was given in terms of the mandatory's accountability to international organs'.[40] Several organs contributed to the implementation of the LoN supervisory action of the hence guaranteeing the rights of the "peoples" under mandates: the Permanent Mandates Commission, the Council, the Assembly and, finally, the Permanent Court of International Justice.

Among these, a few words should be said about the PMC. This advisory body of the Society is mentioned in the last paragraph of Article 22 which states that the Commission 'shall be constituted to receive and examine the annual reports of the Mandatories and to advise the Council on all matters relating to the observance of the mandates'.[41] There is thus a clear division of roles in the Society's control of the management of the territory by the Mandatory Power: 'The Permanent Mandates Commission alone had this advisory role, just as the Council alone had the supervisory function'.[42] The PMC very quickly became the linchpin in the system of supervision of the Mandate Management and supported the Council in its executive activity; in this respect, it must be emphasized that almost all the memoranda, reports and opinions prepared by it were adopted by the Council, which "very generally gave it warm approval and effective support".[43] The PMC met in ordinary session at least once a year and, during this session, it examined the annual reports drawn up by the Mandatory Powers with a view to preparing a report for the Council. Finally, it is important to stress that this institutional monitoring body certainly constituted a landmark innovation in international juridical relations and will end up inspiring other UN organs and international organisations (universal and regional) set up in order to guarantee the respect of the international obligations of their member states.

38 ICJ, Namibia 1971, para. 78 (at 41).

39 Jean Ray, *Commentaire du Pacte de la Société des Nations*, Paris, 1930, 606 [our translation].

40 ICJ, Namibia 1971, para. 48 (at 29–30).

41 It is impossible, in a literary register, not to refer the reader to the first – exhilarating – 100 pages (or so) of Albert Cohen's magnificent novel (*Belle du Seigneur*, Paris, 1968), which depicts in an exhilarating way the daily life of an LoN civil servant attached to the "Mandates Section".

42 ICJ, South West Africa Cases, 1966, para. 22 (at 25).

43 Henri Rolin, "La pratique des mandats internationaux", 19 *RCADI* 1927-IV, 544 [our translation].

iii *Travaux Préparatoires*

On the nature of the Mandate in the light of the holding of sovereignty and its exercise, a distinction must be made between Type A Mandates on the one hand, and Type B and C Mandates on the other. The starting point for reflection is nevertheless common, namely Art. 22(1), according to which the colonies and territories (subsequently placed under mandate) 'have ceased to be under the sovereignty' of the defeated States. The simple literal interpretation (Art. 31 (1) VCLT 1969) leads to the conclusion that the latter no longer enjoy the territorial sovereignty. The question is therefore who the new holders are.

1 Type A Mandates

The peace treaties convey the consent of the defeated States to cede the territories, while by the mandates the occupying Powers accept a conspicuous body of obligations towards the LoN, already contained elsewhere in the Pact. The cession by Germany of all its rights, interests and titles, embodied in Articles 118 and 119 of the Treaty of Versailles, does not constitute a cession *sic et simpliciter*, but a cession by which the cessionary States received the territories under the condition that they would not extend their sovereignty over them, but that they would establish mandates (Art. 118(2)). Should it be noted, therefore, that mandates could be conceived as a voluntary restriction by the occupying Powers not to annex the territories of the defeated States.

The literal interpretation of the relevant texts supports this reading. In the various peace treaties, one finds the expression "Government(s) exercising authority" (120, 122, 127 Versailles; 34 of the 1923 Treaty of Lausanne). The wording chosen by the Parties is rather different from the juridical and diplomatic language of the time used to refer to colonial possessions.[44]

Article 46 of the 1923 Treaty of Lausanne, on the sharing of the (heavy) Ottoman debt, introduces the principle of succession *among* Turkey and 'the States in favour of which territory has been detached from the Ottoman Empire after the Balkan wars of 1912–13 [...] *and the States newly created in territories in Asia which are detached from the Ottoman Empire under the present Treaty* [see Article 16]'.[45] By virtue of this last fragment, the Treaty of Lausanne clearly refers to Syria and Palestine – including Jordan – which, precisely as sovereign states, were imposed a *pro rata* share of the Ottoman debt.

---

44 Notwithstanding certain authors who, based on ideological preconceptions, quickly liquidate the issue by assimilating the B and C mandates to a "regime of pure and simple colonisation", Charles Ayoub, *Les Mandats orientaux*, Paris, 1924, 137–138.

45 Emphasis added.

Article 257 of the Treaty of Versailles is more eloquent in this respect than the Treaty of Lausanne: it refers to the transfer of the territories subject to the mandate "to the Mandatory Power *in its capacity as such*".[46] In its capacity as a Mandatory Power, therefore, and not as a territorial sovereign. Article 312 of the same treaty makes a clear distinction between cession and administration. Again, in the juridical-diplomatic language of the past as well as of nowadays, the former indicates the transfer of sovereignty, the latter the exercise of governmental authority without the administering state being endowed with the *ius disponendi*[47] or the *interversio possessionis*: the ultimate and true feature of sovereignty.[48] Sovereignty was thus recognised to "communities" under Mandate A or, at least, it was unanimously accepted[49] that the Mandatories had not extended theirs, although there were some authors who, especially at the beginning, envisaged a 'shared sovereignty' between the Mandatory and the 'independent community'.[50]

The preparatory works for the Mandate agreements tend to confirm this construction quite clearly. Article 1 of the British Mandate in Palestine originally read: 'His Britannic Majesty shall have the right to exercise as Mandatory all the powers inherent in the Government of a Sovereign State, save as they may be limited by the terms of the present Mandate'.[51] The Italian delegation in London did not fail to point out that this formulation was too "broad and generic" and that it was therefore in contradiction with Article 22 of the LoN Covenant. Moreover, it should be noted that, unlike Syria and Mesopotamia (which Art. 94 of the Treaty of Sevres recognised as "independent States"), in Art. 95, relating to Palestine, such a qualification is absent. This, the Italian delegation argued, could support the (erroneous) interpretation that the legal status of Palestine was different from the first two; such a reading would in any case have been in contrast with paragraph 4 of Article 22, according to which all 'communities formerly belonging to the Turkish Empire' enjoyed an identical status and were placed on an equal footing.[52] The Japanese delegate,

46 Emphasis added.

47 'The Mandatory Power … had no right of disposition, no *jus disponendi*: it was merely a Mandatory on behalf of the League', ICJ, International Status of South-West Africa, 168 (separate opinion of Judge Read).

48 See *supra* Part 3. Chapter 8. Section A.

49 'The situation in the mandated territories is a sobering one', Reply by Mr. Rundstein (Poland) to the Advisory Opinion on *The Free City of Danzig and the International Labour Organization*, vol. C 18-II, 114.

50 Henri Rolin, "Le système des mandats coloniaux", 1 *RDILC* 1920, 348.

51 *Prassi italiana*, Vol. V, 2687.

52 See: *Prassi italiana*, vol. V, 2687–2691.

Mr Adachi, also criticised the British amendments to the draft mandates for not taking into account the ultimate purpose of the institution of mandates, namely political independence and freedom. It was for the accomplishment of this task, he said, that 'Mandatory Powers should assume a temporary responsibility regarding'[53] the administration of the territories concerned.

Eventually, Article 1 of the British Mandate over Palestine would no longer contain a reference to sovereignty, but would merely state "full powers of legislation and administration". Similarly, the wording on the exequatur of foreign consuls was contested, as Palestine was sovereign even if the Mandatory Power exercised its sovereign functions.[54] In response to these critical comments, the draft British Mandate was amended and the phrase 'all the powers inherent in the Government of a Sovereign State' was replaced by 'all the powers of legislation and administration'.

In para. 3 of Article 22, there is a reference to the "wishes" that the mandated country may express to the Mandatory Power. This could lead us to believe that this is not really a protectorate, since the "protection" was implemented without the consent of the country in question, the mandate having been concluded between the LoN and the Mandatory Power. According to Balladore Pallieri, instead, only Type A mandates could be compared to protectorates.[55]

According to Brierly, this would be a "responsible protectorate" insofar as the Mandatory Power had to fulfil certain international obligations (also of an institutional nature) towards both the LoN and the populations under trusteeship.[56] Such thesis was supported by the French Government before the CPJ in the case of the Nationality Decrees Issued in Tunis and Morocco.[57]

It is therefore necessary to distinguish between protectorates[58] and LoN mandates from the point of view of sovereignty.[59] The former is characterised

53 *Official Journal*, June 1923, 20 April 1923 (6th Meeting of the Council (24th session)), 571.

54 The same applies to Syria and Lebanon (*Prassi italiana*, vol. V, 2703–2705).

55 Balladore Pallieri (1962), para. 51 (at 156).

56 Brierly (1963), 182. This jurist makes no distinction in this respect between the different types of mandate.

57 Conclusions of the French Government, cited in *Reports of the PCIJ*, B 4, 13.

58 See *supra* Part 3. Chapter 8. Section G. See generally: Thomas Baty, "Protectorates and Mandates", 2 *BYIL* 1921–1922, 109–121. International case law is in line: Pablo Najera (France) v. Mexico, para. 2 (at 468): "countries under mandate do not constitute protectorates" [our translation].

59 Although domestic jurisprudence that is not very attentive to the specificities of public international law has sometimes hastily come to this conclusion (Cape Law Society v. Van Aardt, Supreme Court of South Africa (Cape of Good Hope Provincial Division), 1926, 2 ILR, 43). See also *supra* Part 3. Chapter 8. Section G.

by a divorce between the exercise of sovereignty by the protecting State and sovereignty itself, whose *ius nudum is in the* hands of the protected state.

LoN mandates present a completely new complexity in this respect. Indeed, at least as far as Type A mandates are concerned, they are very similar to protectorates, with the notable difference that a third party, the League of Nations, plays the role of "guardian", albeit with the limitations we have already noted (revocation and modification of the mandate impossible): 'Palestine had … ceased to be an autonomous province; *it was virtually raised provisionally to the rank of an independent state*, placed under the trusteeship of Great Britain as Mandatory of the League of Nations',[60] thence sometimes referred to as "dormant sovereignty".[61] It is has been rightly asserted that 'Great Britain is not the sovereign of Palestine but simply the Mandatory of the League of Nations'.[62] Therefore, the organs of the "independent community" are not confused with those of the Mandatory administration[63] and the decisions rendered by the Mandatory are considered "foreign judgments" in its internal order.[64]

In a similar vein, and by analogy with the institution of the protectorate, any territorial modification by the Mandatory Power of the territory of the 'community' must be approved both by the representatives of the latter and by the Council of the LoN.[65] The 1939 French transfer of the Sanjak of Alexandretta[66] to Turkey, after a most tortuous and questionable process, is unfortunately the exception that proves the rule.

2 Types B and C Mandates

A different discourse must be held for type B and C mandates, as their arrangement is even more sophisticated. The literal and teleological interpretation of Art. 22 as a whole precludes such an independent status for these other types of mandates. On the other hand, mandates could hardly be equated with

60 Speech of Mr Politis before the P.C.I.J. in the Mavrommatis case, vol. C 5-I, 45.

61 Reply of Sir Cecil Hurst (Great Britain), in the Mavrommatis case, vol. C 5-I, 74.

62 ICJ, Mavrommatis Palestine Concessions Case, Series A 2, 81 (Dissenting opinion of Judge Bustamante).

63 Lebanon Expropriation Case, Court of Cassation of Lebanon, 6 July 1926, 2 *ILR*, 45.

64 District Governor, Jerusalem-Jaffa District and Another v. Suleiman Murra and Another, Supreme Court of Palestine, 25 June 1925, 2 *ILR*, 46.

65 Similarly for Type C Mandates, see *infra* Part 3. Chapter 9. Section A.iii.2.

66 On the history of the attachment of the Sanjak of Alexandretta to Turkey, see: Stéphane Yérasimov, "Le sandjak d'Alexandrette: formation et intégration d'un territoire", 48 *Revue de l'Occident musulman et de la Méditerranée* 1998, 198–212.

colonies: the literal, teleological and jurisdictional interpretation[67] as well as the recourse to the travaux préparatoires converge on this point. According to the teleological interpretation, it seems clear, today as in the past, that the purpose of this innovative institution in international relations was certainly not to transfer the territories concerned from one sovereignty to another, even if it was that of the victorious powers. The literal interpretation would support this reading where it is written, in Article 22 of the Covenant, that the territories will be administered 'as an integral part of its territory'. This fragment should, or at least could, mean 'as if it were, contrary to the fact, an integral portion of the Commonwealth'[68] of the Mandatory Power, for the purposes of the Mandate.[69]

However, the denial of the Mandatory's sovereignty does not automatically answer the question of where it resides. In the light of a teleological reading – in conjunction with recourse to the PMC practice – it is possible to maintain that sovereignty resides with the peoples of the territories concerned by the mandate;[70] only its exercise is entrusted to the Mandatory Power. Territorial regimes are characterised by this divorce between *ius nudum* and *exercitium iuris*.[71] The novelty, and the fundamental difference compared to the simple protectorate and other cases of divorce between the holding of the right of territorial sovereignty and its exercise, is represented by the control exercised by the LoN: in the case of protectorate, bilateral relationship, under the Mandates régime, triangular relationship. Colonial sovereignty is therefore juridically unfit to explain the title of the regalian powers of the Mandatory over the territories over which it exercises "trusteeship". Such a construction of the legal

67 'Palestine ... was not at the time [of the Mandate] a British Colony ... but a Mandated territory', Stampfer v. Attorney-General, Israel, Supreme Court sitting as the Court of Criminal Appeals, 4 January 1956, 23 *ILR*, 289.

68 Jolley v. Mainka, Australia, High Court, 27 April 1933, 7 *ILR*, 48 (*Per* Evatt). Similarly: Rex v. Offen, South-West Africa, High Court, Central Circuit Court, 23/24 August 1934, 7 *ILR*, 53. Similarly: The Administration of the Territory of Papua and New Guinea v. Blasius Tirupia and Others (*In re* Vunapaladig and Japalik Land), Papua and New Guinea, Supreme Court, 1 July 1971, 55 *ILR*, 59. A different reading was advocated, and we believe wrongly, by the New York District Court: "[T]he words 'as an integral part of the United States' which appeared in an earlier draft [of the Trusteeship Agreement] were deleted *to negate any impression that the United States was claiming sovereignty*", Morgan Guaranty v. Republic of Palau, Decision of 10 July 1986, 87 *ILR*, 606 [emphasis added].

69 See Falema'iLesa v. Attorney-General of New Zealand, New Zealand, Judicial Committee of the Privy Council, 28 July 1982, 79 *ILR*, 691.

70 See Edgar Pelichet, *La personnalité internationale distincte des collectivités sous mandat*, Paris, 1932, 108.

71 See *supra* Part 3. Chapter 8. Section A.i.

relationship between the Mandatory Power, population and territory is not conceivable. Since the Mandatory Power exercises regalian functions whose title lies in the Mandate, it does not hold the title of sovereignty over the mandated territory (see above the principle of non-annexation).[72]

iv *The Juridical Context*

1 Doctrine

In this respect, the panorama of the juridical literature[73] is certainly more kaleidoscopic. According to some jurists, 'in any case, countries under mandate are not states',[74] while others erroneously speak of 'delegation of sovereignty'.[75] Still others do not hesitate to assert that sovereignty belongs to the Mandatory Power, for type A mandates as protectorates[76] and for type B and C mandates as colonies.[77] The restrictions on Mandatory sovereignty, namely

---

72 According to Kelsen (1950, 688), the assertion that the Mandatories did not enjoy sovereignty over the territories of which they had "trusteeship" is 'a legal fiction incompatible with the rules of international law'. However, the illustrious Austrian jurist added that the interpretation (based on Article 22(8)) that the LoN "was the sovereign in relation to the mandated territories" could be admissible (689) [our translation].

73 Stoyanowsky, 75 [*passim*]. The author also reviews the different, what he calls "eclectic", theories put forward to address the issue of Mandatory Power sovereignty: a) partial Mandatory Power sovereignty theory; b) shared sovereignty theory; c) suspended sovereignty theory; d) virtual sovereignty [78–86]. An examination of these theoretical explanations is beyond the scope of this study. The (vague) theory of virtual sovereignty was also put forward by Albert Millot (*Les mandats internationaux. Étude sur l'application de l'article 22 du Pacte de la Société des Nations*, Paris, 1924, 117–118); Paul Pic, "Le régime des mandats d'après le traité de Versailles", 30 *RGDIP* 1923-IV, 334. For a critique of the latter view: Comisetti, 106–110.

74 Speech by Mr. Kaufmann (Danzig) at the Advisory Opinion *The Free City of Danzig and the International Labour Organisation*, vol. C 18-II, 94.

75 See for all: PT Furukaki, *Les Mandats internationaux de la Société des Nations*, Lyon, 1923, 180 [our translation].

76 '[T]erritorial sovereignty or the right of government evidently belonged to the Mandating Power, given that the organisation of power that existed in those territories was but an emanation of it and that both the League of Nations through its organs and the Powers individually had recognised as such. All that can be said is that it was a (at least formally) controlled territorial sovereignty, i.e., also qualified by the particular obligations imposed on the Mandatory Powers, obligations that were basically summed up in exercising such power in the interests of the populations subject to the mandate and under the control of a special international body. The formula contained in Article 22 therefore seems excessive whereby the Mandate would be exercised "in the name and on behalf of the League of Nations"', Quadri (1968), 723 [our translation].

77 Rolin (1920), 348–351; Diena (1924), 240–242. *Contra*: *In re* Tamasese, A prisoner, New Zealand, Supreme Court, 21 February 1929, 7 *ILR*, 45; Jolley v. Mainka, Australia, High Court, 27 April and 31 August 1933 (Appeal from the Central Court of the Territory of

the obligations arising from both Article 22 and the Mandate itself (in addition to control by the LoN), were to be configured as servitudes.[78] Lord Balfour did not hesitate to declare that 'a Mandate was a self-imposed limitation by the conquerors on the sovereignty which they exercised over the conquered territory'.[79]

According to Redslob[80] and Lauterpacht,[81] sovereignty belongs to the LoN which exercises it through one of its organs, the Mandatory Power. This construction, however, clashes with the juridical logic and the factual reality that governed the appointment of the mandataries: it was neither the Council nor the Assembly that proceeded to the attribution of Mandates, but the Supreme Council. The renunciation of sovereignty by the defeated powers was made to the benefit of the principal Allied and Associated Powers and not in favour of the LoN[82] which, moreover, did not yet exist. According to Brierly, 'the only possible theory is that the rights of the trustee have their foundations in his obligations; they are tools given to him in order to achieve the works assigned to him. The trustee gets all the tools necessary for such end, but only those'.[83] According to Corbett, the territory under the Mandate must be considered as "never to be incorporated" into the Mandatory's territory.[84] Some speak, for mandates B and C, of 'Mandatory's sovereignty [which] is exercised in its fullness'.[85] Nothing could be further from the truth, given that, in the best-case scenario, the Mandatory Power *exercises* the sovereignty that *resides* with the

New Guinea), 7 *ILR*, 47 (*Per* Starke and Dixon); 'The State exercises full and exclusive sovereignty over the atmospheric space above its territory, including its territorial waters. For the purposes of such sovereignty, the territory of the State shall mean the national, metropolitan and colonial territory, and that of the protectorates and *countries entrusted by mandate* or for any other reason to the Italian State, when special international conventions do not provide otherwise', DL (decree-law) of 20 August 1923 n° 2207 (in: *Prassi italiana*, 3rd series, vol. V, 2378; our translation; emphasis added).

78 See: Rolin (1920), 350.

79 *Official Journal*, June 1922, 17 May 1922 (11th Meeting of the Council), 547.

80 Redslob (1927), 196.

81 Sir Hersch Lauterpacht, "Particular Types of Statehood", in *International Law being the Collected Papers of Hersch Lauterpacht*, vol. 3, Cambridge, 1977, 68–69.

82 See: Olivier Hojer, *Le pacte de la Société des Nations. Commentaire théorique et pratique*, Paris, 1926, 374. This interpretation has been criticised by Millot, 1924, 117.

83 James Brierly, "Trusts and Mandates", 10 *BYIL* 1929, 218, 219.

84 PE Corbett, "What is the League of Nations?" 10 *BYIL* 1929, 135.

85 Ayoub (1924), 121 [our translation]. See also: Baty (1921–1922), 117 ff.; Paul Fauchille, *Traité de droit international public*, vol. 1, Paris, 1925, 298 [only for types B and C Mandates]; Rolin (1920), 338–353.

people of the territory. The hypothesis of a 'suspended sovereignty'[86] was also raised, without really convincing.

Some authors argue that the Mandatories merely enjoys the right to exercise governmental authority without, however, being vested with the right of sovereignty: in one case they exercise sovereignty directly (Mandates of type B and C), in the other "indirectly through Native institutions".[87] This construction is hardly inaccurate, but it fails to answer the question of who is the holder of *ius nudum*; this is not tenable because how can one imagine a subject of international law exercising sovereignty without having received the power to do so from its holder, whoever that may be: 'Sovereignty is not vested in anyone, as in the case of a Native Protectorate'.[88] The exercise of a right can only be done by the holder or by someone juridically empowered by the holder.

Other explanatory hypotheses have been advocated, based, to different degrees and modalities, on 'mixed' or 'divided' sovereignty between: a) the LoN and the Mandatory; b) the LoN and the people; c) the Mandatory and the people.[89] Lord McNair in his Separate Opinion appended to the ICJ Opinion in the International Status of South-West Africa case annotated:

> Sovereignty over a Mandated territory is in abeyance; if and when the inhabitants of the Territory obtain recognition as an independent State, as has already happened in the case of some of the Mandates, sovereignty will revive and vest in the new State.[90]

According to Kelsen, 'an interpretation was possible according to which the League of Nations was the sovereign in relation to the mandated territories'.[91] The interpretation which the illustrious Austrian jurist refers to is articulated around paragraphs 2 and 8 of Article 22 of the LoN Covenant. Such a

86 Stoyanowsky (1925), 90–93.

87 James C Hales, "Some Legal Aspects of the Mandate System: Sovereignty – Nationality – Termination and Transfer", 23 *Transactions of the Grotius Society* 1937, 93.

88 *Ibid.*, 94.

89 For a complete overview, see: Comisetti (1934), 110–112.

90 ICJ, International Status of South-West Africa, 150.

91 Kelsen (1950), 689; also: Georges D Cioriceanu, *Les mandats internationaux. One of the consequences of the fundamental principles of the League of Nations. Le nouveau régime politico-administratif des anciennes colonies allemandes et des territoires ayant appartenant à la Turquie,* Paris, 1921, 35–37 and 85–89; Fauchille (1925), Vol. 1, Part II, 848 ff; Distefano (2006), 188–190.

construction does not seem implausible in our view, but only for type B and C mandates.[92]

Finally, the Institute of International Law, at its 1931 session (Cambridge), adopted Resolution VI, which reads: "Mandated communities [of whatever type, therefore] are subjects of International Law. They have a patrimony distinct from that of the Mandatory State, they enjoy a national status and may acquire rights or be bound by obligations of their own".[93]

2 Practice of the LoN Organs

The League of Nations examined the question for the first time and, in the words of the rapporteur, Mr Hymans (report of 5 August 1920, approved by the Council), avoided the pitfall: 'I shall not enter into a controversy – though this would certainly be very interesting – as to where the sovereignty actually resides. We are face to face with a new institution. Legal erudition will decide as to what extent it can apply to this institution the older juridical notions'.[94] In any case, from the very beginning the PMC went out of its way to condemn any pure and simple claim to sovereignty over the mandated territories; Marquis Theodoli, its President, stated on 23 April 1923 that

> Anything which tended to create confusion between the institution of mandates and a disputed annexation was likely to bring discredit on the general work of the League, and if the principle proposed in the South African amendment were adopted, it would be equivalent to countenancing an act of annexation.[95]

92 For the purposes of demonstrating the international legal personality of the LoN, it was argued that the latter exercised prerogatives of territorial sovereignty, precisely by virtue of art. 22 of the Covenant. In this regard: Sir John Fischer Williams, *Report*, Vienna Conference of 1926 to the *International Law Association*, who insisted in particular on paragraph 2 of this provision: 'the League has Mandatories who act on its behalf, not on behalf of the Members of the League' (*Status of the League of Nations in International Law. The Maritime and Commercial Section*, 683).

93 Our translation.

94 Hymans Report adopted by the Council on 5 August 1920, *Official Journal*, September 1920, 5 August 1920 (2nd meeting, 8th session, Procès-verbal), 339. A completely different attitude was taken by Mr Van Rees, the Dutch member of the PMC, who, in his report on the "Domanial regime in the territories under mandates B et C", stated that this question 'far from having a purely academic significance [is] of essentially practical interest for the assessment of the domanial regulations enacted in the territories under mandate B and C' (PMC, P.V., 3rd session (1923), 217.

95 *Official Journal*, June 1923, 20 April 1923 (6th meeting), 571.

The agreement between the Union of South Africa and Portugal concerning the borders between South West Africa and Angola provided an opportunity for the organs of the LoN (Council and PMC) to consider a concrete case. The preamble to this border treaty read as follows:

> Whereas under a mandate issued by the Council of the League of Nations in pursuance of Article 22 of the Treaty of Versailles, the Government of the Union of South Africa, subject to the terms of the said mandate, *possesses sovereignty over the territory of South West Africa* lately under the sovereignty of Germany.[96]

It was a claim to sovereignty that the Union of South Africa could hardly sustain, as the ICJ will reaffirm decades later. However, such an assertion of sovereignty did not appear at the time to be completely outrageous, as certain internal judicial decisions of the Mandatory Power concerned attest. In this respect, it is sufficient to quote a decision of one of the Appeals Chamber of that State:

> [T]he full power of administration and legislation is vested in the mandatory, that the plenary authority to make laws and enforce them covers the whole sphere of government and that in taking such measures as are calculated to maintain public order the mandatory acts as any other sovereign authority would act in like circumstances.[97]

The Council of the LoN was seized of the question for the first time, at the request of the Commission, but decided 'not to express an opinion on a territory under mandate'.[98] This lack of a position could not satisfy the Commission, which in a way represented the interests of the LoN vis-à-vis the Mandatory. The Council finally gave in to the Commission's pressing demands and appointed a rapporteur in the person of Mr Beelaerts van Blokland (Netherlands). He expressed a desire to receive information from the Union of South Africa Government[99] and stated that:

> It seems to me that, from all practical points of view, *the situation is quite clear*. The Covenant, as well as other articles of the Treaty of Versailles,

96 *Ibid.*, November 1926, 1533 [emphasis added].

97 Winter v. Minister of Defence and Others (Supreme Court, Appeal), 13 December 1939, 9 *ILR*, 45–6 (De Wet J).

98 *Official Journal*, April 1927, 7 March 1927 (1st meeting), 347.

99 *Ibid.*, October 1927, 8 September 1927 (4th meeting, $46t^{h}$ Session), 1120.

> the mandates themselves, and the decisions already adopted by the Council on such points as the national status of the native inhabitants of mandated territories, the extension to the mandated territories of international conventions which were applicable to the neighbouring colonies of the mandatory Powers, the question of borrowing and investment of public and private capital in the mandated territories, the question of loans and the investment of public and private capital in mandated territories , and that of State lands formerly belonging to the German Government, all have had their part in determining or in giving precision to the legal relationship between the Mandatories and the territories under their mandate. *This relationship, to my mind, is clearly a new one in international law and for this reason the use of some of the time-honoured terminology in the same way as previously is perhaps sometimes inappropriate to the new conditions.*[100]

The Rapporteur also asked that his comments be forwarded to the South African Government for its consideration and reaction. The response of the Mandatory Government was cryptic in that it merely acknowledged the report and stated that it 'in view of the opinion of the Council expressed thereon, has no comment to offer'.[101] While the report may have contained some ambiguities and may not have been clear on certain points relating to the sovereignty claim, it was nonetheless categorical in its refutation of the claim. The PMC has always conducted itself according to 'the governing principle that sovereignty has not been acquired and has seen to it that the principle is honoured'.[102]

On the basis of these considerations, the Dutch representative proposed that the Council adopt the conclusions reached by the PMC. The Council did so on the same day (8 September 1927). The matter was then considered again by the Council at its meeting of 13 January 1930, when the Finnish representative remarked that the conclusions of the PMC should be adopted and that 'there

---

100 *Op.cit.* 1120 [emphasis added]. At the 6th Assembly Committee (1929), Dr. Nansen stated that 'The Council has definitively decided this question', i.e., in the sense of the 'absence of sovereignty of the mandatary over the territory under mandate' (A., 10th Assembly, Committee Sessions, 1929, VI, 21).

101 *Official Journal*, May 1928, 709 (Letter from the Government of the Union of South Africa to the Secretary-General of the League).

102 Norman Bentwich, *The Mandates System*, London, 1930, 20. *Contra*: Baty (1921–1922, 119), according to whom Article 22 of the Covenant "reads like a University Extension Lecture" adding that "There is, however, a difference between legal pedantry and ordinary precision. In avoiding the former, the article has drifted many miles away from the latter. We do not We do not subscribe to this view, which is largely unfounded".

is no reason to modify, in any way, this opinion [of the Council] which states implicitly *that sovereignty in the traditional sense of the word, does not reside in the mandatory Power*'.[103] The absence of any real protest from the Mandatory Power thus suggested that the latter was 'prepared to accept in this respect the description of the Mandatory's powers as contained [in the reports]'[104] finally adopted by the Council.

Moreover, in another context, the Dutch member of the PMC, Mr. van Rees, in his memorandum on "The domanial regime in the territories under mandates B and C" presented to the Commission, considered that the issue was 'far from being of purely academic significance'.[105] After sifting through several doctrinal opinions as well as state practice (both Mandatory's and not), Van Rees concluded that Article 22 alone did not provide a clear answer to the question and therefore appealed to the systemic interpretation (now codified in Art. 31 para. 3 lit. (c) VCLT 1969).[106] To this end, he referred in particular to Article 257 of the Treaty of Versailles, which states

> Germany's sovereignty over her overseas possessions has passed to the Principal Allied and Associated Powers. By virtue of their sovereign powers, these Powers have appointed Mandatories to administer the territories ceded by Germany [...] This control, which relates to the entire management and not to certain specific parts of the administration of the Mandatory, who, moreover, acts only in the name of the League of Nations, excludes any idea that the sovereignty of the territory belongs to it.[107]

It is important to stress that, in accordance with a well-established principle of interpretation – already at that time – the practice of an organ of an international organization in the application of a norm concerning it must be taken into account in order to understand its meaning. In this regard, the PMC, as one of its members (van Rees) recalled, 'has always interpreted article 22, paragraph 6, of the Covenant in the sense that the mandated territory must be administered "as *if* it" were an integral part of the territory of the mandating

103 *Official Journal*, February 1930, 13 January 1930 (2nd meeting), 70 [emphasis added].

104 Letter from the Government of the Union of South Africa (16 April 1930) to the Secretary General of the LoN, *Official Journal*, July 1930, 838–839.

105 Memorandum by Mr van Rees, 217 [our translation].

106 Distefano (2019), 487–494.

107 *Ibid.*, 222 [emphasis added].

country'.[108] It follows that the Mandatory did not enjoy sovereignty over the territory of which it was the trustee. The PMC therefore missed no opportunity to reiterate the integrity of the Mandate in the face of attempts by (some) Mandatories to modify it.

V *International and Municipal Case Law*

1 Type A Mandates

The literal interpretation of Art. 22 LoN, corroborated by the internal jurisprudence of third (i.e., non-Mandatory) states,[109] confirms the absence of such sovereignty: 'Syria and Lebanon ... are in accordance with the Covenant of the League of Nations, to be deemed to be independent States and persons of public international law'.[110] Even the domestic jurisprudence of the Mandatories, of the "independent community"[111] as well as the doctrine[112] are adamant in this respect:

> Palestine was not a territory transferred to Great Britain [...] The true effect of this [Article 5 of the British Mandate on Palestine] is that his Britannic Majesty accepted the mandate in respect of Palestine and undertook to exercise it on behalf of the League of Nations in conformity with the provisions contained in it. There was no provision in art. 30 for the transfer of territory to Great Britain. If there had been, there would have been no need for the mandate.[113]

In the light of other domestic court decisions,[114] the lack of *animus domini* and the non *nullius* character of the territory would prevent the establishment of the sovereignty of the Mandatory over the territory concerned. Furthermore,

108 PMC, P.V., 9th session (1926), 33 [emphasis added]. *Contra*: Sir Hersch Lauterpacht (1977), 67, according to whom this phrase meant "a straightforward annexation".

109 Extradition of Criminal to and from Mandated Territories, Alta Corte de Justicia de Uruguay, 7 March 1928, 4 *ILR*, 47.

110 Antoine Bey Sabbagh v. Mohammed Pacha Ahmed and Others, Mixed Court of Mansura (Egypt), 15 November 1927, 4 *ILR* 48–49.

111 'The Crown had not acquired full sovereignty by accepting the Mandate for Palestine', Attorney-General v. Goralschwili and Another, High Court of Palestine, 1925, 2 *ILR* 48.

112 PCIJ, Mavrommatis Concessions Case, 81 (dissenting opinion of Judge Bustamante).

113 The King v. Ketter, England, Court of Criminal Appeal, 21 February 1939, 9 *ILR*, 47, 48; 'Mandated Palestine was not regarded as a British Possession', Stampfer v. Attorney-General, Israel, Supreme Court sitting as the Court of Criminal Appeals, 4 January 1956, 23 *ILR*, 292 (dissenting opinion of Judge Gotein).

114 The Egyptian Enterprise and Development Company v. Minister of War, France, Tribunal civil de la Seine, 1 March 1937, 11 *ILR*, 54.

any such manifestation by the Mandatory would have been invalid as it would have been at variance with Article 22 of the Covenant and the corresponding mandate, which constitutes the title of the Mandatory's presence over the territory concerned. This does not mean, however, that "independent communities" are states in the sense of international law.[115] For them to become so, additional international acts will be required which will have the effect of terminating the mandate, hence accompanying the "country" to independence (as will be the case for Iraq and Trans-Jordan before WWII).

International jurisprudence, on the other hand, did not hesitate to consider the 'independent communities' of the defunct Ottoman Empire as real states, at least from the point of view of succession to the debts of the latter:[116] 'Article 22, paragraph 1, of the Covenant stipulated that "the well-being and development of such peoples form a sacred trust of civilisation". The only limitation imposed by the League's Covenant upon the sovereignty and full independence of the people of Palestine was the temporary tutelage entrusted to the Mandatory Power'.[117]

2 Types B and C Mandates

The domestic jurisprudence of the Mandatory Powers is not uniform. Attempts have been made to distinguish between a transfer as a sovereign and a transfer encumbered by obligations arising from the agency institution:

> Thus the title under which the territory is to be held as a mandated territory is different from that under which a territory transferred by simple cession woud have been held. The article shows that the intention was to achieve a transfer of a territory without making that territory in the ordinary sense a possession of the mandatory. A territory which is a 'possession' can be ceded by a power to another power so that the latter power will have complete authority in relation to that territory [...] A mandated territory is not a possession of a power in the ordinary sense.[118]

115 See Klausner v. Levy, United States, District Court, Eastern District of Virginia, 10 March 1940, 16 *ILR*, 39.

116 Ottoman Debt Arbitration (pres. M Borel), 18 April 1925, 3 *ILR*, 42.

117 ICJ, Wall in Palestine, 2004, 249 (separate opinion of Judge Elaraby). See also: *ibid*, 237 (separate opinion of Judge Al-Khasawneh).

118 Frost v. Stevenson, Australia, High Court of Australia, 13 August 1937, 8 *ILR*, 105 (*Per* Latham).

The *ius disponendi* (the right to dispose of territory)[119] – the litmus test of the right of sovereignty – and the power to change its legal status[120] are lacking with the Mandatory Power. The obligations incumbent upon it, which derive jointly from Article 22 and the mandate itself, are an obstacle to the recognition of this power: 'Consideration of the provisions of the Treaty Peace with Germany shows, I think, the mandated territories did not become possessions, in the ordinary sense, of the mandatory powers';[121] or again: 'The power and jurisdiction is ample, but the supreme principle is that Australia is unable to treat the territories as part of its own dominions, but it is subject to international duties of an onerous kind, including the duties of not attempting to alter or to derogate from the status of the territory under mandate'.[122] The High Court of Australia concluded that 'it is impossible to believe that the acceptance by the mandatory power of its international trust – 'sacred trust' – in the interests of those who are 'not yet' able to stand by themselves in the modern world is to be regarded as a new method of 'acquisition' of territory by the mandatory power'.[123] In the same vein, the New Zealand High Court stated: 'Western Samoa, being a 'trust territory', is not British or New Zealand territory'.[124]

Other internal jurisdictional interpretations do not hide the difficulty of the courts in understanding the institution of the Mandatory Power, thus showing its revolutionary novelty:

> The Mandated Territory occupies a peculiar position: on the one hand it is a foreign country territorially vis-à-vis the Union, on the other hand, the Union Parliament has power of legislation in respect thereof, but the operative effect of such legislation within the Territory is not dependent upon conventions, or treaty or international law, but upon promulgation

119 See: G Distefano (2002), 35.

120 'Thus, it appears that the only probable manner of changing the status of a mandated territory is through action of the League by amending art. 22 by admitting a mandatory community to its membership [...] Thus, the League of Nations seems competent and *alone competent* to change the status of territories now under Article 22', Quincy Wright, *The Mandates under the League of Nations*, Chicago, 1930, 505, 506 [emphasis added].

121 Ffrost v. Stevenson, Australia, High Court of Australia, 13 August 1937, 8 *ILR*, 102 (*Per* Latham).

122 *Ibid.*, 108 (*Per* Evatt).

123 *Ibid.*, 109 (*Per* Evatt).

124 Annandale v. Collector of Customs, New Zealand Supreme Court of Wellington, 8 November 1954, 22 *ILR*, 88.

> of the legislation within the Mandated Territory, or upon the Union Act incorporating the Mandated Territory as part of the Union Territory.[125]

International jurisprudence – on the other hand – has been far more consistent and constant in refuting any Mandatory's sovereignty. As the ICJ puts it:

> The terms of this Mandate, as well as the provisions of Article 22 of the Covenant and the principles embodied therein, show that the creation of this new international institution did not involve any cession of territory or transfer of sovereignty to the Union of South Africa.[126]

B Trusteeship System of the United Nations

i *The Succession of Mandates within the United Nations International Trusteeship Administration*[127]

As the ICJ stated in 1950,[128] the dissolution of the LoN did not extinguish the mandate regime. The juridical effects created jointly by Article 22 and the Mandate Agreements remained. In the absence of special provisions contained in the LoN Covenant and in the specific mandate agreements, the general regime, codified in many respects by the VCLT 1969, applied, notably the customary rule reflected in its Art. 70 para. 1 lit. b).[129]

At its twenty-first and last ordinary session – in 1946 – the UNGA discussed the question of the dissolution of the mandate system. Only one intervention is to be recorded, that of the Egyptian delegate, requesting that the Assembly take into account the fact that Palestine had, from the intellectual, economic and political point of view, 'attained such a degree of development that it should no longer be placed under a mandate or trusteeship system, or under any other such system that may be envisaged'.[130] As the request was not formulated as

125 Faul v. South African Railways and Harbours, South West Africa, High Court, 20–21 September 1948, 16 *ILR*, 40.

126 ICJ, International Status of South-West Africa, 132.

127 In general, against any succession between the LoN and the UN, see: ICJ, Namibia 1971, 227–252 (dissenting opinion of Judge Sir Gerald Fitzmaurice).

128 See *infra* footnote 133.

129 We can say that the general principle underlying this provision was customary at the time of the dissolution of the LoN.

130 A., 21st assembly, 1946, plenary sessions, 59 (session of 18 April 1946).

an amendment, the resolution was eventually adopted unanimously bar the announced abstention of Egypt.[131]

The resolution adopted by the LoN Assembly on 18 April 1946, by which the Geneva-based organisation terminated its existence, merely "noted" the identity between the purposes of the LoN and the UN (in Chapters 12 and 13 of the UNC) regarding the Mandates. This resolution was based on and, at the same time, built a juridical nexus with Article 80 of the Charter. The Mandatory Powers decided to continue the administration of the territories in accordance with the principles of the Mandate. The dissolution of the LoN did not mean the termination of the Mandates:[132] 'it [the Assembly] did not say that the Mandates themselves came to an end'.[133]

The South West Africa saga is a patent example of the problems associated with mandate succession within the UN. The South African government had repeatedly asserted that its mandate obligations in relation to South West Africa remained in force.[134] The supervisory function was taken over, in accordance with the above-mentioned resolution, by the UN, and more specifically by the General Assembly, whose competence 'to exercise such supervision and to receive and examine reports is derived from the provisions of Article 10 of the Charter, which authorizes the General Assembly to discuss any questions or any matters within the scope of the Charter and to make recommendations on these questions to the Members of the United Nations'.[135] Judge Bustamante in his dissenting opinion appended to ICJ's 1963 Judgment in the Northern Cameroons' case, observed in this respect:

> It can accordingly be asserted that, despite the dissolution of the League of Nations, there was unanimous agreement among the Mandatory Powers that the Mandates were to continue to be exercised in accordance

131 The Egyptian attempt to establish a different regime for Mandatory Palestine was evidently repeated in San Francisco, but it also failed (Ruth Russell, *A History of the United Nations Charter*, Washington, 1958, 828–829). For fear 'that this article would rouse Zionist opposition' (829), it was agreed that further consultations would be held, and discussion of the issue was accordingly postponed.

132 Thence one the main differences with the institution of the mandate in civil law (see *supra* Part 3. Chapter 9. Section A.i).

133 ICJ, International Status of South-West Africa, 134.

134 *Ibid.*, 135.

135 *Ibid.*, 137. See *infra* note 152. *Contra*: Kelsen (1950), 598–599.

> with the rules of the Mandate Agreements, until the Trusteeship System had been finally established.[136]

Can we therefore speak of an automatic succession? According to Judge Tanaka, this construction can be comfortably argued:

> Therefore, it is not very unnatural and unreasonable to recognize in the United Nations and the trusteeship system the successor of the League and the mandates system respectively. Nevertheless, we cannot recognize universal succession in the juridical sense in these cases. Universal succession between the two entities, namely the League and the United Nations did not occur. Neither can the application of the provisions of the trusteeship system on the Mandate be recognized without the conclusion of a trusteeship agreement.[137]

Furthermore, the preamble of some trusteeship agreements[138] contains an express reference to mandates: 'in substitution for the terms of the mandate under which the territory has been administered'.[139]

All the Mandatory Powers handed over "their" Mandated territories to the UN Trusteeship administration, with the notable exception of the Union of South Africa in relation to South West Africa.[140] From this refusal, in contrast with the consent expressed by the other Mandatory Powers, it is inferred that

136 ICJ, Case concerning the Northern Cameroons (Cameroun v. United Kingdom), Judgement of 2 December 1963 (Preliminary objections): *ICJ Reports 1963*, 160 (dissenting opinion of Judge Bustamante).

137 ICJ, South West Africa Cases, 1966, 274 (dissenting opinion of Judge Tanaka).

138 Among them: New Guinea and Samoa.

139 "[T]he Mandate has been superseded by the present Trusteeship Agreement by means of which territories originally held under Mandate from the League of Nations can be placed under the international trusteeship of the General Assembly of the United Nations in accordance with Articles 75 and 77 of the United Nations Charter. The text of the present Trusteeship Agreement follows the pattern of the old Mandate", *Maleksultan v. Jeraj*, East Africa, Court of Appeal of Nairobi, 22 January 1955, 22 *ILR*, 86.

140 In this case, 'The System of Trusteeship under the United Nations has not replaced the Mandates System; the latter remains in force so far as South-West Africa is concerned', Voting Procedure on Questions Relating to Reports and Petitions Concerning to the Territory of South-West Africa, Advisory Opinion of 7 June 1955: *ICJ. Reports 1955*, 96–97 (separate opinion of Judge Sir Hersch Lauterpacht). Also: ICJ, *International Status of South-West Africa*, 138. There is no doubt that the dissolution of the LoN (with its system of mandates) a year before the introduction of the trusteeship system left an interregnum that was unscrupulously and abusively used by the Union of South Africa to legitimise the annexation of South-West Africa.

there was no automatic succession, and that the latter required an agreement between the Mandatory Power and the UN.[141] The Court declared in 1950 that there was no obligation on the part of the Mandatory States to *convert* the mandate into a *trusteeship*:[142] 'Territories held under Mandate were not by the Charter automatically placed under the new International Trusteeship System'.[143] Such a reading is corroborated by the consideration of Article 80, para. 2, of the UNC and Resolution of 9 February 1946, by which the UNGA invited the Mandatory States to 'undertake practical steps, in concert with the other States directly concerned, for the implementation of Article 79'.[144] The systemic interpretation of these two texts shows that there is no obligation for the Mandatories to conclude a trusteeship agreement:

> The trusteeship system did not automatically replace the mandate system, and the United Nations did not succeed to the rights of the League of Nations as to the former mandated territories.[145]

Only the B and C Mandates were affected by the succession between international organisations,[146] since all the "independent communities" of the

141 The Court has, however, demonstrated in the various cases in the dispute over the Mandatory Territory that the Union of South Africa has recognised, by its conduct, the supervisory jurisdiction of the United Nations.

142 ICJ, International Status of South-West Africa, 140, 144. *Contra* dissenting opinion of Judge Alvarez, *ibid.* 183–184; dissenting opinion of Judge De Visscher, *ibid.* 186; dissenting opinion of Judge Krylov, *ibid*, 191; ICJ, South West Africa Cases, 1962, 366 (separate opinion of Judge Bustamante), according to whom the obligation of the Mandatory to place the Territory under the trusteeship regime must instead be sought in the membership of the United Nations and to have 'assumed all the obligations therefrom, and, consequently, if one of those Member States is a Mandatory, it at the same time freely accepted the obligation to renew or transform the Mandate into a Trusteeship agreement'.

143 ICJ, International Status of South-West Africa, 138. The Court's decision, expressed in the reply to Question (b), was adopted by eight votes to six. *Contra*: 'There can be no interruption in the continuous performance of this trust' (dissenting opinion of Judge Alvarez, *ibid.*, 182).

144 UNGA Resolution 9 (I).

145 Kelsen (1950), 596.

146 'It must also be borne in mind that Tanganyika was then being administered in accordance with Article 22 of the Covenant of the League of Nations under a Mandate conferred on the King of England, that the Mandate has been superseded by the present Trusteeship Agreement by means of which territories originally held under Mandate from the League of Nations can be placed under the international trusteeship of the General Assembly of the United Nations in accordance with Articles 75 and 77 of the United Nations Charter. The text of the present Trusteeship Agreement follows the pattern of the old Mandate and will be found at page 1 of Vol. V of the current Laws of Tanganyika and one of the

Ottoman Empire, in other words the A Mandates, became independent before the establishment of the UN trusteeship regime (with the notable exception of Palestine). Added to the type B and C Mandates were the colonial territories of Japan and Italy, which the Allied Powers wanted to submit to the administration of the United Nations (art. 77 para. 1 lit. c of the UNC). Only one colonial territory, taken from one of the defeated Powers (Italy),[147] namely Somalia, was placed under the trusteeship regime. Since Somalia was placed under the trusteeship of the former colonial power,[148] the Trusteeship Council, which had drawn up the draft agreement, assumed very extensive powers in accordance with the letter and especially the spirit of the trusteeship regime. This is evidenced by the fact that Italy was assisted (and supervised) in the exercise of its trusteeship function by an Advisory Council comprising the Philippines, Colombia and Egypt.[149]

However, the absence of an automatic succession did not affect the persistence of the obligations of the Mandatory Power who had chosen not to place the territory under the trusteeship regime. The obligations remain the same, with the substitution of the controlling bodies following the dissolution of the LoN.[150] On this last point, the ICJ was repeatedly called upon, thus providing us with an impressive jurisprudential refinement. The absence of an obligation to transfer the Mandates concerned to the Trusteeship system and the refusal of one of the Mandatories (the Union of South Africa) raised the question of continued control. This was a thorny issue, as the Mandate Agreement in question was only the last vestige of a complex system that had in the meantime completely disappeared. Once the persistence of the mandate obligations had been asserted, and for as long as the former Mandatory Power occupied Namibian territory, the question of control over the Mandatory Management thus became acute. It was necessary to reinvent a system of control in which it would have been possible to embed the mandate.

principal objects of the Mandate is the government of the territory in the interest of the inhabitants of the territory', *Maleksultan v. Jerai*, East Africa, Court of Appeal of Nairobi, 22 January 1955, 22 *ILR*, 86.

147 By virtue of Article 23 of the 1947 Peace Treaty, Italy latter renounced all its rights and titles over its former colony.

148 It should be noted that, at the time the trusteeship over Somalia was established, Italy was not a member of the UN.

149 See Resolution 289 (IV) adopted by the UNGA on 21 November 1949.

150 ICJ, International Status of South-West Africa, 137–138; ICJ, Admissibility of Hearings of Petitioners by the Committee on South West Africa, Advisory Opinion of 1er June 1956: *ICJ Reports 1956*, 27.

In its 1955 opinion (*Voting Procedure*), the Court had stated that: 'the authority of the General Assembly to exercise supervision over the administration of South-West Africa as a mandated Territory is based on the provisions of the Charter'.[151] The provisions alluded to by the Court are those relating to the prerogatives of the Assembly, and in particular Article 10 of the UNC.[152] The idea behind this – unprecedented, unpredictable and, for some, "unheard of"[153] – succession was the existence of an International Community[154] represented and acting first by the LoN and then by the UN. Moreover, there was a succession of international organisations, and this at a time when the I.C.J. had only just declared that the United Nations possessed international legal personality, which was moreover objective.[155] The Court is very clear on this point:

> [t]he United Nations, as a *successor to the League, acting through its competent organs,* must be seen *above all* as the supervisory institution, competent to pronounce, in that capacity, on the conduct of the mandatory with respect to its international obligations, and competent to act accordingly.[156]

More recently, the ICJ was keen to clarify that the UN – and in particular, but not exclusively, the UNGA – had a legal interest in the resolution of the Palestinian question:

> The responsibility of the United Nations in this matter has also its origin in the Mandate and the Partition Resolution concerning Palestine [...]

151 ICJ, Voting Procedure on Questions Relating to Reports and Petitions Concerning the Territory of South West Africa, Advisory Opinion of 7 June 1955: *ICJ Reports* 1955, 76. The Court referred to and quoted an excerpt from her 1950 Advisory opinion (*International South-West Africa*, supra note 134 and *infra* 152).

152 'The competence of the General Assembly of the United Nations to exercise such supervision and to receive and examine reports is derived from the general provisions of Article 10 of the Charter, which authorizes the General Assembly to discuss any questions or any matters within the scope of the Charter and to make recommendations on these questions or matters to the Members of the United Nations', ICJ, International Status of South-West Africa, 137.

153 ICJ, South West Africa Cases, 1962, 611–613 (dissenting opinion of Judge ad hoc Van Wyk).

154 'Responsibility for the supervision and proper enforcement of the Mandate for South West Africa lay with the international political community acting under the aegis of the United Nations General Assembly', *Binga v. Administrator-General for South-West Africa and Others*, South West Africa, Supreme Court, 22 June 1984, 82 *ILR*, 466.

155 ICJ, Reparation for Injuries Suffered, 185.

156 ICJ, Namibia 1971, para. 103 (at 49–50) [emphasis added].

> This responsibility has been described by the General Assembly as "a permanent responsibility towards the question of Palestine until the question is resolved in all its aspects in a satisfactory manner in accordance with international legitimacy" (General Assembly resolution 57/107 of 3 December 2002).[157]

The UNGA was hence able to proceed with the partition of Mandatory Palestine because it had inherited the title from the LoN.[158]

ii *Affinities and Differences with the International Trusteeship Administration Established by the UN Charter*[159]

The Negotiating Committee in San Francisco responsible for discussing and drafting the chapters on the UN trusteeship system considered that, in all respects, the terms "trusteeship" and "*tutelle*" were synonymous:[160] 'It is no exaggeration to say that Article 76 on the purposes of the trusteeship system is a direct descendant of Article 22 of the LoN Covenant'.[161] Consequently, this institution was introduced into the Charter by analogy *and* in the wake of the mandate system, even in the absence of any automatic succession (*supra* Part 3. Chapter 9. Section B.i). The ICJ thus expressed itself on the genesis of mandates and trusteeships, as well as on the roles played respectively by the UN and by the UNS:[162]

> The negotiation of trusteeship agreements was entirely different in the United Nations in 1946 and subsequently from the negotiation of the mandate agreements in 1919 and the ensuing years. As has been seen, in 1919 agreement was first reached on which territories were to be placed under mandate. Thereafter the terms of the Mandates were drafted in the Milner Commission in 1919 and then approved by the Council of Heads of Delegations at the Peace Conference. Although there was a later clamour

157 ICJ, Wall in Palestine, 2004, para. 49 (at 159).

158 See *supra* Part 2. Chapter 6. Section B.iv.

159 See Ramendra N Chowdhuri, International Mandates and Trusteeship Systems. RN Chowdhuri, *International Mandates and Trusteeship Systems*, The Hague, 1955; Leo Gross, *U.N. Trusteeship and League of Nations Mandate System*, Oxford, 1948; Andrea Messineo, "Dal mandato all'amministrazione fiduciaria", *Civiltà cattolica*, 1948, 579–645.

160 Eighth meeting of Committee II/4 (22 May 1945), vol. 10, 471.

161 Maurice Glele-Ahanhanzo, "Article 76", in *La Charte des Nations Unies. Commentaire article par article* (ed. Jean-Pierre Cot, Alain Pellet), 2nd edn, Paris, 1991, 1124 [our translation].

162 See in general: Donald S Leeper, "Trusteeship compared with Mandate", 50 *Michigan Law Review* 1951–1952, 1199–1210.

> from the League Assembly to learn the texts of the drafts, the texts of the mandates were agreed by the Principal Allied and Associated Powers and then confirmed by the Council of the League; the Powers did not submit themselves to cross-examination in the Assembly.[163]

In the same case, ICJ's Judge Tanaka recalled, with regard to the South African mandate, that '[a]fter the dissolution of the League, the same idea and principles have been continued in the 'International Trusteeship System' in the Charter of the United Nations'.[164] The LoN Assembly itself, in its resolution of the twenty-first (and last) session extinguishing the mandate system, recognised: 'that the termination of the League's existence, its functions with respect to the mandated territories will come to an end, but notes that Chapters XI, XII and XIII of the Charter of the United Nations embody principles corresponding to those declared in Article 22 of the Covenant of the League'.[165]

Trusteeship was introduced by the Charter with a view to establishing a more advantageous regime than that for "non-self-governing territories", for which the key word "independence" was not used. The territories placed under the trusteeship regime were distinct from the non-self-governing territories in their characteristics and origins: they had already been subject to an *international concern*, since they were under a mandate. However, the acceleration of the emancipation process of the 'non-self-governing territories' (the colonies of the victors) meant that the trusteeship administration eventually benefited from the advances of the former. A few words on the trusteeship system established by the Charter, under which the mandated territories were placed, ought to be spent.

Article 73 plays the same role as Article 22 of the Covenant and even refers to the "sacred" nature of the trusteeship mission. Under this provision, states (colonial powers) undertook to promote the political, economic and social advancement of the populations concerned. The power of control, exercised by the UNGA, was particularly limited and was based on Article 10 of the Charter, i.e., on the general powers of the Assembly. The subsequent practice of the application of these provisions shows an opposition between the states concerned and the UNGA, which aimed at increasingly arrogating itself broad competences with regard to colonial possessions. The practice of the UN

163 ICJ, South West Africa Cases, 1966, 408 (dissenting opinion of Judge Jessup).

164 *Ibid.*, 1966, 265 (dissenting opinion of Judge Tanaka).

165 "Resolution dissolving the Mandate System", adopted on 18 April 1946 by the Twenty-first Assembly of the LoN, A., 21st assembly (7th meeting), plenary sessions, *Official Journal*, supplement, 58 [Annex C].

plenary body has resulted in a norm prohibiting the colonizing states from hindering the access of colonial territories to independence. Indeed, Resolution 1514 (XV) of 14 December 1960 was soon considered to reflect general international law.[166] Moreover, the vague wording of Article 79 of the Charter favoured the UN's "decolonizing mission".[167]

Article 77 was, in the intention of the negotiators in San Francisco, the 'core' provision of this chapter [Chapter XII].[168] This provision lists the categories of territories that may be placed under the system. It introduces the requirement of a 'trusteeship agreement' determining 'under what conditions' these territories will be subject to it. Unlike the mandate system, where the variable typology was established in the Covenant itself, in the Charter system it remains silent in this respect, the typology being defined *à la carte* by each "trusteeship agreement". Although the trusteeship system, unlike the mandate system, established a single regime per se, the territories concerned were therefore ultimately subject to different terms and conditions.

Article 80(1) of the UNC is intended to guarantee the rights of the peoples of the mandate territories that have not yet been placed under the trusteeship system. This provision will be the insurmountable legal obstacle to the annexation by the Union of South Africa of South West Africa (Namibia). It provides that the trusteeship system shall not prejudice the rights which any people or state may have under 'existing international instruments to which the Members of the United Nations may respectively be parties'. In San Francisco, during the discussion of the future Article 80, it was proposed to insert an 'express reference to Article 22(4) of the Covenant of the League of Nations. It was objected that it would be inappropriate to refer expressly to an international instrument to which not all the United Nations were parties'.[169] It is also clear from the *travaux préparatoires*, as well as from the literal and contextual interpretation, that the rights referred to in this provision are *all the* rights arising from Article 22 *and* its subsequent application by States, as well as by the competent organs of the LoN. Article 80 UNC will undergo impressive judicial interpretations, both contentious and advisory (ICJ's advisory opinions of 1950 and 1955, as well as its 1956 judgment). Article 80, since the attainment of by Namibia of its independence, has now become obsolete within the meaning of Article 61 VCLT 1969. In a sense, this provision definitively completes the "sacred trust of civilisation" initiated by Article 22 of the Covenant.

166 See *supra* Part 2. Chapter 6. Section A.i.

167 Jean-Robert Henry, "Article 79", in *La Charte des Nations Unies*, 1152–1153 [our translation].

168 Draft report of the Committee II/4, vol. 10, 626.

169 *Ibid.*, 591.

1 Affinities with the Mandate System

Territorially, the expansion of the UN trusteeship system coincides with that of the mandates, with the notable exception of Type A mandates. Like the mandate system – even more so following the termination of Type A mandates – the trusteeship system is predominantly concentrated on the African continent, with some colonial territories in the Pacific (former Japanese possessions).[170]

At the San Francisco Conference, the political purpose of the trusteeship system dominated the debates on the non-self-governing territories. A divide emerged within the Big Five, with the colonial powers on the one hand and the non-colonial powers on the other. The solution finally adopted reflects the compromise reached in the negotiations: Chapter XII refers to both "self-government or independence" (Article 76 lit. b), while Chapter XI refers only to 'peoples [which] have not yet attained a full measure of self-government' (Article 73).

The system finally established follows a two-stage procedure,[171] formerly introduced by the LoN regarding the Mandates: the first, political, consists of the agreement by the victorious powers of the WWII on the designation of the "administering authority of the territory". The second stage saw the UN take over 'to give its label to this agreement, approve it and possibly correct it'.[172] As for the trusteeship agreement, given '[its] dual contractual and "quasi-statutory" character',[173] it is reminiscent of the mandate agreement, with its dual conventional and institutional nature (*supra* Part 3. Chapter 9. Section A.i).[174] The administration could be entrusted to several States. Nauru was placed under the joint administration of Australia, Great Britain and New Zealand.[175] In

170 'Kwajalein was formerly part of the Japanese mandated group under the League of Nations. Following World War II, the Marshall, Caroline and Marianas Islands (excepting Guam, at that time a possession of the United States) *passed to the United Nations as successor to the League of Nations*', Application of Reyes, United States, District Court, District of Hawaii, 12 April 1956, 23 *ILR*, 36 [emphasis added].

171 "The trusteeship agreement, at its inception, is an institution with a history. It is undoubtedly inspired by the experience of the LoN in terms of the elaboration of mandates, and globally reproduces the two-step mechanism that the provisions of the Pact, corrected by practice, had identified", Henry (1991), 1144 [our translation].

172 *Loc.cit.*

173 ICJ, Certain Phosphate Lands in Nauru (Nauru v. Australia), Judgement of 26 June 1992 (Preliminary Objections), *ICJ Reports 1992*, 278 (separate opinion of Judge Shahabuddeen).

174 "[T]he regime of Trusteeship Administration is *connected* like that under the former Mandate system, with the Anglo-Saxon *legal institution of trusteeship*, which consists in entrusting the full administration of property to a person for the benefit of a third person", *Società A.B.C. v. Fontana and Della Rocca*, Italy, Corte di Cassazione (Sezioni riunite), 10 August 1954, 22 *ILR*, 77 [emphasis added].

175 ICJ, Certain Phosphate Lands in Nauru, paras. 43–47 (at 257–258).

such cases, 'the Administering Authority ... did not have an international legal personality distinct from those of the States thus designated'.[176] Responsibility was thus "joint" and "several".[177]

The purposes of both systems are the same.[178] From a historical perspective, the identity between the two regimes can be seen as a step backwards, since the normative and factual context had changed considerably between the two post-war periods. In other words, maintaining the system means that the trusteeship regime has certainly consolidated the achievements of the LoN, but without improving it or bringing it in line with the new requirements of the International Community. Like the mandate system, the trusteeship system is 'essentially dynamic in nature',[179] in that it was supposed to evolve according to the results to be achieved. The limitations on the exercise of the powers of the administering authority are not dissimilar to those that once encumbered the Mandatory Power.

The administering authority had the primary duty to develop the social and economic progress of the territory. A resolution was adopted by the UNGA on 15 November 1949, in which the plenary body of the UN drew:

> the attention of the Trusteeship Council to the necessity of requesting the Administering Authorities to study the possibility of including in the curricula of schools in the Trust Territories instruction on the United Nations, the International Trusteeship System and the special status of Trust Territories, and to this end to make use, if they so desire, of the co-operation that may be furnished by the United Nations Educational, Scientific and Cultural Organization.[180]

Furthermore, the UN Charter imposes on the states administering the Non-Self-Governing Territories the 'sacred trust [...] to promote [the] well-being of the inhabitants of these territories' (Art. 73 UNC).

ICJ has been vested with the same judicial supervisory power to determine violations of trusteeship agreements as its predecessor: 8 of the 11 Trusteeship agreements contained an arbitration clause identical in every respect to the one formerly inserted in the Mandate agreements. The jurisdictional clause in the Mandates is found in the trusteeship agreements under the Charter

---

176 *Ibid.*, para. 47 (at 258).

177 *Ibid.*, 286 (separate opinion of Judge Shahabuddeen).

178 Brierly (1963), 181.

179 Giuseppe Vedovato, "Les accords de tutelle", 76 *RCADI* 1950-I, 642 [our translation].

180 Paragraph 2 of resolution 324 (IV).

system[181] although, as has been noted, the 'context of the adjudication clause ... is not the same'.[182] The ICJ was called upon – on the basis of the arbitration clause inserted in the South African Mandate Agreement – to entertain no less than 5 times (1950, 1955, 1956, 1962 and 1971), both in its contentious and advisory function, claims based on the LoN Mandate entrusted to the South African Union. The scope of the jurisdictional clause was thus delineated by the ICJ:

> If therefore, the contention put forward by the Applicants in the present case were correct in principle (and this contention is in a major degree founded on the existence and wording of the jurisdictional clause, and also involves the erroneous assumption that it can *per se* confer substantive rights), it would follow that, in the case of some of the trusteeships, individual members of the United Nations would be held to have a legal right or interest in the conduct and administration of the trust, but in relation to others they would not, although these were no less trusteeships,-no less an expression of the "sacred trust of civilization". The implications become even more striking when it is realized that the trusteeships to which no jurisdictional clause attaches are three previous Pacific 'C' mandates - that is to say the class of territory inhabited by precisely the most undeveloped categories of peoples, the least "able to stand by themselves".[183]

The Trusteeship system provided for a questionnaire to be completed by the administering authority as part of the reporting process to the Trusteeship Committee.

With regard to the termination of trusteeship agreements, only China among the Big Five proposed, during the San Francisco negotiations, 'to provide for action against violation of a trust agreement'.[184] Egypt, too, recalling Japan's violation of its mandate obligations and the powerlessness of the UN organs, supported UN's power to unilaterally terminate a trusteeship agreement. Britain and the United States opposed this, arguing that it was a treaty agreement. On this point, the UNC did not mark much progress compared to the mandate system. In the silence of the texts, some have claimed, wrongly, that the trusteeship agreement is irrevocable. This argument, supported by

181 See: ICJ, Northern Cameroons, 25–26.

182 *Ibid.*, 65 (separate opinion of Judge Sir Percy Spender).

183 ICJ, South West Africa Cases, 1966, para. 95 (at 49–50).

184 Russell (1958), 836.

Vedovato,[185] is specious in that it is based on the example of the Italian administration of Somalia. However, as we have observed, this was indeed a *sui generis* situation.

2 Differences with the Mandate System

UN Secretary-General Trygve Lie said at the inauguration of the Trusteeship Council on 26 March 1947: 'The International Trusteeship System is no mere prolongation of the Mandates System under the League of Nations. It is a new system of international supervision. Its scope is wider, its power broader, and its potentialities far greater than those of the Mandates System'.[186] One of the I.C.J. judges added that 'The character, purport, structure and working of the Trusteeship System being different from those of the Mandates System and resulting in a much broader and more effective supervision of the administration of the trust territories than in the case of the Mandates, may render recourse to judicial protection less necessary but the right of another Member to invoke it … subsists'.[187]

Two chapters and 17 articles instead of one: the arithmetic alone betrays the difference in approach between the two institutions. It reflects the two founding treaties: 'The complexity and variety of the Trusteeship problems forced the General Assembly, unlike the League Assembly, to create a multiplicity of subsidiary bodies under Article 22 of the Charter'.[188] This need is difficult to understand: the number of territories under trusteeship had not increased compared to those under mandate. In conclusion, from a strict institutional efficiency point of view, it is not completely wrong to say that the allegedly "ineffective" LoN did not necessarily do less well than the hypertrophic UN. What are the differences between the two systems?

In relation to mandated territories, the prohibition on the erection of fortifications, naval bases and other military installations by the Mandatory Power, as well as the military training of natives, disappears (Art. 22 (5)).

While states were free, in accordance with Article 77 of the UNC, to place certain territories under the trusteeship system, the major Allied and Associated Powers, as reflected in the articles of the peace treaties ending the WWI, had committed themselves to subjecting certain territories, peoples and communities to the mandate system. In many respects, the Charter regime is a

185 Vedovato (1950), 643.

186 Quoted in: Chowdhuri (1955), 300.

187 ICJ, Northern Cameroons 46 (individual op. of Judge Wellington Koo); similarly, Judge Beb A Don's dissenting opinion was appended to the same judgment (*ibid.*, 184).

188 Chowdhuri (1955), 155.

step backwards from the spirit of the 1919 Peace Conference (see *above* Part 3. Chapter 9. Section A.i). Another step backwards is to be noted insofar as Article 22 provided that the "wishes" of the communities (Type A mandates) were to be taken 'must be a principal consideration in the selection of the Mandatory' (para. 4). Nothing of the sort is contained in Article 81 of the UNC, according to which the trusteeship agreement will designate the authority that will administer the territory. The designation is the exclusive joint responsibility of the states directly concerned and the UN. Admittedly, it could be argued that this only concerned "independent communities", whose degree of development was certainly higher than that of any other people inhabiting the territories to be placed under the trusteeship regime. Nevertheless, the text of the Covenant went further than that of the Charter. Moreover, unlike the mandates, the trusteeship agreements merely confirmed the *durante bello* 'possession' of the territory, giving it another legal title, that of *trusteeship*. While the UN must approve trusteeship agreements, in the LoN system the Council had the power to define the content of the mandate agreement in accordance with Article 22(8) (see *above* Part 3. Chapter 9. Section A.ii).[189]

The Charter, unlike the Covenant, does not enumerate the features that the State entrusted with the Trusteeship administration must possess. Unlike the mandates, the administration may be entrusted to a State, a group of States or even the UN itself[190] (Art. 81 UNC). In this respect, the Charter represents a definite innovation compared to the Covenant. It takes up the idea of the internationalisation of Mandates territories, as it had emerged during the preparatory work in Paris before it was finally rejected. As it was commented on the Mandates system: "The evolution of the system must therefore be sought *in the direct exercise of this mission by existing* or future *international organisations*, which unfortunately today have no more than a purely moral right of control, which may be effective, but lacks the coercive forces that it urgently needs".[191] However, the minor hypothesis envisaged by Article 81 of the UNC, providing for the direct administration of "the Organisation itself", was never realised. The closest example was Somalia, where Italy, a former colonial

189 'The San Francisco Charter reveals definite progress beyond the Covenant of the League of Nations in respect of the development of the institution for the protection of dependent, under-developed or former colonial countries', ICJ, South West Africa Cases, 1962, 365 (separate opinion of Judge Bustamante).

190 This last case highlights the anti-colonial character of the UNC and the UN. In addition to a somewhat diluted administration of Congo, the UN assumed direct control, albeit for an interim period, of Dutch New Guinea (or West Irian), before its transfer to Indonesian sovereignty.

191 Comisetti (1934), 153 [our translation].

power, was assisted and monitored by a group of states – Egypt, Colombia and the Philippines – forming all together an Advisory Council.[192]

In all the provisions relating to the trusteeship regime, the noun "administration" and the verb derived from it ("administer") makes its appearance. The vagueness on the question of the holding of sovereignty in the trusteeship regime (see *above* Part 3. Chapter 9.Section A.iv) is definitively dispelled. The administering authority (formerly "the power") does not enjoy sovereignty, but is authorised by the trusteeship agreement as well as by Article 81 to "administer" the territory. More than a few authorities have also correctly supported the sovereignty of trusteeship countries.[193] Some domestic jurisprudence has gone so far as to affirm the sovereignty of the UN: 'Kwajalein Island as part of a Trust Territory, was primarily under the sovereignty and jurisdiction of the United Nations and was accordingly foreign territory for immigration purposes'.[194]

Moreover, the institutional machinery of the mandates has been enriched by a body of norms establishing the rules and purposes pursued. One need only think of the 1960 Declaration (resolution 1514 (XV) of 14 December 1960) on the granting of independence to colonial countries and peoples. There is no doubt that the new human rights paradigm has influenced the UN trusteeship regime.[195] In the same vein, the UNGA reiterated the ultimate purpose and raison d'être of this system in its: 'Inadequacy of political, economic, social or educational preparedness should never serve *as a pretext for delaying independence*' (para. 3).[196] Even more clearly, in paragraph 5: 'Immediate steps shall be taken *in Trust Territories and Non-Self-Governing Territories or all other territories* which have not yet attained independence, to transfer all powers to the peoples of those territories … in order to enable them to enjoy complete independence and freedom'. Depending on the different normative and historical context, the UNGA adopted a very active role in the management of the trusteeship. This new dynamic not only took the form of more forceful interventions towards the administering authorities, but also took concrete form

192 UNGA Resolution 289 (IV) (21 November 1949).

193 Serge Krylov, "Les notions principales du droit des gens: la doctrine soviétique du droit international", in 70 *RCADI* 1947-I, 472; Jean Roche, "La souveraineté dans les territoires sous tutelle", 59 *RGDIP* 1954, 167; Georg Dahm, *Völkerrecht*, vol. 1, Stuttgart, 1958, 71 (speaking of *sui generis* subject).

194 Aradanas v. Hogan, United States, District Court, District of Hawaii, 11 and 29 October 1957, 24 *ILR*, 58.

195 See: René Brunet, *La garantie internationale des droits de l'homme*, Geneva, 1947, 127–140.

196 Emphasis added. See *above* Part 3. Chapter 9. Section A.i.

in the Decolonisation *Manifesto*, namely the aforementioned Resolution 1514 (para. 5).[197]

In this respect, it is worth noting the flexibility of the content of the trusteeship agreements compared to the taxonomic rigidity of the mandate system. This is so even if, as we have already had occasion to point out, the implementation agreements differed somewhat from one another in order to take account of local specificities. Unlike the mandate regime, which established a tripartite typology (community, people, territory), the UN trusteeship system is monolithic. In the Charter, no reference is made to the "inadequacy" of the administered peoples, to their inferior "civilisation" or to the colonies.[198]

Another difference lies with Article 84 of the UNC, which provides that the administering authority 'has the duty to ensure that the trust territory shall play its part in the maintenance of international peace and security. To this end the administering authority may make use of volunteer forces,[199] facilities and assistance from the trust territory', as necessary to fulfil its obligations under Chapter VII of the UNC. The requirements of the collective security system prevail over those of the trusteeship regime. The "sacred mission of civilisation" gives way to the supreme value of maintenance and restoration of international peace and security. The difference with the mandate system is obvious here (*supra* Part 3. Chapter 9. Section A.iii). It is the corollary of the establishment of a system of collective security more integrated than that of the LoN.

Under this angle, it is also worth mentioning the distinction introduced by the UNC between strategic and non-strategic areas within the territory under the trusteeship system (arts. 82–83). The definition of these areas was indicated in the Trusteeship Agreement. In the strategic areas, 'all the functions devolved of the United Nations' with regard to the management of the trusteeship institution 'shall be exercised by the Security Council' (Article 83 (1)). On the other hand, these same functions are exercised by the General Assembly in the non-strategic areas (Article 85 para. 1).

197 'The obscure wording of Article 79 will have two consequences for its *application*. On the one hand, it will not favour the extension of the trusteeship regime outside the indispensable renewal of the system of mandates; and it will be by other means that decolonization will be achieved', Henry (1991), 1147 [our translation].

198 See *supra* Part 2. Chapter 6. Section A.i.

199 See the Report (Mr Mendez Octavio) of the Second Committee to the Plenary Session of the United Nations Conference in San Francisco on International Organisation, Vol. II, 264.

On the need for an oversight system, it was stated that: '[t]he authors of the Charter had in mind the same necessity when they organized an International Trusteeship System'[200] and they were clearly inspired by the mandate system. With regard to the control of trusteeship, the Trusteeship Council, the principal organ of the United Nations – unlike the PMC within the LoN system – is given a more extensive role than its predecessor. Whereas the former Organisation's system of control only provided for the examination of annual reports and, thanks to the subsequent modifying practice, written petitions, the trusteeship system goes significantly further. The experience of the LoN was naturally well alive in the minds of the negotiators in San Francisco. The need to add other means of control in addition to the annual report emerged quite quickly. Article 87 (b) of the Charter introduced the right of petition (including oral), while in the next paragraph (c) the power to make "periodic visits to the administered territories" is stipulated for the Trusteeship Council.

All supervisory functions of the trusteeship system are assumed by the General Assembly. It is thus given a leading role, whereas the LoN Assembly had been marginalised. The chapters of the Charter relating to the trusteeship system provide that the main functions – with regard to non-strategic areas – "including the approval of the terms of the trusteeship agreements and of their modification or amendment, shall be exercised by the General Assembly" (Article 85 (1)). Kelsen goes even further and, based on a strictly literal interpretation, observed that the UNGA 'has an important competence with respect to all strategic areas, whereas the Security Council has no competence with respect to non strategic areas'.[201] State and institutional practice in the application of these provisions will not confirm this interpretation, as the Security Council, together with the administering states, clings to a stricter interpretation. Moreover, if one relies on contextual interpretation, one will not fail to notice that, in accordance with Article 83, 'all functions of the United Nations relating to strategic area, including the approval of the terms of trusteeship agreements and of their alteration or amendment, shall be exercised by the Security Council'. Such – exclusive? – of the Security Council in relation to "strategic areas" is corroborated by Article 76.

Within the LoN, the role of the Assembly was downplayed from the outset by the Council and the Mandatories. The Assembly limited itself to moral action through close cooperation with the Secretariat. Its Sixth Committee acted as a bridge between the two bodies. The role of the UN Security Council is less

200 ICJ, International Status of South-West Africa, 136.

201 Kelsen (1950), 624.

extensive than that of the LoN Council, as the former is limited to approving trusteeship agreements, while the latter was vested with the residual power provided for in Article 22 (8).

The most important difference, however, is the prerogative of the UNGA in establishing and accelerating the process of 'autonomy' and 'independence' of the trust territories. Thus, the UNGA is given a role that goes considerably beyond reviewing annual reports, receiving petitions and hearing petitioners. It can assume a more proactive role and adopt initiatives such as inviting the Trusteeship Council to "recommend" that administering states 'the flag of the United Nations to be flown over all Trust Territories, side by side with the flag of the administering Authority, and, where appropriate, the flag of the Administering Territory concerned'.[202] Furthermore, the UNC recognized the authority of the UNGA to modify the terms of the trusteeship agreement and especially to terminate it *with* the consent of the administering authority, in "non-strategic" trusteeship areas.

The right to petition is included in the Charter from the outset, whereas it was not included in the LoN Covenant, although, as we have seen, it has been developed by the subsequent practice of the organs of the League in the application of Article 22. UNC Article 87, lit. b), establishes the right of petitions that the UNGA "receives". The modalities and functioning of the petition were defined in the rules of procedure adopted by the Trusteeship Council at the 22nd meeting of its 1st session (23 April 1947). According to this resolution, petitions, regardless of their form (written or oral), were to be transmitted to the United Nations through the administering Power (as was the case under the LoN régime) or handed over to the UN representatives present in the territory. According to Article 87 (b), the Trusteeship Council (under the authority of the General Assembly) is empowered by the Charter to 'accept petitions and examine them in consultation with the administration authority'. According to the Trusteeship Council's rules of procedure, 'written petitions may be addressed directly to the Secretary-General or may be transmitted to him through the Administrative Authority'.[203]

In the same vein, mention should be made of the procedure for the oral hearing of petitioners and questionnaires. This possibility, unlike the system of Mandates where it was rejected by the Council (see *above* Part 3. Chapter 9. Section A.iv.2), is contemplated by "Rule 88 of the Rules of Procedure", which provides that the Trusteeship Council 'may designate one or more of its

202 UNGA Resolution 325 (IV) (15 November 1949).

203 Rule 80 of the Rules of Procedure, amended 1995 [emphasis added].

representatives to accept oral petitions the subject-matter of which has been previously communicated to the Trusteeship Council and the Administering Authority concerned. Oral petitions and oral presentations may be examined either in public or in private'.[204] Similarly, on-site visits, the admissibility of which was debated at length within the LoN and eventually rejected, are envisaged by the trusteeship system in Articles 91 to 96 of the Rules of Procedure of the Trusteeship Council. Moreover, the trusteeship administration shows another difference from the Mandate system, one that strengthens UN control over the administering Power and reinforces the protection afforded to the indigenous population. We refer to the right of visitation for the benefit of the Trusteeship Council: 'periodic visits to the respective trust territories at times agreed upon with the administration authority' (Article 87 lit. c.).

The control exercised by the UNGA as well as by the Trusteeship Council differs from the LoN system in that it has significantly greater means of intervention. However, under Article 79, the General Assembly can only *approve* the trusteeship agreements, whereas under Article 22 para. 8, the Council of the LoN was empowered to define the content of the mandate if the principal Allied Powers were unable to reach agreement among themselves.[205] It should be noted, however, that at no time did the Council of the LoN avail itself of this important power.

The sanction for non-compliance with the obligations embodied in the trusteeship agreement and in the relevant provisions of the Charter is, according to Kelsen, expulsion under Article 6 of the UNC.[206] In addition, the sanction mechanisms provided for in Chapter VII of the Charter remain applicable.

iii *The Legacy of the Mandate System in the UN Trusteeship Administration*

An authority rightly asserted that '[t]he mandate system will be in law what it will be in fact'.[207] It is thus time to look at its impact on international relations.

The assessment of the mandate institution can hardly be made in absolute terms. It must be done in the context of the colonial experience (retrospective dimension) and from the perspective of the UN trust administration (prospective dimension). The latter has already been discussed above. It is

204 Rule 88 of the Rules of Procedure, amended 1995 [emphasis added].

205 See *supra* Part 3. Chapter 9. Section A.iv.2.

206 Kelsen (1950), 694. Although he hastened to add that 'Nor has the expulsion the effect to divest a state of the legal power it has over a non-self-governing territory referred to in Article 73'.

207 Rolin (1920), 329 [our translation].

therefore appropriate to consider what the mandate of the LoN represented in the historical panorama of the early twentieth century. The LoN mandate, sometimes referred to by the doctrine as the 'colonial mandate', was inspired, as we have seen, by colonial management, especially in the eyes of contemporaries. However, it also had fundamental structural differences from the notion of colonisation. In particular, the purpose – the civilising mission – and the triangular relationship (LoN, territory, Mandatory Power) are in sharp contrast to the colonial institution, not to mention the absence of sovereignty in the hands of the Mandatory. The triangular relationship refers particularly to the control that is supposed to embody it. Control by the LoN, through its various organs, marks a notable difference from the colonial system. In the latter case, responsibility is a chimera, as the Mandatory is almost always judge and party. Internal responsibility vis-à-vis the parliament is in fact non-existent, as abuses are hardly ever brought to the attention of deputies.

The mandate regime is something else entirely. It may have been conceived, at the beginning, as a makeshift compromise between the demands of Britain and France, who wanted to take away Germany's colonies, on the one hand, and the points of President Wilson, who rejected any territorial annexation, on the other (see *above* Part 3. Chapter 9. Section A.i). The PMC is to be commended for the way in which it understood and carried out its task. Thanks to the dedication of its members, who devoted much of their time to the LoN, there were a few Mandatory territories whose government officials felt constantly under the control of world public opinion. Far from relaxing its vigilance, the PMC became increasingly effective. At first, governments preferred to send officials from their central administrations. They knew little about what was going on in other territories. Subsequently, the governors of the Mandatory Territories became accustomed to coming before the PMC themselves to justify their actions. At its first session, the PMC had expressed the wish that the administrators personally responsible should be instructed to come and present the annual report of the Mandatory Powers themselves.

Among the League's organs, the PMC soon assumed particular importance, not only because of the qualities of its members and the greatness of its mission, but also because its sessions became more and more numerous, eventually taking on a quasi-permanent character.[208] Within a few years, membership of the PMC became a real "international public service"; from 1926 onwards, the PMC held at least two annual sessions. The PMC had an extremely

208 This seems to recall, in a related area, the current evolution of the UN Human Rights Council.

conscientious conception of its role. One could have imagined – and some of the mandatory States had hoped for a while – that the PMC would have confined itself to merely acknowledging the reports submitted, accompanying them with a purely formal examination and a few more or less benevolent comments. This is not what the PMC did. It took the reports and demanded that they be explained to it orally by the competent officials of the Mandatory administration concerned. It investigated each report so thoroughly and in such detail that it was truly impossible for anything important to be missed. In this way, the mandate system, which could well have been a hypocritical charade, became one of the important realities of international life at the time. One of its members had hoped that the work of the Commission would gradually produce a set of rules of administration that could be applied to any colonial country.[209]

Certainly, some criticism of the PMC's methods can be made. One may complain that, entrusted with a *sacred trust of civilisation*, it sometimes shrouded itself in secrecy. The diplomatic tone of its communiqués, its emotion in the face of some information that was not even indiscreet, may have seemed to contradict its real function, which was fundamentally to ensure the control of the LoN (but also of public opinion) over the administration in charge. But this is only a matter of form. Moreover, the public could find out exactly what it was doing, alas with delay, through the publication of its reports to the Council and its detailed minutes in the *LoN's Official Journal*.

It is impossible to deny the direct relationship between the trusteeship system and the mandate system. With the benefit of hindsight, it is also possible to show a sort of Ariadne's thread which, from colonisation to independence, passes through the mandate.[210] Indeed, the creation of the Mandates, with the International Community as Mandator, and the purposes they pursued, had an undeniable influence on decolonisation,[211] which would take place a few decades later.[212] The Mandatory Powers administered the mandated territories (formerly colonies of defeated Germany, in Mandates B and C), while exercising sovereignty over their colonies. The simultaneous presence of the same

209 Working Methods of the PMC, PMC, P.V., 5th session (1924), 150.

210 Some prominent authors did not hesitate to designate the mandate of the LoN a 'colonial mandate'.

211 'Article 22 of the pact establishes for the first time the obligations of the white race with respect to the coloured race', *Journal de Genève*, 21 September 1922, 2 [our translation].

212 "The Court is not unaware of the historical evolution of the old colonial systems and the *new conception of colonial affairs as expressed in the Covenant of the League of Nations and now in the Charter of the United Nations*", *Società A.B.C. v. Fontana and Della Rocca*, Italy, Corte di Cassazione (Sezioni riunite), 10 August 1954, 22 *ILR*, 77 [emphasis added].

Sate – as a colonial and Mandatory Power – over different, and sometimes contiguous, territories undoubtedly accelerated the decolonisation process.[213] Indeed, while on the one hand the Mandatory Power had to accompany the population of the territory concerned to independence (especially for type A and B Mandates), on the other hand this same State had no obligation to this aim over its colonial possessions. The resulting asymmetrical situation highlighted the inanity of this duality: the former colonies of the defeated Powers were enabled to take their destiny into their own hands, whereas the colonies of the victors could hardly benefit from this advance of PIL.[214] The former were assisted by the Mandatory Powers on their way to emancipation, while the latter maintained the colonial system in their overseas possessions. This is a glaring inequality that will persist for some decades. Therefore, it is not too much to say that the mandates constitute the first act in the final eviction of the colonial system.[215] As the representative of the British Empire, Lord Balfour, had prophesied before the first Assembly of the LoN: 'What is done in the Mandated territories will unquestionably have its reaction upon those other colonies which are not mandated and over which neither the Council nor the Assembly have the slightest authority'.[216] All the territories placed under the trusteeship regime eventually regained their independence. In other words, with the emancipation of Namibia, the Mandate system has finally achieved the goal set by Article 22 of the Covenant in 1919.

The trusteeship system was not as successful as had been hoped. It did not in all cases prevent the control of the administering power.[217] In this regard – admittedly in the midst of the Cold War – the Soviet Union withdrew from the Trusteeship Committee in January 1950 to express its disagreement with the draft agreement on Somalia.[218] The trusteeship system was soon overtaken by

213 It should be noted that Roden Buxton (British Empire) proposed an extensive application of the Mandate system, of which Art. 22 was to be considered the "general charter of the colonies". This proposal went unheeded.

214 'The granting of 'self-government' or independence to certain colonial possessions with a partly or mainly European population – especially in the Western Hemisphere – was likely to engender the idea that other colonial dependencies might eventually achieve a similar development in turn', Rolin (1920), 11.

215 Mr Malcolm McDonald's speech to the West African Club (9 October 1935) is indicative of the fears that the (British) colonies would be transformed into mandated territories (*Morning Post*, 10 October; see also *Bulletin d'information coloniale*, 5 December 1935, 3). It is paradoxical to learn that such a change of regime would infringe on the freedom of the natives, who would be treated 'as mere property'.

216 1st Assembly, 18 December 1920, 30th plenary meeting, 721.

217 Rodolfo De Nova, *Il Patto della Società delle Nazioni*, Milan, 1945, 74.

218 *UN Doc.* A/C.4/SR.177, 15 November 1950, 219–220.

decolonisation, made possible by the quasi-legislative work of the UNGA, but also by the experience of the mandate system, which had sown the seeds of the right of peoples to self-determination.

What future can we envisage today for the concept of international trusteeship? Can it be conceived for non-viable entities (such as micro-territories), or even for drowning states?[219] Can it be used pending a final settlement of a disputed territorial situation? These questions remain open.

C International Cities and Territories

The phenomenon of internationalised territory, or if one prefers the internationalisation of territories, whatever their regime, is not new. The ancestor is surely the Free City of Krakow established by the Final Declaration of the Congress of Vienna of 9 June 1815. According to this act (Article 6) it was made perpetually neutral, independent and free under the protection of Prussia, Austria and Russia. This "perpetuity", however, only lasted until 1846 when it was annexed by Austria after agreement with the other interested states (without, however, consulting the organs of the City ...).[220]

However, despite the long history of international practice, can we really speak of a single concept and regime, beyond the panoply of (very) different cases; or is it rather a residual definitional category? That is, negative, in the sense that state sovereignty is *denied* or absent?

As in the other sub-sections, we therefore group together here, for the sake of convenience, highly different territorial situations and regimes. However, they are characterised by elements of internationalisation that distinguish them from other categories of territorial regimes studied elsewhere in this book. Given the relatively large number of these phenomena and because of their extreme variety, we will limit ourselves to examining only some of them, classifying them in descending order of internationalisation.

The Free City of Danzig certainly represents the most advanced example of internationalisation, while the regime over the Memel Territory is at the opposite extreme of the spectrum; the International Zone of Tangier, which survives World War II, can be classified somewhere in between. While in the first case there is a genuine Danzig sovereignty, in the second case Lithuania has full sovereignty over the Memel Territory, but its exercise is encumbered by

219 See *supra* Part 2. Chapter 7. Section D.

220 Does the lack of consultation reveal the make-up of a tripartite protectorate? Perhaps. But even in this case it is worth noting that diplomats frequently resort to this legal "fix".

treaty restrictions for the benefit of the German-speaking minority in particular. In the third case, that of Tangier, Moroccan sovereignty is recognised but its exercise is entrusted, again by treaty, to a group of states which thus form a veritable 'coimperium'.[221]

Finally, for the sake of brevity, we will not examine either the case of the Free Territory of Trieste[222] or the internationalisation of the Holy City of

---

221 See *supra* Part 3. Chapter 8. Section D.

222 Under Article 21 para. 1 of the Peace Treaty between Italy and the (Four) Allied Powers (1947), *UNTS*, vol. 49 (n° 747), 'There is hereby constituted the Free Territory of Trieste' whose 'integrity and independence shall be assured by the Security Council of the United Nations'. The establishment of this Territory should have followed the cessation of Italian sovereignty (para. 2); it is interesting to note that, unlike most similar situations, 'The Free Territory of Trieste shall not be considered as ceded territory' by the defeated Power to the Allied Powers (para. 4). In accordance with Annex VI to the 1947 Treaty, a Governor, appointed by the Security Council, would have been responsible for the administration of the Territory and would have exercised his powers as "representative of the Security Council" (Article 17 of the said Annex). To this end, he would have been supported by an Executive and a Legislature but would have been responsible only to the Security Council. He would have had the power to 'overturn' an act of the Legislative Assembly if he considered it to be contrary to the Statute of the Territory. This status would have had to be 'drafted by the Council of Foreign Ministers [of the Four Allied Powers] and approved by the Security Council' (Article 21 para. 3 of the 1947 Treaty). Furthermore, according to Article 24 para. 1 of Annex VI, the Governor would have managed the foreign policy of the City. The same provision – in its paragraph 4 – prohibited 'Economic union or associations of an exclusive character with any State'. This provision is very reminiscent of Article 80 of the Treaty of Versailles of 1919 and its "twin" Article 88 of the Treaty of St. Germain, concerning the inalienable independence of Austria and the obligation of Germany to respect it. To return to the Free Territory of Trieste, due to the tension between the two blocs, it was impossible to appoint a Governor, so that for 7 years Zone A was occupied by the United States and the United Kingdom and Zone B by Yugoslavia. In 1954, in London, the "Memorandum of Understanding regarding the Free Territory of Trieste" (UNTS, vol. 235, n° 3297) was signed, by which, '[o]wing to the fact that it has proved impossible to put into effect the provisions of the Italian Peace Treaty 2 relating to the Free Territory of Trieste' (para. 1), the Parties (i.e., the United States, the United Kingdom, Italy and Yugoslavia) decided that Zone A would be subject to Italian occupation while Zone B remained under Yugoslav occupation. However, it must be emphasised that the legal situation did not really change, in addition to the political awareness of the impossibility of achieving the Free Territory of Trieste as foreseen by the Peace Treaty of 1947. Of course, Italy succeeded the United States and the United Kingdom in administering Zone A, but as the Italian Council of State put it so well in 1961: 'the Memorandum was not an instrument which could technically achieve such an object for the reason, if for no other, that the other signatories of the Treaty of Peace [of 1947] did not participate in the Memorandum' (Società Teatro Puccini v. Commissioner-General of the Government for the Territory of Trieste, 20 December 1961, 40 ILR, 43, 47–48). It was not until the Treaty of Osimo of 10 November 1975 between Italy and Yugoslavia that the issue was definitively buried, rather than resolved. While it is true that this treaty (Article 7) abrogates the

Jerusalem.[223] Both share the same fate in that they never came into being. On another note, it is important to point out that these two cases, as well as that of the Free City of Danzig, can also be studied and used as examples of direct international administration, which will be discussed later. In this respect, they certainly inspired the UNSC when it shaped the transitional regime for Kosovo established by its resolution 1244 (10 June 1999).[224]

i *The Free City of Danzig*

By Article 100 of the Treaty of Versailles, Germany renounces 'all rights and title' over the territories defined by this same provision in favour of the main Allied Powers who, by Article 102, 'undertake to establish the town of Danzig, together with the territory referred to in Article 100, as a Free City. It will be placed under the protection of the League of Nations'.

The articulation between the renunciation by the defeated Germany, the acquisition by the main allied powers and finally the constitution of a new entity is reminiscent of the creation of the LoN Mandates. Yet, the similarity ends there, since we are dealing here with a different situation and regime.

London Memorandum – although here too there is no total identity between the Parties (the United States and the United Kingdom are missing) – there is no mention of the legal regime relating to the Free Territory of Trieste. In the end, the only two issues that are explicitly remediated by the Treaty of Osimo refer to the nationality of the persons living in the two zones and to the delimitation of the land and maritime boundaries (territorial sea and contiguous zone) in the Gulf of Trieste.

223 According to resolution 303 (IV) of 9 December 1949, following the partition resolution of Mandatory Palestine 181 (II), the UNGA 'Decides ... To restate, therefore, its intention that Jerusalem should be placed under a permanent international regime, which should envisage appropriate guarantees for the protection of the Holy Places, both within and outside Jerusalem, and to confirm specifically the following provisions of General Assembly resolution 181 (II): (1) the City of Jerusalem shall be established as a *corpus separatum* under a special international regime and shall be administered by the United Nations' (para. 1). In accordance with this resolution, the Trusteeship Council was charged with preparing a Statute for the City which was then submitted to Jordan and Israel, the occupying powers. Faced with the refusal of these two States to follow up on it, the Trusteeship Council decided – in its resolution of 14 June 1950 – to submit it to the UNGA for approval. However, the UNGA was unable to reach a decision by the required majority (two-thirds of the votes). Subsequently, both states carried out actions that made the implementation of the International City of Jerusalem illusory. For example, Jordan built representative offices for the Hashemite King in East Jerusalem (1960), while Israel started the transfer of its ministries from Tel Aviv to Jerusalem, notably that of Foreign Affairs (in 1952).

224 See *infra* Part 3. Chapter 9. Section C.i.

The "*sui generis* legal status"[225] of the Free City of Danzig and the legal nature of the relationship between it and Poland gave rise to various pronouncements by the ICJ, which examined these issues from different angles, either in advisory opinions or in judgments. Unsurprisingly, the World Court ended up establishing a genuine internationalisation of the Free City of Danzig, thus excluding any possible form of Polish "protectorate" over it. It is true that the former enjoys rights and prerogatives over and in relation to the latter, but even taken together, they do not allow the legal relationship between Poland and the Free City of Danzig to be considered a protectorate, however slight. Moreover, the 1920 Paris Convention, which the Major Allied Powers undertook to negotiate under Article 104 of the Treaty of Versailles between Poland and the Free City of Danzig, is "an international treaty".[226]

In order to disentangle the Free City of Danzig from Poland, Article 103 (1) of the Treaty of Versailles provides for 'A constitution for the Free City of Danzig [to] be drawn up by the duly appointed representatives of the Free City in agreement with a High Commissioner to be appointed by the League of Nations. This constitution shall be placed under the guarantee of the League of Nations'.[227] The High Commissioner had very extensive powers,[228] among which was the power to deal 'in the first instance with all differences arising between Poland and the Free City of Danzig in regard to this Treaty or any arrangements or agreements made thereunder' (art. 103 (2)). Article 39 of the aforementioned 1920 Paris Convention refers to the High Commissioner's power of arbitration, while adding that the High Commissioner, 'if he deems it necessary, shall refer the matter to the Council of the League of Nations'.[229] It should be noted that the Constitution, adopted by the Dantzig Constituent Assembly on 11 August 1920 and approved by the High Commissioner on 14

225 Treatment of Polish Nationals and Other Persons of Polish Origin or Speech in the Danzig Territory, Advisory Opinion of 4 February 1932, *PCIJ Reports*, A/B 44, 23.

226 PCIJ, Jurisdiction of the Courts of Danzig, advisory opinion of 3 March 1928, *PCIJ Reports*, B 15, 17.

227 See: Treatment of Polish nationals and other persons of Polish origin or Speech in the territory of Danzig, 1932, 21–22.

228 The memory of the figure of the High Commissioner of the Free City of Danzig will resound like a powerful echo when the Security Council shaped the status and prerogatives of the High Representative for Kosovo in 1999.

229 These powers went beyond the mere arbitral dimension since they allowed him to "examine himself and independently of the Parties to the dispute, the factual and legal situation, and to clarify and resolve the points at issue", Opinion of Mr Verzijl, annexed to the Memorandum of the Government of the Free City of Danzig, *ICJ Reports*, C 8 (Polish Postal Service in Danzig), 340.

June 1920, could only be amended with the consent of the Council of the League of Nations.[230]

The consequence of placing the Free City of Danzig and its constitution under the guarantee of the League of Nations is that '[a] violation or an erroneous application of the Constitution by Danzig is, therefore, so far as international relations are concerned, a matter solely between the League, as *guarantor*, and Danzig'.[231]

It is true that Poland was responsible, albeit with restrictions, for the foreign relations of the Free City of Danzig:

> It is now common ground between Poland and the Free City that the rights of Poland as regards the conduct of the foreign relations of the Free City are not absolute. The Polish Government is not entitled to impose a policy on the Free City nor to take any step in connection with the foreign relations of the Free City, against its will. On the other hand, the Free City cannot call upon Poland to take any step in connection with the foreign relations of the Free City which are opposed to her own policy.[232]

Similarly, a decision of the Council of the League of Nations of 22 June 1921 entrusted Poland with the task of defending the Free City and maintaining order on its territory if the Dantzig police forces were not able to guarantee this. It should be noted, however, that the question of a Danzigian army, which had been raised in informal talks, was eventually dropped from the negotiations and hence from the Paris Convention. However, according to an authoritative interpretation of the relevant normative texts, "the League of Nations undertakes to respect and maintain against external aggression the territorial integrity and political independence of the Free City of Danzig in the *same manner as it does for all Members of the League of Nations*, under the *terms of Article 10 of the Covenant*".[233]

230 PCIJ, Treatment of Polish Nationals and Other Persons of Polish Origin or Speech in the Territory of Danzig, 1932, 21; PCIJ, Consistency of Certain Danzig Legislative Decrees with the Constitution of the Free City, Advisory Opinion of 4 December 1935, *PCIJ Reports*, A/B 65, 50.

231 PCIJ, Treatment of Polish Nationals and Other Persons of Polish Origin or Speech in the Danzig Territory, 1932, 24 [emphasis added].

232 PCIJ, Free City of Danzig and ILO, advisory opinion of 26 August 1930, *PCIJ Reports*, B 18, 13. Similarly: Pablo Najera (France) v. Mexico, para. 9 (at 483).

233 "Report presented to the Council of the League of Nations by Viscount Ishii", reproduced in: *PCIJ Reports* C 8 (Polish Postal Service in Danzig), 194 [emphasis added].

However, despite diplomatic representation by Poland, this is far from the unilateral relationship that is normally established between a protecting State and a protected state;[234] rather, it is a case of reciprocal obligations and interests ultimately aimed at reconciling or even shaping a concerted foreign policy between Poland and the Free City of Danzig. These are, as the PCIJ put it, limitations on the 'independence of the Free City, they constitute organic limitations which are an essential feature of its political structure'.[235] Furthermore, and in contrast with the traditional Protectorate situation, there is an international *substantive* guarantee[236] of the Free City of Danzig and its constitution. Similarly, the LoN played an institutional role, for example, in the appointment of the High Commissioner of the City (whose powers and competences are similar to those of the UN High Representative in Kosovo). This interpretation of the legal regime governing the relationship between two diverse territorial subjects, a state and a Free City, is confirmed by arbitral jurisprudence:

> The situation is almost identical, in this respect, to that of the citizens of the Free City of Danzig, placed under the diplomatic protection of the Polish Republic, although this small free state is not a protectorate of Poland either.[237]

In other words, the fact that the citizens of the Free City of Danzig were placed under the protection of Poland did not make the latter the protective state of the former. On another level, the fact that, under the terms of the above-mentioned normative texts, Poland was granted customs facilities on the territory of Danzig and "free access to the sea" did not prejudice the independence of the Free City from Poland.[238] Such rights, which can be described as "servitudes", have existed in relations between independent states without their *status being* affected. In the present case, however, its 'independence' is 'restricted

234 Case of Pablo Najera (France) v. Mexico, para. 9 (at 474).

235 PCIJ, Free City of Danzig and ILO, 11.

236 'It is clear that, though the interpretation of the Danzig Constitution is primarily an internal question of the Free City, it may involve the guarantee of the League of Nations as interpreted by the Council and by the Court', PCIJ, Consistency of Certain Danzig Legislative Decrees with the Constitution of the Free City, 1935, 50.

237 Pablo Najero case, 474 [our translation].

238 Access to, or Anchorage in, the port of Danzig, of Polish War Vessels, Advisory Opinion of 11 December 1931, *PCIJ Reports*, A/B 43, 143–144.

and … its external affairs are subject to the action of two authorities: the League of Nations on the one hand, and the Polish Government on the other'.[239]

In the light of the above, was the Free City of Danzig a state? The answer seems to be yes:[240]

- There was a Danzig's nationality (Article 105 of the Treaty of Versailles);[241]
- The Constitution of the Free City 'despite its peculiarities, is and remains the Constitution of a foreign State';[242]
- It was admitted to appear before the PCIJ[243] and was able to appoint an *ad hoc* judge in a contentious case;[244]
- It could become a member of an IO, although Poland could exercise its veto power (ILO);[245]
- The Free City 'has, on the whole, an independent legislative power';[246]
- It was a party to several international treaties, both bilateral and multilateral, which demonstrates and presupposes its capacity to enter into international treaties and it was therefore 'responsible to other States and … entitled to demand the fulfilment of the international obligations which other States [had] towards it';[247]
- The territory of the Free City of Danzig was not under Polish sovereignty.[248]

---

239 Report submitted by the ILO to the 48th session of the Governing Body, *PCIJ Report* C 18-II, 189 (Free City of Danzig and ILO, 1930).

240 "The regime of the Free City corresponds to that of a state governed by the rule of law (*Rechtstaat*)…", Consistency of Certain Danzig Legislative Decrees with the Constitution of the Free City, 1935, 54.

241 'From the entry into force of the present treaty, German nationals domiciled in the territory … shall lose, *ipso facto,* their German nationality, with a view to becoming nationals of the Free City of Danzig'.

242 PCIJ, Treatment of Polish nationals and other persons of Polish origin or Speech in the territory of Danzig, 1932, 24.

243 On 23 June 1922, the PCIJ communicated to all States parties to its Statute the list of States which, although not "members of the League of Nations", could have recourse to it.

244 PCIJ, Access to, or Anchorage in, the port of Danzig, of Polish War Vessels, 1931, 23–24.

245 PCIJ, Free City of Danzig and ILO, 1930, 15.

246 ILO Memorandum, *PCIJ Report* C 18-II, 165 (Free City of Danzig and ILO, 1930).

247 Speech by Mr Kaufmann (Danzig), *PCIJ Report* C 18-II, 22 (Free City of Danzig and ILO, 1930).

248 PCIJ, Access to, or Anchorage in, the port of Danzig, of Polish War Vessels, 1931, 142: 'The port of Danzig is not Polish territory, and therefore the rights claimed by Poland would be exercised in derogation of the rights of the Free City. Such rights must therefore be established on a clear basis'. According to the "Lotus Principle", which this same Court formulated in 1927 in the case of the same name, restrictions on the freedom of states (in this case Danzig) cannot be presumed. It should be noted that this presumption did not apply in the case of the Memel Territory, and in its favour, since it was not a State. The only State concerned was, in the case in point, … Lithuania.

The end of the Free City of Danzig and its legal status is akin to a situation of implicit termination by the subsequent behaviour of the Parties concerned: the dissolution of the LoN, the acquiescence of the other guaranteeing Parties such as the United Kingdom, which after timidly raising objections, tacitly recognised its annexation by Poland. In 1945, when the Cold War was beginning to take shape, no one was prepared to die for the preservation of Danzig's status as a Free City.

ii *The Tangier International Zone*

When the Western powers began to maintain stable and continuous diplomatic relations with the Sultanate of Morocco, their representatives were not allowed to reside permanently at the Cherifian Court in Fez but had to establish their official quarters in Tangier. The future International Zone of Tangier has its historical roots in this prohibition, while a series of Cherifian dahirs (decrees) built its regime.

On 5 November 1914, France, Spain and Great Britain concluded a treaty laying the foundations for an international city administration, followed by a Cherifian dahir (of application) issued on the same day, but due to the outbreak of WWI, this regime never came into being.

The actual internationalisation of the Tangier Zone was established[249] by the Convention of 18 December 1923 between France, Great Britain, and Spain, successively amended by an agreement of 25 July 1928 between the same States and Italy. In the meantime, the original parties to the treaty invited the United States to accede to the 1923 Convention; however, this request was rejected, even though the United States 'expressed a readiness to consider the possibility of suspending its extraterritoriality rights in the Tangier Zone provided certain assurances were given'.[250]

Some salient provisions of the 1923 Convention (as amended by the Agreement of 25 July 1928) are worth mentioning: a) by Article 25, the sovereign rights of the Sultan over the Zone are recognised; b) the permanent demilitarisation and neutralisation[251] of the Zone are established by Article

---

249 It was preceded and prepared by the Act of Algeciras of 7 April 1906 (Article 61), by the French protectorate treaty on Morocco of 30 March 1912, as well as by the Franco-Spanish Treaty on the French protectorate on Morocco, signed the same year, by virtue of which Spain was recognised as having three zones of influence, in the North, in the South, and around Ifni, in accordance with a secret agreement concluded as early as 3 November 1904 (*RGDIP*, 1912, documents, 18 ff.).

250 *Hackworth*, vol. 1, 94–95.

251 On the meaning of neutralisation and demilitarisation, see *supra* Part 3. Chapter 8. Section H.i and Part 3. Chapter 8. Section H.ii.

3;[252] c) the most extensive legislative and administrative powers are conferred by the Cherifian authority on the administering powers (Article 5);[253] d) by virtue of the Franco-Moroccan protectorate treaty, France protects the interests of Moroccan nationals of the Zone who are abroad (Article 6); e) freedom of religion is guaranteed (Articles 11 and 26); f) the abrogation of the Capitulations following the establishment of the Mixed Courts (Articles 25 and 29); g) economic and fiscal equality or the "open door regime".

The institutional architecture of the Zone's regime consisted of: a) a Legislative Assembly, composed of the Sultan's representative (*Mendoub*), who presided over it, and thirty members representing the foreign and indigenous communities of the Zone;[254] b) an Administrator, appointed by the Control Committee, who exercised executive power and had an international police force at his disposal; c) a Control Committee, composed of eight members, in charge of ensuring the respect of the Statute of the Zone and of economic equality; d) Mixed Courts in charge of the administration of justice towards foreigners.[255]

On 15 June 1940, Spain occupied the Zone, invoking the need to preserve its neutrality as the other Contracting Parties were engaged in WWII. The modus vivendi that had been in place since then[256] did not last very long, however, as on 4 November 1940, Spain unilaterally abrogated the regime and annexed the Zone to its protectorate over Morocco.[257]

At the Potsdam Conference (17 July–2 August 1945), the heads of government of the Soviet Union, the United States and Great Britain decided that the Zone 'which includes the City of Tangier and the area adjacent to it, in view of its special strategic importance, shall remain international'.[258] One cannot help but note in this regard that this decision was taken without the consent of

---

252 Exception made for the right of passage of French and Spanish troops.

253 Exception made for diplomatic matters reserved to France by virtue of Article V of the Franco-Moroccan protectorate treaty of 1912. It is important to note in passing that the International Zone of Tangier must be placed in the more general context of the French protectorate over Morocco (see *supra* Part 3. Chapter 8. Section G).

254 It is important to note that this body exercised its legislative powers by mandate of the Sultan.

255 These mixed courts were reorganised by the Convention of 10 November 1952.

256 Digest of International Law, vol. 1, 595–596.

257 Joyce AC Gutteridge, 'The Dissolution of the International Regime in Tangier', 33 *BYIL* 1957, 296.

258 Digest of International Law, vol. 1, 596.

the other three Parties to the 1923 Convention (France, Italy and Spain),[259] to which, conversely, the United States was not a party.[260]

A few days later (31 August 1945) a treaty was concluded between Great Britain and France – annexed to the Final Act of the Conference – which provided for the temporary re-establishment of the international administration of the Area in accordance with the 1923 Convention, pending the holding of an international conference for the final settlement of the question.

This treaty also officially ended the Spanish occupation by 'requesting' the Spanish government to 'hand over to the Committee of Control the administration of the Zone and the archives of the administration'.[261] Here again, one cannot help but observe that since this treaty was not binding on Spain, it was not bound by its stipulations (*res inter alios acta*) and yet it performed the obligation. The latter could therefore be constructed as a collateral agreement within the meaning of Article 35 VCLT 1969.

This situation lasted for less than 5 years. On 2 March 1956, negotiations between France and Morocco resulted in a joint declaration (with attached Protocol) in which the two contracting parties, having taken note of "the evolution achieved by Morocco on the path of progress", concluded that

> The Treaty of Fez of 30 March 1912 [establishing the French protectorate over Morocco] no longer corresponds to the needs of modern life and can no longer govern Franco-Moroccan relations.[262]

At the same time, France recognised Morocco's independence and affirmed 'its will to respect and ensure respect for the integrity of Moroccan territory, guaranteed by international treaties'.[263] This joint declaration was followed by a declaration (of 7 April 1956) of similar content between Spain and Morocco (regarding the three zones of Spanish influence over Morocco).

While these two joint declarations put an end to both the French protectorate over Morocco and the three zones of Spanish influence, the Tangier International Zone continued to exist.

259 The former was considered a minor partner, the latter a defeated power, the latter having remained neutral during the Second World War. As for Italy, it should be noted that it had given its agreement under Article 41 of the 1947 Peace Treaty.

260 See *supra* Part 2. Chapter 5. Section B.ii.

261 Digest of International Law, vol. 1, 597.

262 https://mjp.univ-perp.fr/constit/ma1956.htm#D%25E9claration_commune_franco-marocaine_du_ [our translation].

263 *Ibid.*

Finally, an international conference was convened in Tangiers by the Sultan of Morocco from 8 to 29 October 1956 'with a view to settling the questions raised by the abrogation of the special regime of the Tangier zone'.[264] The Final Declaration, adopted by the participating states,[265] a) enshrined "the principles of the independence of Morocco and the unity and integrity of its territory"; b) recognised "the abolition of the international regime of the Tangier Zone"; c) the recovery by the Sultan of "all his powers and competences [in the Zone], which shall henceforth be under his entire and sole exclusive sovereignty".

Finally, the International Zone of Tangier can be equated to the "International Settlement of Shanghai" (1845–1944),[266] i.e., an extension and *institutionalization* of the regime of capitulations (inaugurated by France and the Ottoman Empire in 1526). In the case of the International Zone of Tangiers, it constitutes an internationalisation, shouldered by an international administration, of the open-door regime that once prevailed throughout Morocco.

iii *The Memel Territory*

This territorial situation is, as mentioned above, at the opposite end of the spectrum from the Free City of Danzig;[267] however, they both share the same founding act, namely the Treaty of Versailles. This is the territory of Memel (Lithuanian: "Klaipėda"), which until 1919[268] belonged to East Prussia and which Germany ceded to the main Allied Powers by virtue of this treaty. Again, certain German interests – rather the interests of the predominantly German-speaking inhabitants – in the territory had to be reconciled with those of Lithuania, under whose sovereignty it would eventually fall. By Article 99,

> Germany renounces in favour of the Principal Allied and Associated Powers all rights and title over the territories included between the Baltic, the north-eastern frontier of East Prussia as defined in Article 28 of Part II (Boundaries of Germany) of the present Treaty and the former frontier

264 Preamble to the Final Declaration, 29 October 1956, *UNTS*, vol. 263, 166.

265 These are: Belgium, France, Italy, Morocco, the Netherlands, Portugal, Spain, the United Kingdom and the United States.

266 See CF Fraser, "The Status of the International Settlement at Shanghai", 21 *Journal of Comparative Legislation and International Law* 1939, 38–53.

267 Indeed, when in the summer of 1922, rumours spread that the Special Commission for the revision of the status of the Memel Territory had considered transforming it into a Free City like Danzig, the ethnic Lithuanian inhabitants of the region formed an insurrectionary government in collusion with Lithuania, chaired by Mr Simonaitis.

268 On 23 March 1938, the German Reich passed a law for the annexation of the Memel Territory, thus signifying the extinction of the regime associated with it until then.

> between Germany and Russia. Germany undertakes to accept the settlement made by the Principal Allied and Associated Powers in regard to these territories, particularly in so far as concerns the nationality of the inhabitants.

By a mechanism similar to that of the Free City of Danzig and, *mutatis mutandis*, to the Mandates of League of Nations, the territory of Memel was ceded – after a period of international administration – by the major Allied Powers to Lithuania, but *subject to* restrictions relating, inter alia, to the nationality of the inhabitants,[269] formerly German, and to the benefit of the inhabitants of this territory. In other words, the cession of the Memel territory was subject to Lithuania's acceptance of all the clauses contained in a notification which the (five) principal Allied and Associated Powers made to the Lithuanian Government, and which were finally enshrined in the Paris Convention of 8 May 1924 concluded with Lithuania, Annex I of which contains the "Statute of the Memel Territory".[270]

Like the Free City of Danzig, therefore, the Treaty of Versailles envisaged, albeit implicitly, the conclusion of a convention implementing the provision on the Memel Territory.[271] This treaty not only defined the new substantive law regime governing the Territory but, even more importantly, laid down the institutional architecture embodying its autonomy[272] within the Lithuanian legal order. At the top of this structure was the Governor appointed by the President of Lithuania,[273] and then the Directorate, which according to Article 17 of the "Statute of the Memel Territory", exercised executive power.[274] While it is true that '[t]he right of initiating legislation shall belon equally to the Chamber of

---

269 See Article 6 of the Paris Convention of 1924. Similarly: Case between Germany and Lithuania concerning the nationality of various persons (Germany v. Lithuania), Arbitral Award of 10 August 1937, *RIAA*, vol. III, 1751.

270 *LNTS*, vol. 29 (1924), 86–106.

271 *LNTS*, vol. 29 (1924), 95–106. Pursuant to the above-mentioned Convention, Lithuania adopted the Statute on the Memel Territory. Germany did the same by the law of 20 February 1925 "for the implementation of Articles 8 and 10" of the 1924 Convention. Lithuania, by virtue of Article 6, succeeded pro rata to the debts of the German State in respect of the Memel Territory.

272 The preamble to the Memel Territory Statute states in its first paragraph that '[r]ealising the wisdom of granting autonomy to the Memel Territory and *of preserving the traditional rights and culture of its inhabitants*' [emphasis added].

273 Article 2 of the Statute of the Memel Territory (see *supra* note 271).

274 The President was appointed by the Governor, who in turn, as we have seen, was appointed by the President of Lithuania. In contrast to the situation in the Free City of Danzig, there is an unequivocable power of control of Lithuania over the Memel Territory.

Representatives and to the Directorate' (Article 18 of the Statute), it is also true that the Governor had the "right to veto laws passed" by these two bodies, 'if these laws exceed[ed] the competence of the authorities of the Territory as laid down by the present Statute, or if they [were] incompatible with the provisions of Article 6 or with the international obligations of Lithuania':[275]

> When, under the Convention of Paris, these four Powers transferred to Lithuania all the rights and title acquired by them from Germany, under Article 99 of the Treaty of Versailles, over the Memel Territory, and Lithuania undertook to secure to that Territory autonomy within the limits fixed by the Statute of Memel, it certainly was not the intention of the Parties to the Convention that the sovereignty should be divided between two bodies which were to exist side by side in the same territory. Their intention was simply to ensure to the transferred territory a wide measure of legislative, judicial, administrative and financial decentralization which should not disturb the unity of the Lithuanian State and should operate within the framework of Lithuanian sovereignty.[276]

The subject matter of the dispute in the present case was the conclusion of a trade agreement between Germany and the Memel Territory Board. *Mutatis mutandis*, the political issues at stake were akin to those raised by the Austro-German Customs Regime case, in that the commercial aspects *concealed* political implications which the legal texts governing the Territory were intended to avoid, i.e., Germany's control over the territory it had ceded under the Treaty of Versailles.

Indeed, as the PCIJ was keen to observe, the Territory's autonomy, while not insignificant, was hardly complete; for example, the Governor had the power of veto over the Territory's internal laws (Articles 2 and 16) as well as the power to appoint the executive, whose nominees, however, had to be confirmed by the Legislature.

With regard to foreign relations, and unlike the future (and unrealised) Territory of Trieste, it was, according to Article 7 of the Statute of the Memel Territory, are 'within the exclusive jurisdiction of the Lithuanian Republic'.[277]

---

275 Article 16 of the Statute of the Memel Territory [emphasis added].

276 PCIJ, Interpretation of the Statute of the Memel Territory (United Kingdom, France, Italy and Japan v. Lithuania), judgment of 11 August 1932: *PCIJ Reports* A/B 49, 313. See also Article 1 of the Statute of the Memel Territory (see *supra* note 271) as well as Article 2 of the Paris Convention of 1924.

277 Ibid., 325. This is indirectly corroborated by Article 9 (1) of the Statute of the Memel Territory, according to which the citizens of Memel enjoyed 'throughout Lithuanian

The conduct of foreign relations by a territorial entity is certainly a regalian prerogative, and if its exercise can be entrusted to a state, as in the case of the protectorate, it is necessary that this entity possesses the title, which is not the case for the territory of Memel. This proves that Article 99 of the Treaty of Versailles, as well as other international and internal acts, was only intended to establish internal autonomy without affecting Lithuanian governmental authority in its external dimension. This was corroborated by the fact that, according to Article 34 of the Statute of the Memel Territory, contained in the said Convention, in '[t]he passports [issued] by the Directorate of the Territory shall be mentioned both the Lithuanian nationality of the bearer and his status as a citizen of the Memel Territory'.[278] Thus, unlike the Free City of Danzig, there was no nationality of the territory of Memel.

On another note, the Conference of Ambassadors of the Major Powers and Allies decided on 11 March 1920 that the Memel Territory should have its own flag "to facilitate the navigation of the Memel Territory's nationals by river and sea".[279]

It is therefore not incorrect to say that the (unfree) territory of Memel is an example of strong local autonomy[280] – guaranteed by international treaties (which also give the Main Allied Powers an interest in acting) – within the sovereignty of a state. It is therefore not a question of an *internationalised* territory – as was the case with Danzig and Trieste – but rather, let us repeat, of an international guarantee of local autonomy without prejudice to Lithuania's sovereignty. It is in this sense that the statements of the PCIJ referring to Article 1 of the Statute of the Memel Territory stating the "sovereignty of Lithuania"[281] should be interpreted.

territory all the recognized civil rights enjoyed by the *other nationals* of Lithuania' [emphasis added].

278 Conversely, Article 11 of the Convention provided for the protection of minorities living in the Memel Territory. In this connection, the Lithuanian Government had made a declaration before the Council of the LoN in which it undertook to do so.

279 In: *Prassi italiana*, 3rd series, vol. 5, para. 1287, 2877.

280 PCIJ, Interpretation of the Statute of the Memel Territory, 1932, 314. See also Article 5 of the Statute of the Memel Territory, which details the powers which 'shall be within the competence of the local authorities of the Memel Territory', including the maintenance of order by the local police. It is important to stress that the exercise of these powers by the local authorities 'shall conform the principles of the Lithuanian Constitution', 'in the absence of provisions to the contrary in the present Statute' (Article 6 of the Statute).

281 *Loc. cit.*

CHAPTER 10

The Direct International Administration of Territories

At the outset, two words must be spent on the qualifier "direct". They enable us to distinguish the situation currently under consideration from those in which one or more States administer a territory under the supervision – with varying degrees of control – of a competent international organisation. This latter situation includes: a) the mandating administration (LoN); b) the trusteeship administration (UN). Situations that could be described as *indirect* international administration and which we have already reviewed.[1]

Neither do the Free Cities, such as Danzig, which, while under the guarantee of the League of Nations (Articles 47–49 of the 1919 Treaty of Versailles),[2] were administered by the local authorities (albeit under the supervision of the League of Nations), nor the International Zone of Tangiers, whose administration was entrusted to an assembly made up of representatives of states outside any international organisation. Moreover, as we shall see, international cities, including those that never came into being, such as Trieste and Jerusalem, were intended to last in time, whereas in all the cases examined here it is a question of a provisional solution in the context of the maintenance and restoration of international peace and security. This is an element of differentiation whose importance cannot be downplayed.

In the various scenarios we are considering here, it is an international organisation that administers a territory directly, i.e., through its organs. In other words, a further step in the internationalisation of administration is taken by the absence of a State in the wielding of the administration, respectively the Mandatory Power (within the LoN system) and the authority in charge of the trusteeship administration (within the UN system). Accordingly, the element that differentiates these two categories (direct and indirect) lies in the direct exercise by the competent international organisation of the administrative function.

Moreover, this distinctive feature likewise excludes situations in which a group of states – without a mandate from an international

1 See *supra* Part 3. Chapter 9.

2 See *supra* Part 3. Chapter 9. Section C.i.

 | DOI:10.1163/9789004708594_013

organisation – administers a territory. While this scenario is difficult to envisage at present, precisely because of the existence of these competences and powers at the UN,[3] in particular, this could be achieved in the past through de facto international organisations ("de facto international governments") having granted themselves power over territories (notably before 1919 and 1945 respectively).[4]

In this specific case within the broader category of territorial redistribution or planning, it was not uncommon for the Great Powers to entrust the administration of a territory or a country to a state or even to exercise this administration directly. In the first case, this was referred to as *indirect* international administration, which could take the form of a protectorate,[5] while in the second case it was a *direct* international administration.[6] It is curious, but not surprising, to observe that this duality has been reproduced in both the LoN and the UN, i.e., this binary system between *indirect* international administration (Mandates and Trusteeship Administration) and *direct administration,* of which we shall examine here a few examples.

But before doing so, it is important to stress that all these forms of direct international administration – like *indirect ones* – are characterised by being temporary.[7] This feature is also in their genes and reflects the aims of this administration, which are to accompany the country concerned to independence or to resolve or even prevent an armed conflict without prejudging the final solution as to its status.

A Within the League of Nations

i *The Saar Territory Governing Commission and Its Sequel after WWII*

The settlement of the Saar question after WWI summarises some of the aspects of the international law of territory that we have hitherto discussed. Under Article 45 of the Treaty of Versailles, France obtains '[a]s compensation for

3 The principle of the sovereign equality of States, enshrined in Article 2(1) of the UNC, and its corollary, the principle of non-intervention in the internal affairs of a State, are also obstacles to the legality of this practice today.

4 See *supra* Part 2. Chapter 5. Section B.

5 As was the case with the historical example discussed above of the British protectorate over the Ionian Islands.

6 One example is the unprecedented experiment of the "International Government of Crete" between 1897 and 1913, established by the Treaty of Constantinople of 4 December 1897. See *supra* Part 2. Chapter 5. Section B.i.

7 See *infra* note 14.

the destruction of the coal-mines in the north of France … full and absolute possession … of the coal mines situated in the Saar basin'. At the same time Germany "renounces, in favour of the League of Nations, in the capacity of trustee, the government" of the Saar territory (Article 49). We have three legal persons which are holders of rights of different nature and content: France enjoys the possession (and the "fruits" therefrom)[8] of the Saar Territory, which remains under German sovereignty but whose exercise is entrusted to the League of Nations:

> [T]he powers of government over the Saar Territory passed from the German Reich and the States of Prussia and Bavaria, for the period of duration of the Statute, to the Governing Commission of the Saar Territory.[9]

The detachment of the Saarland and the creation of a direct international administration can be compared, in terms of purpose, to the peaceful occupation of territories as a pledge.[10] In this case, it was an occupation that enabled France to ensure that the war damage suffered during WWI was fully repaired by Germany. More concretely, by taking advantage of the coal resources in the Saarland, France provides for the fulfilment of this obligation on the part of Germany.

Two elements allow us to distinguish between direct and indirect administration of territories: under the régime of Mandates, (a) the defeated Powers renounce in favour of the Allied Powers and (b) the trustee is the Mandatory. Here, Germany retains naked sovereignty (*ius nudum*),[11] unlike its former colonies, and its exercise is not assigned to a state under international control but *directly* to an organ of an international organisation.

Paragraphs 16–33 of the Annex to Article 50 of the Treaty of Versailles assign the administration of the Saar to the LoN for a *transitional period of* fifteen years, until a plebiscite is held to decide the fate of this territory: i) to reintegrate Germany in the exercise of its sovereignty; ii) to transfer the territory to France; iii) to maintain the international administration.

Under the terms of the Treaty of Versailles, the exercise of this administration fell to the "Special Commission", composed of five members (one

8 See *supra* Part 3. Chapter 8. Section A.i.

9 Pensions of Officials of the Saar Territory, arbitral award of 4 September 1934, *RIAA*, vol. 3, 1557.

10 See *supra* Part 3. Chapter 8. Section F.

11 In Re Kremer, decision of the Council of State (France) of 12 June 1936, 8 *ILR* 142.

Frenchman, one non-Frenchman from the Saarland and living there, three nationals of states other than France and Germany), appointed with an annual mandate by the Council, which also decided on its president, whom para. 18 (of the aforementioned Annex) described as the "executive of the Commission". The Council examined the reports produced by the Commission. According to para. 19, the latter would exercise "all the powers of government hitherto belonging to the German Empire, Prussia or Bavaria", including, therefore, the three powers of the state: legislative, executive and judicial; indeed, according to para. 25, 'Justice will be rendered in the name of the Governing Commission'.

With regard to foreign relations, it should be noted that the Saar Territory Governing Commission had limited powers in foreign affairs, including membership of the UPU.

Even more interestingly, in accordance with para. 33, the Commission was vested with the power to settle disputes between France and Germany on the interpretation of its powers, imposing its decision on both States. This clearly shows the international character of the exercise of governmental functions, and even their supranationality in relation to Germany, in particular (as holder of naked sovereignty), and France. These powers of the Commission are not unlike those of the High Commissioner of the Free City of Danzig, *mutatis mutandis.*

On another note, the Council of the LoN decided to create a neutral international force to maintain order in the Saarland during the plebiscite period (late 1934-early 1935).

Through the plebiscite, the inhabitants of the Saar Territory eventually chose by an overwhelming majority to join Germany. Consequently, on 28 February 1935, the Commission, because of the decision of the Council of the LoN (by which it had taken note of the plebiscite results), transferred its powers to it, which the Council, in turn, transferred to Germany the following day. Thus, the double divorce, between sovereignty and its exercise (by LoN), and between sovereignty and possession (by France) ended by Germany's absorption of the *exercitium iuris* and enjoyment of the "fruits" of its sovereignty over the Saar Territory.

After WWII, Germany and Austria were subjected to military occupation by the Four Allied Powers. In 1947, part of the territory of Saarland, which was under French occupation as the sixth Land of the FRG, was detached from Germany and established as an autonomous entity under French protectorate on 15 December 1947. Article 60 of the constitution of the "Saarland State", drawn up by a Landtag elected on 5 October 1947, read as follows

> Saarland is an autonomously organised, democratic and social, and economic territory attached to France.

The Basic Law of the Saarland was supplemented by no less than eleven additional agreements concluded in 1950 and finally amended in 1953. The inhabitants of this part of the Saarland acquired a new nationality, separate from the two countries concerned, and this area enjoyed legislative, administrative and judicial autonomy under the general agreement.

France, represented firstly by a High Commissioner and then by an ambassador, was vested with the defence of the territory and the management of its foreign relations. The Saarland was able to participate in several multilateral treaties, including the European Convention on Human Rights of 1950. The admission of the Saarland to the Council of Europe on 20 July 1950 preceded its membership.

Although the status of the Saar zone could in some respects be equated with that of a real union with France, or even a protectorate,[12] its precise definition was never the subject of international treaty regulation. In order to clarify its international status, we must thus turn to international practice.

By virtue of the plebiscite of 23 October 1955 – under the terms of the Franco-German agreement of 23 October 1954 – the inhabitants of the Saarland rejected the "Saar Statute", which was the result of Franco-German negotiations. This Statute provided for the "internationalisation of the political management of the territory at the level of Western Europe" on the one hand and "the maintenance of the Franco-Saarland economic union" on the other.[13] Finally, on 27 October 1956, France and Germany concluded a series of agreements aimed, among other things, at returning this zone to German sovereignty on 1er January 1957. It can be said that the creation of the ECSC ("European Coal and Steel Community") in 1952 and subsequently of EURATOM (1958) and above all the EEC in 1957 not only met French requirements in the energy field but also made such a legal regime in the Saarland inconceivable or even unbearable.

However, if the status of the Saarland in the inter-war period illustrates a form of indirect international administration,[14] the status after WWII is more

12 The genesis of the relationship is, however, somewhat unusual, since it is a trilateral relationship, whereas an international protectorate presupposes two sovereign States (see Part 3. Chapter 8. Section G. *above*).

13 Marcel Merle, "L'accord franco-allemand du 23 octobre 1954 sur le statut de la Sarre", 1 *AFDI* 1955, 129 [our translation].

14 But not a State, of course, as Kaufmann states in his Reply submitted to the PCIJ in the case concerning the Free City of Danzig and the ILO, *PCIJ Reports*, C 18-II, 94: 'I have

like an international zone or city, not dissimilar to the Free City of Danzig, but with much more power from France than from Poland and therefore less emancipation of the Saarland from the Free City of Danzig.

Obviously, the major difference was the treaty instrument establishing this regime; whereas in all the cases hitherto reviewed, the settlement was indeed enshrined in a multilateral convention, here it is a bilateral treaty pending a general peace treaty. France's security needs and interests in the region's mining basins took precedence over any other security and collective interest considerations. This is a far cry from the Free City of Danzig, the International Zone of Tangier, the territory of Memel and other territorial regimes, or the 'European interest' and 'objective Law' of the Åland Islands.

ii *The Leticia Administration Commission (1933–1934)*

The second example of direct international administration by the League of Nations that we would like to briefly discuss here is that of the 'District of Leticia', a slice of Amazonian Forest, populated – during the period in question – by less than a thousand people, of whom about two hundred lived in the small town of the same name. This ingenious solution of temporary international administration was invented by the LoN to avoid a new conflict between Colombia and Peru.[15]

Indeed, following the occupation of this territory by a group of Peruvian private individuals from the neighbouring districts, the LoN had to adjudicate between the Colombian claim to take back the territory and the Peruvian claim to challenge the validity of the 1922 delimitation treaty, under which Colombian sovereignty over the Leticia district had been established.[16]

The proposal of the Council, which was seized of the matter by Colombia under Article 15 of the LoN Covenant, provided for the establishment of a Commission of the Society to administer the territory which Peruvian forces had subsequently occupied, although it had not initially recognised the action of its nationals. This proposal was accepted by Colombia but rejected by Peru. Finally, the Council succeeded in obtaining an agreement between the two states (on 25 May 1933 in Geneva) on the basis of which a Commission (appointed by the LoN Council) 'in the name of the Government of Colombia,

---

heard, not without some surprise, a certain comparison of the extraordinary status of the Saar Basin, which was conceived for a transitional period of fifteen years, with the status of the Free City [of Danzig]. The Saarland ... is not a state'.

15 On the territorial dispute between these two states, see *Hackworth*, vol. 1, 752–754.

16 The Salomon-Lozano Treaty of 24 March 1922, signed in Lima, *roughly* establishes the thalweg of the Putumayo River as the border between Colombia and Peru (Article 1).

shall take charge of the administration of the territory [of Leticia] evacuated by the Peruvian forces' (2). To do so, it was invested with all the necessary powers. In order to maintain order, it 'shall call upon military forces of its own selection, and may attach to itself any other elements as it may deem necessary' (3).[17] In fact, it resorted only to the Colombian armed forces as international forces. The Commission was constituted on 19 June 1933 and composed of three members: American, Brazilian and Spanish (the first two being nationals of non-LoN member states). They divided the administration into sectors: order and security, public works and hygiene, and the examination and evaluation of claims concerning the property lost by the inhabitants of the district during the events of September 1932.

The practice of the Commission shows, even more than the text of the 1933 agreement, that it sought and succeeded in gaining substantial autonomy from the two States, especially from Colombia, and, like the Saarland Special Commission, presented reports to the Council.

The period of international and transitional administration ended with the treaty concluded between the two States in Rio de Janeiro on 24 May 1934, by which, among other things, the Commission transferred the administration of the district to the Colombian authorities on 19 June according to the indications received by the Council of the LoN

B Direct International Administration by the UN: a Very Brief Sampling

UN's practice of direct international administration of territories, which is still unrelenting today, is certainly richer, although it is undeniable that, especially at the beginning, it drew inspiration from that of its predecessor with a view to broadening and fleshing it out. The aims and characteristics are therefore *more or less the same*, especially their temporary nature, as the IDI has rightly pointed out:

> powers of public authority must be returned as soon as possible to the population or people concerned in order to be exercised within the framework of a State respecting democratic principles, the rule of law and human rights.[18]

17 *LNTS*, Vol. 138, n° 3192, 255.

18 Article 3 para. 5 of the IDI Resolution on International Administration (2021), https://www.idi-iil.org/app/uploads/2021/09/2021_online_13_en.pdf.

Leaving aside the otherwise unsuccessful attempts at establishing international cities, such as Trieste and Jerusalem, for the reasons explained above, several examples can be listed in chronological order. It should be noted that in most cases the genesis and status of the administration is decided by the Security Council under Chapter VII of the UNC, while in some cases an international treaty between the parties concerned is the constitutive act.[19]

In this necessarily succinct sampling, it is worth mentioning, first of all, West New Guinea, also known as West Irian Jaya, where administration by the UNTEA ("United Nations Temporary Executive Authority") was provided for by the New York Agreement of 15 August 1962 between the Netherlands, a former colonial power, and Indonesia (its former colony), a newly independent state. Under its Article V, an Administrator, appointed by the Secretary-General, was vested with "full authority to administer the territory" under the direction of the Secretary-General, while security was guaranteed by the United Nations Security Force in West New Guinea (UNSF).

International administration ended with the exercise of the right to self-determination by the people of Irian Jaya, and its incorporation as a province by Indonesia.

Mention should also be made, in passing, of the Council for Namibia, which was established by the UNGA through its resolution 2248 (S-V) of 19 May 1967. However, due to South African opposition, its members were never allowed to enter Namibian territory and perform their functions. This obvious lack of effectiveness was, however, compensated for by the Council's acts of multilateral diplomacy, acting on behalf of the Namibian people. Among these representations made by the Council, one cannot leave unnoticed its participation at diplomatic conferences such as those leading to the 1969 VCLT (1968–1969) and the VCSS 1978 (1977–1978). It is safe to say that through its activity in the international legal arena in support of SWAPO (the Namibian people's national liberation movement), the Council contributed to strengthening the right to self-determination of the Namibian people and thereby to undermining the illegal effectiveness of the South African occupation.[20]

Less fortunate, at least to date, has been the work of MINURSO in Western Sahara.[21] The Security Council gave the Special Representative all the necessary powers to organise and manage the referendum according to UNGA Resolution

19 Article 4 of the IDI Resolution on International Administration (2021), https://www.idi-iil.org/app/uploads/2021/09/2021_online_13_en.pdf.

20 See *supra* Part 2. Chapter 6. Section A.

21 United Nations Mission for the Referendum in Western Sahara (established by Security Council Res. 690 (29 April 1991)).

1514 (Principle VII (a) and ICJ's 1975 Advisory opinion). The referendum has still not taken place to this day … and one cannot really speak of an international administration of the territory, as the territory is under Moroccan military occupation.[22]

In Cambodia, UNTAC (1992–1993)[23] was entrusted, again by the Security Council, with direct control of those parts of the Cambodian administration that could influence the conduct of the post-conflict elections as a central element of the overall settlement in that country.

In Croatia, the UNTAES (1996–1998)[24] was established by Resolution 1037 (15 January 1996) following the "Dayton Peace Accords" eventually signed in Paris on 14 December 1995. The Security Council thus acceded to the request of the various parties to establish a provisional administration with the power to "govern" these parts of Croatian territory. It was technically defined as a peacekeeping operation and included a civilian and a military component, both under the "overall authority" of an interim administrator who also had the legislative function. It was extended once and ended in 1998.

No list of direct international administrations by the UN could fail to mention Kosovo, whose international juridical status has been dealt with in this volume from several angles, to which we refer the reader to add further tesserae to this complex mosaic. UNMIK ("United Nations Mission in Kosovo"), established by Resolution 1244 (10 June 1999), is undoubtedly the most advanced example to date of direct international administration by the UN. Like UNTAES, it comprised both a civilian and military component.[25] Moreover, the practice of the

22 See *supra* Part 2, Chapter 6. Section A.ii.

23 United Nations Transitional Authority in Cambodia.

24 United Nations Transitional Administration for Eastern Slavonia, Baranja and Western Sirmium.

25 By its resolution 1244, the Security Council 'Decides on the deployment in Kosovo, under United Nations auspices, of international civil and security presences, with appropriate equipment and personnel as required, and welcomes the agreement of the Federal Republic of Yugoslavia to such presences (5); […] 10. 'Authorizes the Secretary-General, with the assistance of relevant international organizations, to establish an international civil presence in Kosovo in order to provide an interim administration for Kosovo under which the people of Kosovo can enjoy substantial autonomy within the Federal Republic of Yugoslavia, and which will provide transitional administration while establishing and overseeing the development of provisional democratic self-governing institutions to ensure conditions for a peaceful and normal life for all inhabitants of Kosovo;'. Its Annex II adds an additional brick to the institutional scaffolding of direct international administration in that it provides for the 'Establishment of an interim administration for Kosovo as a part of the international civil presence under which the people of Kosovo can enjoy substantial autonomy within the Federal Republic of Yugoslavia, to be decided by the Security Council of the United Nations. The interim administration to provide

Special Representative as a "proconsul" of the Security Council, together with the acquiescence of the latter, allowed him to assume, with the 1st Regulations adopted by UNMIK (1999/1), very extensive powers of direct administration despite Belgrade's opposition. Section 1.1. of the Regulation provides: "All legislative and executive authority with respect to Kosovo, including the administration of the judiciary is vested in UNMIK and is exercised by the Special Representative of the Secretary General".[26]

UNMIK administered Kosovo for nine years until the declaration of independence on 17 February 2008. The Security Council, divided due to the opposition by Russia and China, failed to adopt a resolution taking into account both this declaration and the 117 international recognitions that have heretofore followed. However, the UN Secretary General, overcoming the Security Council's blockage, downgraded UNMIK's powers and tasks to the promotion of security, stability and respect for human rights in Kosovo. It is clear that there is no longer any international, let alone direct, UN administration of the territory.

Finally, we have to mention Timor-Leste, in many ways a *success story* of direct international administration. On 5 May 1999, Portugal and Indonesia concluded an "Agreement between the Republic of Indonesia and the Portuguese Republic on the question of East Timor"[27] and stipulated two others with the Secretary General on the modalities of holding a referendum in the territory that would eventually allow the Timorese people to choose between broad autonomy within Indonesia or independence. In case of a victory for the second scenario, Article 6 of the Agreement established the institution of a UN Administration to create the governmental structures of the future state of East Timor. The referendum was held on 30 August 1999 and an overwhelming majority opted for independence. As a result, the Security Council established UNTAET by Resolution 1272 (25 October 1999), consisting

---

transitional administration while establishing and overseeing the development of provisional democratic self-governing institutions to ensure conditions for a peaceful and normal life for all inhabitants in Kosovo' (5).

26 In its Advisory Opinion on the Declaration of Independence (2010), the Court emphasised that the Special Representative had, inter alia, prominent legislative powers: 'The Constitutional Framework [established by UNSC Res. 1244 and the UNMIK Regulations] gave the Special Representative the power to oversee and, in certain circumstances, annul the acts of the Provisional Institutions of Self-Government' (para. 108). The Special Representative did not hesitate to find 'a number of acts as being incompatible with the Constitutional Framework on the grounds that they were deemed to be "beyond the scope of [the Assembly's] competencies"' (*ibid.*).

27 https://digitallibrary.un.org/record/1492926.

of a military body (authorised to 'take all necessary means to fulfil its mandate', para. 4)[28] and a civilian body. UNTAET, guided by a Provisional Administrator appointed by the Secretary-General, administered the territory until its independence on 20 May 2002 as Timor-Leste. By the virtue of paragraph 1 of the aforementioned resolution, UNTAET had the power to 'exercise all legislative and executive powers, including the administration of justice'. Among the powers and competencies enjoyed by UNTAET are: '(a) to provide security and maintain law and order throughout the territory of East Timor; (b) to establish an effective administration; (c) to assist in the development of civil and social services; (d) to ensure the coordination and delivery of humanitarian assistance, rehabilitation and development assistance; (e) to support capacity-building for self-government; and (f) to assist in the establishment of conditions for sustainable development' (para. 2 of resolution 1272). It is not difficult to see among these sovereign functions the intention of the Security Council to prepare for the construction of a state that conforms to international ('UN') 'standards', for example in the areas of human rights, environmental law, governance and human development.

As we have just seen, both in the light of LoN practice and that of the UN, direct international administration of territories is one of the instruments that the organised International Community has resorted to and continues to resort in order to maintain and/or restore international peace and security, 'being understood that the ultimate beneficiary of the process must be the population or people concerned'.[29]

To this end, the competent bodies act within the framework of the collective security system and this dimension is yet another illustration of the links between the "New York Law" and international law of territory.

---

28 This formula is not insignificant since it allows this peace operation to be classified as one with the power to 'impose' peace within the meaning of Article 42 UNC.

29 Article 3 para. 5 of the IDI Resolution on International Administration (2021), https://www.idi-iil.org/app/uploads/2021/09/2021_online_13_en.pdf.

Analytical Index

www.ingramcontent.com/pod-product-compliance
Lightning Source LLC
LaVergne TN
LVHW020004031026
849161LV00023B/927